B&T
$30.00

Modern America

Number 4

THE NEW DEAL

Volume One

The New Deal

The National Level

Edited by

John Braeman
Robert H. Bremner
David Brody

OHIO STATE UNIVERSITY PRESS : COLUMBUS

Library of Congress Cataloguing in Publication Data

Braeman, John.
  The New Deal.

  (Modern America; 4)
  CONTENTS: v. 1. The national level—v. 2. The state and local levels.
  Includes index.
  1. United States—Politics and government—1933–1945. 2. United States—Social
conditions—1933–1945. I. Bremner, Robert Hamlett, 1917–   joint author. II. Brody,
David, joint author. III. Title. IV. Series.   1-28-76
E806.B72   320.9′73′0917   74–20843
ISBN 0–8142–0200–4 (v. 1)   0–8142–0201–2 (v. 2)

Contents

Introduction

Despite the passing years, debate over the New Deal continues unabated. But as the New Deal recedes farther into the past, the terms of that debate have changed. Few historians nowadays see Franklin D. Roosevelt as a power-mad demagogue who replaced the free enterprise system responsible for America's progress and greatness with a deadening creeping socialism. Not many more picture FDR as a courageous Saint George who slew the dragon of economic royalism, rescued the nation from depression, and erected a new regime of social justice. Most present-day students of the New Deal recognize its limited aims and even more limited achievements; a minority on the left even charge that the New Deal did no more than patch up and strengthen the old deal. The focus of the current debate is thus upon such questions as how *new* was the New Deal; what alternatives policy-makers had; how successful was the Roosevelt administration in disciplining, liberalizing, and humanizing capitalism; and what was its long-term significance in shaping contemporary America.

One of the more hotly argued questions is to what extent Roosevelt's policies for combatting the Depression differed from Hoover's. In his review of the existing historiography, Albert U. Romasco of New York University shows how contemporary newspapermen and associates of Roosevelt, "liberal" historians such as Basil Rauch, Richard Hofstadter, and Arthur M. Schlesinger, Jr., and even "conservative" critics of the New Deal, all, for their differing purposes, postulated a sharp contrast between the two chief executives. "Each has been made a reference point for comprehending the other." On the other side has been a "dissenting" minority who stress "the similarities in the Hoover-Roosevelt policies."

Romasco himself leans toward the contrast rather than continuity school. Hoover, he acknowledges, did break "with the stoical tradition of previous depression presidents by assuming responsibility for the prosperous functioning of the economy." But his program was limited by "a well thought-out philosophy of government." Thus, Romasco concludes, to argue "that Roosevelt's New Deal was anticipated in its essentials by President Hoover . . . magnifies to disproportion the carefully circumscribed Hooverian policies, while minimizing the profuse outpouring that was Roosevelt's New Deal."

The degree of continuity with Hoover was at its greatest during the first—or NRA—phase of the New Deal. During this phase, James Holt of New Zealand's Auckland University finds, the Roosevelt administration sought to achieve its goal of restoring "*balance* and *coordination*" in the economy through "voluntary cooperation with a minimum of governmental coercion." From 1934 on, however, "when New Dealers talked of the need for cooperative action to meet the needs of a complex 'interrelated' economy, they almost invariably meant nothing more than action by federal agencies." Accompanying this shift were vocal attacks upon "the economic royalists and their political lackeys" and "demands for social justice." At the same time, Holt points out, this apparently more radical tack had its conservative implications. "In the early days of the Roosevelt administration, New Dealers had denounced economic individualism and competitiveness as outworn creeds and had proposed to put cooperation, neighborliness, and national unity in their place." But with the collapse of the National Recovery Administration, "the case for the New Deal came to rest on the more modest claim that positive government could render an individualistic, capitalistic society more stable, more equalitarian, and more humane."

Examining government-business relations, Ellis W. Hawley of the University of Iowa views the New Deal as marking a shift from Hoover's reliance upon "informal business-government cooperation" to a "more formal and coercive attempt" at managing the economy. But he underlines how the New Deal's commitment to change "was clearly limited by fixed ideological boundaries" that ruled out, on the one hand, "stabilizing arrangements involving the open avowal of a 'closed,' 'authoritarian,' or 'monopolistic' system" and, on the other, "liberalizing or democratizing reforms that would seriously jeopardize capitalist incentives, constitutional safeguards, modern technology, or recovery prospects." And even within these limits, the administration shied away from programs "whose implementation would require excessive conflict or some radically new type of politics or administration." The result was a disposition "to adjust differences, make accommodations, and build on existing institutions." Although acknowledging that business "benefited most from the innovations of the period," Hawley denies that the initiative for these policies came from the business community. On the contrary, most business leaders fought "a bitter and expensive delaying action." "What emerged," he shows, "was the creation not of an omnipotent corporate elite but of a complex interaction between conflicting interest groups, resurgent liberal ideals, and the champions of competing reform models. . . ."

Looking at the New Deal from a long-term perspective, Hawley sees the Roosevelt administration as a major transitional stage in a continuing effort "to resolve the tensions between bureaucratic industrialism and a liberal-democratic ethos." No group in American society was more affected by this tension between old ideals and new realities than the farmer. Richard S. Kirkendall, professor of history at Indiana University and executive secretary of the Organization of American Historians, shows how the New Deal cast its weight decisively toward adapting the farmer to what Kenneth E. Boulding has termed "the organizational revolution." In its agricultural policies—as in its policies toward business—the New Deal, Kirkendall finds, was committed to change within the capitalist system. Its immediate aim was "to raise farm prices and restore profits to the farm business"; its longer-range goal was "to fit the farmer into a collectivist type of capitalism." Attempts "to serve more than the business interests of the commercial farmer" were only "partially successful." More successful were the New Deal's efforts to raise prices and restore profitability. But the most significant result of the New Deal in agriculture—as in business —was "to promote further evolution along collectivist lines." "By 1940," Kirkendall concludes, "the American farmer worked in a system that was dominated by the interplay among large public and private organizations."

New Deal agricultural policies accelerated developments long under way. In contrast, the Roosevelt administration's labor policies brought about what Milton Derber of the Institute of Labor and Industrial Relations at the University of Illinois regards as "a fundamental restructuring of the industrial relations system." Although the immediate effect of New Deal policies was to benefit labor—and make possible the unionization of the mass-production industries—Derber sees their more significant long-run result as making the federal government the "rule-maker and umpire" in the labor-management process, laying down and enforcing "the rules of the game for the chief actors—organized labor and management." At the same time, the federal government assumed the responsibility for setting minimum labor standards, providing "social security" for the nation's citizens, and guaranteeing—whatever the shortcomings of its efforts in practice—against unemployment. And these new roles for the federal government brought organized labor more actively than ever into the political arena in a still-continuing alliance with the Democratic party.

Almost as revolutionary was what Jerold S. Auerbach of Wellesley College describes as the "wrenching change" undergone by the legal profession during the Roosevelt years. On the one hand, lawyers faced sharp attack for their alleged bondage to business. On the other, the New Deal "enabled a new professional elite to ascend to power"—an elite drawn from those lawyers whose social and ethnic backgrounds had excluded them from the white, Anglo-Saxon Protestant legal establishment and/or whose ambitions for public service found an outlet in the Roosevelt adminstration. "Between 1933 and 1941," Auerbach writes, "professional power in the public arena shifted from a corporate elite, served by Wall Street lawyers, to a legal elite, dominated by New Deal lawyers." The central role played by lawyers in the New Deal had its drawbacks as well as its benefits. The commitment of this new legal "counter-elite" to "flexibility, to instrumentalism, to skeptical realism and to administrative discretion . . . freed the New Deal from the debilitating paralysis" of the Hoover years. But, Auerbach adds, the "lawyer's obsession with process" was a major factor in the New Deal's opportunism, its readiness to compromise, and its willingness to accept "the existing balance of power between competing interest groups."

The Roosevelt administration's disposition to accept "the existing balance of power between competing interest groups" was nowhere more evident than in its treatment of the nation's most distressed group, the Negro. Raymond Wolters of the University of Delaware portrays how the two major New Deal recovery programs—the Agricultural Adjustment Administration and the National Recovery Administration—worked to the disadvantage of the Negro. Other New Deal agencies—such as the Civilian Conservation Corps and the Tennessee Valley Authority—practiced and enforced racial segregation and discrimination. Roosevelt himself shied from endorsing any civil rights legislation; he even refused to put a federal anti-lynching bill on his "must" list. And though such other New Deal agencies as the Farm Security Administration, Public Works Administration, Works Progress Administration, and National Youth Administration did attempt to assure blacks fair treatment, their efforts fell short of meeting the desperate needs of the country's black citizens. Part of the difficulty, Wolters explains, was southern influence in Congress; but perhaps even more important were the "fundamental and basic deficiencies of 'broker leadership' " whereby the most benefits went to "those who are well organized and politically influential." Yet despite its shortcomings, Wolters concludes, "the New Deal offered Negroes more in material benefits and recognition than had any administration since the era of Reconstruction." The result was a massive shift of black voters from their traditional loyalty to the Republican party to the Democrats—a shift that subsequent developments have reinforced and solidified.

There was perhaps no stauncher friend of the Negro within the ranks of the New Dealers than Aubrey Willis Williams. Williams, a social worker turned bureaucrat, was, according to John A. Salmond of Australia's La Trobe University, "a radical." Unlike, however, so many of similar views, he hoped to achieve his goal of a more just and decent social order by working within the Roosevelt administration. As an official of the Federal Emergency Relief Administration and Civil Works Administration, then as deputy administrator of the Works Progress Administration and executive director of the National Youth Administration, Williams was one of the administration's leading champions of federally financed and administered work relief instead of the demoralizing and dehumanizing dole. His outspoken liberalism so outraged Capitol Hill that Roosevelt passed him over for head of the WPA to succeed Harry Hopkins. But what most outraged southern lawmakers, liberals as much as conservatives —and cost him Senate confirmation of his nomination as head of the Rural Electrification Administration in 1945—was his uncompromising advocacy of Negro rights. Despite his disappointments and frustrations, Williams "never lost his faith in FDR; he never seems to have doubted for a minute that they shared the same social goals, had the same dream of what America could become." Nor was Williams atypical. "There were," Salmond reminds us, "thousands like him" in the New Deal agencies, "people who saw themselves as the local agents of general social change and who believed implicitly in its value."

Williams, as late as 1945, continued to believe that "a revival and a widening of the New Deal was imminent." But the reform impulse sparked by the depression had long since waned. Richard Polenberg of Cornell University shows how the decline began paradoxically in the wake of

Roosevelt's landslide 1936 victory. The court-packing fight "divided the liberal coalition," "exposed Roosevelt to the charge of seeking dictatorial power," and led to the formation of a powerful bipartisan conservative coalition in Congress. At the same time, proposals such as low-cost public housing, wages and hours regulation, and civil rights legislation appealing to the northern, urban wing of the Democratic party alienated southern and rural congressmen. Perhaps even more important was the growing popular sentiment "that the Roosevelt administration follow a more conservative course"—a sentiment stimulated by the New Deal's success in improving economic conditions, but then reinforced by the disillusionment with the New Deal produced by the recession of 1937–38. Popular support for the New Deal was further weakened by "the appearance of a virulent strain of nativism." And, Polenberg points out, "the administration had itself begun to draw in its horns" by 1939 as Roosevelt's preoccupation with foreign policy and national defense led him "to court southerners" and seek "a rapprochement with the business community."

Nor did the American involvement in World War II, in striking contrast with Great Britain's experience, bring "a new thrust forward" in reform legislation. David Brody of the University of California-Davis finds part of the explanation to lie in the external limitations facing the Roosevelt administration: the strength of the southern Democratic-Republican coalition in Congress; the compulsion upon Roosevelt before Pearl Harbor of gaining support for his foreign and defense programs from among opponents of his domestic programs; the importance of gaining the cooperation of industry in the mobilization effort; the reliance upon executives drawn from business to run the defense program; "the conservative perspective of the military men" who came to "play a central role" within the War Production Board; the war-bred prosperity; and the satisfaction of organized agriculture and labor with the existing mechanisms established by the New Deal—"the system of price support written into the Soil Conservation and Domestic Allotment Act" and the "effective protection of the right to organize and engage in collective bargaining" guaranteed by the Wagner Act—as the means of advancing their interests during wartime. But much of the blame, Brody argues, must be ascribed to the intellectual and ideological limitations of the New Deal itself: its ad hoc and "*reactive*" character, its lack of "a comprehensive blueprint for change," its failure to have "any clear vision of a new society"; Roosevelt's preference for accommodation, his eagerness "to win the approval and cooperation of the groups affected by his programs, his reliance "on broker politics, shaping policy by a close calculation of the relative power of claimant groups."

One might expect the novelists of the day to have provided for a later generation insights into the meaning and impact of the New Deal. Yet, Eric Solomon of San Francisco State College shows, such was not the case. Some novelists did deal with "the facts of life in the United States" during the 1930s in their nonfiction and journalistic efforts; "a few conservative novelists," such as William Faulkner and John Dos Passos, "attacked the premises of, and participants in, the New Deal"; and the depression itself—with its accompanying sense of despair and impending doom—"was an omnipresent subject." But "most fiction written throughout the 1930s reflected . . . disinterest at the efforts of the federal government to discover remedies." Even "the novelists of social protest" failed to deal with "the world of the New Deal, its reforms and legislation." At least part of the explanation for this lack of interest was the tradition that the writer should take "a stance of opposition to authority, to institutions, usually to government." And perhaps even more important was that novelists, by the nature of their craft, "seemed more interested in problems—which allowed full play to the creative urge for detailed description and deep sympathy—than in solutions—which would have demanded political and economic analysis." Whatever the reasons, Solomon concludes, "the important fictional portrait of the New Deal remains to be written."

Looking at these essays as a whole, what common themes emerge? First, there is a turning away from the value judgments about the New Deal implicit and too often explicit in the appraisals by conservative detractors, liberal admirers, and contemporary and more recent left-wing critics. Second, there is the recognition that the New Deal was a complex, multifaceted phenomenon that can not be summed up in any single and sweeping generalization. Third, there is an attempt to place the New Deal within its larger context—in the context not simply of its own time and place but of what had gone before and what would follow. The result will hopefully be to contribute to the reassessment of the New Deal currently under way.

JOHN BRAEMAN
ROBERT H. BREMNER
DAVID BRODY

THE NEW DEAL

Albert U. Romasco

Hoover-Roosevelt and the Great Depression: A Historiographic Inquiry into a Perennial Comparison

THE EXPERIENCE OF THE GREAT DEPRESSION ERA, FROM 1929 TO 1941, was one that seared itself deeply in the American mind. For contemporaries, it was often a personal trauma as well as a profound national crisis. This double impact in turn provoked a heightened awareness among Americans concerning a host of expectations suddenly called into doubt. There was scarcely an assumption, a value, or a traditional institution that escaped close scrutiny. And as the assurances of a familiar world dissolved in the face of a plunging economy, a frightened people groped for ways out of their dilemma. Although this national search took many forms, the major attention undoubtedly centered upon the necessity of presidential leadership. By the outset of the Great Depression, Americans clearly had already learned to look to the presidency for leadership and remedial action in resolving major crises.

One measure of the enduring impact that the depression experience has had upon American thought is the continuing fascination that these years hold for American historians. This is particularly noticeable in the voluminous literature dealing with President Franklin Delano Roosevelt and the New Deal. For the Roosevelt scholars, the main attraction in their accounts of the depression drama has been understandably Roosevelt himself. But in their attempts to comprehend Roosevelt, they have managed to say a good deal peripherally about President Herbert Clark Hoover as well. In part, this coupling of Hoover-Roosevelt was the result of historical accident. They simply happened to share the Great Depression between them. Beyond this, however, the device of comparing the two presidents served the useful purposes of illuminating Roosevelt's complexity and providing historical location for the bewildering changes of the New Deal. For Roosevelt followed no one path, nor did the New Deal proceed in an orderly fashion, now in one direction, then in another. Instead, it went many ways simultaneously, drawing upon a wide and often conflicting series of ideas, traditions, and strains culled from the American experience. Thus, the Roosevelt specialists, in their attempts to deal with the complexity of their subject and to make it intellectually graspable, have resorted to a variety of historical devices, not the least of which is the Hoover comparison.

My purpose in this essay is to explore this comparative interplay; that is, the ways in which Roosevelt scholars have relied upon—explicitly or implicitly—the perennial comparison drawn between the Hoover and the Roosevelt administrations during the Great Depression. Daniel J. Boorstin has demonstrated how Americans have utilized a negative comparison to establish their own self-image or self-identity, that is, the concept of America as a non-Europe.[1] My interest here is in the ways historians have employed a similar form of thinking to define Hoover and Roosevelt not positively by what they were but negatively by what they were not: Hoover as a non-Roosevelt, and Roosevelt, conversely, a non-Hoover. There are also a number of more specific issues related to this problem in the historiography of Hoover-Roosevelt and the Great Depression that will be discussed. Principally, they are the extent to which historians have relied upon this comparison, the degree of consensus in its use, the complex of conclusions deduced from it, and, lastly, for lack of a better name, the dissenters—those writers who rejected, in part or in full, the antithetical view and treatment of Hoover and Roosevelt. The dissenters, particularly the more recent ones, clearly present a fundamental challenge not only to the customarily held interpretation of Hoover but of Roosevelt as well. I will also suggest some conclusions regarding the historical credibility of the Hoover created by the antithetical approach, as well as of the emerging Hoover of the dissenters who insist upon closely identifying Hoover and Roosevelt instead of sharply distinguishing them. And, finally, since historians seldom write of the past without exposing something of themselves and the intellectual currents of their day, some observations on this tendency among Roosevelt historians seem warranted.

Politically, Hoover was the greatest casualty of the events precipitated by the Great Crash and the subsequent slide of the economy down into the Great Depression. His reputation literally catapulted from a pinnacle to an abyss. He had entered the presidency at the full tide of Republican ascendancy, one of the authentic heroes of the optimistic New Era, a man of immense personal achievement—an engineer, a highly successful international businessman, a world-renowned humanitarian, and a vigorous, efficient administrator and public servant.[2] Four years later, he left the presidency with little more than a shattered reputation. It was a classic fall from eminence that can hardly be fully explained solely by reference to Hoover's political failure to overcome the depression and to restore prosperity. That failure was a fact, and certainly it played an important part, especially considering the high expectations that Hoover's 1928 presidential campaign and election had aroused. But the implications of that historical fact were decisively aided, abetted, and perpetuated by the labors of the first historians of the Hoover presidency—contemporary newsmen and political commentators. Their work, as it has turned out, was far more enduring than they could have imagined. They set the mold for the historical judgment of Hoover, a legacy that has endured, only slightly modified, until relatively recent times.

National reputations, in the modern world of technology and the mass media, are the product of genuine achievement plus extensive publicity. Hoover was fortunate in entering the presidency with a good press. His accomplishments and successes did not pass his fellow Americans unnoticed. During his years as secretary of commerce, he found ways to be helpful to newsmen in search of a story, and they were grateful. In return, Hoover's stature soared like a well-touted stock on the bull market. He was advertised as a new-type politician, a scientist in government, a man who would bring the latest business efficiencies to the arts of governing a nation. With this kind of publicity build-up, it is understandable why no one laughed when Herbert Hoover solemnly dedicated himself to the monumental objective of abolishing poverty from the land. After all, he had always succeeded before in big enterprises; and besides, Americans were in a euphoric mood at the twilight of the twenties.

Events were cruel to Herbert Hoover. Everyone knows that he did not abolish poverty. Neither did he deal scientifically or successfully with the catastrophic economic malaise that settled upon the country. His press boosters became disillusioned; they realized that they had, so to speak, backed a lemon. And they took their revenge by completely changing course, systematically, pitilessly dismantling the overblown reputation they had helped build in the public's eye. Hoover became the negative of his old self. The real Hoover, thus deflated and exposed, was now presented as an incompetent politician unable to control his own party, a pseudo-scientist who avoided decision-making under cover of countless fact-finding commissions, a thin-skinned man overly sensitive to public criticism but insensitive to the human suffering that engulfed so many of his fellow citizens. All had been misled, including themselves, the newsmen claimed with unblinking effrontery, by Hoover's genius at public relations.[3]

The dismantling job on President Hoover's reputation, started by contemporary newspapermen, was eagerly taken up by partisan Democratic politicians and completed with high glee. They would make Hoover into the Democratic counterpart of the Republican party's famed bloody shirt, and scare generations of the children of the Republic quadrennially with invocations of poor Hoover's specter. And they succeeded beyond expectation. Under the direction of Charles Michelson, publicity director for the Democratic National Committee and a newspaper reporter who was an expert at political publicity and image-making, the committee provided a flood of releases for Democratic politicians intent upon belittling Hoover. In short order, Hoover was publicly reduced to the status of a do-nothing president.[4] It is an image faithfully cherished by Democratic politicians, periodically resurrected through the years in the byways of the nation's hustings, and given varying degrees of historical legitimacy by latter-day historians.

"No cosmic dramatist," Robert E. Sherwood, a dramatist himself, remarked in 1948, "could possibly devise a better entrance for a new President—or a new Dictator, or a new Messiah—than that accorded to Franklin Delano Roosevelt." "Herbert Hoover," he continued, "was, in the parlance of vaudeville, 'a good act to follow.' "[5] It was a prophetic insight, one that historians have seized upon and exploited both before and since Sherwood articulated their method into words. For the dramatic possibilities of a stark contrast and comparison between Hoover and Roosevelt were obvious once the dynamic activity of the First Hundred Days was under way. To understand and explain Franklin Roosevelt, a challenge that historians have always found difficult, they would use Hoover as their foil. The subtle, elusive, and complex Roosevelt surely could be better comprehended in juxtaposition to the straightforward, plodding, obvious Hoover. Actual events thus helped to typecast Hoover for a role that he performs yet in the Roosevelt literature. It is time now to show how the comparison was used at first, then subsequently built upon, altered, and elaborated, so that ultimately the historical Hoover, who lives on in our histories, was formed.

With singular appropriateness, one of the first historical accounts of President Roosevelt and the unfolding New Deal was the work of a journalist turned historian. Ernest K. Lindley was one of Roosevelt's favorite correspondents, a man who had tried his hand as a Roosevelt speech-writer during the 1932 presidential campaign. The thesis of his book is in its title, *The Roosevelt Revolution* (1933). "The Roosevelt Revolution," he explained, "is democracy trying to create out of American materials an economic system which will work with reasonable satisfaction to the great majority of citizens." Essentially defined as a drastic reordering of economic institutions and arrangements, the New Deal was placed in the context of the past by the judgment that it represented the culmination of the political dissent and reform that had emerged in the late nineteenth century. Roosevelt himself was presented as a vibrant personality and strong leader—buoyant, vital, self-confident, and gay—a nondoctrinaire who was remarkably free from the deadening inhibitions of orthodox economics.[6] He was, in brief, precisely the man needed to restore the people's badly battered confidence.

Lindley disposed of Hoover with rather short shrift. A true believer of the tenets of orthodox economics, Hoover stoically responded to the depression crisis by awaiting the next upswing of the business cycle. "Mr. Hoover could not control Congress," Lindley observed, "and neither Congress nor Mr. Hoover had a domestic program worthy of mention." The result of this lassitude was the opportunity for a dramatic new beginning for the incoming administration. Or in Lindley's words, "Mr. Roosevelt took office at the very moment that the old system was crumbling to the ground. He propped it up and began remodelling operations."[7] In a sequel study, *Half Way with Roosevelt* (1937), Lindley abandoned the revolutionary designation of the New Deal as too controversial, but he found the comparison with Hoover still useful. Hoover, unlike the flexible, pragmatic, experimental Roosevelt, was a man restrained from forceful action "by his respect for principles." But even if he somehow mustered the resources to act, the intellectual acuity essential to inform and direct action was absent. "Mr. Hoover," Lindley concluded, "had only the vaguest conception of the forces at work in the depression and no conception whatsoever of how to overcome them."[8] And thus was Sherwood's law first perceived and applied.

Lindley was merely the first of a long and distinguished line of Roosevelt's intimates, advisers, and former associates who would publish accounts of the New Deal. Two of them are particularly pertinent to this study—the personal accounts and semi-histories written by Raymond Moley and Rexford G. Tugwell. Moley's *After Seven Years* (1939) came out roughly six years after he had broken with Roosevelt over the London Economic Conference; subsequently, he became more disillusioned with the New Deal as a new group of advisers gained ever increasing influence. Despite these reservations, however, Moley had not become a friend in the enemy's camp. Hoover, in his pages, continued to serve the effect of dramatic contrast.

Moley conceded that Hoover was exceedingly well informed, but that was no asset; in fact, it was one of Hoover's gravest liabilities. For this man, who was "full of information and dogmas," had become "imprisoned by his knowledge," and incapable of forceful leadership. The times called desperately for a president with "a fluid mind." Roosevelt clearly filled that bill. Furthermore, he would not be diverted from freely experimenting, as he had promised in the campaign, by Hoover's badly disguised efforts to maneuver Roosevelt during the interregnum into adopting his own international thesis on the origins of the depression, his own practice of issuing reassuring statements in a vain gambit for restoring confidence, or his own faith in such sacred symbols as the balanced budget and the traditional gold standard.[9] Such cooperation would really mean capitulation—the premature abortion of the New Deal and a continuation of the tired, futile Hoover policies.

Moley's clean-cut comparison in delineating the difference of mind, style, and policies between Hoover and Roosevelt were later taken up by his fellow brain-truster Rexford Tugwell in *The Democratic Roosevelt* (1957). Tugwell had had no similar falling out with Roosevelt, although like Moley, but for different reasons, he disapproved the directions taken by the later New Deal. Tugwell's Roosevelt is nothing less than an American version of the hero in history—the man peculiarly attuned to his times and driven by some inner force to realize new potentialities. Understandably, then, Hoover's stature in comparison to such a giant became of necessity even more diminutive.

"Herbert Hoover," Tugwell asserted, "stands in almost classic contrast to Franklin, however he is looked at; but in his characteristic reaction to economic disaster the contrast is at its very sharpest." For Hoover, who was characterized as a "moral man," the depression was "a cross to be borne"; and though he had taken some action, he went only so far as his principles would permit. He was further restrained by his conviction that a period of crisis was not the proper moment for reform.[10] Instead, he tried repeatedly to resort to words of encouragement as a means of restoring the nation's sense of confidence—that elusive but essential first Hooverian condition for recovery. In Tugwell's account, Herbert Hoover had become, in addition to the usual failings ascribed to him, an object to be pitied.

The 1940s were a pivotal period in the historiography of Hoover-Roosevelt and the Great Depression. For it was during this decade that a number of secondary accounts centering on the Great Depression, Roosevelt, and incidentally, on Hoover first appeared in print—among them important works by Basil Rauch, Dixon Wecter, Richard Hofstadter, and Broadus Mitchell.[11] Collectively, the new literature marked a transition from accounts written by contemporary newspapermen and associates of Roosevelt, who had witnessed or participated firsthand in the events they described, to studies by professional historians and scholars. Freed from any apparent direct commitments, and separated by a longer time interval from the New Deal, these historians enjoyed the potentiality of greater detachment and objectivity. Their histories, in fact, were more disinterested and considerably more factual and complete in their treatment of Hoover; and though the perennial comparison was still much in evidence, their handling of it was clearly more refined and subtle. Moreover, though Hoover was decidedly of lesser interest to them, he received more than a slighting, perfunctory notice.

Rauch in *The History of the New Deal, 1933–1938* (1944) and Wecter in *The Age of the Great Depression* (1948) both acknowledged that Hoover was more than a do-nothing president who merely sat on his hands waiting for the depression to turn the corner toward recovery. Hoover did respond to the depression, and they described his initial program of attempting to maintain the high levels of precrash wages, production, and new construction by the voluntary action of business leaders. These voluntary measures were buttressed by some governmental action, principally a tax reduction and a federally supported public works program. Yet, this policy proved woefully inadequate, and Hoover reluctantly was forced to greater reliance upon further governmental authority and power. In the latter half of 1931 and continuing through 1932, Hoover moved with greater vigor to protect the superstructure of American business and finance. This program, whose principal measures included the moratorium on intergovernmental debt, the creation of the Reconstruction Finance Corporation, the Glass-Steagall Bank Credit Act, the Home Loan Bank Act, and the Emergency Relief and Construction Act, though far more forceful than Hoover's first response to the crisis, proved nonetheless to be a failure.[12]

Rauch, an ardent admirer of Roosevelt, nonetheless pointed out that some of the early New Deal policies were partially anticipated by Hoover—notably, in the fields of federal relief for the unemployed, public works, and stock exchange regulation. But even here, Hoover's innovations were marred by a combination of timid execution and a biased predeliction for policies that favored "only one major sectional-class interest group"—the eastern business and financial interests. Beyond this, there was the greater failure of mind—"Hoover's stubborn adherence to principle," his refusal to accept wholeheartedly the imperative need to take the next big step toward policies that frankly marshalled direct government power and regulation.[13]

Wecter echoed many of the insights that Rauch had explicated. Hoover, though he took action, relied primarily upon self-help and cooperation among the top strata of American society. In his later, more forceful policies, Hoover's efforts were undercut by his inability to dramatize his program to the people, to engage the popular imagination with the facility that his brilliant successor later demonstrated. "For all of [Hoover's] abilities," Wecter concluded, "he lacked the gifts which his successor possessed in such abundance—political camaraderie, communicable personal warmth, a comprehensible program, thrilling leadership."[14] By dwelling at some length upon Hoover's actions and hesitations, even though it was done in the context of a critical comparison with Roosevelt, both Rauch and Wecter thus succeeded in adding a good deal more historical substance to what had been previously little more than a shadowy and polemicized Hoover.

These scattered strands of fact and insights regarding Hoover were gathered up by Richard Hofstadter in separate influential essays on Hoover and Roosevelt in his *The American Political Tradition* (1948). In his comparison of the two men, Hofstadter was not uncritical of what he regarded as Roosevelt's limitations, especially his intellectual shallowness and his helter-skelter brand of pragmatism. But it was precisely these

Rooseveltian qualities of openness and flexibility that set him off so clearly from his predecessor.

In the Hoover essay, Hofstadter produced a brilliant synthesis, the classic formulation and statement of the liberal interpretation of the man. Without disparaging Hoover's extraordinary personal achievements, Hofstadter showed how great personal success within the context and values of nineteenth-century America helped fashion Hoover into an ideologue, a devoted exponent and defender of the old American way and its traditions. Although Hoover was hampered by personal traits that made him an ineffectual politician, his greatest handicap, however, was his philosophy. Hoover was a man imprisoned by old-fashioned, outmoded principles. Not even the shock of national disaster could shake him loose from these moorings of belief. "Almost overnight," Hofstadter remarked, "his essential beliefs had become outlandish and unintelligible. The victim of his faith in the power of capitalism to survive and prosper without gigantic government props, Hoover was the last presidential spokesman of the hallowed doctrines of laissez-faire liberalism."[15] And Hoover failed; he could do no other than fail as long as he held faithfully to his beliefs, and he would not give them up. Hofstadter's imaginative recreation of the mind and character of Herbert Hoover was an exercise in compassionate historical criticism—a criticism that elevated Hoover to a truly tragic figure.

Broadus Mitchell's *Depression Decade* (1947) was an equally significant work historiographically, but for quite different reasons. Mitchell's account of Hoover and Roosevelt in the Great Depression broke new ground in several significant aspects of the subject. Mitchell was unique among American historians in his insight and approach to the Great Depression in that he placed American developments squarely in a worldwide context. From this perspective, he advanced an internationalist interpretation that located the origins of the world depression in the economic dislocations—particularly in international trade and monetary arrangements—caused by World War I and its aftermath. In analyzing the American response to this crisis, Mitchell emphasized the Hooverian antecedents to early New Deal policies to an extent that called into serious question the validity of the sharp contrast that this comparison usually elicited. Besides citing Federal Farm Board activities, such as the creation of national cooperatives and its suggestion of removing land from use, the establishment of the RFC, and the beginning of federal relief to the states, Mitchell also identified the overriding objective sought by both Hoover and Roosevelt as identical—the preservation of American capitalism. The only difference here was one of degree—Roosevelt was the more realistic of the two in understanding that governmental power had to be used to protect individuals as well as corporations against loss if capitalism were to survive. Roosevelt thus went an important step further than Hoover in his analysis and program.

Mitchell was also unusual in the evenhanded manner with which he bestowed criticism on both Roosevelt and Hoover. By far the most important critical judgment made of Roosevelt was that he, like Hoover, failed to end the depression. It took World War II to provide the impetus and the levels of spending to attain that objective. This crucial fact is acknowl-. edged in the general studies of the New Deal, but it has not been dwelt upon or explored with the attention that it demands as the central economic and political problem of these years. Mitchell's position here was entirely consistent—a depression that was international in its origins and scope required an internationally oriented recovery program; but Roosevelt, on the contrary, was initially an economic nationalist, and his policies reflected that orientation. Furthermore, Mitchell deplored Roosevelt's reliance upon scarcity economics as much as he did Hoover's percolation theory of recovery from the top down. The deliberate curtailment of commodity production and the destruction of food, in Mitchell's view, simply defied common sense, and exposed the limitations of Roosevelt's policies and the continued viability of American capitalism. Perhaps, he suggested, policies that leaned more heavily upon collectivist methods were required.[16] Mitchell's suggestions were pregnant with implications for a critical appraisal of Roosevelt and a reappraisal of Hoover, but they were long to remain unexplored until time and a new climate of opinion offered a more receptive environment for them.

The 1950s and 1960s witnessed a proliferation of scholarly studies on Roosevelt and the Great Depression. Most of them included some comment upon Hoover and a historical judgment of his presidential tenure. With few exceptions, and these will be discussed later, the Roosevelt specialists built upon Hofstadter's rather than Mitchell's foundation and ground plan. What emerged clearly during these two decades was the final touching up of the liberal interpretation of Hoover. It is an interpretation involving political assumptions and preferences, coupled with a distinctive analysis of twentieth-century America's major problems and the preferred solutions that together constitute the characteristic markings of recent liberal historiography. This way of thought and its implicit values are well illustrated in the liberal historians' treatment of the familiar comparison between Hoover and Roosevelt.

The Great Depression was both a profound national crisis and an inviting opportunity for political reform. The crisis undercut reputations and institutions, notably those of the nation's business and financial leaders as well as their favored political instrument, the Republican party. The complacency and self-celebration of the party during the era of its political dominance in the twenties, the unequal distribution of prosperity's rewards, and the ideological insistence upon a minimum of federal interference in the nation's economic life while the party was actively promoting the interests of the business class—these were the chief staples in the liberal condemnation of Republican socioeconomic policies. And Hoover was the heir and spokesman of that tradition.

And, indeed, ever since his *American Individualism* (1922), Hoover had articulated a distinct political philosophy that emphasized the primary role of self-help and voluntary action while he emphatically warned against the dire consequences of an expanded federal establishment. As president, Hoover was guided and restrained by his beliefs; after the crash, he took up the double burden of devising policies that would both overcome the depression while still preserving cherished American behavioral patterns and traditions—what he called the American System. Whether such a tradition ever existed in actuality is beside the point, since Hoover certainly thought and acted on that belief.[17] And in so doing, he was on a perfect collision course with liberal opinion.

The liberal analysis of most contemporary national problems, including the Great Depression, is that their resolution requires an ever more active federal initiative and intervention. Liberals have called precisely for what Hoover deplored and strenuously attempted to block—the steady enlargement of federal authority and power, particularly in the presidential office. Instead, the Hoover administration offered them an illustration of an alternative approach, one grounded in reiterated homilies on the virtues of individual initiative, self-help through voluntary association, and local and state governmental action. There was a distinct conflict of ideology here, one that President Hoover himself had sought to dramatize in his 1932 campaign criticisms of Roosevelt's proposed New Deal. Hoover, in short, was no fabricated, imaginary antagonist; he was a genuine target for the liberal historians' criticism. And he received that criticism in full measure.

Among the major works of the 1950s and 1960s, which collectively spanned American history from the 1920s through the Great Depression, were studies by Arthur M. Schlesinger, Jr., William E. Leuchtenburg, John D. Hicks, and Walter Johnson.[18] These accounts are, in part, a historical justification of the liberal critique of business government. Schlesinger, for example, in *The Crisis of the Old Order* (1957), was highly critical of the Republican presidents of the twenties for fostering business interests to the neglect and detriment of all other major components of the American population. In regard to Hoover, he remarked that "the administration's special concern for business was natural enough. . . . Let business recover, Hoover believed, and recovery for the rest of the nation—the worker, the farmer, the unemployed—would come in due course." Even in the face of a paralyzing economic disaster, Hoover could not be forced to accept a more comprehensive, expanded federal role. He remained, for example, adamantly opposed to all schemes for active government planning despite the growing support for this idea not only among liberal economists and progressive senators but among important figures in the business class itself.[19]

William Leuchtenburg—in two books, *The Perils of Prosperity, 1914–32* (1958), and *Franklin D. Roosevelt and the New Deal, 1932–1940* (1963)—dealt extensively with both presidents as well as the background to the depression since World War I. Here was strong support for the liberal view of business misgovernment by the string of presidents from Harding through Hoover. "The 1920's," Leuchtenburg observed, "represent not the high tide of laissez faire but of Hamiltonianism, of a hierarchical concept of society with a deliberate pursuit by the government of policies most favorable to large business interests." Business, in effect, was given its head with the confident expectation that the entire nation would benefit. When the validity of this Republican policy was exploded, Hoover stood amid the debris attempting to salvage some remnants of the party's faith in business leadership. Leuchtenburg fully acknowledged the range of Hoover's activities, commenting that "he used governmental power to check the depression in an unprecedented manner." But doing more than previous depression presidents—who had done practically nothing—was far from enough. "Hoover's failure," Leuchtenburg concluded, "lay in his refusal to admit the collapse of his program and in his rigid rejection of the need for a new course."[20]

John Hicks's *Republican Ascendancy, 1921–1933* (1960), stopping short of Roosevelt and the New Deal, effectively disposed of a decade of GOP leadership. As for Hoover, "He was the prisoner of his economic views; his strong convictions on the subject of what government had no right to do greatly narrowed the field of his possible activities." What Hoover did find permissible were invariably policies that favored the nation's great corporations. The dismal results not only discredited Hoover but the whole concept of business leadership itself.[21]

In *1600 Pennsylvania Avenue: Presidents and the People, 1929–1959* (1960), Walter Johnson applied the liberal critique to Hoover in one of his more vulnerable spots—the arts of strong presidential leadership. "Hoover's difficulties in coping with the depression," Johnson concluded, "were increased . . . by his failure to grasp the full powers of the presidency." Hoover lacked the skills and temperament of the strong party leader—a first necessity for effective presidential leadership. Failing to exploit the potentialities of the national pulpit that he occupied, Hoover forfeited powerful opportunities to mobilize the Congress, the press, and public opinion in support of his policies. But there was slight prospect that Hoover ever would have tried such dramatic techniques of leadership. It was a style that would have rubbed against his grain, and, besides, he did not see any need for it. As Johnson has remarked, "He did not feel that a major adjustment was necessary in America between democracy and capitalism."[22]

The counterpart, of course, of Hoover's low estate among the liberal historians has been the vastly different conclusion that results when liberal tenets were applied to the chief protagonist of the perennial comparison. In this case, a seesaw effect applies: when Hoover goes down, Roosevelt comes up. For Roosevelt, unlike Hoover, was moving the federal apparatus and the presidential office decisively in the direction that conformed with the liberal view. Consequently, as an instrument of reform he won high praises from the liberal camp. It is not that Roosevelt escaped entirely from all criticism by mainstream historians. But those criticisms tended to be secondary details in the historical portrait they drew—such matters as the court-packing plan, the attempted party purge, or the 1937 collapse of the economy. These, indeed, were the unfortunate consequences of misguided decisions, but they amounted to no more than disagreements within the liberal consensus. They hardly rippled the mood of celebration of Roosevelt's leadership.

During the long years of the making of the liberal analysis of Hoover-Roosevelt, there appeared occasionally a study highly critical of Roosevelt. Two of these are particularly relevant here because, besides attacking Roosevelt, they completely reversed the order of priority in the liberal comparison. They elevated Hoover's wisdom and stature high above its usual low place as a means of criticizing Roosevelt. The comparison was still in full operation, but as Herodotus said of the ancient Egyptians, they did all things backwards. From the liberal point of view, that is precisely what both John T. Flynn and Edgar E. Robinson managed to do as well.[23]

John T. Flynn's *The Roosevelt Myth* (1948) appeared a number of years after he had become personally disillusioned with Roosevelt. He readily admitted that a major purpose of his study was to reduce Roosevelt to size. Since Flynn felt that Roosevelt's gargantuan reputation had been created by the mass media and a host of partisan books by the president's friends, he would exercise an equally critical license. His book is a monument to his resolve. Roosevelt became a man with no economic knowledge, which, added to the charge that he had no fundamental philosophy either, meant that he was governed by expediency. Roosevelt, as Flynn put it, was "purely an opportunist," primarily preoccupied with garnering votes. As for the myriad Rooseveltian policies, they were disposed of with dispatch: "The Second New Deal was a flop. The First New Deal had been abandoned . . . immediately after his inauguration."[24]

What Roosevelt lost here in girth and height, Hoover gained. For Hoover thoroughly understood economics and had fashioned a comprehensive plan to end the depression. And that plan—essentially, strengthening the banking system and restoring the flow of credit and new investment—would have succeeded had Hoover not been consistently blocked by the Democratic-controlled House of Representatives.[25] Here, in short, was the familiar comparison turned on its head. Flynn's Hoover was dramatically built up in order to scale Roosevelt down drastically to less than great man size.

The conservative critique of Hoover-Roosevelt was more fully argued by Edgar Robinson, a professional historian, in *The Roosevelt Leadership, 1933–45* (1955). Although his stated purpose was to evaluate Roosevelt's political leadership, Robinson was as much preoccupied with Hoover as with Roosevelt. Hoover, in fact, served as the ideal type by which Roosevelt and all his works were measured and condemned. For Robinson, Hoover's "New Day" program offered the best of two worlds: preserving the cherished traditions of "Old America"—honesty, self-reliance, hard work, equal opportunity, and private enterprise—as well as incorporating the modern techniques of scientific intelligence. The promise of continued American progress—prosperity for the masses, social justice, and greater opportunity for all—was assured only when properly grounded in the traditions of the American way.[26]

But Roosevelt's political methods and objectives constituted a radical departure from the American way. He wrought no less than a revolution. "His revolution," Robinson explained, "consisted in making over the government itself." Its major ingredients included "a tremendous concentration of power in the Executive; . . . destroying the idea that much could be achieved for the people, by the government as umpire." Roosevelt not only believed in the all-powerful government, he also deliberately fanned class antagonisms, and on occasion used the methods of a "would-be dictator." One important consequence of New Deal policies was that "Roosevelt was assured of the active opposition of all those who still held to the view that the chief duty of government was merely to hold the balance for a competitive system of free enterprise." Conservatives, whom Robinson defined as those who adhered "to the basic principles of Constitutional government," could only look upon Roosevelt's new America with anguish and foreboding.[27]

The conservative critique of Hoover-Roosevelt was thus fashioned from assumptions and values opposite to those operating in the liberal historiography. It was also informed by a different vision of America. Predictably, its analysis of the depression crisis and the range of its preferred solutions were markedly more complacent and circumscribed than those of the liberals. Like Hoover, the conservatives felt that the basic structure of the American system was sound. An extensive reform program was neither necessary nor desired. Little wonder that in their historical rendition of the Hoover-Roosevelt dichotomy, it was Hoover who was vindicated.

Liberal and conservative historians hold little common ground beyond their mutual conviction that Hoover and Roosevelt represented antithetical forces in American history. Both have freely used the perennial comparison, but they have deduced from this common procedure widely divergent conclusions. However, the very basis of this approach has been directly challenged by one other school of thought that disputes the liberal-conservative focus on differences and insists on the similarities in the Hoover-Roosevelt policies. This dissenting viewpoint has been argued (with a considerable degree of individual variation) by Walter Lippmann, Broadus Mitchell, William A. Williams, and, most recently, by Barton J. Bernstein.[28]

Lippmann introduced dissent early in the game—in 1935 while the New

Deal itself was still in mid-course, with his article "The Permanent New Deal." He undertook there a direct assault upon what he termed "partisan mythology," the contention by partisans of both presidents that fundamental differences separated the Hoover-Roosevelt depression programs. In Lippmann's view, this reiterated belief was untenable—a myth pure and simple. Once the issue was historically analyzed, he believed that all vestiges of a stark contrast evaporated.

Lippmann, in his analysis, attempted to penetrate the confusing variety of New Deal activities by isolating its essential core. He resolved this problem by identifying two major categories of New Deal policies: measures that were essentially intended as reforms, and those that aimed principally at economic recovery. New Deal reforms included new ventures in the federal regulation of private business and government entry into business in direct competition with private enterprise. Lippmann argued that the regulatory functions, such as those authorized by the Securities Act, the Stock Exchange Act, and the Banking Act of 1933, were merely a continuation of governing techniques that had been urged and partially applied during the progressive era. And the new efforts in government business enterprise, such as the Tennessee Valley Authority and the idea of social insurance, were explained as basically extensions of earlier federal or state precedents. In short, as far as reform went, the New Deal was neither creative nor radical. It trod a familiar path cut by the past.

The recovery program, on the other hand, was both new and radical. New in the sense that it broke with past precedent—the laissez faire attitude of previous depression presidents; radical because of the federal assumption of an important new function. As Lippmann put it, "The national government undertook to make the whole economic order operate prosperously." This commitment was a genuine, sharp break with past traditions, but the innovator here was Hoover, not Roosevelt. For it was Hoover who first "committed the government to the new function of using all its powers to regulate the business cycle." Furthermore, in the main recovery policies—those involving the budget, agriculture, industry, and labor —there was "no break in principle" between Hoover and Roosevelt. From this analysis, Lippmann concluded that "apart from the Roosevelt measures of reform . . . all the main features of the Roosevelt programme were anticipated by Mr. Hoover."[29] Thus, by a process that perhaps can best be described as an exercise in historical subtraction, the New Deal was reduced to a near cipher. Roosevelt's policies, in sum, were no more than an elaboration, an evolution from the policies of Theodore Roosevelt, Wood-

row Wilson, and, contrary to the prevailing belief, Herbert Hoover.
There is little in common between Lippmann and William A. Williams beyond the fact that both dispensed with the traditional contrast. Both closely identified the Hoover-Roosevelt policies, but in different ways and for different reasons. Williams, in *The Contours of American History* (1961), dealt only briefly with Hoover, but he buttressed this concise account with a number of provocative assertions that offered an alternative hypothesis of Hoover-Roosevelt and the Great Depression from all that came before.

Williams did not attempt a one-to-one correlation between the Hoover-Roosevelt policies; instead, he dealt with both presidents in the larger historical context of twentieth-century America. According to Williams, the distinguishing economic and political fact of recent America, particularly since the progressive era, was the dominating position of "corporation capitalism." It was a system of political economy that in order to survive and prosper needed the careful tending of its essential requirements: an expanding foreign market for its surplus production, and the capital accumulation to finance its operations. The successful functioning of such a system transcended the domestic market and domestic politics; it required a rationalized, stable world economy open to American investment and trade. Twentieth-century presidents understood and responded to the needs of the corporate economy with greater or lesser perception, and in the process America moved perceptibly toward what Williams termed a "syndicalist nation."[30]

Hoover, in Williams's judgment, possessed a penetrating understanding of the system that was almost prophetic. As the "key leader" of a group of enlightened, class-conscious corporation executives, Hoover knew how the corporate economy functioned, its vital requirements, the socioeconomic inequities it had produced, and its potentiality for slipping into one or another form of authoritarian government. That is, if any one of its major functional components (corporate, labor, or political leaders) individually gained control of the federal government, the result would be, respectively, fascism, socialism or "bureaucratic tyranny." If the three blocs instead ended up by collaborating together to dominate the state, the outcome would be the oligarchic control of a syndicalist nation.

Hoover, once in the executive office, had intended to remedy the functional defects of the system, distribute its rewards more equitably as one means of preventing the growth of popular radicalism, and, at the same time, avoid all tendencies leading to authoritarianism. But these plans were disrupted by the immediate necessity of resolving the depression crisis. The outcome of that venture anticipated the future in several highly significant ways:

> The policies that Hoover did finally employ in his efforts to halt the depression provided the rudiments of Roosevelt's program. And Hoover's analysis of the propensity of the corporation political economy to produce "a syndicalist nation on a gigantic scale" was ultimately verified by the results of Roosevelt's New Deal.

Hoover's failure, in a crucial sense, was the outcome of deliberate, conscious choice. "He refused to save the system," Williams concluded, "through means that he considered destructive of its values and potential."[31]

Roosevelt, on the other hand, lacked Hoover's awareness of the potential pitfalls of the corporate economy, and the result of Roosevelt's intellectual shortcomings was the final consolidation of the syndicalist system. Roosevelt's pragmatic exercise of power had blundered the nation into an economic and political structure where, as Williams gloomily observed, "the citizen was almost wholly dependent upon the definition of public welfare that emerged *inside* the national government as a consensus among the leaders of the various functional-syndicalist elements of the political economy."[32] Hoover's forebodings had become America's reality.

More recent critics of Roosevelt and the New Deal—New Left historians such as Howard Zinn, Paul K. Conkin, and Barton J. Bernstein —have used a totally different perspective and standard of evaluation than that of the well-worn Hoover comparison.[33] "When we compel the past to speak," Zinn has frankly remarked, " . . . we would like the past to speak wisely to our present needs."[34] It is thus from a radical appraisal of present-day America, not the olden days of Herbert Hoover, that their historical scales are set—and the balance weighs heavily against Roosevelt. For the achievements of Roosevelt's welfare state, seen from the vantage point of the late 1960s, seemed to them a meager sop. The details of their critique fall beyond the scope of this essay, which is concerned with the Hoover-Roosevelt comparison. Hoover is not much mentioned in their pages; and when he does briefly appear, there is hardly a step missed in the hot pursuit of Roosevelt. Bernstein, for example, moved Hoover from the nineteenth century, where he had long been consigned by liberal historians, into the twentieth, and, following Lippmann and Williams, ascribed much of the innovative aspects of the New Deal to Hoover.

"Rather than the last of the old presidents," Bernstein remarked, "Herbert Hoover was the first of the new." As for Roosevelt himself, he was "a charismatic leader and a brilliant politician, . . . [who] expanded federal activities on the basis of Hoover's efforts."[35]

This passing attention to Hoover, however, is really incidental to the main objective of the New Left historians, that is, clearing the field of fire for their principal target, Roosevelt. For it is the liberal Roosevelt, not the conservative Hoover, whom they hold responsible for the persisting, multiple injustices of a modified capitalist state. In their view, Roosevelt did enough to save the system, but not enough to redeem it. The chief beneficiaries of New Deal reform simply were not the rhetorical "bottom third of the nation." One of the great opportunities for significant socioeconomic change had been contained by a clever combination of large, generous promises and half measures. And they hold Roosevelt accountable for the results.

The Hoover-Roosevelt comparison has thus served a variety of purposes since it was first employed during the years of the Great Depression. Both presidents in good measure have been given historical definition by this way of thought. Each has been made a reference point for comprehending the other. When Roosevelt, for instance, is conceived as a political leader highly receptive to new ideas and willing to experiment, or as a bold innovator from past traditions, a president who greatly extended executive authority and power, or as the patron of new power blocs, and the responsible agent for the burgeoning presence of a vast federal bureaucracy in American life—it is invariably Hoover, as the symbol of the past, who serves as a measure for these changes. It is one of the heavier burdens that Hoover has had to bear. Yet conservative and liberal historians alike have followed this method, even though they part company emphatically once they turn to assessing the meaning of the difference.

The Hoover-Roosevelt comparison has also served to give historical legitimacy to contending political viewpoints, methods, programs, and personal visions of the ideal. For liberal historians, Roosevelt was their wish come true: an energetic, resourceful chief executive who fully understood the imperative need of federal power for the resolution of national problems. And because he boldly augmented the powers of his office while thrusting the federal presence into new, wider areas of responsibility, they applauded Roosevelt unstintingly for his wisdom and his political finesse. America was finally moving once again, and in the right directions after the nadir of the twenties. And by this process of change and reform, the liberal critique of modern America was finding its justification—a fact of sufficient import to soften, sometimes to dissolve entirely, in rationalization the critical perception of some of the more questionable Rooseveltian methods, the unexpected consequences of policy, or the unfulfilled promises.

Conservatives, whose literature is quantitatively slight in comparison with that of the liberals, have also found a vindication of their own assumptions and values in the Hoover-Roosevelt comparison. More sensitive to the grave dangers of concentrating unchecked power in one office than to any potential benefits, they viewed the fashioning of a powerful presidency as one of the preconditions of an American totalitarianism. Roosevelt was jettisoning the sacrosanct individualistic heritage and the republic's wise restraints on the scope and exercise of power for the sorry mess of a collectivist-state porridge. And all this was done in blind disregard of the lessons so obviously apparent in the European experience. For them, it was Hoover's deliberate restraint in the use of power that was wisdom, his warnings prophetic. The realities of Roosevelt's New Deal America, on the other hand, simply confirmed their most dire prognostications. The qualities of life that they fondly associated with the old American way were recklessly, needlessly being swept away.

The most recent critical appraisals of Roosevelt and the New Deal were ones grounded in a radical framework. It is not Hoover and the older America associated with him that provide the central basis of this critique. The New Left is not informed by nostalgia but by a radical stance toward a contemporary America besmirched with injustices foreign and domestic. And these are seen as the direct legacy of Roosevelt's limited vision and commitment. In these accounts, there is no muting of the unfulfilled promises of Roosevelt's welfare state to the bottom third of the nation because it is precisely these shortcomings that constitute the heart of their indictment. And though the radicals break with the liberal and conservative practice by stressing the similarities in the policies of the Hoover and Roosevelt administrations, their treatment of the precursor of the New Deal is relatively sympathetic. Roosevelt is clearly the main concern, the main quarry.

Thus, liberals, conservatives, and radicals have each looked at Hoover-Roosevelt from their own chosen perspectives: the conservatives from a past they preferred; the liberals, seeing that same past in a different light, welcomed the break from it as necessary and beneficial; and the radicals, largely disregarding the past, concentrated upon the consequences of action and inaction for the present. Further, in each of these perspectives there are embedded distinct sets of conflicting values and personal hopes and fears. The two factors taken together largely determine the disparate judgments that have been rendered by historians of the Great Depression era.

Yet in making the Hoover-Roosevelt comparison, whichever way it has been treated, no one has argued that the two presidents were similar in such matters as personal temperament, political style, or methods of leadership. The differences here have been taken for granted. It is in the realm of *policies* that the dispute has been formulated and argued. The liberal-conservative consensus on this point has been directly challenged by the dissenters, not all of whom are radicals, but who are joined by their common insistence upon continuity. Unlike the subjective factors of perspective and values, the disagreement over whether Roosevelt's New Deal represented a dramatic break from the preceding administration or was merely an elaboration of Hoover's policies is an issue permitting analysis on other than the basis of a counterassertion of personal bias.

Hoover's initial program for containing the effects and repercussions of the stock market crash was largely an exercise in presidential exhortation. His strategy called for businessmen to continue their normal operations, maintain their current work force at prevailing wages, and to expedite new investment in capital improvements. Meanwhile, the bankers were to see to it that the necessary credit was readily available, and labor was to stay on the job and avoid all strikes. There was, in short, to be none of the customary retrenchment and liquidation characteristic of periods of business uncertainty in the past. The nation's normal business was instead to go on normally.[36]

It was a program that required only a minimum of federal action for its implementation. Beyond Hoover's promise to reduce taxes, expand public works, and ease credit through the traditional devices of the Federal Reserve—lowering the discount rate and improving the banks' reserve position by open-market purchases of bonds—the national government had little to do beyond persuasion. For the ultimate success of this first program depended upon its faithful execution by private groups. It is a classic illustration of Hoover's philosophy of government practically applied. The nation was to surmount a major economic crisis by the enlightened cooperation of organized associational groups. This is what Hoover meant by voluntarism—action taken outside of government—a method he regarded as infinitely preferable to programs based upon federal authority and implementation. By such means he hoped to preserve the national genius for individual initiative and responsibility while avoiding all danger from governmental paternalism.

Hoover's political act of faith in voluntarism was based upon an economic theory for controlling, or mitigating, the fluctuations of the business cycle. This held, in brief, that if the nation could maintain a high level of spending, business confidence would be quickly restored, and the duration of the cycle's trough significantly shortened. But in his insistence that *private* means accomplish this end, Hoover surrendered the success of his program to agents beyond his command. He could only trust in the good will, the courage, and the enlightened self-interest of his chosen instruments to make his program work.

It was more than the business leaders could do, and, when the program failed, Hoover confronted new and more serious economic consequences. The immediate issue was no longer restoring prosperity, but of preventing the utter collapse of the nation's business and banking structure. For Hoover, at least, this became a necessary precondition for the success of his larger program. He turned to avert this catastrophe with energy and resourcefulness.

In his determination to attain this vital objective, Hoover was much more disposed to bend his scruples against reliance upon the direct action of government. The immediate aims of this second program (involving the moratorium, the RFC, the Glass-Steagall Bank Credit, and the Home Loan Bank acts), were, first, to preserve and strengthen the banking and business structures; and, second, by effectively shoring them up, to permit businessmen to resume the nation's prosperous level of business. He succeeded in the one and failed in the other. With direct government assistance, he prevented a collapse (at least until just before Roosevelt's inauguration), but the leaders of the private sector were too frightened to start the requisite level of private spending for recovery. One possibility open to Hoover, of course, was to offset this failure of private enterprise by turning to a program of public spending. Congress was vehemently urging a variety of schemes for this purpose. Hoover strongly rebuffed all such efforts to carry direct government action any further; instead, he fell back once again upon the familiar expedient of voluntarism.[37] Hoover's policies had come full circle.

To what extent, then, were Roosevelt's policies anticipated by Hoover? That Hoover broke with the stoical tradition of previous depression presidents by assuming responsibility for the prosperous functioning of the economy is undeniable. However, in his attempts to meet that responsibility, Hoover was guided and restrained by a well thought-out philosophy of government. And this certainly circumscribed the methods and the means that he regarded as acceptable. His legislative proposals were carefully designed to achieve defined and limited ends; he successfully refused to permit proposals to pass that went beyond his own conception of what was necessary and permissible. To say that he was willing to use *all* the powers of government to restore the economy is to misunderstand both the man, what he did, and, equally important, what he stubbornly refused to do as a matter of principle.

And when one recalls, even fleetingly, the vast array of New Deal policies, the assumption and concentration of power in Washington, the new intrusion of the federal presence in the everyday life of farmers, businessmen, bankers, and others—the assertion that Roosevelt's New Deal was anticipated in its essentials by President Hoover is staggering. It magnifies to disproportion the carefully circumscribed Hooverian policies, while minimizing the profuse outpouring that was Roosevelt's New Deal. None of this is said to discredit Hoover. He would be the last person to claim such credit. In the Hoover-Roosevelt historiography, the two principals have often been less than their admirers claimed, more than their critics conceded, but the comparison itself has been enduring.

1. Daniel J. Boorstin, *America and the Image of Europe: Reflections on American Thought* (New York, 1960), p. 36.

2. Harris Gaylord Warren, *Herbert Hoover and the Great Depression* (New York, 1959), pp. 20–32.

3. Albert U. Romasco, *The Poverty of Abundance: Hoover, the Nation, the Depression* (New York, 1965), pp. 204–12. Craig Lloyd, *Aggressive Introvert: A Study of Herbert Hoover and Public Relations Management, 1912–1932* (Columbus, Ohio, 1972), is an excellent account of Hoover's use of public relations techniques.

4. Walter Johnson, *1600 Pennsylvania Avenue: Presidents and the People, 1929–1959* (Boston, 1960), p. 27.

5. Robert E. Sherwood, *Roosevelt and Hopkins*, 2 vols. (New York, 1950), 1:48.

6. Ernest K. Lindley, *The Roosevelt Revolution: First Phase* (New York, 1933), pp. 4, 6, 15, 272, 372.

7. Ibid., pp. 14–15, 327.

8. Ernest K. Lindley, *Half Way with Roosevelt* (New York, 1937), pp. 10, 48, 97.

9. Raymond Moley, *After Seven Years* (New York, 1939), pp. 11, 139–42.

10. Rexford Tugwell, *The Democratic Roosevelt* (Garden City, N.Y., 1957), pp. 197, 251.

11. Basil Rauch, *The History of the New Deal, 1933–1938* (New York, 1944); Dixon Wecter, *The Age of the Great Depression* (New York, 1948); Richard Hofstadter, *The American Political Tradition: And the Men Who Made It* (New York, 1954); Broadus Mitchell, *Depression Decade: From New Era through New Deal, 1929–1941* (New York, 1947).

12. Rauch, *History of the New Deal*, pp. 15, 19–21; Wecter, *Age of the Great Depression*, pp. 43–44, 46–49.

13. Rauch, *History of the New Deal*, pp. 15, 18–19, 71–72, 236.

14. Wecter, *Age of the Great Depression*, pp. 43, 44.

15. Hofstadter, *American Political Tradition*, pp. 286, 293–94.

16. Mitchell, *Depression Decade*, pp. 3–7, 27, 57, 59, 69–71, 76, 89–90, 114, 132–33, 180, 190, 341, 367–68, 405.

17. For a more extended discussion of Hoover's political philosophy, see Romasco, *Poverty of Abundance*, chap. 2.

18. Arthur M. Schlesinger, Jr., *The Crisis of the Old Order, 1919–1933* (Boston, 1957); William E. Leuchtenburg, *The Perils of Prosperity, 1914–32* (Chicago, 1958), and *Franklin D. Roosevelt and the New Deal, 1932–1940* (New York, 1963); John D. Hicks, *Republican Ascendancy, 1921–1933* (New York, 1960); Johnson, *1600 Pennsylvania Avenue*.

19. Schlesinger, *Crisis of the Old Order*, pp. 226, 238.

20. Leuchtenburg, *Perils of Prosperity*, pp. 103, 251, 255.

21. Hicks, *Republican Ascendancy*, pp. 217, 223, 273.

22. Johnson, *1600 Pennsylvania Avenue*, pp. 25. 28.

23. John T. Flynn, *The Roosevelt Myth* (New York, 1948); Edgar E. Robinson, *The Roosevelt Leadership, 1933–1945* (Philadelphia, 1955).

24. Flynn, *Roosevelt Myth*, pp. vii, 33, 77–78, 119.

25. Ibid., pp. 124–26.

26. Robinson, *Roosevelt Leadership*, pp. 36–37.

27. Ibid., pp. 153, 187, 211, 381.

28. Walter Lippmann, "The Permanent New Deal," *Yale Review* 24 (1935), reprinted in Richard M. Abrams and Lawrence W. Levine, *The Shaping of Twentieth-Century America* (Boston, 1965); William Appleman Williams, *The Contours of American History* (Chicago, 1966); Barton J. Bernstein, "The New Deal: The Conservative Achievements of Liberal Reform," in Bernstein, ed., *Towards a New Past: Dissenting Essays in American History* (New York, 1968).

29. Abrams and Levine, *Shaping of Twentieth-Century America*, pp. 430, 433, 435, 437–39.

30. Williams, *Contours of American History*, pp. 418–21.

31. Ibid., pp. 415, 425–28, 438.

32. Ibid., p. 448.

33. Howard Zinn, ed., *New Deal Thought* (Indianapolis, 1966); Paul K. Conkin, *The New Deal* (New York, 1967).

34. Zinn, *New Deal Thought*, p. xvi.

35. Bernstein, "The New Deal," p. 267.

36. For a more extended discussion of the material in this and the succeeding four paragraphs, see Romasco, *Poverty of Abundance*, chaps. 3, 9, 10.

37. Jordan Schwarz, *The Interregnum of Despair: Hoover, Congress, and the Depression* (Urbana, Ill., 1970), pp. 43, 177, 206.

James Holt

The New Deal and the
American Anti-Statist Tradition

WITHIN A YEAR OF FRANKLIN D. ROOSEVELT'S FIRST INAUGURATION AS president of the United States, a vociferous and apparently powerful conservative opposition had launched a vigorous assault on the new administration's programs. Though all kinds of charges were made against the New Deal from the right, one basic theme pervaded the rhetoric of conservatives during the 1930s and gave coherence to their indictment. The expansion of federal power under the auspices of the Roosevelt administration, they repeated endlessly, was undermining individual freedom and enterprise in the United States. Americans had enjoyed greater freedom and greater prosperity than any other people because in the United States men had been given the greatest possibile opportunity to work out their lives with a minimum of restraint and coercion. Freedom could be misused, and occasionally government, preferably at the state or local level, was required to step in and correct abuses. But the dead hand of government could never be a substitute for the hard work and individual initiative of free men. Prosperity would only return to the United States and freedom would only be preserved if the New Dealers would abandon their bureaucratic, socialistic, spendthrift schemes, which were shackling the energies and undermining the confidence of liberty-loving Americans.

It was not only Liberty Leaguers and business rhetoricians who based their critique of the New Deal on this anti-statist, individualistic credo. Even Republican politicians who were regarded as "moderate" or "liberal" because they had endorsed many of the Roosevelt administration's programs, or near substitutes, commonly laced their speeches with eulogies to American individualism and dire warnings that freedom was being throttled by the New Deal. "The choice before us is clear," Alfred M. Landon warned the voters in the 1936 campaign. "On one side is the system of free competitive enterprise, which while not perfect, at least does not dole out opportunity according to a governmental yardstick—a system under which this country is still a freer, happier place to live in than any other country in the world. . . . On the other side is a system under which the minutest doings of every citizen are scrutinized and regulated. . . . There is no halfway house between these two systems."[1]

It has been suggested that the Roosevelt administration, by failing to respond to this assault in clear and consistent terms, lost the ideological battle of the 1930s by default. "The New Dealers," William Leuchtenburg has written, "were never able to develop an adequate reform ideology to challenge the business rhetoricians." By 1937, when a measure of prosperity had been restored, it is argued, conservatives were able to appeal successfully to traditional anti-statist doctrines and individualistic values that had not been systematically assailed in more opportune times.[2]

It is hard to see how it could ever be determined what part attachment to traditional values and doctrines played in the decline of the New Deal, if any. Historians, however, cannot afford to ignore what they find difficult to verify, and it seems at least plausible that the difficulty of explaining and defending a complex and novel program of federal action in the face of deeply entrenched anti-statist traditions impeded the Roosevelt administration's efforts at reform. This essay sets out to examine just how the New Deal was defended by the president and his supporters, and to offer some tentative judgements about the "adequacy" of what they said.

Though the men whose words are the subject of this study are referred to at times as "New Dealers," it is not intended to imply, by the use of this term, that they were all committed to a common ideology, or even that all of them supported the whole of the president's program. A New Dealer, for the purposes of this essay, is simply a prominent executive official or a congressman who defended the New Deal, or was defending it on the occasion when he is quoted. It is not suggested that either the programs of the Roosevelt administration or the public utterances of its supporters were marked by ideological coherence or consistency, but simply that many speeches were delivered in defense of the New Deal, and that certain themes were prominent in this body of rhetoric.

In one of the more striking phrases of his first campaign for the presidency, Franklin Roosevelt called for "bold persistent experimentation" to meet the challenge of the depression; and once in office, he and other administration figures continued from time to time to characterize their programs as "experimental." Old ideologies, it was suggested, had clearly failed America, and some new methods of dealing with the nation's problems would have to be found even at the risk of occasional failure. For the New Dealers, this approach had the merit of providing both a justification for the novelty and diversity of their programs and a useful alibi for any setbacks that occurred.[3]

On the other hand, a heavy emphasis on the experimental nature of the new programs could well create the impression that the government lacked any sense of direction and was merely groping in the dark for some way out of the economic crisis. Furthermore, conservative critics fastened on the notion of experimentation and accused the administration of using the American people as guinea pigs for the benefit of woolly-minded radicals in the president's brain trust.

This was a charge that New Dealers were at great pains to refute, and rather than develop the idea of experimentation in any rigorous fashion, they usually coupled it with an emphasis on practicality and vigorous action. To experiment was "to take a method and try it. If it fails, admit it frankly and try another. But above all try something."[4] The Roosevelt administration, Solicitor General Robert Jackson declared in 1939, was an administration "of action, of experiment, of determination that our people, by some means or another, 'eat Regular.' "[5] Conversely, though conservative critics were sometimes condemned by New Dealers as sterile ideologues full of "bland and meaningless statements about returning to first principles,"[6] they were more commonly accused simply of negativism. The opposition, complained Secretary of the Interior Harold Ickes, "were full of admonitions. We mustn't do this, we mustn't do that. Don't, don't, don't."[7] When the Republicans had been in power in the 1920s, President Roosevelt said in 1936, "this Nation was afflicted with hear-nothing, see-nothing, do-nothing Government. The Nation looked to Government but the Government looked away." Since 1933, however, "you have had an Administration which instead of twirling its thumbs has rolled up its sleeves. We will keep our sleeves rolled up."[8]

These plaudits for activism were commonly supplemented with evidence that the administration's programs were in fact producing results. In speech after speech, Democratic orators catalogued at great length the visible material benefits that the New Deal was conferring on the nation: relief for the destitute, jobs for the unemployed, price supports for the farmers, and so on. Whatever the ultimate meaning of the new array of federal programs might be, they provided their sponsors with a feast of practical accomplishments that were so specific and so tangible that their impact could even be measured by locality—so many public works projects for state X, and so much farm credit for district Y.[9]

Similarly, Democratic orators were forever pointing to a mass of evidence demonstrating improvements in the economic situation to prove that the administration's program was a practical success. The resolution of the national banking crisis during President Roosevelt's first few days in office provided his supporters with an immediate economic achievement to applaud at the very onset. After that, most economic indicators began to climb upward; and although full recovery was not achieved until the 1940s, Democrats could contrast the general upswing of the economy between 1933 and 1937 with the disastrous deflationary spiral of the Hoover years. "The constantly rising tide of national prosperity is the answer to all attacks on the Roosevelt administration," Postmaster General James A. Farley remarked in December 1935. "The contrast between the state of the Nation today and what it was on the advent of Franklin D. Roosevelt to the White House is all the retort required."[10]

An emphasis on specific material benefits also typified most discussion of the New Deal's goals. The purpose of the government's programs in the first instance, of course, was to alleviate distress and promote recovery. Beyond that the New Deal's vision of the future was commonly presented as a series of such socially desirable conditions as the elimination of slums and sweatshops, the abolition of child labor, improved standards of health, and social security.[11] For some Democrats, it was enough to recite these wholesome objectives in order to rebut conservative charges that the New Deal was dangerously radical. If old age pensions, full employment, and social security were socialism, one Democratic congressman said, then let us have socialism.[12]

In emphasising their activism and dwelling on the practical purposes and accomplishments of their programs, New Dealers made it abundantly clear that they were looking to positive action by the federal government to solve the nation's problems. What the deeper meaning of an expansion of federal power might be for the nation's economic and political systems, however, was a question that the practical-men-of-action approach ignored entirely. Indeed, it was possible to supplement a stress on good deeds and good intentions with an explicit denial that any fundamental change in the economic and political systems was intended or was occurring under the New Deal.

On the right flank of the Roosevelt administration, some conservative Democrats, torn between suspicions of the direction in which the New Deal was headed and loyalty to a Democratic administration, took such a position. They made the assumption that the depression was the product of some temporary external pressure on the economic system and not an indication of any fundamental breakdown. They took refuge in the fact that Congress had established many New Deal agencies for a limited period of time. They anticipated that much of the New Deal would disappear after "the emergency" had passed. As soon as such organizations as the AAA and the NRA had achieved their goals, Senator James Byrnes assured a South Carolina audience in January 1934, "the very people who have been most urgent in their demands for government regulation will be most urgent in demanding that government cease its regulation of business and the people of the United States have the happy assurance that their Government will respond to the will of the people."[13] As soon as the situation permitted, a Missouri congressman assured his constituents, he would favor repealing laws that gave extraordinary powers to executive officials. "Had it not been for the great emergency that confronted us, I never would have voted for such legislation."[14]

The notion that the depression had created an emergency that justified the adoption of otherwise undesirable policies on a temporary basis was employed by Democrats of all persuasions on the critical issue of deficit spending. This was a particularly difficult question for the Democrats to deal with. Not only was the ideal of the annually balanced budget endorsed by most financial experts and buttressed by common-sense attitudes toward the value of thrift, but the Roosevelt administration was itself committed to orthodox fiscal principles. In the 1932 campaign, Roosevelt had made the unbalanced budgets of the Hoover administration a primary target of attack and had promised a 25 percent reduction in federal expenditure. One of his first legislative proposals was an economy bill that he accompanied with a message deploring the tendency toward greater deficits and blaming it for a variety of economic ills.[15] As late as July 1933, President Roosevelt referred to the Economy Act as "the base of the whole recovery plan," and the administration continued to praise itself for its economizing activities throughout the year.[16]

The president's budget message of January 1934, however, destroyed

the credibility of this posture, for it anticipated what contemporary observers saw as a huge deficit for the coming fiscal year. During 1933, the
administration had made much of the distinction between regular government expenditures, which were supposedly being pruned, and "extraordinary" expenditures, which were admittedly rising. After the 1934 budget
message, it was clear that the distinction had little meaning. Total spending
was rising faster than revenue, and from this point on the fiscal policies of
the Roosevelt administration were under constant fire from the right.

Democrats responded to these attacks in part by pointing to the value of
their projects. The government's outlay had gone to provide relief for the
suffering, jobs for the unemployed, and a host of other worthwhile projects. Recovery itself had been procured, the president said in 1936, "by
spending money to put people back to work and second by lending money
to stop people from going broke."[18] With this kind of argument, New
Dealers came close to making a positive case for deficit spending; but at
least until the recession of 1937, they stopped short of that point.[19] What
they argued was not that deficit spending was promoting recovery but that
the programs the government was spending money on were promoting
recovery, and the beneficial effects of these programs had to be weighed
against the undesirable effects of the budget deficits.

Far from challenging fiscal orthodoxy, Democrats produced a variety of
arguments designed to show that the Roosevelt administration had not
moved so far away from "sound financial principles" as its critics alleged.
The nation's credit was still sound, they said, as was demonstrated by the
Treasury's continued ability to raise money at a reasonable cost. Much of
the debt the administration had incurred consisted of securely invested
loans that in due course would be repaid. Though the debt was increasing,
it had increased faster under Hoover and to less purpose. The United States
still had a much lower debt than Britain and other countries and indebted-
ness was growing more slowly than national income. As the economy
recovered, the need for emergency expenditures would decrease, and the
budget would move back into balance.[20] The goal of the annually balanced
budget was not abandoned but temporarily postponed.

Outside the area of fiscal policy, the New Deal was not for the most part
presented as merely a temporary expedient. It was possible to emphasize
practical achievement and activism while disavowing any long-term reformist goals, but in fact prominent executive officials rarely chose to do
so. The president himself stressed continuously the need to go beyond
"immediate tasks of relief and recovery . . .   [and] safeguard these

tasks by rebuilding many of the structures of our economic life and . . . reorganizing it in order to prevent a recurrence of collapse."[21] Just how and to what purpose American life was to be "reorganized" were questions to which the Roosevelt administration proffered a number of answers during the 1930s.

For a time, during the early years of the New Deal, "cooperation" was the Roosevelt administration's watchword. People acting together in a group, the president explained, "can accomplish things which no individual acting alone could even hope to bring about."[22] Under the auspices of the New Deal, Americans would work together in a spirit of neighborliness and unity to overcome their common problems. Rugged individualism would give way to teamwork, disunity would be replaced by harmony, and order would emerge from chaos.

At the heart of this new order, according to New Dealers, lay the National Recovery Administration, established in June 1933. Although, as Ellis Hawley has demonstrated, the NRA did not represent a single economic strategy but rather provided a framework within which a number of persuasions and interest groups competed for supremacy,[23] New Dealers were able to agree in a general way what it was all about, at least for rhetorical purposes. Moreover, whatever disagreements existed within the administration about the principles and purposes of the agency, virtually all the leading New Dealers seemed to see it as the key to recovery and the core of their program for the first few months after its establishment. Other programs were discussed and praised, but when the general principles of the New Deal were under review, the focus was almost invariably on the NRA.

The economic goals that New Dealers emphasized in this period were *balance* and *coordination*. Somehow, the various sectors of the economy had lost any rational relationship with one another. The list of factors that required balancing varied from one speaker to another. Sometimes it was agriculture and industry; sometimes production and consumption; sometimes wages and profits; sometimes all these and more. In any case, the formulation of the nation's economic problems in terms of dislocation and imbalance was a common theme in the rhetoric of the early New Deal.[24]

At this stage, no particular groups or institutions were held responsible for the loss of balance in the American economy. Even Hoover and the Republican party were rarely mentioned by administration spokesmen in 1933. Instead, the Great Depression was attributed to the inadequacy of "rugged individualism" as an economic credo for a modern industrial society. Such a concept might have been perfectly appropriate to the United States in its pioneer days, it was commonly said, but it had proved to be anomalous in the increasingly complex "inter-related" world of the twentieth century.[25] What was required, Secretary of Commerce Daniel Roper explained, was "a more cooperative setup."[26]

In describing the kind of action that would be necessary to turn individualistic anarchy into cooperative stability, New Dealers sometimes spoke of the need for planning, or used phrases like "conscious control," "social control," or "intelligent direction."[27] Occasionally they said quite explicitly that the need for planning, control, and direction would require an expansion of federal power.[28]

However, at this stage most New Dealers were at pains to deny that the new cooperative order was synonymous with statism. The essence of the recovery plan, and especially of the NRA, was voluntary cooperation with a minimum of governmental coercion. The NRA was to be, in the president's language, "a great spontaneous cooperation," "democratic self-discipline," "cooperative action in industry."[29] NRA officials Hugh Johnson and Donald Richberg saw "the gist of the President's program" as "cooperation and not compulsion," and "an adventure in the self-government of industry," rather than rigid state control.[30]

Admittedly, the federal government was to play a leading role in the workings of the NRA, but this role would be that of a supervisor, a senior partner, a coordinator, a referee, not a dictator. The federal government, Daniel Roper explained, "is not to dictate but to coordinate, guide and stimulate all to wisely help themselves." The NRA, Hugh Johnson said, was committed to the least possible interference with industry. "The idea is that industry shall govern itself." The Roosevelt administration, according to Donald Richberg, was "seeking to establish a half-way house of democratic cooperation for the common good, midway between the anarchy of unplanned, unregulated industrialism and the tyranny of State control of industry."[31]

Since coordination and balance were to be restored to the economic system without coercion, it was essential that a spirit of unity prevail. Traditionally antagonistic interest groups must put aside their differences in the interest of the common good. Businessmen must work together and with the government. The industrial east must support measures to help agriculture. Labor and capital must join together in the battle against the depression. Workers, employers, and consumers must unite in a drive against misery and depression.[32]

For President Roosevelt in particular, cooperation meant not just an alliance of social and economic interest groups but a new moral tone for American society that would bind men and women together as individuals. At times, he compared the new spirit to that which America had experienced in wartime, but the virtues on which he placed most emphasis were those of the Good Samaritan rather than the soldier at war. "A spirit of justice, a spirit of teamwork, a spirit of sacrifice," was what the New Deal insisted on, he said, "but above all a spirit of neighborliness." Through the changes that were taking place in America, "we are extending to our National life the old principle of the local community; the principle that no individual, man, woman, or child, has a right to do things that hurt his neighbors."[33]

The establishment of a new moral climate was what principally distinguished the New Deal era from previous decades, the president often suggested. The twenties had been "an unfortunate decade characterized by a mad chase for unearned riches, and an unwillingness of leaders in almost every walk of life to look beyond their own schemes and speculations." Industrial relations in many cases resembled "the gang wars of the underworld." Such an unhealthy moral climate had caused or contributed to the onset of the depression. The dangerous situation the United States had got itself into was an outcome of "the general attitude 'every man for himself; the devil take the hindmost,' " an attitude that had permeated American life in the 1920s. "If every American were to make fair play his objective in his dealings with others," the president declared in February 1934, "most of our problems would disappear, many of which have arisen because of greed and selfishness."[34]

This rationale, if rationale is not too strong a term to describe the cluster of themes developed by the New Dealers in 1933, was soon undermined by economic and political developments. Within a few months of its inception, it had become apparent that the NRA had produced no miraculous recovery, and few of the programs introduced in 1934 or 1935 could by any stretch of the imagination be described as exercises in voluntarism. By the winter of 1933–34, moreover, the grand coalition of interest groups the administration had attempted to assemble was collapsing. Bitter disputes had broken out over various aspects of the NRA's policies, and business leaders and prominent Republicans were assailing the whole New Deal program with increasing vigor. To continue to wax enthusiastic about the value of voluntary cooperation and national unity when the most powerful economic interest groups in the nation were attacking the government's whole program made less and less sense.

The notion that the purpose of the New Deal was to introduce some new cooperative order to replace an outmoded individualism was never entirely abandoned. New Dealers continued to say that "this modern economic world of ours is governed by rules and regulations vastly more complex than those laid down in the days of Adam Smith or John Stuart Mill,"[35] and that social and economic institutions must be adjusted "from the individualistic era of the past to the interrelated, coordinated era in which we are now living."[36] They continued also to stress the decline of local self-sufficiency and the rise of national interdependence as the crucial element in this process of modernization.[37]

From 1934 onward, however, when New Dealers talked of the need for cooperative action to meet the needs of a complex "interrelated" economy, they almost invariably meant nothing more than action by federal agencies. In a speech at Green Bay, Wisconsin, on 9 August 1934, for example, President Roosevelt attacked "the forces which disregard human cooperation and human rights in seeking that kind of individual profit which is gained at the expense of his fellows," and pleaded for "the submerging of individual desires into unselfish and practical cooperation." As an example of noncooperation, however, he chose the case of a man who opposed government regulation of business. In December 1935, in a speech to the Farm Bureau, the president declared that "the people of the nation have learned more about effective cooperation in the past two and a half years than in the previous 25 years"; but he offered this remark as the conclusion to a speech that applauded the New Deal for putting "the power of government behind" all sections of the community.[38]

Once cooperative action came to mean governmental action, the idea that the New Deal was inaugurating an entirely new set of social values was bound to wither. During the heyday of the NRA, the appeal for cooperation had involved fairly specific demands on the American citizen. He was to buy only from stores displaying "The Blue Eagle," abide by the NRA codes, and so on. But if "learning about cooperation" meant learning what federal agencies could achieve, it was no longer clear how the individual citizen was supposed to express his devotion to the cooperative ethic other than by voting the straight Democratic ticket.

On occasions, the president suggested that Americans should replace grasping individualism with a more restrained pursuit of affluence. "Americans must forswear that conception of the acquisition of wealth which . . . creates undue private power over private affairs and . . . public affairs as well," he said in his annual message of 1935, and content themselves with "a proper security, a reasonable leisure, and a decent living throughout life." The objectives of young people had changed, the president told Young Democrats in August 1935.

> In the older days a great financial fortune was too often the goal. To rule through wealth, or through the power of wealth, fired our imagination. This was the dream of the golden ladder—each individual for himself. It is my firm belief that the newer generation of America has a different dream. You place emphasis on sufficiency of life rather than a plethora of riches. You think of . . . security for yourself and for your family. . . . Your advancement, you hope, is along a broad highway on which thousands of your fellow men and women are advancing with you.[39]

No doubt, in the depressed 1930s, it was not unreasonable to describe security and a modest living as "a dream"; but unlike the earlier call for cooperation, the thrust of these passages was largely negative. Americans must give up the search for great wealth, but no alternative goal was offered except less wealth. Moreover, even the forswearing of antisocial activity hardly called for any specific individual response, since by now it was clearly the government that bore the responsibility for suppressing exploitation and protecting the needy.

Another approach was to abandon the assault on individualism and to argue instead that New Dealers, and not their conservative opponents, were its true guardians. In his speech to Young Democrats in August 1935, the president had suggested that individual effort was acceptable as long as it did not impinge on the efforts of others. "These words 'freedom' and 'opportunity' do not mean a license to climb upwards by pushing other people down." Government did not seek to establish a complete paternalism but to provide a "minimum security . . . and to restrain the kind of individual action which in the past has been harmful to the community."[40]

With a slight shift of emphasis, the argument became a positive one —government action to protect the weak and restrain the strong would create true equality of opportunity and thereby open the competitive race to all. Far from restricting individual effort, the government was sustaining it. "To a great extent the achievements of invention, of mechanical and of artistic creation, must of necessity . . . be individual rather than governmental," the president said in San Diego on 2 October 1935.

> It is the self-reliant pioneer in every enterprise who beats the path along which American civilization has marched. Such individual effort is the glory of

America. The task of government is that of application and encouragement. A wise government seeks to provide the opportunity through which the best of individual achievement can be obtained. . . . Our common life under our various agencies of Government, our laws, and our basic Constitution exist primarily to protect the individual, to cherish his rights, and to make clear his just principles. It is this conception of service to the individual with which the Federal Government has concerned itself these two and a half years just passed.[41]

The purpose of liberal reform was not to transform American values but to regenerate them according to this formula. The president continued to talk about the value of cooperation in later addresses, but the San Diego speech indicated the general direction in which the New Dealer's rhetoric was heading in the middle and late 1930s.

When, toward the end of President Roosevelt's first year in office, business leaders and prominent Republicans began accusing the administration of throttling private enterprise and undermining American liberty, many Democrats responded by blasting their conservative opponents as apologists for exploitation and spokesmen for vested interests. As social and political divisions deepened in the following years, the antiprivilege theme assumed a more and more prominent place in New Dealers' rhetoric. By 1936, the war against the depression seemed to be turning into a war against reactionaries.

In general, it was Democratic congressmen rather than executive officials who were first to revive the familiar slogans of the progressive era in the service of the New Deal. The opening of the regular session of the Seventy-third Congress in January 1934 coincided with the beginnings of the conservative assault on the Roosevelt administration, and many congressional Democrats and some cabinet members seized upon these attacks as evidence that once more "the people" were at war with "the interests."

In the 1920s, Republican administration had blindly followed the lead of "so-called captains of industry and of big business." An "oligarchy of greed" had been fastened upon the country. Corruption and special privilege had been in control. Only banks, railroads, and big business had benefited from federal policies. In November 1933, "a bloodless revolution . . . had occurred, turning out from the seat of power the representatives of wealth and privilege." For the first time in years, Wall Street no longer enjoyed free access to the White House. At last, the

American people had a government that guaranteed "equal rights to all and special privileges to none."[42]

Unlike many of his subordinates and supporters, President Roosevelt made very little use of the antiprivilege theme until 1936, though he occasionally made jabs in that direction during 1934 and 1935. In March 1934, addressing the General Conference of Code Authorities, he declared that for a number of years "the machinery of democracy had failed to function" in the United States. Public inertia had allowed government to fall into the hands of "special groups," some of which were seeking "special advantages for special classes and others led by a handful of individuals who believed in their superhuman ability to retain in their own hands the entire business and financial control over the economic and social structure of the Nation."[43] This sally, however, was incidental to the main thrust of the speech, which stressed the need for planning, economic balance, and "the social point of view." Much the same could be said for the president's rhetoric in general during 1934 and 1935. Though he occasionally denounced "Tories" and spoke of "weaning out overprivilege," he generally preferred to emphasize less divisive themes at this stage.

In January 1936, the president took a new political tack when he devoted the bulk of his annual message, specially timed to reach the largest possible radio audience, to a thundering attack on "economic autocrats." The message began with a discussion of the international situation which concluded that "the evidence before us clearly proves that autocracy in world affairs endangers peace and that such threats do not spring from those nations devoted to the democratic ideal." If this were true in world affairs, the president continued ominously, "it should have the greatest weight in the determination of domestic policies." Within the United States, "popular opinion is at war with a power-seeking minority." Similar battles had been fought at the constitutional convention of 1787 and under Jefferson, Jackson, Theodore Roosevelt, and Woodrow Wilson. "In these latter years we have witnessed the domination of government by financial and industrial groups numerically small but politically dominant in the twelve years that succeeded the World War." In 1933, power had been restored to the people, but in doing so the government had "earned the hatred of entrenched greed." Now this "minority in business and industry" was seeking to restore its lost power and "gang up against the people's liberties."[44]

The president kept up this attack on the "economic autocrats" and their political allies throughout 1936. On 8 January, he compared the New Deal to Andrew Jackson's "many battles to protect the people against autocratic or oligarchic aggression." In his acceptance speech, at the Democratic convention in June, he dwelt at great length on the sins of "economic royalists" who had subverted political liberty by building "new kingdoms" through "control over material things" and who had then "reached out for control of Government itself." In his final campaign address in Madison Square Garden on 31 October, the president lashed out once more at "government by organized money."[45]

As the antiprivilege theme came to the fore, New Dealers began charging that the depression itself had been brought on by the selfish policies of the economic royalists and their political lackeys. The Republican party, according to James Farley, had followed "a policy of favoritism to special interests which, while it brought vast profit to those special interests, ignored the general public interest and so finally brought about a collapse of the whole economic structure." The country had "been brought to desperate straights by exploitation, by centering all processes on the increase of profits, legitimate or illegitimate, until production had sped far beyond the limits of consumption, and with little or no regard to the primary necessity of keeping the purchasing power of the country at large up."[46]

What was novel here was not the economic analysis itself but the terms in which it was presented. When New Dealers had spoken of an imbalance in the economy in 1933, they had meant, in part, that profits had been too high and wages and farm income too low. There was a significant difference, however, between attributing the depression to a lack of balance between wages and profits and blaming it on the fact that "our so-called captains of finance had skinned the country alive" or that the country had been governed for years by a "concealed dictatorship" that had been "skimming the cream off of American prosperity for a bunch of Brahmins in the pious hope that something would trickle down through fat fingers to the mass of people below."[47] In the one case, the problem was conceived of as the malfunctioning of a system; in the other, as the malpractices of men.

Implicit in this talk of exploitation and maldistributed wealth was another version of the administration's social goals. A plea for neighborliness was giving way to a demand for social justice. It must become "less possible for the powerful ones, whether they be in business, agriculture, or labor," said Secretary of Agriculture Henry Wallace, "to profiteer in terms of wages or prices at the expense of those at the bottom of the heap." The New Deal's principle objective, Senator Joseph O'Mahoney of Wyoming declared in February 1934, is "the liberation of our people from economic exploitation."[48]

Though these demands for social justice were commonly expressed in negative terms—exploitation must end, the maldistribution of wealth must be corrected—New Dealers also laid stress on the positive side of the question by insisting that such things as decent working conditions, reasonable wages, and full employment were not merely desirable objectives but essential prerequisites for the fulfilment of human rights. Donald Richberg spoke of a "new liberty which includes the right of every man to earn a living, the freedom of industrial workers from sweatshop wages and hours, the freedom of farmers from being compelled to sell their products below cost." Senator Robert F. Wagner of New York saw the New Deal's economic and social goals as "the twentieth century's bill of rights for the American people." President Roosevelt talked of guaranteeing "old and sacred possessive rights for which mankind has constantly struggled —homes, livelihood, and individual security."[49]

In tracing the various themes that appeared in New Dealers' rhetoric during the 1930s, it is easy to make the various changes that occurred from time to time appear more orderly and more complete than they were in fact. Soothing talk about cooperation and unity had never come easily to a pugnacious man like Harold Ickes, and from the outset he had stressed the need to root out privilege and redistribute income. Other New Dealers, such as Donald Richberg, never made much use of the antiprivilege theme, and talk of interdependence and cooperation did not disappear altogether from New Dealers' pronouncements even after the demise of the NRA. Nevertheless, the over-all trend between 1933 and 1936 is clear enough. In the early days, New Dealers had often compared the economic crisis to a wartime situation, especially the war of 1917–18. By 1936, they found a more congenial analogy in Andrew Jackson's war on the Bank of the United States. Having failed to unite the country, they now embraced divisiveness. Instead of summoning a united people to battle against a common enemy, New Dealers were now calling the common people to war against an enemy within.

In one obvious sense, the switch from cooperation and national unity to assaults on economic royalists and demands for social justice represented a turn toward a more radical appeal. The reconstruction of American society would rest on conflict and the coercive power of the state rather than harmony and voluntarism. Antiprivilege egalitarianism, on the other hand, was quite compatible with the kind of capitalistic individualism New Dealers had condemned so vigorously in 1933, and increasing emphasis on the antiprivilege theme coincided with less and less talk about a new cooperative order. Both approaches, then, may be said to have had a conservative aspect: the one insisted that change could occur without social strife or coercion; the other did not challenge the basic institutions and values of society but merely promised to distribute the benefits more equitably.

New Dealers themselves were well aware that the doctrines they were propagating were something less than revolutionary, and their speeches contained many assurances to this effect. President Roosevelt's address to the Democratic state convention at Syracuse, New York, on 29 September 1936, was perhaps the fullest and most eloquent statement of the conservative intent of the New Deal's reform measures. It was the Democrats and not the Republicans, the president declared, who were the real enemies of communism in the United States, because it was the Democrats who had acted decisively to relieve the social distress that bred communism. "The true conservative seeks to protect this system of private property and free enterprise by correcting such injustices and inequalities as arise from it. The most serious threat to our institutions comes from those who refuse to face the need for change. Liberalism becomes the protection for the far-sighted conservative."[50]

The idea that the Roosevelt administration, and not its right-wing opponents, was the true conservator of American institutions and traditions was one that New Dealers most commonly invoked to rebut the charge that they were undermining individual liberty in the United States. Liberty, as far as the conservatives were concerned, meant the absence of oppression by the state; and since this was the commonly accepted definition, and since there could be little doubt that the Roosevelt adminstration had extended the power of the federal government, the question of "liberty" was not an easy one for New Dealers to handle.

At times, they admitted that their programs did involve placing restrictions on the freedom of individuals to do as they chose, but denied that any truly important freedom had been abridged by such restrictions. What the conservatives called freedom, they argued, was really "antisocial license," the kind of freedom "one takes in running by a red traffic light in an automobile."[51] In the modern world, the complexity of life demanded greater restrictions on individual action to protect the common interests of the community. "No civilized community ever existed without restraints," Joseph Kennedy argued. The president "is merely continuing a long established evolutionary trend of balance between individualism and social control." The important freedom in the modern world, Donald Richberg said, was "not the freedom of a wild beast to hunt alone and fight a world of enemies." Certainly, "ancient liberties for which mankind has always struggled are just as precious . . . as they ever were. But we must restrain and discipline ourselves more and more in order to enjoy the advantages of modern life and to protect our freedom and security." Surely it was indefensible, Assistant Attorney General John Dickenson pleaded, to treat economic restrictions as "interferences with personal freedom in its essential or spiritual sense." Economic freedom was far less important than religious freedom or freedom of speech, and at the same time "it is in the field of economic conduct that the action of one individual may most adversely affect the interests of others."[52]

If some freedoms were more desirable than others, how could one know whether the suppression of the latter would not tend to undermine the former? What assurances could there be that increased federal power would always be used for benevolent purposes? Insofar as they attempted to answer this sort of question, New Dealers stressed the notion that government in America was an instrument of the people and hence could not endanger the people's liberties. The pioneers, the president said, had believed they "could create and use forms of government that would not enslave the human spirit but free it and nourish it throughout the generations. They did not fear government because they knew that government in the new world was their own." Government was not to be looked upon as "something apart from the people . . . [but] something to be used by the people for their own good." Should the people come to distrust the intentions of government, the solution lay in the electoral process. "The essential democracy of our Nation and the safety of our people," the president declared in his second inaugural address, "depend not upon the absence of power but upon lodging it with those whom the people can change or continue at stated intervals through an honest and free system of elections."[53]

This line of argument left unresolved the problems of individual and minority rights, since "free and honest elections" did not preclude the possibility of tyranny by the majority. It was also an argument that was difficult to reconcile with the contention that the federal government had been dominated by nefarious vested interests during the 1920s, and quite impossible to reconcile with one striking passage in President Roosevelt's annual message of 1936. The economic autocrats, the president warned on that occasion, "realize that in thirty-four months we have built up new instruments of public power. In the hands of a people's Government this power is wholesome and proper. But in the hands of political puppets of an economic autocracy such power would provide shackles for the liberties of the people."[54] The Republican opposition was quick to seize upon this admission by the president that strong centralized government was indeed a threat to "the people's liberties,"[55] and the president did not repeat the mistake.

Now and again some New Dealers confessed publicly that the expansion of federal power might pose some threat to individual liberty, but such occasions were rare. Henry Wallace, speaking at the University of North Carolina in 1937, expressed concern that "if government marched into the economic field decisively and directly at the top, the result can be regimentation of all types of activity in a manner completely abhorrent to the American temperament." The answer, as Wallace saw it, was an "economic democracy" modeled on the AAA but involving a reorganization of all sections of the economy on syndicalist lines—a scheme that went far beyond any administration proposal.[56]

Clearly, all this was dangerous ground for New Deal rhetoricians; and, rather than dwell at length on how liberty might be protected from some malevolent administration, they much preferred to stress ways in which individual freedom had been preserved and extended under the benevolence of the present administration. In the first place, they argued that the New Deal had saved liberty in America by curing the economic and social problems that had produced anarchy and dictatorship elsewhere. "I suppose there does not exist in the whole country a more committed believer in the democratic process than I am," Rexford Tugwell assured the American Society of Newspaper Editors on 21 April 1934. "But I happen to be really interested in its survival. . . . For this something more than windy eulogies to liberty is necessary."[57]

At times, New Dealers claimed that the Roosevelt administration had extended liberty in the United States by striking down the power of the economic autocrats who had supposedly dominated the government in the 1920s. "My reply to the assertion of Mr. [Ogden] Mills that liberty has been slain during the present administration," said Senator Joseph Robinson of Arkansas, "is that insofar as the masses of our population are concerned, there is far more liberty now than was enjoyed by our citizens generally when he stood close to the seat of power and whispered to the head of the Government the dubious course to be taken to strengthen and to build up privilege and monopoly at the sacrifice of the common citizen's liberty and welfare." Regimentation, Congressman John W. Flanagan of Virginia declared, had been practiced by Wall Street before Trotsky, Stalin, Hitler, and Mussolini were born. The nation was moving away from dictatorship, not toward it, according to Congressman Samuel B. Pettengill of Indiana. "We had a dictatorship. It was the dictatorship of the dollar." The nation had moved toward greater democracy, President Roosevelt claimed in his second inaugural speech, because "we have begun to bring private autocratic powers into their proper subordination to the public government."[58]

Most commonly, however, New Dealers based the argument that they were extending freedom on the idea that "necessitous men are not free men." According to this view, Americans had lacked complete freedom under Republican rule not so much because at that time they had been controlled or regimented by big business but because they had been abandoned by a heartless government to poverty and insecurity. Some of the New Deal's opponents, Senator Wagner said, claimed that man had become a pawn of the state, but did they not realize "that under the system which they defend, the individual is a pawn of fate—buffeted and torn like the wandering and lost Ulysses." Liberty, in the conditions of 1932, said a Democratic congressman, meant only "the liberty to starve in a land of plenty."[59]

The people had their own notions about liberty, Harold Ickes declared. "To them it means the right of every man who is willing to work to have a job at wages adequate to support in decency and comfort his family, to educate his children, and to give him a modest surplus. . . . Liberty means to him protection by the State of the individual from exploitation. It means the abolition of child labor; the end of sweatshops; healthful and sanitary living conditions; the clearance of slum areas; adequate school facilities." A man who was denied the right to work, Donald Richberg said, had been effectively denied his liberty. "Liberty and security are inseparable." In the 1940s, President Roosevelt was to build on this theme in his appeals for the "four freedoms" and the "economic bill of rights."[60]

The idea that economic and social security were essential underpinnings of political and civil liberties was not, of course, entirely novel. It can be traced back at least as far as late nineteenth-century critics of laissez faire economics and Social Darwinism in the United States. Nevertheless, it was an idea that had gained little currency at the level of national party politics until New Dealers made such play with it in the 1930s. For them, it represented an ideal way of introducing an essentially radical notion in a rather conservative guise. Major extensions of federal power in the spheres of economic and social policy were justified as means of preserving and extending individual rights guaranteed by the Constitution. It was a characteristically American way of defending the welfare state.

In effect, New Dealers did not present a case for the New Deal but several cases. Whether or not the voters found them less persuasive for this reason is impossible to tell, but it is clear that each of the strands that ran through the rhetoric of the New Deal bore some obvious relationship to the major concerns of the 1930s. The emphasis on activism, on results, on getting practical things done was calculated to appeal both to a traditional American value and to the demand for a government that could cope with the economic crisis more effectively than Hoover's had. The need for national unity, cooperation, and social solidarity was urged at a time when the economic and social structures of the country seemed to be on the verge of collapse and when millions had learned the bitter lesson of what rugged individualism could mean on the downward slide of a deflationary spiral. Assaults on privilege and social injustice were as old as the Republic and as serviceable in the bitter social climate of the middle thirties as they had ever been. The idea that a man had a right to social and economic security in the same way that he had a right to civil and political liberty must have been particularly appealing to a generation that had suffered from the most severe economic collapse in the nation's history.

By contrast, the conservatives' diatribes against positive government, and their insistence that economic individualism was as relevant to the depressed 1930s as it had ever been, seem to have been maladroit and inappropriate. It is not surprising that politicians who emphasized the glorious achievements of unregulated capitalism during the worst slump in history and who emphasized thrift, enterprise, and competitiveness at a time when the exercise of these bourgeois virtues had saved few from some measure of deprivation, went down to such resounding defeats in 1934 and 1936.

Nevertheless, the conservatives recovered from the electoral disasters of the middle 1930s, and anti-statist individualism survived the New Deal as a popular political credo. A welfare state generates not only gratitude from those who gain from its beneficence but resentment from those who do not, or are jealous of those who appear to have gained more. A government that extends the scope of its activities is bound to create enemies as well as friends. Even before the recession of 1937, the Roosevelt administration had accumulated many enemies who responded warmly to the anti-statist appeals of the conservative opposition.

Moreover, despite the New Deal, life in postdepression America remained essentially competitive and individualistic. A corporation might depend for its existence on federal armaments contracts or more distantly on the purchasing power generated by government expenditure. Yet the men and women who worked for that corporation would be hired, fired, or promoted on the basis of their talents and industry in competition with others. A farmer's prosperity might rest ultimately on federal crop control programs, but he would still be a property-owning entrepreneur; and how prosperous he became under the umbrella of federal protection would still depend upon his entrepreneurial talents. Certainly, it would gratify him to think so.

The Roosevelt administration created a new role for the federal government in the 1930s, and the expansion of federal power was accompanied by significant social and economic changes. Yet, American society had not been transformed so fundamentally that an entirely new set of cultural values emerged to displace the old. In the early days of the Roosevelt administration, New Dealers had denounced economic individualism and competitiveness as outworn creeds and had proposed to put cooperation, neighborliness, and national unity in their place. Any substance that may have lain behind these slogans, however, collapsed with the NRA; and the case for the New Deal came to rest on the more modest claim that positive government could render an individualistic, capitalistic society more stable, more equalitarian, and more humane.

These propositions were widely accepted in the United States after the 1930s. In the generation that succeeded the New Deal, it never seemed very likely that many of its major innovations, such as social security and farm price supports, would be abandoned. Rather, they were extended and supplemented by new agencies and programs of the welfare state variety. Nevertheless, resistance to welfare statism remained much stronger in the United States than in any comparable capitalist nation, and the suspicion lingered that there was something rather un-American about big government. Many Americans who clung to their social security benefits and the TVA continued to believe in their hearts that Barry Goldwater was right.

The writer wishes to thank the American Council of Learned Societies for generous financial support, and the administrative committee and staff of the Charles Warren Center for Studies in American History, Harvard University, for their help and hospitality, while research for this paper was being carried out. An earlier version was presented to a conference of the Australian and New Zealand American Studies Association at La Trobe University, Victoria, Australia, in August 1970.

1. *New York Times*, 13 Sept. 1936.

2. William E. Leuchtenburg, *Franklin D. Roosevelt and the New Deal, 1932–1940* (New York, 1963), p. 273.

3. Samuel I. Rosenman, ed., *The Public Papers and Addresses of Franklin D. Roosevelt*, 13 vols. (New York, 1938–50), 2:165, 490; 5:164–65; Rexford Tugwell, *New York Times*, 28 June 1934; Robert Jackson, 28 Jan. 1938, *Congressional Record*, 75th Cong., 3d sess., Appendix, p. 379.

4. Rosenman, ed., *Public Papers of FDR*, 1:646.

5. *Congressional Record*, 76th Cong., 1st sess., Appendix, p. 3462.

6. James A. Farley, 2 Mar. 1936, ibid., 74th Cong., 2d sess., p. 3246.

7. *Vital Speeches*, 6 May 1935, p. 500.

8. Rosenman, ed., *Public Papers of FDR*, 5:568.

9. See, for example, James A. Farley, *The New Deal and Old Hickory* (Washington, 1935), in which Farley detailed the benefits received by Pennsylvania from the New Deal, including the amount spent there by specific federal agencies.

10. *Congressional Record*, 74th Cong., 2d sess., p. 640.

11. See, for example, speeches by Harold Ickes, *New York Times*, 24 May 1934, and Roosevelt in Rosenman, ed., *Public Papers of FDR*, 5:566–67.

12. Rep. Matthew A. Dunn, Pennsylvania, *Congressional Record*, 74th Cong., 1st sess., p. 209.

13. Ibid., 73d Cong., 2d sess., p. 70.

14. Rep. John J. Cochran, ibid., 74th Cong., 2d sess., p. 10827.

15. Rosenman, ed., *Public Papers of FDR*, 2:49–54.

16. Ibid., 2:296; William Woodin, James A. Farley, Franklin D. Roosevelt, *New York Times*, 16, 19 Sept., 11 Dec. 1933.

17. *New York Times*, 5 Jan. 1934.

18. Rosenman, ed., *Public Papers of FDR*, 5:333, 444.

19. After 1937, spokesmen for the Roosevelt administration did, on occasions, advocate the deliberate creation of budget deficits to stimulate the economy. See speeches by James Roosevelt, *Congressional Record*, 75th Cong., 3d sess., 1665-67; Roosevelt in Rosenman, ed., *Public Papers of FDR*, 8:9–11; Henry Wallace, *Congressional Record*, 76th Cong., 1st sess., Appendix, pp. 85–87.

20. Rosenman, ed., *Public Papers of FDR*, 4:478; 5:488; Joseph P. Kennedy, "The Administration and Business," *New York Times Magazine*, 6 Sept. 1936, p. 1; Senators Joseph T. Robinson, Arkansas, and Alben W. Barkley, Kentucky, *New York Times*, 4 Mar., 24 June 1936; Senators James F. Byrnes, South Carolina, and Frederick Van Nuys, Indiana, *Congressional Record*, 73d Cong., 2d sess., p. 11345; 74th Cong., 2d sess., pp. 2280–81; Representatives Henry T. Rainey, Illinois, and Joseph T. Byrns, Tennessee, ibid., 73d Cong., 2d sess., pp. 6660–61, 11835–37; James A Farley, ibid., p. 4052.

21. Rosenman, ed., *Public Papers of FDR*, 3:287.

22. Ibid., 2:299.

23. Ellis W. Hawley, *The New Deal and the Problem of Monopoly* (Princeton, N.J., 1968), pp. 19–146.

24. Henry Wallace, Sen. Robert F. Wagner, New York, Hugh Johnson, *New York Times*, 10, 22 May, 2 Sept. 1933: Donald Richberg, "Balance, Not Planning, Is Richberg's Aim," *New York Times Magazine*, 9 Sept. 1934, p. 3.

25. Senator Wagner, Assistant Secretary of Commerce John Dickenson, Attorney General Homer Cummings, Hugh Johnson, *New York Times*, 22 May, 1 Sept., 11 Oct. 1933.

26. Ibid., 22 May 1933.

27. Henry Wallace, Harold Ickes, Donald Richberg, *New York Times*, 10, 22 May, 10 Dec. 1933; Rosenman, ed., *Public Papers of FDR*, 2:518; 3:124.

28. Henry Wallace, *New York Times*, 22 May 1933.

29. Rosenman, ed., *Public Papers of FDR*, 2:252, 298.

30. *New York Times*, 13 Sept. 1933; Donald Richberg, "NRA Ideals: A Reply to Critics," *New York Times Magazine*, 25 Feb. 1934, p. 1.

31. *New York Times*, 22 May, 19 Oct., 10 Dec. 1933.

32. Henry Wallace and Frances Perkins, ibid., 10 May, 5 Oct. 1933; Rosenman, ed., *Public Papers of FDR*, 2:156–57, 385–87.

33. Rosenman, ed., *Public Papers of FDR*, 2:380, 340.

34. Ibid., 3:10, 123, 313; *New York Times*, 13 Feb. 1934.

35. Rosenman, ed., *Public Papers of FDR*, 4:339.

36. Daniel Roper, *New York Times*, 23 June 1935.

37. Rosenman, ed., *Public Papers of FDR*, 4:209–10; 5:178, 334, 462, 483–85, 496–97.

38. Ibid., 3:372–73; 4:490.

39. Ibid., 4:17, 339.

40. Ibid., 5:341–42.

41. Ibid., 4:406–7.

42. Representatives Wright Patman, Texas, and Henry T. Rainey, Illinois, Senator Bennett Champ Clark, Missouri, *Congressional Record*, 73d Cong., 2d sess., pp. 495, 6899–901, 6944–45; James A. Farley, ibid., p. 4051; Harold Ickes, *New York Times*, 9 Feb. 1934.

43. Rosenman, ed., *Public Papers of FDR*, 3:124.

44. Ibid., 5:8–18.

45. Ibid., 5:38–44, 230–36, 566–73.

46. *Congressional Record*, 73d Cong., 2d sess., pp. 5093–94.

47. Hugh Johnson, *New York Times*, 8 Dec. 1933, 9 June 1934.

48. Ibid., 25 Nov. 1933; *Congressional Record*, 73d Cong., 2d sess., p. 2722.

49. *New York Times*, 6 Sept. 1934; *Vital Speeches*, 14 Jan. 1935, p. 248; Rosenman, ed., *Public Papers of FDR*, 3:292.

50. Rosenman, ed., *Public Papers of FDR*, 5:389.

51. Henry Wallace and Senator Wagner, *New York Times*, 6, 27 Sept. 1934.

52. Joseph P. Kennedy, *I'm for Roosevelt* (New York, 1936), p. 107; *Vital Speeches*, 3 Dec. 1934, p. 136; John Dickenson, *Hold Fast the Middle Way: An Outline of Economic Challenge and Alternatives* (Boston, 1935), pp. 219–21.

53. Rosenman, ed., *Public Papers of FDR*, 3:370–71; 5:387; 6:2; 9:437; Robert Jackson, *Congressional Record*, 76th Cong., 3d sess., Appendix, p. 3930.

54. Rosenman, ed., *Public Papers of FDR*, 5:16.

55. See, for example, the remarks of former Secretary of the Treasury Ogden Mills, *Vital Speeches*, 15 July 1936, p. 657.

56. Henry Wallace, *Technology, Corporations, and the General Welfare* (Chapel Hill, N.C., 1937), p. 75.

57. Rexford Tugwell, *The Battle for Democracy* (New York, 1935), p. 200; see also Kennedy, *I'm for Roosevelt*, chap. 10.

58. *Congressional Record*, 73d Cong., 2d sess., pp. 1567, 10716, 11247; Rosenman, ed., *Public Papers of FDR*, 6:2.

59. *New York Times*, 27 Sept. 1934; *Congressional Record*, 73d Cong., 2d sess., p. 12285.

60. Harold Ickes, *The New Democracy* (New York, 1934), pp. 45–56; *Congressional Record*, 74th Cong., 1st sess., p. 2716; *Vital Speeches*, 11 Feb. 1935; Rosenman, ed., *Public Papers of FDR*, 9:671–72; 13:40–41.

Ellis W. Hawley

The New Deal and Business

As depicted by most American historians in the 1950s, the "mixed economy" of the United States was a superlative blend of two worlds, a system that combined rational direction, organizational security, and stable growth with a large measure of democratic decision-making, individual liberty, and local and private initiative. While bringing competitive excesses and harmful fluctuations under administrative control, it had also developed a system of "countervailing powers," a "corporate conscience," and a vigorous "inter-industry competition," all of which had enabled it to retain the dynamism and safeguards associated with free markets and competitive enterprise. And though it was still far from perfect, its amazing productivity had all but solved the quantitative problems of production and distribution, thus providing the material base for a new type of qualitative and cultural reform.[1] Looking back, moreover, these writers credited Franklin D. Roosevelt and his New Deal with much of the historical development responsible for this happy state of affairs. By modernizing and defending the American political system, they argued, and by using it to stabilize, democratize, and humanize an unruly corporate capitalism, the pragmatic New Dealers had provided the basic framework within which the nation's liberal-democratic ideals could be preserved and realized.[2]

More recently, as views of the economy have changed, this older image of the New Deal has become somewhat tarnished. The central development in recent American history, according to a new group of institutionalist scholars, has been the rise of bureaucratic industrialism, not the further advance of liberal democracy; and the chief impetus to reform, they insist, has come from organizational elites in search of stability and order, not from liberal democrats seeking equality and social justice.[3] Hence, the New Deal was more the product of corporate capitalism rather than the shaper of it. In essence, it provided a threatened managerial elite with the political tools needed to maintain social stability, rationalize market behavior, and solve the problems of aggregate demand and developmental capital.[4] And the results, according to another group of younger and more radical scholars, have been tragic.[5] Out of the failure of "reform," they contend, came a bastard liberalism, a "corporate" variety, which, in the name of "progress," built illiberal and undemocratic institutions that have, in effect, perpetuated social injustice and economic tyranny, required constant involvement abroad, and transformed what should be a free people into mindless bureaucrats and earnest consumers.[6]

These divergent views, of course, may well tell us more about the 1950s and 1960s than about the 1930s. Yet, they do raise major questions concerning the nature of the political economy that was hammered out during the New Deal years, who it was that did the hammering, and how such conflicting estimates of it could be made. They also suggest that New Deal activities might be profitably explored within a broader perspective, one that would see them as part of a continuing but never wholly successful effort to resolve the tensions between bureaucratic industrialism and a liberal-democratic ethos. In the 1930s, as the political arena became a confusing battleground for conflicting industrial groups seeking stability and salvation, rival groups of reformers seeking to remedy a "defective" and "oppressive" economic structure, and competing models of how one could reconcile a techno-corporate order with America's democratic heritage, the tensions became particularly acute. But the dilemma that underlay them was not new. Nor would it disappear with the passing of the New Deal.

For business-government relations, in fact, the period of the New Deal is probably best viewed as a time when one resolution of these tensions between organizational capitalism and the liberal-democratic ethos, the resolution that emerged in the 1920s, broke down, lost credence, and was rejected as being both unworkable and tyrannical. The result was an intense but confused search for another synthesis, one, so most agreed, that would necessarily involve a larger role for government. And New Deal policy, as it fluctuated between competing models and built new bureaucracies, did lay the groundwork for the point of resolution that was lauded in the 1950s. In this sense, it represented a new departure. Yet it was also tied to the past, both in the sense that it was trying to cope with a continuing problem, one that antedated the depression, and in the sense that most of the competing models offered as solutions derived from past experience, particularly from conflicting progressive visions, variants of the "planned economy" of World War I, or logical extensions of the cooperative associationalism that had been hailed as the answer during the New Era but found wanting after 1929. Seen in perspective, the origins, formulation, and effects of New Deal policy fit into a broader framework of long-standing tensions and repeated efforts at resolution; and it is to the task of examining them within this framework that the remainder of this essay will be devoted.

In recent years, historians have disagreed sharply about business-government relations during the progressive era.[7] But from all they have said, two things seem to stand out. One was the rapid rise of an organizational economy, which brought with it large areas of "private government," new bureaucratic-scientific-professional values, and a persistent search for order and stability, primarily through the creation of ever larger associative and hierarchic structures, the infusing of these with a new set of managerial attitudes and group loyalties, and the use of the state, where necessary and expedient, to further the process.[8] The other was an ambivalent cluster of reform efforts, striving in general to resolve the tensions between the new order and the liberal-democratic-village values that it threatened,[9] yet deeply divided over the point at which this should take place, the degree of centralization needed, and the method by which liberty could best be advanced.[10] Not surprisingly, different reform models appeared; and around these, as seekers of order and both "old" and "new" liberals clashed, compromised, and merged into one another, many of the period's debates swirled.

Four models, in particular, were significant. The first, best known as Wilson's New Freedom and best articulated by Louis Brandeis, held that bureaucratic centralism had gone beyond technological needs, that this "new tyranny" rested chiefly on special privilege and "unfair" or "unnatural" behavior, and that the state could best advance freedom by removing these aids to concentration and forging an economy that was not only modern and scientific but competitive, ethical, and decentralized as well.[11] The second model, the New Nationalism of Herbert Croly and Theodore Roosevelt, held just the opposite: that concentration and cooperation did stem from technological needs, and consequently, to liberate and democratize, the state must forge national controls and use them to advance social justice, promote cooperation in the public interest, and provide the material base for a new and higher individualism.[12] The third model, generally labeled the New Competition and associated particularly with the trade association promoter and spokesman for business progressivism Arthur J. Eddy, held that through self-regulating associations, codes of ethics, and schemes of "industrial betterment," the new economy was itself developing an "industrial democracy," a "purer" competition, a "higher individualism." Hence, it needed only encouragement and guidance, not regulation and restructuring.[13] And finally, implicit in much agitation and explicit with a few theorists, was an incipient model of interest-group liberalism, one that would allegedly advance liberty by balancing groups against each other and allowing this to take the place of classical competition.[14]

All of these designs were and would remain influential, but none succeeded at the time in becoming completely dominant. On the surface, to be sure, the New Freedom came closest. Such measures as the Clayton, Federal Trade Commission, and Federal Reserve Acts were all officially based upon it. Yet, special measures reflecting rival views were also enacted; and of greater significance, the machinery established by the New Freedom laws could be and was used to alter their basic thrust. The Federal Trade Commission, in particular, was potentially an instrument of national control, a promoter of the New Competition, or a defender of the status quo as well as a market restorer. And in practice, the fluctuating policies reflected a continuation of earlier debates.[15] As Robert Wiebe has noted, progressivism established "no more than a framework," the assumption being that "the right men in the right offices" would do the rest.[16]

What these men would do was also affected by the war experience of 1917 and 1918. For war purposes now, an emergency government took shape, private organizations became arms of the state, and leaders from the private power structure, serving for the duration as public officials, proceeded through a burgeoning network of administrative controls, cooperative arrangements, and promotional-advisory-educational organs to mobilize and direct the nation's resources. As a result, organizational elites and values were strengthened; notions of national management, social engineering, and cooperative commonwealths excited wartime dreamers; and for some, another model of business-government relations emerged. An efficient and purposeful yet allegedly democratic order, they would remember, could be created by a mixture of national planning, public relations techniques, industrial self-government, and massive injections of state capital.[17]

At war's end, however, not many wanted to retain the wartime system intact. Portions of it had produced strong irritations. Mass sentiment, reflecting postwar disillusionments, seemed bent upon a "return to normalcy." And corporate leaders, after testing public opinion, quickly concluded that the resurgent hostility toward "monopoly," "profiteering," and political capitalism was likely to make the "benefits" that could be derived from a "Peace Industries Board" far too costly. Accordingly, the strategy upon which they soon settled was essentially one of seeking national coordination without an enlarged state bureaucracy, insisting that the resulting enlargement of "private government" was the "American way," and channeling most of the reaction against centralization into attacks on "big government," "big labor," and "un-American" radicals.[18] Reform, moreover, quickly adjusted to the changed climate. Although advocates of enforced competition, governmental management, and interest-group liberalism did not disappear, the leadership in the "progressive" camp passed to champions of the New Competition and cooperative associationalism.[19]

Viewed through the depression wreckage, of course, this approach to reform seemed futile, hypocritical, and sinister. Yet for Americans in the 1920s, benefiting as they were from rapid industrial expansion and a technological breakthrough into a mass consumption economy, associationalism did seem to resolve the tensions between industrial needs and fulfillment of the national heritage. By fostering welfare capitalism and cooperative institutions—particularly trade associations, professional societies, and subordinate farm and labor groups—such policy-makers as Secretary of Commerce Herbert Hoover were allegedly meeting the needs for stability, efficiency, and security, all without sacrificing the safeguards and creativity inherent in individual initiative and "healthy" competition. And through a "cooperative system," one in which "progressive" federal agencies used "scientific" inquiries and promotional-advisory techniques to generate "constructive action" on the part of enlightened economic leaders, self-governing associations, and local communities, they were also meeting the needs for over-all direction and coordinated attacks on national problems, again without resort to such freedom-destroying methods as government regulation, public enterprise, or politicized cartels.[20] Some dissenters there were, but as the leading advocate and promoter of such policies, Hoover seemed the logical choice for president in 1928. To many of his fellow citizens, he had become the supreme embodiment of a higher synthesis of the old and the new; and judging from the election returns, most of them seemed satisfied with his interpretation of the "American way."

Steady progress toward a capitalist utopia, however, was not to be. Even if the New Era system had continued to expand economically, its failure to cope with a variety of social problems would probably, in time, have produced insistent demands for "democratization." And, as it turned out, the system was unable to generate the mass purchasing power and steady flow of new capital needed for continued expansion. The result, beginning in 1929, was contraction; and once this began, the old tensions between bureaucratic industrialism and the liberal-democratic ethos reasserted themselves in acute form. On one hand, the industrial champions of the "higher individualism" and "cooperative system" gradually lost confidence in their own solutions and were soon urging that they be given new powers or that the state help them to plan, rationalize, and stabilize their operations. On the other, the notion that "private government" combined expert efficiency with liberal, democratic, humane, and uniquely American values came under increasing attack. Associationalism, many more came to believe, was merely a facade behind which selfish "monopolists" had concentrated and abused their power, thus plunging the nation into the depression. And in the wake of this disillusionment came insistent demands that liberal-democratic ideals be made good, demands for dismantling, restructuring, regulating, supervising, or nationalizing the controls that "private governors" had abused.[21]

Caught in the middle, Hoover resisted both sets of demands, claimed that yielding to either would destroy the basis for further progress, and stayed, for the most part, within his cherished framework of voluntary associationalism. Building on devices he had championed during the recession of 1921, he called the nation's economic leaders together, set up appropriate committees, and secured pledges of wage maintenance, economic stabilization, and expanded construction, all designed to short-circuit the business cycle and generate the needed investment and purchasing power. To implement these, he again turned to private groups; and to supplement them, he tried, again primarily by means of promotional-advisory techniques, to expand local and federal public works, make needed credits and investment funds available, and reestablish business confidence.[22]

A failure, however, in checking economic contraction, such efforts could not halt the conflicting demands for a new approach, some recommending a reversion to laissez faire,[23] but many more urging proposals based on resurrected progressive models, memories of the war, or more coercive styles of business-government cooperation. From liberal "planners," for example, came a revived New Nationalism, blended now with war memories, an admiration for some aspects of the Russian "experiment," and much talk about "scientific management," "functional syndicates," and "democratic collectivism."[24] From farm and labor spokesmen came arguments that "balancing" the economy would advance both recovery and liberty.[25] From neo-Brandeisians and rural "progressives" came calls for an updated New Freedom.[26] From men who recalled the effects of wartime financing and who had later argued that public spending could become an economic "balance wheel" came plans for massive bond issues and public works programs.[27] And from business leaders and their political allies, a few of whom seemed to admire some aspects of the Italian "experiment," came numerous proposals for antitrust revision, compulsory industrial codes, or new agencies based on the war models. By late 1931, the National Civic Federation, the Chamber of Commerce, and a Congress of Industries were all pushing specific plans; Gerard Swope of General Electric had attracted wide attention with his vision of "planning" by compulsory trade associations; and in industry after industry, similar schemes were appearing.[28]

Actually, as later historians would note, the Hoover administration was clearing the way for such proposals, particularly by demonstrating the inadequacy of "cooperation" and fostering the necessary institutional machinery. Given its experience, the "logical next steps" seemed to require that an ineffective associationalism be strengthened by governmental sanctions and controls, that the supplementary public spending and lending programs and the "gestures" toward protecting farm and labor income be greatly expanded, and that responsibility for social welfare be shifted further to the federal level.[29] Yet, given Hoover's commitments and outlook, these steps would not come in 1931 or 1932. His approach, he convinced himself, had not failed. Success had merely been delayed by adverse developments abroad and political sabotage at home. And in the name of "true" progressivism, he threw his energies into blocking both the business advocates of "industrial dictatorship" and the "new liberals," people, he was convinced, who were really "totalitarians," "socialists," or irresponsible "demagogues" and "spendthrifts."[30]

In fighting these "challenges to liberty," moreover, the president remained for a time a formidable obstacle to any new departure. His "second program," as it took shape in 1932, was limited mostly to shoring up the financial system, supporting relief activities with federal loans, and trying, even at the cost of higher taxes and the risk of further contraction, to defend those alleged "pillars" of business confidence, the gold standard and a balanced budget. The "new liberalism," as embodied in a variety of planning, spending, and regulatory proposals, made little headway.[31] And neither did the numerous schemes for a more coercive style of business-government cooperation. The antitrust laws, Hoover conceded, could stand some revision, particularly for natural resource industries. But anxious to prevent a system of "closed cartels," mindful of rising antibusiness sentiment, and convinced that smuggling the techniques of European facism through a "back door" would lead either to a rightist tyranny or to the eventual triumph of a sterile socialism, he would endorse neither repeal, suspension, special exemptions, nor the type of supervised "business planning" envisioned by Swope and like-minded corporate leaders.[32] By 1932, much of the early New Deal was waiting in the wings, but not until Hoover had been blasted away by the voting returns could the "experimentation" begin.

The shift from Hoover to Roosevelt, then, did bring a new departure in business-government relations. After three years of deepening depression climaxed by a banking crisis, demands for change had become insistent; and under an administration committed to "doing something," the government's role in the economy quickly became a larger one. The novelty of this "new deal," however, has often been exaggerated.[33] The shift was not from laissez faire to a managed economy, but rather from one attempt at management, that through informal business-government cooperation, to another more formal and coercive attempt. The tensions that had reappeared, although altered somewhat by the economic situation and the relative decline of an older middle class of small capitalists and independent professionals, were essentially the same ones that earlier policymakers had tried to resolve. And the guiding models for a new order were mostly inherited ones, not alien imports or instant improvisations. They derived from what innovators had envisioned during the progressive period, from the experience during World War I, from agitation outside the consensus of the 1920s, and from what seemed to be the "lessons" of Hoover's experience or "logical extensions" of his approach.[34]

The new administration, moreover, despite its critics' charges and its own claims of "pragmatism," was committed to change only within a relatively rigid "middle way," one that, to be sure, was broader than Hoover's, but at the same time was clearly limited by fixed ideological boundaries.[35] Ruled out on one side were stabilizing arrangements involving the open avowal of a "closed,"[36] "authoritarian," or "monopolistic" system. Ruled out on the other were liberalizing or democratizing reforms that would seriously jeopardize capitalist incentives, constitutional safeguards, modern technology, or recovery prospects.[37] And ruled out, even when they came within these limits, were programs whose implementation would require excessive conflict or some radically new type of politics or administration. The disposition, by and large, was to adjust differences, make accommodations, and build on existing institutions.[38]

Still, within these elements of continuity, there was a commitment to change, or at least to "action." And once the government had changed hands, a variety of different types of activists began pushing their particular visions of what should replace the Hoover approach to business-government relations. Some, ranging from Rexford Tugwell on the left to Hugh Johnson on the right, were either national or business-oriented "planners." Deriving their models from either the New Nationalism, the war experience, or the vision of an associational capitalism, they were ready now to accept an organizational as opposed to a competitive system, restructure it somewhat in the interests of better "balance," and then "manage" it so as to insure sustained expansion and make possible a reflowering of the liberal-democratic heritage. Others, including western "antimonopolists" like William Borah and Wright Patman, Brandeisian-oriented lawyers like Thomas Corcoran and Benjamin Cohen, farm leaders like Edward O'Neal and John Simpson, and spokesmen for urban labor like Robert Wagner, were either decentralizers or balancers. Heirs of the New Freedom or spokesmen for disadvantaged interest groups, they were insistent now that recovery and freedom must come not by centralizing power but by dispersing it, revitalizing the market system, or strengthening a previously exploited group. And still others, men like the agricultural economist George Warren, the Oklahoma inflationist Elmer Thomas, and the Utah banker Marriner Eccles, were "reflationists," concerned not with structural reform but with using monetary-fiscal levers to "reflate" the economy or "compensate" for its defects.[39]

Within each camp, moreover, further divisions existed. Small-business decentralizers of both the populist and Brandeisian types disagreed at times with those pushing consumer, farmer, or labor welfare; permanent spenders clashed with "pump primers," "currency tinkerers," and "budget balancers"; and leftist "planners" differed sharply with those of the center and right. "Planning," as men like Tugwell saw it, must be done by "public men," not by corporate interests, who almost always opted for scarcity profits. But as envisioned by others, particularly by a man like Adolf Berle, a "regenerated" business could be used in the public interest. And for still others, men like Hugh Johnson, George Peek, or Raymond Moley, all of whom seemed to believe that a more powerful "private government" could deliver on the New Era promises, the answer was a "partnership" with federal authority in a supportive role.[40]

On the business side, too, similar divisions existed. Now flirting with corporate statism were substantial numbers of association officials, former war chieftains, spokesmen for "sick" industries, and other leaders of the corporate "enlightenment."[41] Included in their ranks, for example, were trade association lawyers like Benjamin Javits, Gilbert Montague, and David Podell, economists like Edgar Heermance and Philip Cabot, wartime administrators like Bernard Baruch and Howard Coffin, corporate paternalists like Gerard Swope and Henry Dennison, and prominent association officials like Charles Abbott of the Structural Steel Institute, Wilson Compton of the National Lumber Manufacturers Association, and Walker Hines of the Cotton Textile Institute. Yet these people did not, as some revisionists would have it, constitute a united, omnipotent elite moving confidently toward a corporate order. Among themselves they frequently despaired of agreeing on a specific scheme.[42] Unlike assured rulers, they worried constantly about creating an apparatus that might be used against them. And clearly, they did not speak for all businessmen, particularly not for those who tended to cling either to entrepreneurial modes of thought or to the dream of private coordination. Groups like the American Trade Association Executives, under the leadership of Leslie C. Smith, and the National Association of Manufacturers, with its long history of attacks on "big government" and business-labor cooperation, had not endorsed antitrust revision, chiefly for fear it would lead to unfriendly controls or powerful labor unions.[43] Hard-pressed independents, especially in retail fields and the "sick" or chaotic industries, complained bitterly about their "monopolistic" rivals. Most of the talk about planning, as they saw it, amounted to schemes through which "predatory interests" hoped to join with "big government" and "big labor" to crush "independent enterprise."[44] And intermingled with these views was a discordant medley of others, sentiments ranging from such stout defenses of "rugged individualism" and "natural law" as those set forth by the financier Albert Wiggin or the banking economist Benjamin Anderson to the support for "reflationary" schemes that emanated from James Rand's Committee for the Nation[45] and to time-hallowed calls for tax relief, economy, union-busting, and tariff adjustment.

For a leader who valued consistency, such divided counsels might have required either a choice or a delay in the promised action. But for Roosevelt, with his penchant for resisting ideological systems, mixing opposites, and administering by conflict,[46] the answer was to give "something" to everyone, institutionalize the divisions, and avoid, at least for the time being, a definite commitment to any one reform model. Consequently, what most of the recovery-reform program did as it took shape in 1933, was to create new administrative frameworks, give them vague or ambivalent mandates, and leave it to clashing administrators, competing ideologies, and conflicting pressure groups to fill in the details. This was true, for example, of the act creating the Tennessee Valley Authority, of the Emergency Transportation Act, of the farm law, and, to some extent, of the financial legislation. But it was true, above all, of the National Industrial Recovery Act. Its formulators, by setting forth vague goals, giving industrial code–makers a virtually blank check, and adding licensing provisions and public works, Section 7a for labor, and a mixture of antitrust exemptions with incantations against "monopoly," had provided an "economic charter" rather than a definite policy, a framework that different sets of administrators could use to build quite different versions of an "industrial democracy."[47] Reform through administration, a route upon which the progressives had embarked, had seemingly come into its own.

In the imagery that surrounded the program, moreover, quite inconsistent goals could be discerned. For associational theorists like Benjamin Javits, corporate liberals like Gerard Swope, and Chamber of Commerce leaders like Henry I. Harriman, all of whom saw the NRA as the logical extension of "industrial self-government" and "business planning," there was the dream of creating a rationalized corporatism that would allegedly serve democratic ends—a new order, in other words, in which "enlightened" business groups engaged in cooperative "planning" and social improvement; labor, as a junior partner, aided and shared in the process; and government, by taking care of the "chiselers" and providing a temporary construction market, made it possible for the "planners" to generate new investment and purchasing power. For the leftist intellectuals who became involved—men, for example, like Tugwell, Lewis L. Lorwin, or George Galloway—there was the dream of building a "collectivist democracy" through "national planning," a system, as they visualized it, in which powerful "public men," acting in pursuit of democratically determined goals, would restructure a "defective" corporate capitalism and make it serve the "public interest." For Brandeisian lawyers like Corcoran and Cohen or market-oriented economists like Leon Henderson and Corwin Edwards, most of whom thought in terms of an updated and broadened New Freedom, there was the notion of helping "independent-minded" businessmen to revitalize, "purify," and preserve the decentralized market structure needed for real progress. For laborites and social workers, there was the dream of organizing and protecting the exploited, thus making for a more "balanced" system, more equitable distribution, and new checks against oppression. And for those interested chiefly in "reflation," there was the public works appropriation that could serve as a "pump primer."[48]

It was the war model, however, that seemed to have the most initial influence, to come through the strongest, and to be uppermost in the minds of the top administrators. Roosevelt himself looked back to his war experience, and it was only natural that Hugh Johnson, the former WIB member who had helped to write and was now to administer the act, should try to reestablish the type of business-government cooperation and public relations activities that had been successful in meeting the wartime crisis.[49] Given his efforts to do so, moreover, it was virtually inevitable that the initial attempt to build an effective "industrial democracy" would approach the design of the "business planners." It did not, to be sure, completely duplicate it. The conflicts within business, the power of a few unions, and the protests from other types of reformers meant that a few codes would contain strong labor provisions, a very few would show some concern for consumers, and almost all would make some effort to disguise their cartel arrangements, hold forth vague "antimonopoly" clauses as window dressing, and maintain some semblance of governmental supervision. But still, the codes that had emerged by late 1933 contained the essential features of what men like Javits, Swope, and Harriman had been advocating. Typically, they contained numerous anticompetitive provisions; and typically, they delegated the power to devise and enforce controls to industrial leaders, envisioned labor cooperation on business terms, and included almost nothing that could be used to protect consumers or develop central planning instruments.[50]

In practice, though, this brand of business-government cooperation, like

Hoover's earlier brand, failed to generate expansion and was therefore quickly charged with being tyrannical and oppressive. Perhaps, if the public works side had been rapidly expanded, if business had been massively subsidized with cheap credit and guarantees against loss, or if the initial psychological lift could have been sustained, the outcome would have been different. But this was not the way it happened. On the contrary, "reflation" was stymied by a mixture of fiscal orthodoxy, excessive red tape, and unsuccessful attempts at currency tinkering;[51] expectations of rising sales and profits quickly evaporated; and under the circumstances, the codes were used to raise prices along with wages and restrict new investment rather than encourage it.[52] What seemed for a moment to be the making of a new consensus quickly dissolved. Like Hoover's system, "business planning" had been tried and found wanting; and though industrialists reacted by asking for greater autonomy and blaming the failure on "chiselers," bureaucrats, and labor,[53] they could no longer convince large numbers of their fellow citizens that the approach was either workable or the "American way." With increasing support, advocates of other approaches were soon demanding major changes. And since Roosevelt, unlike Hoover, had not committed himself to one model, he could let others take the blame for the initial failure, watch over the resulting policy debates, and wait for another version of "industrial democracy" to take shape.

In 1934, then, the gap between promise and performance brought the New Deal's initial approach, that embodied in the NRA codes, under increasing attatck, particularly from farm and labor leaders, dissident businessmen, "market restorers," and "national planners." Measures like the Securities Exchange Act, the Air Mail Act, and the new trade law, based as they were on competitive models and ideals, were all indications that this initial approach was in retreat. So were the opening shots in a campaign to dismantle the "power trust." And within the NRA, the shift in sentiment and political pressure was reflected in drives to scrap the price and production provisions, strengthen the labor clauses, and restructure the code authorities. A coherent alternative, however, was slow to emerge. Throughout 1934, the conflicting thrusts—the battles between internationalists, nationalists, and intranationalists in trade policy, between regulators, nationalizers, and decentralizers in the utility and financial fields, and between the "business planners" and their critics in the NRA—tended to cancel each other out and bring stalemate and confusion rather than a new synthesis.[54] The NRA, in particular, became a study in frustration. There the agitation for reform succeeded in hampering formal cartelization, forcing Johnson out, and producing new policy statements, but the agitators were unable to reshape the code structure and use it to implement a new reform model.

During the first half of 1934, for example, those who would restore competition as the regulator did make their influence felt. Picking up support from discontented groups, academic economists, and progressive politicians, from other governmental agencies, and from such inquiries as that conducted by Clarence Darrow's National Recovery Review Board, the "market restorers" within the NRA's technical and advisory divisions were able to block various code provisions from going into effect and eventually to put through Office Memorandum 228 reaffirming faith in competitive goals and renouncing price-fixing and production control. Yet, against the entrenched opposition of the existing code authorities and their supporters, a group whose cooperation the administration seemed anxious to retain, the champions of the new policy found that they could not even revise codes that violated it, much less write new provisions to achieve its goals. The most they could do was to complain vigorously about the gap between policy and practice, thus making administrators reluctant to defend openly or enforce very actively many of the trade practice provisions. For groups needing strong government support to keep "chiselers" in check, the result was renewed competition; but for those needing only tacit cooperation, it was not. Conflicting lines of action, it seemed, although they might provide a sense of movement and involvement, had reduced the effects of government intervention to little more than an equivalent of laissez faire.[55]

A similar inability to translate policy into practice was also characteristic of those who would build "industrial democracy" by strengthening organized labor, particularly now by preventing the independent unionism desired by a majority of employees from being undercut by company organizations or individual bargaining. Here again, official policy, as set forth by the National Labor Board and its successor, the National Labor Relations Board, did interpret Section 7a as requiring a "majority rule," an arrangement, in other words, under which the labor organization that received a majority of employee votes would be recognized as the bargaining agent for all workers in the bargaining unit. Yet, when confronted with the antagonism of NRA administrators, the desire to avoid legal tests, and the tendency of Roosevelt to split the differences, the champions of this interpretation were unable to swing the NRA's enforcement machinery behind it or to prevent special presidential interventions from exempting key industries.[56] Consequently, they were unable to create much of a countervailing force. Throughout the NRA period, increased unionization came chiefly in fields where strong industrial unions were already active, and employee benefits still tended to approximate those considered necessary by "enlightened" industrialists. The rise of "big labor" as a major force would await the type of law that Senator Robert Wagner would finally secure in 1935.[57]

Even less successful and more frustrating was the experience of those who hoped to turn the NRA into an instrument for collectivist planning, one in which broad policy goals would emerge from restructured code authorities representing all interests, strong technical agencies would provide the data and "plans," and powerful "public men," using the licensing provisions if necessary and exercising control over profits and investment as well as pricing and production, would put the "plans" into effect. Only through such a system, ran the argument of men like Tugwell, Lorwin, and Galloway, could Americans have abundance, efficiency, and democracy, all at the same time, and supporting this general view now were detailed memorandums from such economists as Gardiner Means and Mordecai Ezekiel. Unlike the "market restorers," however, these "collectivists" were regarded by many of their fellow citizens as being either un-American or impractical. They lacked popular or political support; and because Roosevelt was both dubious about their approach and unwilling to antagonize the opponents of it, their influence was minimal. The licensing power expired without being invoked. Agitation for such things as profit controls, quality standards, tripartite code authorities, or systematic "expansion plans" was mostly in vain. And the limiting of code authority powers and functions that did take place seemed to stem mostly from complaints about abuse and discrimination, not from efforts to facilitate central planning.[58]

To this agitation for change in 1934, some of the supporters of "business planning" were willing to accommodate themselves. In some fields, the need for government support was still strong enough to override the reluctance to pay a higher "price," and as some business leaders saw it, reform could still be kept in conservative channels that would promote stability and improve rather than threaten the corporate structure.[59] More typically, however, as resentment against, or fear of, the critics mounted and as their influence with Roosevelt seemed more evident, the reaction was one of outrage, alarm, and bitter resistance. Some, still desirous of antitrust immunity and willing to pay some "price" for it, dug in along the line of the existing code structure. Some, convinced that things had already gone too far in opening the door to "socialism," "anarchy," and "labor monopolies," demanded revisions that would guarantee industrial autonomy and allow the open shop. Some, thoroughly disenchanted with the workings of the NRA or deeply frightened by the directions in which its official policies might take it, joined with those who had opposed it from the start to demand that the whole program be scrapped.[60]

Increasingly, it seemed, as the year 1934 drew to a close, the greatest villain in business circles was becoming not "destructive competition" but "New Deal tyranny," or, for those inclined to personalize matters, "that man in the White House." Those opposed to, or disenchanted with, "business planning," those who believed that it had not been given a fair trial, and those frightened by the attacks on it could all agree that top priority now must be given to limiting or rolling back the power of a threatening, unpredictable, and potentially dangerous state bureaucracy. It was this power and its potential misuse, they decided, that were the real sources of instability, the things that frightened investors and blocked recovery. And in attacking it, they were soon invoking, with varying degrees of sincerity, either the ideals of the New Era or those of entre-preneurial capitalism, classical economics, and Jeffersonian liberalism. Many, to be sure, still felt that excessive competition and chaotic disorder were major problems; but with crisis conditions surmounted, the pos-sibilities of solving them privately seemed greater again. Or, at least, they seemed preferable to relying upon public tools that were not properly delimited or were capable of great "abuse" when wielded by ill-informed, impractical, or hostile bureaucrats.[61]

Such fears and beliefs also led most businessmen to oppose the deficit financing, work relief projects, and social insurance programs that might have solved most of their problems. To later generations, such measures would appear as basically conservative, designed, it seemed, to bring stable prosperity without structural change and to undercut the power bases of the system's critics. But with a few exceptions, corporate leaders in 1934 did not view them as such. Instead, they were seen as burdens upon business, as immoral departures from the "American way," as preludes to crippling taxes, capital levies, and economic disaster, or as devices to elect corrupt politicians and strengthen a menacing and wasteful bureaucracy. Recovery and security, according to numerous business speeches now, must come by shrinking government and insisting upon sound finance, not by expanding it and taking risks with the public credit.[62] And partly in response to such criticism, partly because Roosevelt himself remained basically a "budget balancer," the administration coupled its expansion of social services and subsidies with a fiscal orthodoxy that kept the expansionary power of federal deficits far below what was needed to achieve full employment.[63]

As the year 1935 dawned, then, the New Deal had not yet discovered the arrangements that would allow an effective corporate capitalism to function within a liberal-democratic framework. The form of business-government cooperation adopted in 1933 was under severe attack as being both unworkable and tyrannical. Yet most of its supporters, instead of modifying their model to remedy the defects, seemed bent upon resurrecting the discredited models of the 1920s or 1890s. Their rivals, moreover—the "market restorers," "collectivist planners," and "counter-organizers"—were still too weak to force a trial of their solutions. And as yet, no new philosophy had arisen capable of reconciling the conflicting thrusts into what Americans might accept as a new and superior synthesis. In a sense, to be sure, the maze of contradictory activities, particularly those of the NRA, had brought an institutionalization of conflicting pressures; but the result for most participants was a feeling of stalemate and frustration, not one of having broken through to a desirable and satisfying arrangement. That Roosevelt's optimism and "experimentation" might yet produce one, the critics of "business planning" seemed convinced. But the stalemate that the NRA had become by 1935 had few real friends, and to many the Schechter decision, sweeping away the codes and their appendages, seemed to remove an obstacle rather than block needed reforms.[64] At least, it made possible fresh starts.

As one might expect, however, the program that eventually took shape in 1935 clearly had its seeds in earlier developments, particularly in the efforts of those who would limit or check business power rather than trying to use it in the public interest. It was to these groups that Roosevelt now swung his support, partly, it seems, because the end of the NRA afforded him room to maneuver, partly because business hostility had led him to shift his political base toward farm and labor groups, partly because he wished to prevent antibusiness demagogues from making inroads on his left flank.[65] He was limited, moreover, by the political, legal, and ideological obstructions that now lay in the way of other options. Business planning under government auspices, even if it could be made to pass legal muster, was a discredited approach, not only with the public and most "liberals" but also with the business elements that had been frightened and irritated by their NRA experience. The small group that kept trying to revive such an arrangement found itself unable to develop much support in either business or political circles. And "collectivist planning" was even less feasible. Although a few of its advocates—notably, men like Tugwell, Mordecai Ezekiel, and Jerome Frank—worked out and agitated for an "NRA in reverse," so constructed as to bring about "planned expansion," their chances of implementing such a vision seemed to dwindle rather than grow. Added to their encumbrances now was the argument that any planning program must of necessity follow the pattern of the NRA and be dominated by "selfish monopolists."[66]

What emerged, then, as the "market restorers" and "counter-organizers" moved to the fore, was essentially a mixture of selective "trustbusting," government-backed unionization, limited expansion and nationalization of social services, and continued but disguised cartelization for "exceptional" groups willing to pay the "price" and able to pull the right political and ideological levers. To some, particularly those impressed by the antitrust or prolabor rhetoric, the official villification of "economic royalists," and the rejection of "business planning" as a general policy, the mixture seemed to represent a new radicalism.[67] But the changes it could produce would still be limited ones, and to such thwarted "collectivists" as Rexford Tugwell or TVA director Arthur E. Morgan, it appeared as a renunciation of social engineering in favor of the conservative outlook of the lawyer. Its guiding vision, they pointed out, was not a cooperative commonwealth based on an optimistic view of human nature but rather a system of checks and balances based on the view that man would always remain basically selfish, power would inevitably corrupt, and the public interest could best be defined through institutionalized conflict. Perhaps, they conceded, such measures could check abuses or keep conflict within the bounds of human decency; but they could not bring an over-all, organic, operational approach such as the NRA, if properly reconstructed, or the TVA idea, if properly implemented, might have produced.[68]

Experience would soon show, moreover, that "market restoration" of the post-1935 variety could not really destroy the "private socialism" that the president kept denouncing or make much headway toward reestablishing "independent enterprise." Most of the "market restorers," after all, were not ready to outlaw corporate organization or sacrifice modern technology.[69] And this limitation, when coupled with the power still held by the "private socialists," meant that "reform" focused chiefly on particularly vulnerable groups, on such popular demons, for instance, as the Power Trust and the Money Power, or on those industries, like motion pictures or petroleum marketing, where one business group could be enlisted in efforts to "reform" another. This is not to say, of course, that nothing changed. Fierce political and legal struggles did bring simplification of utility holding companies, cheaper and more plentiful electrical power, stronger tools of monetary management, more reliable security exchanges, limited removal of trade restrictions, and broader definitions of "monopolistic" behavior. But even in these vulnerable areas, the changes can be easily exaggerated. And when all was said and done, the area of "independent enterprise" had not been substantially broadened. The network of supercorporations, industrial associations, and oligopolistic understandings that constituted the heart of the corporate system remained substantially intact; and efforts to reach for real weapons, for steeply graduated taxes on "bigness," wealth, and undistributed profits, for example, or for major changes in corporate law, had all either been thwarted or diverted into measures that had little real effect.[70]

In part, too, "market restoration" was blunted by the willingess to make "exceptions." In special cases, many of its advocates would concede, particularly where the overriding need was for conserving natural resources, protecting public health and safety, maintaining essential services, or stopping exploitation as quickly as possible, it was sometimes necessary to rely upon direct administrative controls or counterorganization rather than a revitalization of market mechanisms. And in practice, these cases became loopholes for groups still in need of government-backed market controls and still capable of securing them without paying what they considered to be an exorbitant "price." The oil industry, for example, through special legislation and an interstate compact, remained a "partner" of the government, allegedly promoting conservation by stabilizing its output at profitable levels.[71] The coal industry, using a similar rationale, revived its NRA code but still had great difficulty in making it work.[72] The farmers, by stressing the yeoman ideal, conservation of the soil, and the need for economic "balance," managed to preserve, both for themselves and for agricultural processors, an elaborate system of state-supported production controls, marketing cartels, and minimum-price guarantees.[73] Small merchants, by denouncing mass distributors as "monopolists," put through anti–chain store legislation and "fair trade" laws.[74] Transportation industries, by accepting friendly "regulation" as public utilities, secured both federal subsidies and government-backed cartelization.[75] Opponents of reciprocal trade agreements succeeded in restricting them mostly to commerce with underdeveloped nations.[76] And even where the impetus toward "regulation" came from consumer-minded bureaucrats rather than business leaders, as it did for the food, drug, and cosmetics industries, the resulting imposition of higher "standards" did more than protect consumers. It also strengthened established groups and private market controls.[77]

By 1937, in fact, the conflicting pressures shaping antitrust policy had produced a pattern resembling that of late 1934. The official goal, as under Office Memorandum 228, was "market restoration." Yet in large and crucial areas, the government was doing nothing to restore competition; and in still others, fields that in 1937 were remarkably similar to those in 1934, it was actively supporting anticompetitive arrangements. The major differences now were, first of all, that the gap between policy and practice was no longer advertised in formal codes; second, that the openly supported cartelization was more elaborately justified in terms of social-democratic goals; and third, that the attacks on particularly vulnerable groups were stronger, thus providing a larger outlet for popular antitrust feeling. That the 1937 system was much more liberal or democratic was debatable. But it appeared to be, and this helped to satisfy liberal-democratic critics while allowing a continuation or elaboration of measures protecting invested capital and organizational commitments. Most corporate leaders, moreover, seemed to prefer mild antitrust threats and the somewhat higher "price" extracted from needy industries to the potential threats they had discerned in the NRA of 1934. Although still highly critical of "attacks on business" or aid to rival groups, they were not anxious to revive a formal code system.[78]

Most of them, however, would have preferred going back to the earlier labor arrangements. For federal power now, beginning with the Wagner Act in 1935, was being used to promote unionization, curb union-busting, and expose managerial intransigence. And these uses of it, operating in conjunction with labor's own militancy, the emergence of the CIO, and the shift to industrial unionism, were creating a new set of organizational leaders, who, generally speaking, were making the most serious inroads of the decade on the decision-making power of corporate managers. In broad areas, such men were becoming real partners in determining wage rates, working conditions, and other terms of employment.[79] Significant as this change was, however, its implications for the political economy as a whole were something less than revolutionary. Union leaders did not win a share of the corporation's power over production, pricing, and resource allocation. For the most part, they did not even reach for it; and, as a result, their rise did not bring much redistribution, much restructuring of business itself, or much of an increase in consumer purchasing power.[80] Concentrated industries could still offset higher labor costs through administered inflation, as they did in 1937.[81] Union members, once assured of greater security and a chance to share in future economic growth, could be and eventually were converted into a conservative element. And business organizations, by enlisting union support in their price maintenance and "stabilization" activities,[82] adopting "modernization" programs that eliminated unprotected jobs, and reducing the shares going to nonunion workers and competitive producers of raw materials, found that it was possible to shift the general impact of labor power to the unorganized. Looking back on the period, later observers would have difficulty in understanding why most corporate leaders had fought the change so bitterly.

The other major aspect of the Second New Deal was the expansion and nationalization of social services, exemplified particularly in the Social Security Act, the work relief program, the housing and conservation activities, and the protective labor and rural rehabilitation measures. In one sense now, "welfare capitalism," community-centered welfare, and the patronage-oriented welfare of urban political machines were all giving way to a larger and broader "welfare statism." Yet again, significant as this change was, the patterns adopted worked in some respects to strengthen rather than displace existing institutions. Local communities still remained key units in dispersing welfare; political machines strengthened themselves by becoming intermediaries;[83] business groups benefited from the public investments or were "bribed" into becoming "partners" along the welfare frontier; discontented elements, potentially disruptive, were converted into more conservative citizens; and frequently, despite the humanitarianism involved, groups needing aid and protection the most were the ones exempted. Again, the degree of business opposition seemed disproportionate to the extent and nature of "reform" or "socialization." Logically, the "enlightened" group of corporate leaders willing to go along with, or join in, most of the social program should have been much larger.

Logically, too, both corporate leaders and Second New Dealers might have moved quickly now from the mixture taking shape in 1937 to the "mixed economy" that seemed so satisfactory to similar groups in the 1950s. The latter synthesis, after all, did contain many of the same elements, particularly the same curious blend of private controls and pressure-group "planning" with antitrust ideals, selective "trustbusting," capitalistic labor unions, and modest measures of seminationalized social services. What it contained beyond this was, first of all, a general conviction that such a blend did represent a new and superior synthesis, and second, a more effective set of techniques for promoting and regulating economic growth. Had those shaping policy in 1937 been willing to make the required psychological adjustments, divert somewhat more resources to trade expansion and technological development, and seize the theory of supplementary public investment being advanced by a few New Dealers and Keynesians, it seems possible that the new "American system" might have come in the late 1930s rather than the 1950s.

This development, however, was not to be. Instead, the great majority of corporate leaders and their political allies continued to blame the lack of new investment and the failure to achieve sustained expansion on the New Deal's "shackling," "burdening," and "frightening" of business, whereas various groups of New Dealers continued to see a defective corporate structure in need of income redistribution, "market restoration," or systematic "coordination" and "balancing." By many in both camps, Keynesianism was seen as being either counterproductive, wasteful, dishonest, or a type of "artificial" solution, designed by their opponents to perpetuate "unnatural" structures and controls in need of change.[84] And the result, since nothing done so far had really remedied the system's inability to generate the needed investment and purchasing power, was another breakdown and contraction. In the first half of 1937, as tax increases offset the expansionary effects of the Bonus Act and the administration pursued a deflationary policy, one intended to check a wage-price spiral, curb a speculative inventory boom, strengthen the market for government bonds, and bring the long-sought balanced budget, the stage was set for a new collapse. In the fall, limited recovery and what had seemed to be an emerging equilibrium gave way to the "Roosevelt depression" and to another round of policy conflicts.[85]

As conditions worsened in late 1937, a few business leaders began once more to urge some type of government-backed "business planning." For them, the source of instability had again become "destructive competition." For the great majority, however, the source was political in nature. It lay particularly in the undistributed profits tax of 1936, the federal labor policy, and unwarranted "attacks upon business." And the way to eliminate it and start the needed flow of new investment funds, so the argument ran, was to revise taxes, unwind much of the New Deal, and roll back federal power. Again there were exceptions, but much of organized business, it seemed, had not yet come to view the arrangements of the Second New Deal as really being "stabilizers" and "balance wheels." Nor was it ready yet to adopt the view that contraction called for larger federal deficits. Although the tax revision that business groups lobbied through Congress in early 1938 did mean a larger deficit and thus a dose of Keynesiansim, this was not the intention. In the business theory of recovery, subscribed to by most supporters of the legislation, tax cuts were supposed to be accompanied by reduced governmental expenditures and a return to balanced budgets.[80]

Meanwhile, various groups in the government were also analyzing the breakdown and urging changes in policy, again largely in terms of what they had been advocating earlier. One group, for example, represented by men like Secretary of Commerce Daniel Roper, RFC Director Jesse Jones, and Secretary of the Treasury Henry Morgenthau, Jr., seemed willing now to adopt the business formula and try to restore "confidence" by balancing the budget, revising the tax laws, and declaring a recess on reform. A second, led by Donald Richberg and other former NRA officials, wanted to check the new outbreak of "destructive competition" by setting up a new program of "business planning" through industrial codes. A third, consisting of "collectivist planners" like Ezekiel and congressional "mavericks" like Thomas Amlie, advocated an Industrial Expansion Act, a measure, in other words, that would create machinery similar to the code structure of the NRA but this time with proper safeguards and with mechanisms that would insure its use to underwrite full production rather than restricted output. A fourth, led by men like Harold Ickes, Thomas Corcoran, Leon Henderson, and antitrust chief Robert Jackson, urged that the "market restoration" activities of the Second New Deal be drastically broadened, primarily to deal with the "monopolistic" groups whose "administered" price increases had brought a new failure of purchasing power and a subsequent "strike of capital." And finally, an increasingly influential but still small group, spearheaded by men like Lauchlin Currie and Alvin Hansen, was now ready to pronounce the existing structure acceptable and use planned deficits as a way of stabilizing it. Armed now with Keynes's *General Theory*, this group had acquired a new confidence and cohesion; but much of its support in the subsequent debate still came from people who wanted to spend on humanitarian or social grounds, who saw spending as an aid to other types of reform, or who viewed it as a temporary expedient until something better could be done.[87]

As in 1933, Roosevelt himself seemed reluctant to choose and inclined to give everyone "something." While promising a balanced budget and urging business to take up the slack, he also authorized a resumption of some spending and lending activities, encouraged those who were attacking "concentrations of economic power," discussed the need to "manage" price relationships, and talked about reviving some kind of "business planning." For a time, confusion prevailed. But gradually, some options were ruled out and others limited. "Planning," after all, was still politically unfeasible; "budget-balancing" seemed completely ineffective and would not long remain possible without tax increases; and since few could agree on just what a "decentralization" effort should include, the demands for it were channeled into the protracted studies of a Temporary National Economic Committee. This left a program consisting chiefly of the mixture of 1937 plus two major additions. One was the attempt, under Thurman Arnold's direction, to use the Sherman Act as a weapon of price control. In key areas now, where high prices and costs were felt to constitute economic "bottlenecks," an enlarged Antitrust Division set out to bring them down through highly publicized enforcement "drives" and the negotiation of numerous consent decrees. The other innovation, much more significant for the future, was Roosevelt's acceptance of planned deficits as a way of expanding the economy. Having decided in favor of a new spending program, he proceeded to justify it in Keynesian terms and to claim credit for the upturn that followed it.[88]

As the decade drew to a close, both of these innovations engendered heated debates, and what would have happened to them had there been no World War II is difficult to say. Probably, considering the defeat of the new spending bill in 1939, it would have taken another severe recession or two before Keynesianism became the established way of regulating and stabilizing aggregate demand. And probably, considering Arnold's flair for the dramatic and the initial expansion of his program, it would have taken somewhat longer before corporate planners and other organizational leaders managed to move the antitrust enterprise back into the relatively safe areas of checking marginal abuses and protecting one business group from another. As it turned out, the war hastened both processes. The Arnold program, after coming into sharp conflict with the business-oriented war agencies, was finally shelved and forgotten, at least to the extent that there have been no subsequent efforts to use the antitrust apparatus as a major and continuing tool of price management.[89] And Keynesianism, vindicated by the impact of the war spending, quickly became a part of the "American way," particularly since the war debt, the wartime expansion of the public sector, and the "need" for spending on armaments, technology, and foreign aid all made possible a type of fiscal management that business leaders found more palatable. Instead of being dependent on fluctuating public expenditures that could "subvert" capitalist virtues and create "competition for private enterprise," they could now rely upon a stable core of "desirable" spending and depend upon fluctuations in government revenue to regulate aggregate demand.[90] Corporate capitalism, so "liberal" spenders seemed to think, had finally been "liberalized"; but the reverse effect, a "corporatization" of the "liberals," seemed to be somewhat closer to what had actually happened.

In the 1940s, partly because of their new "partnership" with government during the war, partly because of their subsequent success in scrapping reconversion controls and checking labor power, most corporate leaders also came to accept the other innovations of the New Deal. A mixture of properly limited "welfare statism" with "responsible" labor unions, pressure-group "planning," and devices to maintain "workable" competition," they concluded, did make for a stable environment in which corporate organizations could prosper and grow.[91] And on the other side, deeply impressed by the wartime and postwar performance of the economy, by the changing attitudes of corporate leaders, and by the need to protect a going system from the "mindlessness" of a "radical right," those who had set out to "democratize" and "liberalize" the corporate order came to the conclusion that they had been successful. Admittedly, they noted, much power remained in the hands of a corporate elite. But now, in view of the "corporate conscience," the "workable competition," and the system of "countervailing powers" that reform had created, the power would aid rather than threaten the continued advance of liberty and democracy.[92]

Seemingly, the tensions between corporate values and those of the liberal-democratic creed had been resolved into a new and higher synthesis, that of "democratic pluralism," the "mixed economy," or the "vital center." But the broad belief that such was the case would not endure. Deeply dissatisfied with the type of society that the new "American way" appeared to be creating, a new generation of critics would soon proclaim it to be a "new tyranny" controlled, or at least "manipulated," by an irresponsible "power elite" and a modern set of "feudal fiefdoms." "Reform," so the lament ran, had not only failed to "democratize" the area of "private government"; it had aided the "interests" and the "machine" to take over the public apparatus as well. And though the result had been prosperity for the corporation and its dependents, it had also been an expansion of "imperialism" and "exploitation," an organizational society that left the individual "alienated" and "powerless," and inaction or "repression" in the face of festering social problems.[93] Like New Era associationalism, the pluralistic theories of the 1950s had been merely a smoke screen to hide an undemocratic system of decision-making; and like progressive reform, the New Deal had been another "triumph of conservatism."

That this tarnished image of the New Deal innovations overcompensated for the glowing view of the 1950s seems fairly obvious. The criteria of judgement, after all, were frequently unrealizable ideals or expanded definitions of what constituted "democracy," not the arrangements that preceded the New Deal, the experience of other nations, or the realistic assessment of available alternatives. Roosevelt, it must be conceded, was not the ideal philosopher-politician who might have clarified and resolved the dilemmas of industrial America, but it is hard to conceive of any political figure in the 1930s who could have filled this role. It is also difficult, considering the experience of the Hoover years and of other nations, to argue that rational systematization would have produced better results; and it is doubly difficult, considering the previous pace of reform and what preceded the New Deal innovations, to argue that the period brought a setback rather than a significant advance for democracy. Clearly, the new labor structure, despite its "corporatist" and oligarchic tendencies, was a more democratic arrangement than the company unionism of the New Era.[94] And most believers in democracy, it would seem, would prefer the "new welfare," the expanded federal bureaucracy, and the stabilized, subsidized corporate capitalism that finally emerged, "manipulative," "elitist," and "impersonal" though they might be, to the welfare, governmental, and economic structures that existed in 1932.

The tarnished image, moreover, frequently carried with it an erroneous impression concerning the role of business groups in policy-making. Since they seemed to have benefited most from the innovations of the period, the temptation was strong to conclude that they must have planned it that way and used the New Dealers either as their tools or as camouflage for their operations. In reality, so the evidence at hand indicates, they had neither the power, the unity, nor the vision to do this. They could, to be sure, push an initial program upon the new administration, limit the efforts at structural reform, and secure desired stabilization measures for certain types of industries. But they could not make the initial program work or retain the initiative; and instead of seeing that their long-range interests lay with the pattern taking shape after 1934 and moving quickly to adopt it, most of them spent the next six years fighting a bitter and expensive delaying action. What emerged was the creation not of an omnipotent corporate elite but of a complex interaction between conflicting interest groups, resurgent liberal ideals, and the champions of competing reform models, all of which, after all, contemplated the salvation and stabilizing of corporate capitalism as well as the democratizing of it.

If the revised image overcompensated, however, it did bring into focus some glaring defects in the earlier one, particularly its magnification of the degree of change, its search for continuities only in "reform" rather than in business circles, and its assumptions that the New Deal had solved the problems of power and maldistribution, transformed corporate capitalism into an obedient servant of the people, and found the way to reconcile a techno-corporate order with competitive and democratic ideals. The innovations of the 1930s, significant though they were in strengthening the economy and bringing new groups and beneficiaries into the political process, had not altered the fundamental dilemmas confronting earlier reforms. They had merely shifted them into somewhat different settings. And probably, despite the disillusionment of many critics with a "middle way," the conflicting traditions and drives that underlay the dilemmas would persist, producing, along with some "progress," another confused search for a synthesis and new but transitory claims that one had been found. Significantly, the new concern with "abuses of power," with "overorganization," and with subversion of the "public interest" was producing not only fringe rejections of liberalism and technology but also revivals of the Brandeisian model, new dreams of associationalism, and updated notions of "public men" independent of the tug and pull of interest groups.[95] History, of course, did not run in cycles, but surely there were parallels.

1. See Bernard Sternsher, "Liberalism in the 1950's,"*Antioch Review* 22 (1962): 315–31. As examples, see also: Arthur S. Link, *American Epoch: A History of the United States since the 1890's* (New York, 1955), pp. 595–602; Arthur M. Schlesinger, Jr., "The Future of Liberalism," *Reporter*, 3 May 1956, pp. 8–11; John D. Hicks, "The Third American Revolution," *Nebraska History* 36 (1955): 227–45; Richard Hofstadter, *The Age of Reform: From Bryan to F.D.R.* (New York, 1955), pp. 254–55, 314–16; and Peter Viereck, "A Third View of the New Deal," *New Mexico Quarterly* 26 (1956): 44–52. Particularly persuasive for historians, it seemed, were such works as Adolf A. Berle, *Twentieth Century Capitalist Revolution* (New York, 1954); John K. Galbraith, *American Capitalism: The Concept of Countervailing Power* (Boston, 1952); David Lilienthal, *Big Business: A New Era* (New York, 1953); and A. D. H. Kaplan, *Big Enterprise in a Competitive System* (Washington, 1954).

2. The emphasis, however, differed. Liberals stressed the New Deal's success as a reform movement, neo-conservatives its success in preserving unique and superior American traditions, and men like Hofstadter its success in overcoming outmoded traditions and devising a managerial state.

3. See Louis Galambos, "The Emerging Organizational Synthesis in Modern American History," *Business History Review* 44 (1970): 279–90. Key works reflecting the new outlook include Robert H. Wiebe, *The Search for Order, 1877–1920* (New York, 1967); Samuel Haber, *Efficiency and Uplift: Scientific Management in the Progressive Era, 1890–1920* (Chicago, 1964); Louis Galambos, *Competition and Cooperation: The Emergence of a National Trade Association* (Baltimore, 1966); and John K. Galbraith, *The New Industrial State* (Boston, 1967).

4. See, for example, Galbraith, *New Industrial State*, pp. 302–10.

5. The new radicals tend to differ from the neo-institutionalists in that they see conspiracies and villains rather than amoral or inevitable processes, the subversion of democracy rather than pragmatic problem-solving, and unimaginative failure rather than social improvement. For unsympathetic discussions of the view, see Jerold S. Auerbach, "New Deal, Old Deal, or Raw Deal: Some Thoughts on New Left Historiography," *Journal of Southern History* 35 (1969): 18–30; and Irwin Unger, "The 'New Left' and American History: Some Recent Trends in United States Historiography," *American Historical Review* 72 (1967): 1237–63.

6. See, for example, Barton J. Bernstein, "The New Deal: The Conservative Achievements of Liberal Reform," in Bernstein, ed., *Towards a New Past: Dissenting Essays in American History* (New York, 1967), pp. 280–82; Charles Reich, *The Greening of America* (New York, 1970), pp. 41–58; Paul Conkin, *The New Deal* (New York, 1967), pp. 71–81; and Howard Zinn, ed., *New Deal Thought* (New York, 1966), pp. xv–xxxvi.

7. For summaries of the controversy, see Peter Filene, "An Obituary for 'The Progressive Movement,' " *American Quarterly* 22 (1970): 20–34; and David M. Kennedy, ed., *Progressivism: The Critical Issues* (Boston, 1971), xii–xiv.

8. Wiebe, *Search for Order*, pp. 111–223, is highly persuasive in this regard. See also Samuel P. Hays, *Response to Industrialism, 1885–1914* (Chicago, 1957), pp. 48–70.

9. There were, of course, some groups who favored destroying the industrial order and others, including certain corporatists, technocrats, socialists, and syndicalists, who would abandon the heritage of democratic capitalism. But these groups were and remained marginal to the mainstream of policy-making.

10. For discussion of the division, see John Braeman, "Seven Progressives," *Business History Review* 25 (1961): 581–92; Wiebe, *Search for Order*, pp. 133–63; and George E. Mowry, *The Era of Theodore Roosevelt and the Birth of Modern America, 1900–1912* (New York, 1958), pp. 52–58.

11. For expositions of the view, see Woodrow Wilson, *The New Freedom* (New York, 1913), pp. 163–222; Osmond Fraenkel, ed., *The Curse of Bigness: Miscellaneous Papers of Louis D. Brandeis* (New York, 1934), pp. 104–24, 129–36; and J. B. and J. M. Clark, *The Control of Trusts* (New York, 1914), pp. 187–202.

12. For expositions of the view, see Herbert Croly, *The Promise of American Life* (New York, 1909), pp. 358–81; Charles R. Van Hise, *Concentration and Control* (New York, 1912), pp. 248–78; and Theodore Roosevelt, *The New Nationalism* (New York, 1911), pp. 3–33.

13. See, for example, such books as Arthur Jerome Eddy, *The New Competition* (New York, 1912); Edward Hurley, *The Awakening of Business* (Garden City, N.Y., 1917); and E. H. Gaunt, *Co-operative Competition* (Providence, 1917).

14. See, for example, Arthur F. Bentley, *The Process of Government* (Chicago, 1908). One might note also the tendency for each of these groups to see its model as being the "natural" solution. One saw concentration as having reached artificial proportions; one viewed efforts to decentralize as running against nature; one held that society was gradually evolving toward an associational phase; and one visualized an emerging group equilibrium.

15. See Robert H. Wiebe, *Businessmen and Reform: A Study of the Progressive Movement* (Cambridge, Mass., 1962), pp. 127–56; Arthur S. Link, *Woodrow Wilson and the Progressive Era, 1910–1917* (New York, 1954), pp. 66–75, 225–29; Gabriel Kolko, *The Triumph of Conservatism: A Reinterpretation of American History, 1900–1916* (New York, 1963), pp. 255–78; and G. Cullom Davis, "The Transformation of the Federal Trade Commission, 1914–1929," *Mississippi Valley Historical Review* 44 (1962): 437–55.

16. Wiebe, *Businessmen and Reform*, p. 4.

17. For the nature and effects of the war government, see William E. Leuchtenburg, "The New Deal and the Analogue of War," in John Braeman, Robert H. Bremner, and David Brody, eds., *Change and Continuity in Twentieth-Century America* (Columbus, Ohio, 1964), pp. 84–92; Charles Hirschfield, "National Progressivism and World War I," *Mid-America* 45 (1963): 139–56; Paul A. C. Koistinen, "The 'Industrial-Military Complex' in Historical Perspective: The Interwar Years," *Journal of American History* 56 (1970): 819–39; and Robert Cuff, "Organizing for War: Canada and the United States during World War I," in Canadian Historical Association, *Historical Papers, 1969*, pp. 141–56.

18. Robert F. Himmelberg, "Relaxation of the Federal Anti-Trust Policy as a Goal of the Business Community during the Period, 1918–1933" (Ph.D. diss., Pennsylvania State University, 1963), pp. 17–36; Robert Cuff, "Business, the State, and World War I" (paper presented at Conference on War and Society in North America, Montreal, Canada, 1970), pp. 21–23.

19. Hundreds of articles in the 1920s on "associational activities," "industrial self-government," and the "cooperative system" bear out this interpretation. So does research in the Hoover papers. Both have convinced me that the views found in Grant McConnell's *Private Power and American Democracy* (New York, 1966) and William A. Williams's *Contours of American History* (Cleveland, Ohio, 1961), pp. 425–33, are more valid than the conventional interpretation of the period.

20. See, for example, Herbert Hoover's Addresses to the Chamber of Commerce, 1923, 1924, 1926, Public Statements 306, 378, 579, Hoover Papers (Hoover Presidential Library); E. E. Hunt, "The Cooperative Committee and Conference System," 14 December, 1926, Hunt File, Commerce Department Official Files, Hoover Papers; Evans Clark, "Industry is Setting Up Its Own Government," *New York Times*, 21 March 1926, and Merle Thorpe, "The Business Revolution," *Nation's Business*, March 1927, pp. 27–28.

21. For reactions following the crash, see Joseph Dorfman, *The Economic Mind in American Civilization*, 5 vols. (New York, 1946–59), 5:607–58.

22. The best account of Hoover's cooperative program is in Albert U. Romasco, *The Poverty of Abundance: Hoover, the Nation, the Depression* (New York, 1965), pp. 24–65.

23. See, for example, Benjamin Anderson in *Commercial and Financial Chronicle* 132 (1931): 4524, and John Oakwood in *Barron's*, 29 June 1931, pp. 3, 8.

24. Arthur M. Schlesinger, Jr., *The Crisis of the Old Order* (Boston, 1957), pp. 191–202. For representative plans, see Stuart Chase, "A Ten Year Plan for America," *Harper's* 163 (1931): 1–10; Charles A. Beard, "A 'Five-Year Plan' for America," *Forum* 86 (1931): 1–11; and George Soule, "National Planning," *New Republic* 64 (1931): 61–65. For the influence of the Russian model, see Lewis S. Feuer, "American Travellers to the Soviet Union, 1917–1932: The Formation of a Component of New Deal Ideology," *American Quarterly* 14 (1962): 119–49.

25. *Monthly Labor Review* 33 (1931): 1044–47; *Wallace's Farmer*, 16 April 1932, pp. 4–5.

26. "Program of the Progressive Conference," 11–12 March 1931, George W. Norris Papers (Library of Congress).

27. Schlesinger, *Crisis of the Old Order*, pp. 186–88; Dorfman, *Economic Mind*, 5:691–93, 708–11, 743–44; Jordan Schwarz, *The Interregnum of Despair: Hoover, Congress, and the Depression* (Urbana, Ill., 1970), pp. 142–51.

28. Himmelberg, "Relaxation of Anti-Trust Policy," pp. 223–41, 249–51; Robert Bruere, "Swope Plan and After," *Survey* 67 (1932): 583–85; Schlesinger, *Crisis of the Old Order*, pp. 181–83; *Review of Reviews*, November 1931, p. 64; John P. Diggins, "Mussolini and America," *Historian* 28 (1966): 559–85.

29. See Romasco, *Poverty of Abundance*, pp. 231–34; and Carl Degler, "The Ordeal of Herbert Hoover," *Yale Review* 52 (1963): 573, 582.

30. Herbert Hoover, *The Memoirs of Herbert Hoover: The Great Depression, 1929–1941* (New York, 1952), vi–vii, 2, 38–39, 61–62; William Myers and Walter Newton, *The Hoover Administration* (New York, 1936), pp. 488–89; Hoover to A. W. Shaw, 17 February 1933, File 938, President's Personal Files, Hoover Papers.

31. Romasco, *Poverty of Abundance*, pp. 186–201, 221–29; Schwarz, *Interregnum of Despair*, pp. 88–105, 142–78.

32. Himmelberg, "Relaxation of Anti-Trust Policy" pp. 209–18; Eugene Lyons, *Herbert Hoover* (Garden City, N.Y., 1964), p. 294; Myers and Newton, *Hoover Administration*, p. 119; Hoover to Thomas Thacher, 12 September 1931; to Malcolm Whitman, 11 February 1932; to Howard Coffin, 3 June 1932, all in File 172, White House Official Files, Hoover Papers.

33. I would disagree, for example, with the interpretations in Carl Degler, *Out of Our Past* (New York, 1959), pp. 379–416; Hofstadter, *Age of Reform*, pp. 302–28; and Louis Hacker, *The Shaping of the American Tradition* (New York, 1947), pp. 1125–42.

34. I find persuasive the views in Richard S. Kirkendall, "The Great Depression: Another Watershed in American History?", in Braeman et al., *Change and Continuity*, pp. 147–89; Henry S. Commager, "Twelve Years of Roosevelt," *American Mercury* 40 (April 1945): 391–401; and Bernard Sternsher, "The New Deal 'Revolution,' " *Social Studies* 57 (April 1966): 157–62. In my opinion, however, each underemphasizes the continuity between the New Era, the Hoover administration, and the New Deal, especially in the areas of business policy. More perceptive in this regard is Herbert Stein, *The Fiscal Revolution in America* (Chicago, 1969), pp. 6–38. The continuity has also been stressed by the New Left and by the laissez faire right. See Bernstein, "New Deal," pp. 265–67, and Murray Rothbard, *America's Great Depression* (Princeton, N.J., 1963), pp. 167–85.

35. These are discussed in detail in Theodore Rosenof, "Roads to Recovery: The Economic Ideas of American Political Leaders, 1933–38" (Ph.D. diss., University of Wisconsin, 1970). See also Conkin, *New Deal*, p. 33.

36. Although it was frequently argued that the passing of the frontier and the maturing of the economy threatened stagnation and rigid controls, there was little disposition to accept this as a desirable solution. Instead, "new frontiers" were to be found through raising mass purchasing power, expanding trade, developing new technologies, increasing public investment, or some other means.

37. Those outside these limits, that is, the noncapitalist left, the far right, and various groups of agrarian reactionaries, occasionally exerted a bit of influence, but there was no serious consideration of their proposals. They were useful chiefly, it seems, as bogeymen with which New Dealers, conservatives, and progressives tried to frighten or discredit each other.

38. For a discussion of recent works stressing the resistance to change, see Richard S. Kirkendall, "The New Deal as Watershed: The Recent Literature," *Journal of American History* 54 (1968): 846–52.

39. William E. Leuchtenburg, *Franklin D. Roosevelt and the New Deal, 1932–1940* (New York, 1963), pp. 33–38; Ellis W. Hawley, *The New Deal and the Problem of Monopoly: A Study in Economic Ambivalence* (Princeton, N.J., 1966), pp. 35–52. See also the discussion of each group in Rosenof, "Roads to Recovery,"

40. See Leuchtenburg, *Roosevelt and the New Deal* p. 35. See also Bernard Sternsher, *Rexford G. Tugwell and the New Deal* (New Brunswick, N.J., 1964), pp. 98–106; and Richard S. Kirkendall, "A. A. Berle, Jr., Student of the Corporation, 1917–1932," *Business History Review* 35 (1961): 56–58.

41. The best discussion of business moves leading to the NRA is in Galambos, *Competition and Cooperation*, pp. 181–202. See also his "The Cotton Textile Institute and the Government," *Business History Review* 38 (1964): 202–11.

42. Galambos, "Cotton Textile Institute," pp. 206–7; Edwin B. George, "Anti-Trust Laws as to National Economic Planning," 20 January 1933, Feiker Papers, Box 103, Records of the Bureau of Foreign and Domestic Commerce, R. G. 151 (National Archives).

43. Himmelberg, "Relaxation of Anti-Trust Policy," pp. 245–55. My own research in the business press, the Commerce Department archives, and the Hoover papers also bears out Himmelberg's findings in this regard.

44. See, for example, C. A. Bintliff to Hoover, 24 November 1930, File 277, White House Official Files, Hoover Papers; C. H. Chatten to Julius Klein, 3, 21 October 1932, File 80357, Commerce Department Records (National Archives); and Watson Snyder to J. L. O'Brien, 9 December 1932, File 60-57-32, Justice Department Records (National Archives). To some extent, such complaints were responsible for the increased antitrust activities of the Hoover administration. The initial impetus, however, came from a group who hoped that stronger enforcement would generate more sentiment for revision. See Himmelberg, "Relaxation of Anti-Trust Policy," pp. 176–82, 189–93, 198–200.

45. See Romasco, *Poverty of Abundance*, pp. 82–85; and Herbert M. Bratter, "The Committee for. the Nation," *Journal of Political Economy* 49 (1941): 532–36.

46. For discussions of these qualities and sharply divergent estimates of them, see Arthur M. Schlesinger, Jr., *The Coming of the New Deal* (Boston, 1959), pp. 192–94, 527–32; Rexford G. Tugwell, "The Compromising Roosevelt," *Western Political Quarterly* 6 (1953): 320–41; James M. Burns, *Roosevelt: The Lion and the Fox* (New York, 1957), pp. 474–75; and Conkin, *New Deal*, pp. 11–15.

47. For a further discussion of the birth of the "charter," see Hawley *New Deal and Monopoly*, pp. 19–34.

48. See Schlesinger, *Coming of New Deal*, pp. 87–102; Hawley, *New Deal and Monopoly*, pp. 26–28, 35–52.

49. Leuchtenburg, "New Deal and Analogue of War," pp. 117–35; Gerald Nash, "Experiments in Industrial Mobilization: WIB and NRA," *Mid-America* 43 (1963): pp. 157–74.

50. Hawley, *New Deal and Monopoly*, pp. 55–71; Leverett S. Lyon et al., *The National Recovery Administration* (Washington, 1935), pp. 93, 123, 166, 212, 224, 267, 275, 280, 458–61; 568–77, 585–89, 610–11, 623–37, 653–69, 689–94.

51. Stein, *Fiscal Revolution*, pp. 39–57.

52. The conclusions on this in Lyon, *National Recovery Administration*, pp. 621, 744–45, 804–9, 871–77, still seem persuasive.

53. Hawley, *New Deal and Monopoly*, pp. 69–70, 78–79.

54. See Henry J. Tasca, *The Reciprocal Trade Policy of the United States: A Study in Trade Philosophy* (Philadelphia, 1938), pp. 82–93; Claude M. Fuess, *Joseph B. Eastman* (New York, 1952), pp. 211–21, 232–44; Thomas K. McGraw, *The TVA and the Power Fight, 1933–39* (New York, 1971), pp. 67–90; Hawley, *New Deal and Monopoly*, pp. 91–110.

55. Hawley, *New Deal and Monopoly*, pp. 79–103, 114–18.

56. Irving Bernstein, *Turbulent Years: A History of the American Worker, 1933–1941* (Boston, 1970), pp. 172–205, 318–30; Sidney Fine, *The Automobile under the Blue Eagle* (Ann Arbor, Mich., 1963), pp. 219–30.

57. Foster Rhea Dulles, *Labor in America* (New York, 1966), pp. 267–73; Jerold S. Auerbach, "The Influence of the New Deal," *Current History* 48 (1965): 335–36.

58. Schlesinger, *Coming of New Deal*, pp. 214–17; Hawley, *New Deal and Monopoly*, pp. 89, 102–33; Lewis L. Lorwin and A. Ford Hinrichs, *National Economic and Social Planning* (Washington, 1935), pp. 164–65; Lyon, *National Recovery Administration*, pp. 212–15, 272–76.

59. One might include here such men as Thomas Watson, Joseph Kennedy, W. Averell Harriman, Allie Freed, Henry Harriman, and Gerard Swope. See Bernstein, "New Deal," p. 275, for an attempt to make the group synonymous with "big business."

60. By early 1935, this three-way split was clearly apparent. Groups like the Business Advisory and Planning Council and the Industry and Business Committee for NRA Extension wanted a simple extension of the National Industrial Recovery Act. The Chamber of Commerce and various other

groups wanted extension only if the act was drastically revised. And the Committee for Elimination of Price-Fixing and Production Control, formed by businessmen who were attacking government "shackles," wanted no extension at all. See Hawley, *New Deal and Monopoly*, pp. 120–22; and William H. Wilson, "How the Chamber of Commerce Viewed the NRA: A Re-examination," *Mid-America* 44 (1962): 95–108.

61. For accounts of the changing business attitudes, see Schlesinger, *Coming of New Deal*, pp. 472–88; George Wolfskill and John Hudson, *All But the People: Franklin D. Roosevelt and His Critics, 1933–1939* (New York and Toronto, 1969), pp. 144–49; Frederick Rudolph, "The American Liberty League, 1934–1940," *American Historical Review* 56 (1950): 19–33; and Burns, *Roosevelt*, pp. 202–8, 239–40.

62. See, for example, Carl P. Dennett, "What Is Delaying Recovery"; Virgil Jordan, "Problems Facing America"; Alfred P. Sloan, Jr., "Important Questions of National Policy"; and Winthrop Aldrich, "The Financing of Unemployment Relief," all in *Vital Speeches* 1 (1934): 150–55, 144–46, 163–68, 176–81.

63. Stein, *Fiscal Revolution*, pp. 56–57, 74–76; E. Cary Brown, "Fiscal Policy in the 'Thirties: A Reappraisal," *American Economic Review* 46 (1956): 863–68.

64. On reactions toward the ending of the NRA, see Arthur M. Schlesinger, Jr., *The Politics of Upheaval* (Boston, 1960), pp. 283–91; Burns, *Roosevelt*, pp. 222–23; Wallace E. Davies and William Goetzman, eds., *The New Deal and Business Recovery* (New York, 1960), p. 38.

65. See Burns, *Roosevelt*, pp. 224–26.

66. The post-1935 activities of both business and collectivist planners are discussed in Hawley, *New Deal and Monopoly*, pp. 159–86.

67. See, for example, Basil Rauch, *A History of the New Deal* (New York, 1944), pp. vi–vii, 156–90.

68. Rexford G. Tugwell, "The New Deal: The Progressive Tradition," *Western Political Quarterly* 3 (1950): 390–427. This is also the view in Schlesinger, *Politics of Upheaval*, pp. 389–92.

69. Again, a few agrarians and distributists were ready to do this. But their influence was still minimal.

70. For a detailed discussion of the antitrusters and their influence, see Hawley, *New Deal and Monopoly*, pp. 283–379. For the nature of the business system at the end of the decade, see David Lynch, *The Concentration of Economic Power* (New York, 1946), pp. 111–42, 173–238. For the best account of the changes in the securities field, see Michael E. Parrish, *Securities Regulation and the New Deal* (New Haven, Conn., 1970), pp. 228–32.

71. See Gerald D. Nash, *United States Oil Policy, 1890–1964: Business and Government in Twentieth Century America* (Pittsburgh, 1968), pp. 146–56.

72. See James P. Johnson, "A 'New Deal' for Soft Coal: The Attempted Revitalization of the Bituminous Coal Industry under the New Deal" (Ph.D. diss., Columbia University, 1968); and Waldo E. Fisher and Charles M. James, *Minimum Price Fixing in the Bituminous Coal Industry* (Princeton, N.J., 1955).

73. See Murray R. Benedict, *Farm Policies of the United States, 1790–1950* (New York, 1953), pp. 349–401; and John E. Dalton, *Sugar: A Case Study of Governmental Control* (New York, 1937).

74. See Ewald T. Grether, *Price Control under Fair Trade Legislation* (New York, 1939); and Joseph C. Palamountain, Jr., *The Politics of Distribution* (Cambridge, Mass., 1955).

75. See Ernest W. Williams, Jr., *The Regulation of Rail-Motor Rate Competition* (New York, 1958); Henry L. Smith, *Airways* (New York, 1942); and Paul M. Zeis, *American Shipping Policy* (Princeton, N.J., 1938).

76. Tasca, *Reciprocal Trade*, pp. 74–80, 97–98.

77. See Charles O. Jackson, *Food and Drug Legislation in the New Deal* (Princeton, N.J., 1970), pp. 201–21.

78. Donald Richberg and several other former NRA administrators kept trying to revive something similar, but they did not have any strong business support. For a discussion of their activities, see Hawley, *New Deal and Monopoly*, pp. 164–65.

79. Bernstein, *Turbulent Years*, pp. 786–93; Auerbach, "Influence of the New Deal," pp. 337–39, 365; David Brody, "The Emergence of Mass Production Unionism," in Braeman et al., *Change and Continuity*, pp. 244–56.

80. See Arthur Smithies, "The American Economy in the Thirties," *American Economic Review Proceedings* 36 (1946): 21–23; and Alfred Chandler, "The Role of Business in the United States," *Daedalus* 98 (1969): 37–38. Perhaps the chief structural changes in business organization were a larger role for personnel departments and industrial relations specialists and less power for foremen.

81. Smithies, "American Economy in the Thirties," pp. 21, 23.

82. Thurman Arnold would later find numerous cases where the pattern of labor-management relations approached that of collusion against the public rather than conflict in its behalf. See Arnold, Statements before the Temporary National Economic Committee, 12, 13 February 1941, Book 45, Arnold Papers (University of Wyoming).

83. See, for example, Bruce M. Stave, *The New Deal and the Last Hurrah: Pittsburgh Machine Politics* (Pittsburgh, 1970), p. 182.

84. Stein, *Fiscal Revolution*, pp. 87–93, 119.

85. Ibid., pp. 93–102; Douglas A. Hayes, *Business Confidence and Business Activity* (Ann Arbor, Mich., 1951), pp. 118–26; Kenneth D. Roose, *The Economics of Recession and Revival* (New Haven, Conn., 1954), pp. 234–41.

86. Stein, *Fiscal Revolution*, pp. 103–4, 113–14; Hawley, *New Deal and Monopoly*, pp. 357–58; Leuchtenburg, *Roosevelt and the New Deal*, pp. 256, 260.

87. Leuchtenburg, *Roosevelt and the New Deal*, pp. 244–47; Stein, *Fiscal Revolution*, pp. 102–3; Hawley, *New Deal and Monopoly*, pp. 388–403.

88. Hawley, *New Deal and Monopoly*, pp. 390–91, 394, 396, 399–402, 404–14, 428–40; Leuchtenburg, *Roosevelt and the New Deal*, pp. 248–49, 254–64; Stein, *Fiscal Revolution*, pp. 103–15; Gene M. Gressley, "Thurman Arnold, Antitrust, and the New Deal," *Business History Review* 38 (1964): 224–25, 230.

89. Hawley, *New Deal and Monopoly*, pp. 441–43; Richard Hofstadter, *The Paranoid Style in American Politics and Other Essays* (New York, 1967), pp. 231–36.

90. Stein, *Fiscal Revolution*, pp. 169–90; Galbraith, *New Industrial State*, pp. 226–32.

91. Even business attitudes toward Roosevelt as a historical figure seemed to change. In a representative poll taken in Philadelphia in 1951, almost as many businessmen as laborers expressed admiration for Roosevelt and his achievements. See Fillmore H. Sanford, "Public Orientation toward Roosevelt," *Public Opinion Quarterly* 15 (1951): 204.

92. See again the works cited in footnote 1.

93. See again the works cited in footnote 6.

94. See Milton Derber, "The Idea of Industrial Democracy in America: 1915–1935," *Labor History* 8 (1967): 3–29.

95. See, for example, Mark Green et al., *The Closed Enterprise System* (Washington, 1971); Anthony Lewis, in *New York Times*, 5 June 1971; Alvin Toffler, *Future Shock* (New York, 1970), pp. 108–31; Warren G. Bennis, *Changing Organizations* (New York, 1966); and Theodore J. Lowi, *The End of Liberalism: Ideology, Policy, and the Crisis of Authority* (New York, 1969), pp. 297–314.

Richard S. Kirkendall

The New Deal and Agriculture

THE NEW DEAL FOR AGRICULTURE ILLUSTRATED THE ROOSEVELT administration's commitment to capitalism and its determination both to preserve and to change the system. Farming was extremely depressed in 1933, and New Dealers worked, with some success, to raise farm prices and restore profits to the farm business. They tried to do even more: to fit the farmer into a collectivist type of capitalism. Again, their efforts succeeded. The federal government became more important in American agriculture, seeking among its objectives to regulate farm production, and farm organizations grew in membership and importance. The individual farmer came out of the 1930s less independent than he had been before the New Deal. Some New Dealers also hoped to serve more than the business interests of the commercial farmer. Although their efforts were partially successful, they encountered major obstacles that limited their accomplishments. Farm politics during the 1930s was dominated by men interested, first of all, in higher farm prices.

American capitalism had been moving in a collectivist direction for more than half a century before 1933. Large organizations, both public and private, had been taking shape and gaining power in the economic system. Businessmen had moved first, breaking with individualism and forming giant organizations before the end of the nineteenth century. Antitrust laws had been passed in hopes of restoring the old system, but they had failed. Somewhat more successful efforts had been made in pre–New Deal days to bring government and various economic groups into harmony with the collectivist trends. Government regulatory agencies, such as the Interstate Commerce Commission and the Federal Trade Commission, had been established; and a labor movement, with the American Federation of Labor as its largest component, had developed.[1]

Although farmers often battled against the drive away from individualism, they too were caught up in the trend. Long before the 1930s, they had joined organizations such as the Grange and the National Farmers' Union. In 1920, the American Farm Bureau Federation was formed,[2] and it quickly became the largest farm organization, with a membership of more than 300,000 farm families throughout the 1920s, most of them in the Middle West.[3] The federation devoted a large portion of its time to the formation of other organizations—cooperatives—for the marketing of agricultural commodities.

The Farm Bureau made no effort to organize all of the people who lived on the land. It was interested only in the rural businessman, the farmer who produced and sold a substantial crop. And the "farm problem," as the organization defined it, was the most obvious problem faced by this type of farmer: low farm prices. The organization's aim was to make the farm business profitable once again.

Farming was not a highly profitable business during the 1920s. During World War I, farmers had enjoyed prosperity and had increased their acreage and their production, raised their standard of living, and gone into debt; but the price break of 1920 had dropped farm income from nearly seventeen billion dollars in 1919 to less than nine billion in 1921. Throughout the 1920s, farm income never reached twelve billion; and in 1929, the purchasing power of farm goods was only 91 percent of the prewar level. The price problem was a consequence of an increase in production, due largely to a greater use of fertilizer and machinery, and a drop in demand both at home and abroad.

During the 1920s, the Farm Bureau devoted much of its energy to efforts to get help for the farmer from the federal government, and the organization championed a plan—the McNary-Haugen plan—that was designed to bring the farmer into harmony with practices of the urban business world. In fact, an urban businessman, George Peek, was chiefly responsible for the development of the plan.[4] The president of the Moline Plow Company, a company that was severely damaged by the farm depression, Peek had turned to farm relief to solve his economic problems. "You can't sell a plow to a busted customer," he explained. The basic problem of the rural businessman, as Peek saw it, was that he bought in a protected market and sold in a highly competitive one. Rather than propose the destruction of the protective tariff system, he advocated a plan to get the tariff to do for the farmer what it did for the industrialist. The government, Peek suggested, should help farmers relate supply to domestic demand as industrialists did. According to the plan, the farmer would sell in the American market the amount of his production that could be sold at a price that would give him the purchasing power he had had before the war; and then a government corporation, financed by the participating farmers, would purchase the surplus at the American price and "dump" it abroad at the world price. Helped by the tariff, industrialists had long behaved in a similar fashion, charging one price at home and another abroad, and Peek encouraged the farmer to conform to the practices of the urban business world.

Peek's plan did not gain an opportunity to demonstrate that it could raise farm prices and, by doing so, help other parts of the economy. Congress passed the McNary-Haugen bill in 1927 and again in 1928, but President Coolidge successfully vetoed the measure both times.

By 1933, the farm business was one of the most seriously depressed parts of the American economic system.[5] Few farmers, large or small, were prosperous. When the general depression hit, it had reduced demand for farm products below the unsatisfactory levels of the 1920s, and farm income fell to five billion dollars. The price of cotton, which had averaged 12.4 cents per pound from 1909 to 1914 was only 5.5 cents in February 1933; the price of wheat had dropped from 88.4 to 32.3 cents per bushel; but the farmer's tax burden had doubled since 1914. His debts remained high, and the prices of goods he needed to buy had not dropped nearly as far as farm prices. While agricultural prices fell 63 percent from 1929 to 1933, industrial prices slipped only 15 percent. Industrialists could control production more effectively, so that agricultural production declined only 6 percent while industrial production dropped 42 percent. Thus, by February 1933, farm commodities could purchase only half as much as they could before the war.

Under the impact of the depression, the Farm Bureau suffered a sharp drop in membership. It had had more than 320,000 members in 1930, but it had fallen below 165,000 by 1933.[6] As membership dropped, the organization resumed its battle for the McNary-Haugen plan.

Suffering was intense in rural America, and some farmers expressed their frustration and resentment in loud and at times violent protests. Many corn-hog farmers in the Middle West, who had known prosperity but were now faced with falling income and threatened with the loss of property, joined the Farmers' Holiday Association and participated in "the most aggressive agrarian upheaval of the twentieth century" and "a final great attempt by the family farmer to save himself from absorption and annihilation."[7] The association organized a farm strike that began in August and ran into November 1932, and the participants, though usually peaceful, did employ violence on several occasions in their efforts to keep farm products off the market. The FHA and Wisconsin dairy farmers, who staged a strike in February 1933, threatened new strikes in the spring if the new administration failed the farmer. In addition, there were many protest marches and meetings during the fall and winter of 1932–33, including one in Washington in December by the Farmers' National Relief Conference that demanded immediate action to halt debt payments, evictions, and property seizures; raise prices; distribute food to the needy; and cut the profits of middlemen. Furthermore, farmers took direct action, including "penny" and "Sears-Roebuck" sales to halt the great wave of foreclosures and sales for tax delinquency that was turning landowners into tenants or farm laborers or placing them on relief rolls. Neighbors would appear at forced sales, intimidate those who wished to make serious offers, buy the property at very low prices, such as $1.18 for a farm, and return it to the owner. Mobs also moved against judges, police officers, and lawyers; troops were called into action against farmers; insurance companies suspended foreclosure suits; and farm states passed moratorium laws.

For devotees of "law and order," the situation seemed filled with dangerous possibilities. The Communist party participated in the protest movement,[8] and farm leaders warned of "a revolution in the countryside in less than 12 months" and suggested that the "mental attitude of the farmer is strained to the breaking point." According to a careful student of the "agricultural crisis," revolution was "not outside the realm of possibility," and "the immediate prospect was for a more widespread, and possibly increasingly violent, reaction."[9]

The New Deal's response to the crisis testified to the administration's commitment to capitalism and to its determination to promote further evolution along collectivist lines. The New Dealers discarded the view that farming is a highly individualistic enterprise and insisted that it must be dealt with on a collective basis. They also ignored romantic notions of the farmer as a self-sufficient yeoman,[10] defined him as a businessman, rejected proposals of farm groups of an earlier day designed to destroy the power and change the practices of big business, and broke with the traditional emphasis upon the expansion of agricultural production.[11] Instead, New Dealers urged farmers to imitate the production control methods of the most successful businessmen and brought the power of government to the aid of the farmer so that he could behave like the urban businessman who benefited from the corporate form of organization. The federal government became much more important in decisions about agricultural production, devising production plans designed to coordinate the work of the nation's farmers and establish a profitable balance between supply and demand.

The production control scheme was developed by social scientists, not by farm organization leaders or politicians.[12] The largest contribution came from M. L. Wilson, an agricultural economist from Montana State College who had firsthand knowledge of the critically depressed conditions of Montana's wheat farmers and was permitted by his college to work for agricultural legislation.[13] Wilson was helped by other economists, including William J. Spillman, John D. Black, Howard Tolley, and Mordecai Ezekiel. The result was the Voluntary Domestic Allotment Plan.

To Wilson and his associates, the leading alternatives to the allotment plan, though valuable for their recognition of the importance of farm purchasing power and their endorsement of action by the federal government to raise farm prices, had fatal flaws. One alternative was the McNary-Haugen plan. It seemed certain to encourage the farmer to increase production and thus worsen his situation. Cuts in production seemed necessary. Production now, according to the advocates of the allotment plan, should be limited to the effective demands of the domestic and foreign markets, and no efforts should be made to dump surpluses abroad because dumping would force other countries to push their tariff walls even higher.

Another alternative was the effort of the Hoover administration to encourage farmers to reduce output. Those efforts emphasized persuasion, rejected stronger methods of control, and assumed that the chief role of government in agricultural production was to supply advice so that farmers could devise sound production plans as industrial corporations did. Wilson proposed that the government should do more than talk to farmers: it should employ its taxing and spending powers to promote reductions in output. His plan involved a tax on farm commodities to be paid by the processors when they handled these products and to be used to finance a system of payments to farmers who agreed to adjust production. Each farmer would be free to refuse to participate, but would be encouraged to do so not merely by the promise of higher prices in the market but by payments to him from the government.[14]

Although the leading farm organizations in 1932 preferred other farm relief schemes,[15] production control became the major New Deal program for the farmers before the end of 1933. In achieving this result, Wilson received essential support from Franklin Roosevelt.[16] Another economist with access to the candidate, Rexford Guy Tugwell,[17] introduced Roosevelt to Wilson and his scheme, and the campaigner provided a somewhat vague endorsement of the plan in his major speech on agriculture. He committed himself sufficiently to promote willingness among some of the farm leaders to accept production control as at least one way to attack the farm problem. Roosevelt's support had limits, however. He was reluctant to press any one plan too hard for he hoped to have the support of all farm groups.[18]

He did select an advocate of the allotment plan as secretary of agriculture; he rejected Peek and other opponents of the plan and chose Henry A. Wallace of Iowa,[19] an agricultural journalist, scientist, and businessman who had often advised farmers to reduce their production. Wallace had concluded before 1932 that McNary-Haugen would hurt farmers and had helped Wilson promote interest in his plan. And he selected two other advocates of the plan, Ezekiel and Tugwell, as his top lieutenants. Ezekiel, who had worked for the department and the Farm Board for a decade, became the secretary's economic adviser, and Tugwell became assistant secretary.[20]

In spite of these favorable developments, the advocates of the allotment plan did not achieve a complete victory during the "Hundred Days." The Agricultural Adjustment Act that was passed in May 1933[21] included major Wilsonian features: production control, voluntary participation encouraged by rental or benefit payments, self-financing through processing taxes, and a role for farmers in administration. But the law also included two programs with which Peek was most closely associated. One would sell surplus commodities in foreign markets, and the other would allow processors and distributors of farm products to reach agreements concerning the prices they would pay to farmers.[22]

Advocates of production control, including Wilson, now moved into important positions in the new Agricultural Adjustment Administration, but Peek was appointed to the top spot. The appointment meant that the battle over farm policy would now rage inside government.[23] Although Peek was forced to accept cuts in production, he did so reluctantly, resisted pressures to make this the main feature of the program, emphasized marketing agreements as the means of raising farm prices, and continued to seek ways to sell the surplus. Wallace, however, believed that marketing agreements divorced from production control could make only small increases in farm purchasing power. In the fall of 1933, he publicly criticized Peek's agreements; Peek challenged Wallace's authority to control the A A A; and Wallace and Tugwell vetoed Peek's plan to dump butter in Europe and pressed the president for a decision that would indicate clearly where authority lay. Forced at last to make a choice between representatives of different farm policies, Roosevelt moved Peek into a new post as special adviser to the president on foreign trade.

Wallace had crushed Peek's attempt to make the A A A an independent agency, free from control by the secretary and subordinate only to the president; and now he placed it under the direction of Chester Davis, who believed in production control. Although Davis had been Peek's top lieutenant in the McNary-Haugen fight, he had concluded that the growth of economic nationalism had invalidated that plan and that the United States must reduce its cropland. Now, under his vigorous leadership, which lasted until 1936, production control emerged clearly as the major program to raise farm prices.[24]

Production control illustrated the New Deal's commitment to collective capitalism,[25] and defenses of the program often emphasized its similarities to the practices of large corporations. This line was developed elaborately in 1934 by one of Wallace's advisers, Gardiner Means, a Columbia University economist who had collaborated with Adolf A. Berle on *The Modern Corporation and Private Property*, published in 1932. Means's studies of industrial prices revealed the ways in which giant corporations used their power to control production in order to uphold prices and disclosed the weaknesses of the farmer in such an economic system. The more individualistic farmer could not exercise the same control over production and thus "administer" prices. For him, in contrast to the corporation, price rather than production was the flexible factor. Furthermore, the farmer suffered from the industrialists' ability to restrict production because it led to higher industrial prices and reduced the demand for agricultural products. Factories working at less than full capacity needed fewer agricultural products, and unemployed workers had little purchasing power.

Means's work was highly regarded and frequently drawn upon by members of the Department of Agriculture, including Wallace, Tugwell, Ezekiel, and Wilson. They argued that developments in the distribution of power within the economy had placed the farmer in a disadvantageous position, and thus he needed help from the government so as to be able to imitate industrial practices. The AAA helped farmers achieve the results that industrialists achieved through corporate organization. If the industrialist could adjust production to demand, was it wrong to use government power to help farmers do the same? Had not the industrialist, by cutting back on his production and thereby reducing the demand for farm products, forced the farmer to reduce output?[26]

The argument implied that the New Deal farm program was not a radical program. Farmers were merely behaving like urban businessmen. Farmers were not trying to destroy the production-control practices of the corporate giants. Instead, the rural businessmen were accepting and seeking to employ an established feature of collective capitalism.

At the same time that the farm program promoted the further development of an organized type of capitalism, the program protected the system by undercutting agrarian protest. Farm protest had erupted once again in the fall of 1933 because relief had come more slowly than farmers expected, and the administration had then supplemented production control with crop loans, relief purchases, and moderate monetary inflation. As benefits began to reach the farm and prospects brightened, they sapped the strength of the protest movement. Few farmers had had revolutionary aspirations; they had protested in hopes of improvements in the farm business. The New Deal had made some and had thereby robbed the radicals of support.[27]

Given the character of New Deal farm programs, it is not surprising that some business leaders were strong supporters of them. Among the most important were Henry I. Harriman, the president of the United States Chamber of Commerce from 1932 to 1935, R. R. Rogers, an official of the Prudential Life Insurance Company, and Robert E. Wood, the president of Sears, Roebuck and Company. These men were influenced by both economic and political considerations. They were troubled by the economic breakdown and convinced that farmers must have greater purchasing power in order to pay their debts and buy industrial products, and they were alarmed by the possibility that farmers would repudiate their debts and join radical movements. A successful farm program would promote general economic recovery and check radical action. It would protect the capitalistic system and promote its recovery. Such men helped Wilson gain support for his ideas in 1932 and applauded New Deal farm programs as they developed.

American business in the 1930s was not a solid power bloc, however, and some businessmen opposed the production control program. The processors and distributors of farm products were especially active foes. They had large sums invested in facilities designed to handle farm products, depended upon large sales, and would be harmed by cuts in farm production. Furthermore, they disliked the processing tax. Some of them advocated plans for the expansion of sales and suggested that the government should allow farm prices to drop and either work to reduce barriers to international trade or dump products abroad; and they tried to promote a sense of identity between their interests and those of wage-earners and urban consumers by arguing that the tax would promote unemployment in the processing plants and increase the cost of living. Some processors also favored marketing agreements that would exempt them from the antitrust laws, enable them to work out agreements to pay higher prices to the farmer, and allow them to enlarge their profits by charging consumers higher prices. Policy, these businessmen suggested, should be shaped by men who had "spent their lives in the accumulation of expert knowledge of the handling, processing and marketing of the country's grain crops—those engaged in the highly specialized business of grain marketing, and who know most about it," not by "pedagogues . . . who are without practical experience in handling grain, nor are possessed of any comprehension of the divergence from theory involved in the actual transaction of business of this kind."

These critics also challenged the constitutionality of the farm program, charging that it taxed processors (and ultimately consumers) in order to pay producers. The food industries led a legal battle in 1935, seeking injunctions against the collection of the processing taxes. Then, on 6 January 1936, the Supreme Court in *United States* v. *Butler* declared that the processing tax and the production controls violated the Constitution. The case grew out of hostility toward the AAA in the textile industry and the refusal of the receivers of the Hoosac Mills to pay the tax.[28]

The New Deal for agriculture served important interests that were plagued with serious problems in depressed America. Commercial farmers were suffering and needed help, and small as well as large commercial farmers benefited from the farm programs.[29]

Some of the New Dealers concerned with agriculture hoped to produce more than higher prices and higher profits for the commercial farmers. The farm organizations were interested chiefly in raising farm prices, but economists such as Wilson and Tugwell were interested, most of all, in establishing a permanent program of agricultural planning. They were not fully satisfied with the production control program for it simply took part of each farm out of production and did not guarantee that the best use would be made of farmland. Wilson assumed, however, that the farm relief scheme could lead to something better. By calling upon farmers to reduce their acreage, the scheme offered a way to stimulate discussion and planning and thus could open the way for long-range programs in which he had greater confidence. Tugwell hoped that the emergency efforts would evolve into a system of complete control that would restrict commercial agriculture to "the most efficient farmers operating the best of our lands," convert the other lands to other uses, and move the other farmers into other occupations.

After Davis became administrator of the AAA, he established a Division of Program Planning. Headed by Howard Tolley, who had left the University of California to join the AAA, it became the main planning agency in a department that for the first time had authority to plan a national agricultural program and to put the plan into effect. The assignment gave the economist a chance to move the existing program beyond mere reduction in production and to substitute the idea of adjustment.

Plans for reorganizing agriculture so that it could supply all Americans with a proper diet provided a significant illustration of the division's thinking. The Bureau of Home Economics had prepared recommendations for four diets at different levels of nutritive content and cost; and Tolley organized a study that converted the diets into their implications for agricultural production and concluded that, when prosperity and better knowledge of nutrition enabled Americans to consume the diet recommended as best, the United States would need more, not less, land in farms and would need to increase output of some crops and to reduce production of others.

The diet studies represented the planners' emphasis on "planned" or "balanced abundance." This concept implied that the long-run solution to the "farm problem" depended heavily on efficient and expanded industrial production, low industrial prices, full employment, migration to the cities, and high wages. Ezekiel was the department's leading promoter of this theory of the farmer's dependence on the cities, and Wallace both encouraged the economist's work and was influenced by it. It helped him move away from "agricultural fundamentalism," a belief "that agriculture is *par excellence* the fundamental industry, and that farmers are, in a peculiar sense and degree, of basic importance in society."[30]

As head of the Planning Division in 1934 and 1935, Tolley frequently criticized the AAA, arguing, as did Wilson and Tugwell, that it was not producing the most desirable changes. Many features troubled him. The AAA paid little attention to regional and individual differences and did not allow the colleges and farmers to contribute as much as they could to planning. The farm program seemed likely to become rigid and to freeze existing patterns of farming rather than promote conservation and shift the production of crops into the regions in which they could be grown most successfully. The AAA treated each commodity separately, whereas the planners hoped for a regional approach that would recognize that the adjustments needed varied from region to region. Tolley also hoped to use the payments in a positive rather than a negative way. He wanted to pay farmers to improve farm management and to conserve the soil, rather than merely to reduce output.

Tolley's greatest fear was that the farm program would serve only the interests of established commercial farmers. He watched them organize and press their demands, and he warned against the "frequent tendency" of pressure groups "to think in terms of group monopoly rather than public welfare." He had confidence that "thorough education along economic and social lines" could prevent such a development. This education would teach farmers that a nation must import if it wished to export, and that the public interest required soil conservation and low-cost farming. Commercial farmers would also learn that tenants and laborers who were considered undesirable aliens in the industry they served could not be expected to function as "good citizens" within that industry and that the success of the farm program depended heavily upon increased purchasing power among city laboring people.

In line with these ideas, Tolley's division, working closely with Wilson, who was now assistant secretary of agriculture, developed four new projects in 1935. A regional adjustment project brought department and college officials together to study what adjustments in production were needed. The officials concluded that the production of cash crops should be reduced, the output of soil-conserving crops should be increased, and the adoption of soil conservation methods throughout the country would bring production in line with existing markets. A county planning project organized farmers into nearly 2,500 county planning committees in the hope of educating farmers and giving them a chance to shape the adjustment programs. These projects were supplemented by two educational programs, a discussion group program for farmers and "schools of philosophy" for extension workers, which were designed to broaden the outlook of people involved in planning and administering farm programs.

In spite of these encouraging developments, Tolley grew unhappy with the attitudes of officials in his department and returned to his post at the University of California in September 1935. It seemed to him that the AAA had become complacent. Many of its administrators seemed interested only in reducing production, making payments to farmers, and increasing their income. Satisfied with the program, these administrators did not welcome his proposals for change. Furthermore, his superiors, Davis and Wallace, were unwilling to apply pressure, and raised doubts about the political implications of Tolley's proposals and the wisdom of trying to move at the moment.

The Supreme Court, however, accomplished what Tolley could not. It forced the officials to make changes in their program and gave the social scientists a new opportunity to push their ideas successfully. After the decision in January 1936, Davis called Tolley back to Washington to help in the emergency, and the economist found that the justices had revived the old willingness to experiment among those administering the AAA and benefiting from it. Thus, he was able to achieve things he had been trying to achieve. He became the "driving personality" behind the development of the new legislation. Even the farm leaders, who had responded to the Court's action with determination to get new price-raising legislation, listened to the social scientist and endorsed his recommendations. The specific ideas about method came chiefly from the work of the Planning Division, and that work enabled the administration to move rapidly to a new type of program.

Congress quickly passed a new farm law that seemed capable of both conserving the soil and controlling production without running into trouble with the Court. The law established a scheme whereby payments obtained from general revenue were made to farmers who shifted acreage from soil-depleting to soil-conserving crops and employed soil-building practices. Because the soil-depleting crops happened also to be the surplus crops, including wheat and cotton, and the soil-conserving ones, such as grasses and legumes, were not surplus commercial commodities, production seemed certain to be shifted away from surplus crops and brought into line with domestic needs and anticipated exports. Tolley, who replaced Davis as administrator, was convinced that the new program would bring more benefits to the farmer and the nation than its predecessor had.

The new legislation enabled the AAA to participate more actively in the large-scale attack upon land problems that was under way by 1936 and to associate itself more closely with the increasingly popular efforts to conserve the soil. The great drought of the mid-thirties did much to stimulate interest and action. "The states and the nation are now unleashing the greatest broadside attack on land-use problems of our history," Tugwell announced enthusiastically. "If this task is completed, our national heritage will be secure," he prophesied. "If not, we shall go the way of Mesopotamia, Egypt, and China, and part with our collective birthright for a mess of individualistic potage."

The Soil Conservation Service was another agency involved in this work. It had been established in 1935 as part of the Department of Agriculture and was headed by Hugh Bennett, a veteran crusader for conservation. Also in 1935, a model statute was drafted that was designed to enlarge the work of the SCS and enable farmers to work together in the battle against erosion. The proposed statute authorized the establishment of soil conservation districts to carry on erosion control work, help farmers control erosion on their lands, and enforce needed conservation practices on lands of uncooperative farmers. A district was to be established after a majority of the farmers living there endorsed it in a referendum, and the district was to be controlled by them. In 1937, Roosevelt sent letters to all governors urging passage of the legislation; and in the next four years, nearly all states passed soil conservation laws and 548 districts were established.[31]

Also in the mid-thirties, Tugwell developed other programs designed to serve more than the interests of commercial farmers. His efforts followed a dramatic "purge" in the AAA that revealed the difficulties involved in efforts to serve other interests. By 1930, over 45 percent of the nation's farms were operated by tenants; and most of them, especially the sharecroppers in the South, seemed to be caught in a system of permanent poverty. And the AAA did not rescue them. Although nearly three-fourths of the cotton farms were operated by tenants, they were not represented in the development and administration of the cotton program, and it harmed rather than helped many of them. Many received only a small share or no share at all of the benefit payment from the government because the landlords kept all or most of it, and many tenants were demoted from sharecropper, the lowest form of tenancy, to day laborer or evicted from the land as the cuts in production were made.

One group in the AAA developed a strong interest in the cotton tenants. Closely allied with Tugwell, the group was headed by Jerome Frank, an eastern lawyer and legal philosopher serving as head of the agency's Legal

Division. Urban rather than rural in background, he and his associates looked upon the AAA as an opportunity for reform.

Early in 1935, the reformers made a bold move. The Southern Tenant Farmers' Union, a new, biracial group developed by Socialists and other critics of the southern way of life and the cotton program, was organizing tenants in the Mississippi delta, and some planters responded by evicting tenants who had joined the union and recruiting substitutes. The official interpretation of the contract between the government and the landowners in the program suggested that they were obligated to keep their normal number of tenants but were not required to keep the same people that had been on their land before 1933. In December 1934, the union took one of the landlords into court to test his right to make such changes. Informed of the episode and of the way in which the contract was being interpreted, the Legal Division issued a reintepretation that required landlords to keep the same people, not just the same number. The ruling could help both the union and the tenants.

This was an attempt to use the farm program to provide greater security for these low-income people. The lawyers justified their efforts as needed to realize the basic purpose of the legislation. They argued that the goal was the economic welfare of all rural groups, not just the landowners, and that the alternative interpetation of the contract did not provide adequate protection for the tenants.

To Davis, the entire farm program seemed to be threatened by the ruling. It struck him as a dishonest distortion of the meaning of the contract and but another in a long series of impractical acts by the lawyers that had harmed the AAA, preventing it from operating efficiently and effectively and risking the hostility of the leading groups in farm politics. He believed that his agency existed to bring higher prices to commercial farmers, not to reform the southern social system, and he resented the view that the farm program was "entirely worthless so long as it did not result in a social revolution in the South." The AAA's task was economic recovery, a task that seemed to him to be of fundamental importance and one that had to be completed before progress along other lines could take place. He feared attempts to mix social reform with the recovery program. In addition, he had doubts about the ability of the federal government to develop a new social order in the South. Influenced by these beliefs, Davis decided that he must either dismiss the reformers or resign.

Fortunately for Davis, Wallace shared his views of political realities. The secretary had been working for more than a decade to develop a program capable of raising farm prices and had close ties with commercial farmers and their organizations and representatives. He had been growing concerned about the political difficulties the lawyers were generating, and now he believed that they had "allowed their social preconceptions to lead them into something which was not only indefensible from a practical agricultural point of view but also bad law." He denied that the farm legislation gave the department the power "to change the undesirable social system in the South," and, familiar with the "habits and customs" of southern farm leaders and congressmen, he feared that if he followed "the extreme city group there would be such a break with the men on the hill that the agricultural program might be destroyed."

Thus, on 5 February 1935, Davis "purged" Frank and several others from the AAA. The top officials were reluctant to challenge power arrangements in farm politics and were heavily influenced by concern about their relations with the leading farm groups and their allies. A week after the purge, Wallace ruled that the cotton contract did not bind landowners to keep the same tenants. Thereafter, landowners remained dominant in the AAA and received most of the benefits; and the administration, in spite of widespread criticism, remained reluctant to press for change and hopeful that many tenants and farm workers would find better opportunities in the cities.[32]

After the purge, the Roosevelt administration, pressed by criticism from the Tenant Farmers' Union and others and troubled by conditions in the cotton country, did develop a larger and more active interest in the rural poor, but that development took place outside the AAA, as almost all department officials believed it must. In April 1935, Roosevelt established the Resettlement Administration, headed by Tugwell, one of the boldest of the New Dealers and now a vocal critic of the AAA. The new agency combined and added to the small efforts on behalf of the rural poor that had developed during 1933 and 1934. The RA tried to improve land-use practices and help those who suffered seriously from past mistakes in the use of the land, such as destitute groups living in once-thriving but now exhausted lumbering, mining, and oil regions, sharecroppers in the South, and farmers on poor land in the drought area of the Middle West and in the Appalachians. Although Tugwell personally favored resettlement of the rural poor, his agency placed heavier emphasis on rehabilitation of them in the places they occupied.

The RA's programs assumed that rural poverty demanded an attack upon its causes, not just relief. The situations had taken many years to develop, and only long-run programs could correct them. Nor could solutions come entirely from indirect action, such as the expansion of urban employment. Rural poverty had to be dealt with directly through specially devised programs. And these programs needed to be devised because all Americans, not just the rural poor, suffered from poverty in agriculture, for it meant inadequate purchasing power, destruction of land, disease, and costly social services.

Most important, the planned attack needed to be made because worthy human beings suffered directly from rural poverty. The programs rested on democratic rather than business assumptions, looking upon all men, not just those who had demonstrated abilities in business, as worthy of help from government. Involved was a concept of man that stressed environment rather than innate qualities.

This democratic concept of man did not mean that all of the rural poor should be treated in the same way. Not all of them could be made into commercially successful farmers, for some knew only self-sufficient or plantation agriculture and some had physical or mental deficiencies. Nevertheless, the government should take action. It could help them form cooperatives or obtain more secure tenure arrangements, or it could provide relief. And nearly all of the poor should be provided with the guidance needed to raise their status. All but a few had capacity for improvement, and all were worthy of help.

Resettlement Administration officials agreed that rural America should be approached as something more than simply the home of rural businessmen and that government should do more than increase their profits. The program, in other words, challenged the dominant orientation of farm policies. Not surprisingly, therefore, Tugwell and the Resettlement Administration came under heavy attack and were forced to tackle vast problems with small sums of money.[33]

His experiences in the RA and other frustrations helped to persuade Tugwell to resign after the 1936 election,[34] but programs for the rural poor did not stop with his departure from Washington. In 1937, a President's Special Committee on Farm Tenancy made a comprehensive analysis of the problems associated with low-income farm groups and a set of proposals relating to them; the Bankhead-Jones Farm Security Act was passed, with provisions on rural rehabilitation and the retirement of submarginal lands and an emphasis on loans to tenants to enable them to buy farms; and a new agency, the Farm Security Administration, was established as a substitute for the RA.[35]

Reflecting the influence of agrarian traditions,[36] the efficient family farm became the main goal of FSA activities. The rehabilitation program, the largest FSA activity, dealt chiefly with poor farmers—owners as well as tenants—who needed loans, grants, guidance, and other forms of help to maintain and improve their farm operations; and the tenant purchase program, the second-largest activity, helped tenants and laborers acquire and develop farms of their own.[37]

The FSA became a significant participant in farm politics, especially in the South, challenging the "*status quo* in American agriculture" and putting pressure on others "to match the FSA in its fight against rural poverty and ignorance, and in its efforts to convert the ideals of democracy into democratic reality."[38] Yet, its concrete accomplishments were small relative to the size of rural poverty. While the rehabilitation program grew for several years, Congress provided only small support for efforts to increase the number of family farmers. In its early years, the FSA was able to provide loans for fewer than 5 percent of the applicants and only 2 percent of the nation's tenants. The number of tenants in the South declined from 1.8 million in 1935 to 1.4 million in 1940; but the number of farm operators also dropped by four hundred thousand while the number of day laborers increased by nearly three hundred thousand, and many southerners moved out of agriculture. Although there were more than a million Negro tenants and day laborers in the South, the FSA made less than 2,000 tenant purchase loans to blacks. Nationally, tenant farmers were increasing at the rate of 40,000 per year, and the law allowed the FSA to make fewer than 10,000 loans per year. "Obviously," the director of the budget informed Roosevelt, "this . . . program can be regarded as only an experimental approach to the farm tenancy problem."[39]

The administrator of the FSA, Dr. Will Alexander, had a strong interest in poor blacks as well as poor whites. His agency and the RA distributed a significant share of its benefits to blacks; but these agencies did discriminate against Negroes, dealt cautiously with racial problems, and seldom challenged the system of segregation, fearing that boldness would reduce still further their ability to grapple with the problems of poverty. Yet they were bold enough to arouse opposition.[40] In June 1940, Alexander resigned, in part because his appearances before the congressional appropriations committees were being "made increasingly difficult by the opposition of certain powerful southerners and reactionary northerners who concentrated on FSA their ire against the New Deal and their fear of its threat to white supremacy."[41]

Those who hoped to develop large programs for the rural poor had to struggle against the major pressures of farm politics.[42] As a leading student of the subject has observed, "government agricultural policy . . . is largely designed and administered for the benefit of commercial farmers."[43] Two historians of the rural poor in the 1930s have concluded that "the New Deal definitely preserved more than it changed" in the lives of "the lowest economic level of society—the sharecroppers and the tenant farmers" and "allowed the basic pattern of subsidy for landlords and poverty for rural workers to become permanent."[44] And Leonard J. Arrington has concluded from a careful statistical analysis of the operations of agricultural agencies:

> New Deal expenditures were directed not so much toward the poor farm states but at those states which, though with comparatively high farm incomes, experienced the greatest drops in income as the result of the depression. New Deal loans and expenditures, in other words, were primarily relief-oriented. They were not, at least in their dollar impact, reform-oriented or equality-oriented. The prime goal would seem to have been the restoration of income for individual farmers rather than the achievement of a greater equality.[45]

While the FSA was taking shape, Tolley and other ambitious New Dealers obtained a new opportunity to promote their hopes for agricultural planning. In the fall of 1938, Wallace elevated the Bureau of Agricultural Economics to the role of central planner for the department and appointed Tolley chief of the bureau. During 1939 and 1940, Tolley and his lieutenants, with assistance from Wilson, first as under secretary and then as director of the Extension Service, devoted most of their time and energy to the construction of a planning program involving cooperation among the national agricultural agencies, the agricultural colleges and their extension services, and the farmers.

Tolley and his aides hoped to change both farm policy and the way it was made. The bureau pushed many proposals for change in the AAA. Believing it had not done nearly enough to improve the lot of lower-income groups, the social scientists pushed for changes in this area. Recognizing that AAA officials were interested first of all in making payments to farmers and raising farm prices and farm income, the BAE battled for proposals designed to get more conservation from the program.

The efforts to change the policy-making process included efforts to enlarge the role of the farmers, and was illustrated most significantly by the county planning committees. They were organized by the extension services and composed of farmers and state and national officials serving in the counties. Most members were farmers, and a farmer served as chairman.

One feature of the committees troubled Tolley and others: they did not represent all groups in their communities. The county agent usually selected the farmers who served on the committees, and because those agents tended to work most closely with the more substantial members of their communities, the committees seldom included representatives of the rural poor. Early in 1940, Bushrod W. Allin, the head of the BAE's Division of State and Local Planning, listed efforts to improve representation as one of the "next steps" that could "improve the planning process." He had long been interested in establishing "truly representative" planning committees and regarded elected committees as preferable to ones appointed by county agents. Wallace, Wilson, and Tolley also preferred elected committees.

The promoters of the planning program, however, proceeded cautiously in promoting their theory that all rural groups should be represented in the formulation of agricultural programs. The tendency was to try to influence the extension and farm leaders to take the necessary steps. Frequently, however, these leaders resisted. Allin tolerated slow progress, believing that there were several practical reasons why the less-advantaged groups could not now be adequately represented. Some of them moved too frequently; many were not interested; and social barriers blocked participation. Consequently, farmer membership on the planning committees was drawn "too largely from the ranks of the more prosperous farmers and landowners, particularly in those areas where small farmers, tenants, sharecroppers, and farm laborers comprise a heavy majority of the agricultural population." Although he denied that this prevented the committees from developing an interest in the poor, he believed that "the formulation of plans without participation of the people for whose benefit they are made is not all that might be desired in a democratic process." He and his associates were restrained, however, by fear that vigorous attempts to stimulate mass participation in the committees might only alienate the groups whose cooperation seemed essential.

Although the planning activities failed to conform perfectly with the planners' ideals and many officials in the agricultural agencies and the colleges resisted their efforts, Tolley and his colleagues were optimistic. Farmer participation was growing; planning committees were taking shape and participating actively in the planning process; and various educational programs were at work, seeking to promote participation in, and support for, planning. The work of the planning committees, the schools of philosophy, and the discussion groups might change the ideas of enough farmers, county agents, and administrators and generate enough support for planning to enable it to triumph over hostility and to develop a better farm program. "It may be some time yet before the full significance of this program will be well understood in the majority of the counties, but I believe we are making real progress," Tolley wrote to a college official early in 1940. And he reported later in the year:

> Excellent results have been attained in many of the 1,540 counties where the work had been started by July 1, 1940. These results indicate that the method adopted is a sound one, that the program is developing in the right direction, and that farmers are willing to assume the responsibility and local leadership necessary for the work.[46]

Yet the ambitious efforts to improve the lot of the rural poor and develop a system of agricultural planning had alienated the most influential farm organization, the American Farm Bureau Federation.[47] This organization of rural businessmen had worked hard for the passage of the Agricultural Adjustment Act in 1933 and then had provided strong support for the farm program as it developed during the early years of the New Deal. The president, Edward A. O'Neal, was, Wilson informed a friend, "always Johnny on the spot when it comes to fighting battles in defense of these policies."[48] When a group of prominent businessmen formed the Farmers' Independence Council to try to draw farmers away from the AAA, O'Neal had labeled them men who "farm the farmers" and "Wall Street Hayseeds" masquerading as farmers while trying to defeat legislation real farmers wanted.[49] He had seen "too much rugged individualism" and believed that the nation needed "a national plan for agriculture" and "cooperation instead of competition."[50]

For O'Neal, one of the most attractive features of the New Deal was the many opportunities it provided to strengthen his organization. He applauded the administration's practice of working with farm leaders in drafting the farm laws and claimed credit for obtaining the legislative benefits for the commercial farmers. He liked the use made of the Farm Bureau's allies—the extension services with their agents in each agricultural county—in the administration of the program and the efforts to organize farmers into committees to look after it on the local level, seeing them as "a challenge and an opportunity" for the Farm Bureau and urging

Farm Bureau leaders to "take the lead in organizing and coordinating these production control committees and associations." Often, extension officials helped the Farm Bureau recruit new members; and as the committees developed, Farm Bureau members became very influential in them. He also saw the discussion program as an opportunity to increase "the effectiveness of our Farm Bureau units in molding public opinion" and in "stimulating interest and participation in local Farm Bureau meetings." He was alert to every opportunity to increase the size and power of his organization.[51]

In the second half of the 1930s, however, the AFBF grew increasingly unhappy with the New Deal. To the organization's leaders, it seemed that the Roosevelt administration had become dominated by the forces of urban liberalism, especially organized labor, and had become biased against the farmer. Wallace and his department seemed to be drawing away from the Farm Bureau, developing new ties with the Farmers' Union, and rejecting the view that their job was to serve the interests of commercial farmers. The officials seemed too interested in the rural poor and the urban consumers. Furthermore, the department's tendency to develop committees of farmers to plan and administer farm programs seemed capable of creating groups that would replace the farm organizations in the policy-making process, depriving the Farm Bureau of its status as the leading spokesman for the farmer and providing department officials with the power needed to dominate farm politics and alter the orientation of farm policy.[52]

Thus, in the late 1930s, Farm Bureau leaders began to make suggestions for changes in the planning and administration of the farm programs. O'Neal and others criticized the participation of nonfarm groups and called for heavy reliance on the farm organizations and the extension services.

In 1940, the farm organization perfected its proposals. Its Washington office supplied O'Neal with a report charging that the administration of the farm programs was characterized by duplication and overlapping and denying that the planning project had ended duplication. The project, in fact, involved, according to the report, the danger of federal domination of state and county planning and usurped functions of the farmers' own groups by developing new organizations rather than relying on existing ones to deal with problems normally handled by them. The report charged that the project duplicated objectives that earlier had prompted the department to promote the development of the Farm Bureau. Finally, in December, the farm group proposed the establishment of a five-man nonpartisan board, representative of agriculture, to plan and administer farm programs on the national level and reliance on the extension services in handling those functions on the state and local levels.[53]

The farm organization felt both threatened and capable of expanding its power. "The fundamental aim," Christiana Campbell has demonstrated, "was to take control of agricultural programs away from the Department of Agriculture, which was believed to be no longer the farmers' advocate, and give it to the farmers themselves (i.e., the organized farmers)."[54] As a consequence of the power of the Farm Bureau among farm organizations and its influence upon the extension services, the recommendations, if put into effect, would inevitably produce an especially large increase in the power of that farm organization. It did not want to remove the government from agriculture. The organization wanted only to guarantee that it would shape the role that the government played.[55]

The Farm Bureau that had become highly critical of the New Deal was a larger, stronger group than the one that had supported it earlier. Massive membership drives, involving efforts to exploit the organization's ties with the AAA and Extension, had been very successful after 1932, especially in the South. "In all four regions," Campbell writes, "the increase in membership during the New Deal period was striking, but the percentage increase in the South was by far the greatest."[56] In 1933, the organization had but slightly more than 150,000 members; by 1940, it had nearly 450,000.[57] By then, as Grant McConnell had written, it "had established itself in a position of preeminence among farm organizations."[58] In the South especially, George Tindall writes, no farm group "had the durability or influence to offer an alternative to what the *Louisiana Union Farmer* called the 'company union' headed by 'Ed O'Neal, big Alabama cotton planter.' "[59]

The Farm Bureau had become a very substantial obstacle in the path of New Dealers who hoped to serve more than the business interests of commercial farmers, and it could count on very strong support in Congress. The organization had significant links with the conservative coalition that had taken shape there and was strong enough by the end of the 1930s to block major extensions of administration programs.[60] Many members of the coalition were southern Democrats, although not all southerners were conservative and not all conservatives were southern. Most conservatives represented rural areas; resented the sharp increase in the power and influence within the Democratic party and the national administration of urban groups, especially organized labor and northern Negroes; disliked many features of the New Deal, such as deficit spending and welfare programs; and distrusted organized labor and feared prospects for the future, including the possiblity that major efforts would be made to alter race relations. Thus, New Dealers who advocated additional innovations faced opponents who offered powerful resistance to further change.

The New Deal for agriculture had, in a sense, created its own strong opponent. The New Deal farm programs had at least created a situation that O'Neal and other hard-driving men were able to exploit successfully in order to develop a large organization.

The growth of the AFBF, like the development of the production control program, represented ways in which the New Deal protected and promoted the development of collective capitalism. Rather than attempt to destroy business organizations and business power, the New Deal tried to fit the farmer into the system. He was advised to organize as other businessmen organized and to regulate production as powerful corporations did. Above all, the New Deal made government much more important in his life. Public organizations such as the AAA and the Soil Conservation Service became very active in rural America and moved the farmer several giant steps farther away from an individualistic economic system. He emerged from the 1930s more dependent on others than ever before. Encouraged to move with rather than against the development of a collectivist type of capitalism, he had done so.

The Roosevelt administration was committed to capitalism. It did not try to break with that aspect of the American past. But the administration did not merely accept the system that had evolved by 1933. It was determined to make changes in it, as well as to preserve it, and the changes in American agriculture were some of the New Deal's more important accomplishments. American agriculture did not welcome all attempts to change it, however. The most ambitious New Dealers discovered that as the period moved forward. By the end of the thirties, their heads were still filled with ideas for change, but the forces of resistance had become very strong. The New Deal for agriculture challenges Barton Bernstein's suggestion that the New Deal "ran out of fuel not because of conservative opposition, but because it ran out of ideas."[61]

Agricultural developments in the 1930s suggest that the New Deal promoted significant though not revolutionary changes. It did not promote a social revolution. Rural poverty remained a large part of American life at the end of the decade as it had been at the beginning. If the New Deal rescued farmers who had been impoverished by the depression, it did not provide much help for rural people who had lived below the poverty line before the depression hit. Furthermore, the New Deal did not replace capitalism with another system. Washington in the 1930s looked upon the farmer as a businessman, worked to make his business profitable, and worked also to persuade him not to move in radical directions. Nevertheless, as its farm policies also suggest, the New Deal did change the structure of American capitalism. This was its most important and fundamental accomplishment. The federal government became much more important in agriculture, and more farmers than ever before were drawn into organizations. Similar changes took place elsewhere. The federal government became more important in many areas of American life, and other groups were organized. The substantial enlargement of the labor movement was one of the most significant developments of the decade. At the same time, business organizations survived the depression crisis. Thus, the New Deal for agriculture was part of a larger story involving, above all, the continued and accelerated evolution of a collectivist or organizational type of capitalism. By 1940, the American farmer worked in a system that was dominated by the interplay among large public and private organizations.

I am grateful for the research assistance of Thomas F. Soapes and Michael J. Cassity, doctoral candidates at the University of Missouri, Columbia, and for financial support from Dean Armon F. Yanders of the University's College of Arts and Science.

1. John Kenneth Galbraith, *American Capitalism: The Concept of Countervailing Power* (Sentry Edition; Boston, 1962); Kenneth E. Boulding, *The Organizational Revolution: A Study in the Ethics of Economic Organization* (New York, 1953); Calvin B. Hoover, "The American Organizational Economy," reprinted in Abraham Eisenstadt, ed., *American History: Recent Interpretations* (New York, 1962), pp. 480–90; W. Lloyd Warner, *The Corporation in the Emergent American Society* (New York, 1962).

2. On the early years of the AFBF, see Grant McConnell, *The Decline of Agrarian Democracy* (Berkeley, Calif., 1953), pp. 1–65.

3. Robert L. Tontz, "Memberships of General Farmers' Organizations, United States, 1874–1960," *Agricultural History* 38 (1964): 147, 150.

4. See Gilbert C. Fite, *George N. Peek and the Fight for Farm Parity* (Norman, Okla., 1954), for a valuable account of Peek's activities in farm politics.

5. Van L. Perkins, *Crisis in Agriculture: The Agricultural Adjustment Administration and the New Deal, 1933* (Berkeley and Los Angeles, 1969), includes an excellent account of the farm situation in 1932–33.

6. Tontz, "Memberships of General Farmers' Organizations," p. 156.

7. John L. Shover, *Cornbelt Rebellion: The Farmers' Holiday Association* (Urbana, Ill., 1965), p. 2. This section draws upon Shover as well as Perkins.

8. Shover, "The Communist Party and the Midwest Farm Crisis of 1933," *Journal of American History* 51 (1964): 248–66.

9. Perkins, *Crisis in Agriculture*, p. 18.

10. Romantic views of rural life did exert a small influence on the New Deal. See Paul Conkin, *Tomorrow a New World: The New Deal Community Program* (Ithaca, N.Y., 1959), and William H. Issel, "Ralph Barsodi and the Agrarian Response to Modern America," *Agricultural History* 41 (1967): 155–66.

11. See Galbraith, *American Capitalism*, chap. 11, and Kirkendall, "L. C. Gray and the Supply of Agricultural Land," *Agricultural History* 37 (1963): 206–14. The New Deal enlarged rather than cut back on one source of the expansion of production—agricultural science—and also expanded reclamation, in spite of the desires of the USDA and its allies. Carroll W. Pursell, Jr., "The Administration of Science in the Department of Agriculture, 1933–1940," *Agricultural History* 42 (1968): 231–40; Donald C. Swain, "The Bureau of Reclamation and the New Deal, 1933–1940," *Pacific Northwest Quarterly* 61 (1970): 137–46.

12. This essay draws heavily on my *Social Scientists and Farm Politics in the Age of Roosevelt* (Columbia, Mo., 1966).

13. William D. Rowley, *M. L. Wilson and the Campaign for the Domestic Allotment* (Lincoln, Neb., 1970), is the most thorough study of Wilson's career in the 1920s and early 1930s.

14. Kirkendall, *Social Scientists*, pp. 24–28.

15. On the farm organizations, see William R. Johnson, "National Farm Organizations and the Reshaping of Agricultural Policy in 1932," *Agricultural History* 37 (1963): 35–42.

16. See Gertrude Almy Slichter, "Franklin D. Roosevelt and the Farm Problem, 1929–1932," *Mississippi Valley Historical Review* 43 (1956): 243–59.

17. Tugwell's activities in the New Deal are discussed at length by Bernard Sternsher in *Rexford Tugwell and the New Deal* (New Brunswick, N.J., 1964). See also Tugwell's own writings, especially *The Democratic Roosevelt* (Garden City, N.Y., 1957), and *The Brains Trust* (New York, 1968).

18. Kirkendall, *Social Scientists*, pp. 31–32, 41–52.

19. Edward L. and Frederick Schapsmeier, *Henry A. Wallace: The Agrarian Years, 1919–1940* (Ames, Iowa, 1968), is a useful though unsatisfactory biography. For other attempts to describe and interpret his career, see Russell Lord, *The Wallaces of Iowa* (Boston, 1947); Malcolm O. Sillars, "Henry A. Wallace's Editorials on Agricultural Discontent, 1921–1928," *Agricultural History* 26 (1952): 132–40; and Theodore Rosenof, "The Economic Ideas of Henry A. Wallace, 1933–1948," *Agricultural History* 41 (1967): 143–53.

20. Kirkendall, *Social Scientists*, pp. 50–51, 53–55.

21. On the bill and the passage of it, see Shover, *Cornbelt Rebellion*, chap. 6, and Perkins, *Crisis in Agriculture*, chaps. 3–4.

22. Kirkendall, *Social Scientists*, pp. 56–58.

23. The best discussion of the first year of the AAA is Perkins, *Crisis in Agriculture*, chaps. 5–8.

24. Kirkendall, *Social Scientists*, pp. 63–68.

25. See also Paul Abrahams, "Agricultural Adjustment during the New Deal Period, the New York Milk Industry: A Case Study," *Agricultural History* 39 (1965): 92–101, and Gould Colman, "Theoretical Models and Oral History Interviews," ibid. 41 (1967): 255–66.

26. Kirkendall, *Social Scientists*, pp. 89–91.

27. Shover, *Cornbelt Rebellion*, p. 167; Perkins, *Crisis in Agriculture*, pp. 6, 190–95.

28. Kirkendall, *Social Scientists*, pp. 33–38, 52, 103–4, 119–20, 133–35, 145, 148–49.

29. Perkins, *Crisis in Agriculture* p. 7; Leonard J. Arrington, "Western Agriculture and the New Deal," *Agricultural History* 44 (1970): 337–53; Theodore Saloutos, "The New Deal and Farm Policy in the Great Plains," *Agricultural History* 43 (1969): 345–55; Don F. Hadwiger, *Federal Wheat Commodity Programs* (Ames, Iowa, 1970), pp. 130–31; George B. Tindall, *The Emergence of the New South 1913–1945* (Baton Rouge, La., 1967), p. 409.

30. On Wallace and "agricultural fundamentalism," see Don S. Kirschner, "Henry A. Wallace as Farm Editor," *American Quarterly* 17 (1965): 187–202, and Kirkendall, "Commentary on the Thought of Henry A. Wallace," *Agricultural History* 41 (1967): 139–42.

31. Kirkendall, *Social Scientists*, pp. 28–29, 45, 60, 77–81, 135–48.

32. On tenant farming and the AAA, see especially David E. Conrad, *The Forgotten Farmers: The Story of Sharecroppers in the New Deal* (Urbana, Ill., 1965), and Donald H. Grubbs, *Cry from the Cotton: The Southern Tenant Farmers' Union and the New Deal* (Chapel Hill, N.C., 1971). See also Arthur M. Schlesinger, Jr., *The Coming of the New Deal* (Boston, 1959), pp. 77–81; M. S.

Venkataramani, "Norman Thomas, Arkansas Sharecroppers, and the Roosevelt Agricultural Policies, 1933–1937," *Mississippi Valley Historical Review* 47 (1960): 229–40; Kirkendall, *Social Scientists*, pp. 97–103, 107–8, 152, 204; Jerold S. Auerbach, "Southern Tenant Farmers: Socialist Critics of the New Deal," *Labor History* 7 (1966): 3–18; Tindall, *New South*, pp. 410–21; Sidney Baldwin, *Poverty and Politics: The Rise and Decline of the Farm Security Administration* (Chapel Hill, N.C., 1968), chap. 1, and Louis Cantor, *A Prologue to the Protest Movement: The Missouri Sharecropper Roadside Demonstration of 1939* (Durham, N.C., 1969).

33. Kirkendall, *Social Scientists*, pp. 107–18; Baldwin, *Poverty and Politics*, pp. 58–76, and chap. 4; Sternsher, *Tugwell,* especially chaps. 21 and 22; Conkin, *Tomorrow a New World*, especially chap. 7.

34. Kirkendall, *Social Scientists*, pp. 120–23; Sternsher, *Tugwell*, p. 238; Baldwin, *Poverty and Politics*, pp. 120–21.

35. Kirkendall, *Social Scientists*, pp. 126–29; Baldwin, *Poverty and Politics*, chap. 6.

36. A. Whitney Griswold, *Farming and Democracy* (New York, 1948), pp. 163–65.

37. Kirkendall, *Social Scientists*, pp. 129–30; Baldwin, *Poverty and Politics*, chaps. 7–8, p. 317.

38. Baldwin, "The Farm Security Administration: A Study in Politics and Administration" (Ph.D. diss., Syracuse University, 1955), pp. 404, 406. See also Baldwin, *Poverty and Politics*, chap. 9; Tindall, *New South*, p. 426, and Cantor, *Protest Movement*.

39. Kirkendall, *Social Scientists*, pp. 130–31; Baldwin, *Poverty and Politics*, pp. 196–97, 199; Tindall, *New South*, pp. 431–32; Cantor, *Protest Movement*, chap. 4, p. 151; Donald Holley, "The Negro in the New Deal Resettlement Program," *Agricultural History* 45 (1971): 192.

40. Holley, "The Negro in the Resettlement Program," pp. 179–93; Robert E. Nipp, "The Negro in the New Deal Resettlement Program: a Comment," *Agricultural History* 45 (1971): 195–200; Baldwin, *Poverty and Politics*, pp. 196–97, 200–203, 211, 250, 254–55, 260, 279–80, 282, 297, 307, 332, 407; Cantor, *Protest Movement*, pp. 144–45.

41. Wilma Dykeman and James Stokely, *The Seeds of Southern Change: The Life of Will Alexander* (Chicago, 1962), p. 248.

42. For another illustration, see Kent Hendrickson, "The Sugar-Beet Laborer and the Federal Government: An Episode in the History of the Great Plains in the 1930s," *Great Plains Journal* 3 (1964): 44–59.

43. Charles Hardin, "The Politics of Agriculture in the United States," *Journal of Farm Economics* 32 (1950): 573.

44. Cantor, *Protest Movement*, p. 161; Grubbs, *Cry from the Cotton* , p. xi.

45. "Western Agriculture and the New Deal," p. 352.

46. Kirkendall, *Social Scientists*, chaps. 9, 10, p. 223.

47. The most important book on this subject is Christiana M. Campbell, *The Farm Bureau and the New Deal: A Study of the Making of National Farm Policy, 1933–1940* (Urbana, Ill., 1962). See also McConnell, *Agrarian Democracy*; Orville M. Kile, *The Farm Bureau through Three Decades* (Baltimore, 1950); and William J. Block, *The Separation of the Farm Bureau and the Extension Service: Political Issue in a Federal System* (Urbana, Ill., 1960).

48. Kirkendall, *Social Scientists*, pp. 50–52, 91, 145, 147.

49. James C. Carey, "The Farmers' Independence Council of America," *Agricultural History* 35 (1961): 70–77; Wesley McCune, *Who's behind Our Farm Policy?* (New York, 1956), pp. 12, 15, 30, 32, 346.

50. Quoted in Tindall, *New South*, pp. 398–99, 428.

51. Kirkendall, *Social Scientists*, pp. 58, 91, 93, 135, 141–42, 153, 154, 180.

52. The best account of the split between the Roosevelt administration and the Farm Bureau is in Campbell, *Farm Bureau*, chap. 10. On this and related matters see also Baldwin, *Poverty and Politics*, pp. 205, 238–39, 286–92, 298–302, and Schapsmeier and Schapsmeier, *Agrarian Years*, chap. 15.

53. Kirkendall, *Social Scientists*, pp. 127, 196–97; Baldwin, *Poverty and Politics*, pp. 171–74.

54. *Farm Bureau*, p. 178; see also McConnell, *Agrarian Democracy*, pp. 118–19, and Block, *Farm Bureau and the Extension Service*, p. 35.

55. Kirkendall, *Social Scientists*, pp. 197, 199, 214, 216, 217.

56. *Farm Bureau*, p. 102.

57. In addition to Campbell and McConnell, see Tontz, "Memberships of General Farmers' Organizations," pp. 147, 156.

58. *Agrarian Democracy*, p. 79.

59. *New South*, p. 428.

60. James T. Patterson has contributed an unusually significant book on this subject, *Congressional Conservatism and the New Deal: The Growth of the Conservative Coalition in Congress, 1933–1939* (Lexington, Ky., 1967). See also, Patterson, "A Conservative Coalition Forms in Congress, 1933–1939," *Journal of American History* 52 (1966): 757–72; Frank Freidel, *F.D.R. and the South* (Baton Rouge, 1965); Dewey W. Grantham, Jr., *The Democratic South* (Athens, Ga., 1963); Grantham, "The South and the Reconstruction of American Politics," *Journal of American History* 53 (1966): 227–46; John Robert Moore, "Senator Josiah W. Bailey and the 'Conservative Manifesto' of 1937," *Journal of Southern History* 31 (1965): 21–39; Moore, *Senator Josiah William Bailey of North Carolina: A Political Biography* (Durham, N.C., 1968); Tindall, *New South*, pp. 618–31; Baldwin, *Poverty and Politics*, pp. 316–22, 335–42, 407–12; Kirkendall, *Social Scientists*, pp. 197–98, 208–10.

61. "The New Deal: The Conservative Achievements of Liberal Reform," in Barton J. Bernstein, ed., *Towards A New Past: Dissenting Essays in American History* (New York, 1968), p. 277.

Milton Derber

The New Deal and Labor

THE BASIC FACTS ABOUT LABOR IN THE 1930s ARE WELL KNOWN. THE interpretation of these facts, however, requires periodic reexamination in the light of changing times. Perspective is vital. Measured by one standard, an event may be relatively insignificant; by another standard, it may be of paramount importance.

The central aim of this essay is to subject the labor events and relationships of the New Deal period to a set of multiple perspectives in order, hopefully, to provide some insights that previous writings may not have fully yielded. The reader will be asked to consider the New Deal and labor from the viewpoint of three time periods. First is the contemporary view. How did the developments of the thirties look to the actors and observers of their day? Given the economic, social, and political conditions of the decade, what meanings did they attach to the Wagner and Social Security acts, the rise of industrial unionism, or the sit-down strikes—to cite a few phenomena of common knowledge?

A second perspective is offered by examining the thirties from the standards of an earlier period—I have selected the 1918–19 World War I years because they were the previous high point in the advance of governmental labor policies, reflecting much of the progressive ideas expressed in the reports of the U.S. Commission on Industrial Relations, 1913–15. Considering where labor and labor relations stood in 1919, what meanings might an observer from that period have attributed to the New Deal and labor?

A third perspective is provided by assessing the thirties within the frame of today, the early 1970s. In the three decades since Franklin Roosevelt pronounced the end of the New Deal and the beginning of the win-the-war effort, what new images have we acquired about the New Deal and labor?

In attempting this multilateral analysis, I have no illusions that I write as the proverbial "man from Mars." My views on the thirties inevitably are affected by the fact that I was a university student during that decade and wrote master's and doctoral dissertations on the current labor scene. It has been said that no one who experienced the Great Depression escaped its psychological impact, and I believe that to be true of myself. By the same token, and with all due respect for the writings on the World War I years, my assessment of that period has been shaped by my experiences during World War II and the events since then. As for contemporary standards, I rely largely on personal experiences and judgments stemming from my role as an academic specialist in this area.

Because of space limitations I shall confine my discussion of the New Deal and labor to four broad topics—labor-management relations policy, social security and labor standards, employment and unemployment, and labor in politics. These are among the labor topics with which the New Deal was most concerned and where its activities were most visible. Moreover, abundant facts are available for a discussion of them.

LABOR-MANAGEMENT RELATIONS POLICY

Labor-management relations policy was a major preoccupation of the New Deal administration that neither Franklin Roosevelt nor Labor Secretary Frances Perkins initially pursued with pleasure. As Secretary Perkins wrote in her biography of Roosevelt, the National Labor Relations Act "did not particularly appeal to him when it was described to him. . . . He always regarded the Social Security Act as the cornerstone of his administration and, I think, took greater satisfaction from it than from anything else he achieved on the domestic front."[1] Madame Perkins herself made no reference to labor relations legislation in her first program proposal to Roosevelt. Her orientation was likewise mainly along social welfare lines.

The principal architect of the New Deal labor relations policy was New York's Senator Robert F. Wagner, who was largely responsible for Section 7a of the National Industrial Recovery Act in 1933 as well as for the adoption of the National Labor Relations Act of 1935 (appropriately labeled the Wagner Act). Wagner served as chairman of the National Labor Board that attempted to implement the labor provisions of the

Recovery Act. His experience with this board, his close ties with AFL leaders, and his impassioned concern for industrial democracy sensitized him to the need for federal legislation that would give employees the right to form organizations and to select representatives for collective bargaining without any interference or domination by management. Wagner's democratic principles also led him to support the idea of majority rule, the holding of secret-ballot elections among employees to determine exclusive representation rights.

The NLRA reflected a set of major role changes on the part of the trade union movement, organized management, and the federal government. The unions won legal protection against employer interference with their right to organize and to bargain collectively. In return, however, they agreed to submit to the government's determination of appropriate bargaining units and, as events would soon demonstrate, of the structuring of the labor movement itself. Employers lost their traditional power to deal with their employees on a unilateral basis; they also were deprived of their ability to shape the structure of labor-management relations. Government shifted from what was essentially a laissez faire position (intervening mainly to prevent violence or major economic disruptions) to the role of rule-maker and umpire in the collective bargaining game. Although the immediate effect was to promote the cause of labor (both organized and unorganized) against resistant employers, the more basic, long-run role became that of setting and enforcing the rules of the game for the chief actors—organized labor and management.

These profound role changes did not come about simply through the debates and votes of congressmen. They were accompanied by a series of dramatic and sometimes violent conflicts within the ranks of labor and at the nation's major workplaces, and (more peacefully but no less dramatically) within the chambers of the federal courts.

The story of labor's regeneration, the phenomenal rise of industrial unionism under the leadership of John L. Lewis of the United Mine Workers and Sidney Hillman of the Amalgamated Clothing Workers, the split in the labor movement, the formation of the Congress of Industrial Organizations and the counter-reformation of the AFL—this story has been told many times.[2] Although labor's upsurge (especially in some of the older sectors of unionism—the mines and needle trades) preceded the Wagner Act, the evidence seems clear that without government support, unionism and collective bargaining in the mass production industries probably would not have taken hold in a period of mass unemployment.

Contemporary accounts portrayed the CIO as the wave of the future in part because most labor historians and journalists of the day sympathized with the underdog factory workers, found industrial unionism more congenial to their personal (often radical) leanings, were critical of the long-entrenched, conservative, craft-minded leaders of the AFL, and were convinced from past experience that the mass production industries could only be organized on an industrial union basis. The public limelight focused on the emergence of the great industrial unions in steel, autos, rubber, electrical products, glass, textiles, meat packing, and other industries that in 1939 claimed a membership of some 4 million (although according to Leo Troy, CIO dues-paying members probably numbered only 1.8 million).[3]

There were good grounds for the enthusiasm. The public image of the great industrial corporations that had shown so brightly in the twenties was badly tarnished by the failure of industrial leadership in the 1929–32 Republican years. Moreover, this was the first time (except briefly during World War I) that mass production workers, mobilized by a unique combination of experienced national leaders and new rank-and-file spokesmen, displayed a sufficient solidarity to mount and maintain a successful organizational momentum. The excitement of organization and strikes also helped brighten the lives of many working-class families to whom the depression had brought the anguish of prolonged unemployment or part-time work and poverty. They had a "cause."

It was not an easy victory; there were periods of serious setback, and at several critical points the movement almost collapsed. The New Deal government—despite its internal divisions, its lack of a clear program or ideology, and its administrative weaknesses—provided the decisive counterforce to the corporate resistance, which was powerful and bitter. It also furnished a much-needed procedure for resolving interunion conflict.

The first employer challenge to the new labor movement came in 1933 and 1934 in response to section 7a of the National Industrial Recovery Act, which gave employees the right to bargain collectively through representatives of their own choice and without employer interference. Many of the major companies reactivated or established new employee representation plans or company unions of the type that had flourished during the twenties but had largely been destroyed in the depth of the depression. By 1935, some 2.5 million workers were covered by such plans, as compared with the 4.1 million members of trade unions. The growth rate of the company unions was actually much faster than that of the unions.

In a few industries, notably steel, the unions set out to capture control of the employee representation plans from within. More commonly the unions attacked the plans from without. But the deathblow to most company unions came from two governmental sources. One was Section 8a (2) of the Wagner Act, which declared that it was an unfair labor practice for any employer to "dominate or interfere with the formation or administration of any labor organization or contribute financial or other support to it." The other was the two-year investigation by the La Follette subcommittee of the Senate Committee on Labor and Education revealing interferences by employers with worker efforts to organize and bargain collectively that shocked public opinion and greatly embarrassed top corporate officials.

A second major threat to the union movement came from the challenges by many employer groups, including the American Liberty League and the National Association of Manufacturers, to the constitutionality of the Wagner Act. Spurred by their successful legal campaigns against the NRA, the AAA, and several other New Deal laws, corporate lawyers advised their clients to reject NLRB awards and to press their cases through the courts, up to the U.S. Supreme Court. The vice president in charge of industrial relations for U.S. Steel told the American Management Association in 1935 that rather than obey the Wagner Act he would "go to jail or be convicted as a felon."[4] The issue of constitutionality, however, was finally resolved in April 1937, and U.S. Steel actually signed its first agreement with the Steel Workers Organizing Committee several weeks earlier.

A third threat to union success was the internecine warfare that broke out in 1933 between the advocates of industrial unionism and the craft-minded leaders of the AFL, reaching its climactic point in 1935 and 1936 with the suspension and expulsion of the industrial unions from the Federation and the establishment of the Congress of Industrial Organizations in 1938. It can be argued that the competition between the two factions proved to be of benefit to the labor movement as a whole by stimulating both sides to exert additional drive, to expend greater resources, and to improve organizational efficiency. One reason that the competition was converted to positive rather than negative ends was the availability in the National Labor Relations Board of a mechanism to resolve representation disputes through the ballot box.

Unfortunately, the New Deal was unable to heal the split between its labor allies. Serious efforts at reconciliation occurred in 1937 and 1938, but they appear to have been frustrated by John Lewis, who preferred the greater power and freedom that separation gave him.

Like most of their publicists, the leaders of the CIO saw their organization in 1938 as the dominant force for labor. They underestimated their old associates. The challenge raised by the CIO led to a revitalization of the AFL. Although the craft unionists held firm to their traditional jurisdictions, they recognized the futility of continuing to emphasize narrow craft lines in the mass production field. Unions like the International Association of Machinists, the International Brotherhood of Electrical Workers, the Meat Cutters and Butcher Workmen, and even the Carpenters, under John Lewis's archrival William L. Hutcheson, broadened their jurisdictional scope to compete with the CIO unions in metalworking, electrical manufacturing, meatpacking, lumber, and furniture manufacture. More important, the nonmanufacturing unions were spurred by the new organizational climate to expand their efforts. The Teamsters, for example, grew from 95,500 members in 1929 to first rank in the Federation with 440,000 in 1939; the Hotel and Restaurant Employees rose from 38,000 to 211,000; the Retail Clerks went up from 12,000 in 1935 to 51,000 in 1939. As a result, the AFL more than made up for the losses suffered by the expulsion of the CIO unions and exceeded the CIO by a margin of 3.9 million to 1.8 million in 1939.[5] Even if allowance is made for the attachment of large numbers of non-dues-paying workers to the CIO in the 1938–39 depression years, the AFL advantage is clear.

Although most of the AFL leaders supported President Roosevelt politically, they were often unhappy with the NLRB, which they accused of favoring the CIO in the determination of appropriate bargaining units and in administrative practices. Studies of the board's activities in the thirties, and particularly of the roles of board member Edwin S. Smith and of its secretary and chief executive officer, Nathan Witt, in the 1937–40 years lend weight to this criticism.[6] Smith and Witt were, reportedly, either Communist party members or fellow travelers. They were closely associated with Lee Pressman, then general counsel of the CIO and the Steelworkers, who admitted to being a party member in 1933–35 with Witt; and there is evidence that the CIO at times benefited from these relations. The efforts of the AFL to secure changes in the Wagner Act were not successful; but in 1939, William M. Leiserson was appointed a board member by President Roosevelt to "clean up" the situation, and he was instrumental in bringing about Witt's resignation in 1940. Despite the advantages that the CIO may have gained, many AFL unions relied upon the assistance of the Wagner Act to advance their positions.

In general, the New Deal gave warm encouragement to union growth and the expansion of collective bargaining. Administration leaders resented the tactics of many major and middle-sized corporations to resist union recognition by all possible means, including the use of labor spies, strikebreakers, and court-delaying procedures. The rapid growth of strikes and particularly the use of the sit-down strike, however, generated friction between the administration and some CIO officials. Worker "occupation" of auto and rubber factories in the mid-thirties as a pressure tactic against General Motors, Goodyear Tire and Rubber, and other employers for recognition initially won public sympathy; but its repeated use in plants as a bargaining or pressure tactic, often after recognition had been won, soon created alarm. To many in government as well as among the general public, the "sit-down" loomed as an attack on private ownership and the capitalist system. To others, it represented anarchy and disrespect for law and order. Even national union leaders rapidly discovered that it undermined their organizational control and authority. There were widespread approval and relief when the Supreme Court in 1939 declared the "sit-down" strike illegal in the Fansteel Metallurgical Corporation case.

More conventional strikes also sometimes led to recriminations. Perhaps the most serious were the "Little Steel" strikes of 1937, during which ten workers at the Republic Steel Company's South Chicago plant were killed by Chicago police in the so-called Memorial Day Massacre. Frustrations flowed from the failure of the Steel Workers Organizing Committee to cope with the bitterly resistant "Little Steel" companies, despite the "Big Steel" agreement negotiated by U.S. Steel board chairman Myron Taylor and John Lewis in February 1937 and the Supreme Court verdict upholding the constitutionality of the Wagner Act in April. When President Roosevelt expressed criticism of both sides for being unwilling to compromise, he was bitterly attacked by Lewis for lack of gratitude for labor's political and financial support. It was not until after the outbreak of war in Europe in 1939 and the development of a substantial military defense program that most of the major antiunion corporations yielded to union and government pressures and accepted collective bargaining.

The most significant achievement of collective bargaining during the 1930s was the establishment of formal grievance procedures for the settlement of disputes during the lifetime of an agreement. Such procedures had worked effectively for decades in certain industries like printing, coal mining, the railroads, and the needle trades. They had also been a major feature of the company-dominated employee representation plans. They were now extended to the bulk of organized industries and occupations. During World War II, the National War Labor Board not only strengthened and improved grievance procedures but also made binding arbitration the final step in most grievances.

From the perspective of World War I, the New Deal represented a natural extension of a process that had been evolving since the turn of the century in respect to national labor-management policy. The U.S. Commission on Industrial Relations, 1913–15, had expressed the need for a law to prevent employer interference with the right of employee organization. President Wilson's War Labor Conference Board formulated a set of principles and policies that affirmed the right of workers to organize in trade unions and to bargain collectively through representatives of their own choice, and that prohibited employers from discharging workers for membership in unions or for legitimate union activities. The War Labor Board introduced the idea of secret-ballot employee elections to select shop committee representatives in plants where unionism was not accepted. The trend toward a governmentally supported system of collective bargaining, however, came to an abrupt halt with the end of World War I and the determination of big business (as represented by Judge Gary, the head of U.S. Steel) to oppose unionization in peacetime. The defeat of the steel strike in 1919 was one key indication. The collapse of Wilson's first postwar labor conference on the issue of employee representation by spokesmen of their own choice, i.e., outside union representatives, was another sign. Except for the railroad industry, government labor-management policy retreated to its prewar status. It is interesting to note that the percentage of nonfarm employees who were unionized in 1930 was virtually the same as in 1910—about 10 percent. Thus, section 7a of the NRA and the principles of the Wagner Act could be viewed as a resumption and extension of a trend after a 12-year hiatus.

Looking back at New Deal labor policy from the vantage point of 1973, one may conclude that it was a decisive stage in the development of the American collective bargaining system. The policy has since been revised in several important respects, but the fundamental affirmation of labor's right to organize and to bargain collectively without employer interference remains intact. So too does the role of the federal government in structuring the collective bargaining system by the determination of appropriate bargaining units and the application of the majority rule principle in representation disputes. The major revisions in the policy occurred in the enactment of the Taft-Hartley Law of 1947 and the Landrum-Griffin Law of 1959. The former added to the Wagner Act a set of unfair practices by unions to parallel the earlier unfair practices by management. It also introduced a new fact-finding procedure to deal with national emergency disputes. The 1959 law established a "bill of rights" for labor union members, regulating the internal structure and government of unions so as to eliminate corruption and to promote democracy.

What a retrospective view of New Deal policy reveals most sharply, however, is its significance for the legalization of American labor-management relations. Prior to the 1930s, labor relations, except for the railroad industry, functioned with a minimum of governmental constraints. Government intervention was limited mainly to the use of court injunctions as a weapon against the unions—a process that was finally checked by the passage of the Norris-LaGuardia Act in 1932. Otherwise, laissez faire prevailed. The New Deal provided a legal basis for collective bargaining and, at the same time, opened the door to government regulation of the collective bargaining process as well as the internal life of trade unions. As a result, lawyers and courts have come to play a role matched only under the Australian arbitration system, a condition that some observers, including the writer, view with considerable concern because it detracts from the responsibility of managers, workers, and union officers to develop effective systems of industrial self-government in the workplace.

SOCIAL SECURITY AND LABOR STANDARDS

The virtual revolution in national labor-management relations policy during the New Deal was paralleled by the dramatic advances in protective federal laws on social insurance and labor standards. Two laws—the Social Security Act of 1935 and the Fair Labor Standards Act of 1938—were the cornerstones, with a number of other laws meeting more specialized needs.

The United States had lagged badly behind the major European industrial countries in providing governmental programs for old age retirement, unemployment compensation, and health care.[7] Despite more than three decades of agitation for such programs, largely by middle-class reformers who established the American Association for Labor Legislation, the National Consumers' League, and the American Association for Old Age

Security, little success was achieved until the Great Depression. Wisconsin pioneered the first state unemployment insurance act in 1932. Limited old-age pension laws were adopted by some ten states in the 1920s, but the first compulsory old-age insurance law for private industry employees did not materialize until the federal Railroad Retirement Act of 1934.[8] The only area in which respectable progress had been made prior to the New Deal was workmen's compensation for industrial accidents and later for occupational disease. Nonwork-related injuries and illness, however, were not covered.

Two major reasons for this generally lamentable picture were the opposition of national AFL leaders to social insurance laws (other than workmen's compensation) and the narrow interpretation by the U.S. Supreme Court of the Constitution with respect to interstate commerce. These were reinforced by widespread employer opposition to state compulsory insurance plans and by the hostility of the American Medical Association to federal health schemes. The "voluntaristic" ideology of the AFL ("what the state gives, it can take away") began to change in 1932 when for the first time its national convention endorsed the principle of a federal unemployment insurance program, provided the costs were covered by the employers as part of the costs of production. The constitutionality question, however, weighed heavily on reform efforts until the historic court reversal in 1937.

In contrast to the Wagner Act, the Social Security Act was a favorite objective of Franklin Roosevelt and Labor Secretary Perkins from the outset of the New Deal (and earlier), and its passage was largely an administration effort to which the union leaders contributed only secondarily. The extent of unemployment after the great crash of 1929 and the dire straits in which many older people found themselves generated widespread public support for social security measures. The Townsend movement for a monthly government payment of $200.00 to all persons aged sixty or more was the most notable of many evidences of popular support.[9]

The Social Security Act provided a federal compulsory old-age insurance program, a system of state unemployment compensation plans encouraged by a federal tax-offset, and a joint federal-state program of financial assistance to needy old people, the blind, and fatherless children. Conspicuously absent, however, was health insurance, which could not hurdle the barrier raised by the AMA with its attacks on "socialized medicine."

Whereas the Social Security Act encompassed almost every sector of the population (despite serious exclusions, such as farm and domestic workers), the Fair Labor Standards Act, like the Wagner Act, focused on the worker and the workplace. The aim of its supporters was to establish certain legal basic or minimum standards for work hours, hourly wage rates, the employment of children and adolescents, and industrial homework. Although such standards might help organized workers to avoid cutthroat competition and to eliminate sweatshops (it is not surprising that its main union advocates were Sidney Hillman and David Dubinsky, spokesmen for the highly competitive garment trades), their chief benefit was for the unorganized and the difficult-to-organize.

This explains why FLSA, like Social Security, was primarily an administration rather than a union product. Elizabeth Brandeis, a leading student of protective labor legislation, concluded that the AFL attitude toward FLSA "probably delayed passage of the law for nearly a year and weakened it materially."[10] The CIO, she noted, supported the administration bill but was not the prime mover. Apparently, the chief reason for union antagonism (a sentiment shared by John Lewis as well as building and metal trades leaders) was a fear that general minimum wage-fixing for adult males by the government would remove a major function of collective bargaining. In contrast, the setting of a maximum work week standard was viewed by labor as a desirable way to cope with unemployment and had been strongly advocated by the AFL in supporting a thirty-hour-week law in 1932. Although the National Industrial Recovery Act provided for the inclusion of minimum wages and maximum hours in each industrial code, the main AFL concern appears to have been with the collective bargaining provision of section 7a.

Like Social Security, the Fair Labor Standards Act was a multilateral law. It established a standard work week (initially of 44 hours, reduced to 40 after two years), with time-and-a-half premium pay for any work beyond the standard. It set a minimum wage of 25 cents per hour the first year and 30 cents per hour the second year, to rise to 40 cents after seven years. The administrator of the law could set rates above 30 and up to 40 cents upon recommendation of special industry committees. Child labor below the age of 16 was generally prohibited, as was industrial homework of a sweatshop variety—both NRA targets.

Two other regulatory bills won the enthusiastic support of organized labor. One actually preceded the New Deal—the Bacon-Davis Act of 1931, which provided a basic eight-hour day on public construction projects and the payment of "prevailing wages" (which, practically speaking, meant union wages) as determined by the Department of Labor. The Bacon-Davis Act was extended and strengthened in 1935. The following year, after the NRA had been declared unconstitutional by the Supreme Court, the administration introduced and pushed through Congress the Walsh-Healey Public Contracts Law that provided for the establishment of minimum wages and overtime premium pay as well as the elimination of child and prison labor on all federal contracts costing $10,000 or more.

As in the case of the National Labor Relations Act, the leaders of business and industry and their conservative supporters strenuously, often bitterly, opposed adoption of these New Deal protective labor laws. The economic costs placed upon the employer, the record-keeping and reporting requirements, the steadily mounting power and "interference" of the government, and their general attitude of hostility toward "the man" in the White House were major elements of the conservative attack on the Social Security and related programs. The votes were against them.

In a famous speech to the Teamsters Union, widely regarded as a turning point in his campaign for a third term in 1940, President Franklin Roosevelt summed up the labor achievements of the New Deal. The right to organize and bargain collectively, he said, was the foundation of industrial relations for all time.

> With that foundation, the last seven years have seen a series of laws enacted to give labor a fairer share of the good life to which free men and women in a free nation are entitled as a matter of right. Fair minimum wages are being established for workers in industry; decent maximum hours and days of labor have been set, to bring about the objective of an American standard of living and recreation; child labor has been outlawed in practically all factories; a system of employment exchanges has been created; machinery has been set up and strengthened and successfully used in almost every case for the mediation of labor disputes. Over them all has been created a shelter of social security, a foundation upon which we are trying to build protection from the hazards of old age and unemployment.[11]

It was a sentiment shared by the great majority of the American people despite the well-recognized gaps and limitations of the program.

If we look at the New Deal record in setting labor standards from the angle of World War I, the picture remains most impressive. Despite a giant increase in unionization and collective bargaining under wartime conditions, governmentally protected labor standards had then made only limited progress. Under threat of a national railroad strike, the Congress in 1916 passed the Adamson Act establishing a basic eight-hour day for operating rail employees. The Supreme Court upheld the constitutionality of the act under the interstate commerce provision. But federal laws governing factory and most other types of workers were consistently declared to be unconstitutional. Thus, when Congress in 1916 passed a child labor law, the Court rejected it in 1918 as an improper regulation of commerce.[12] Responsibility for labor standards was left mainly in the domain of the states, where the results were spotty. The best, although far from universal, results were obtained on the limitation of work hours of children and women (mainly on health grounds) and on workmen's compensation for industrial accidents. Minimum wage legislation for women and minors was adopted in some fourteen states between 1912 and 1919, but not for men. Outside of workmen's compensation, social insurance laws were conspicuously absent.

President Wilson's War Labor Conference Board, in setting guidelines for the National War Labor Board, tried to fill a few gaps. It enunciated the policy of equal pay for equal work for women; it supported the basic eight-hour-day principle where existing law required it and urged all other cases to be treated "with due regard to governmental necessities and the welfare, health, and proper comfort of the workers"; and it adopted the principle of a living wage, declaring that "in fixing wages, minimum rates of pay shall be established which will insure the subsistence of the worker and his family in health and reasonable comfort." War Labor Board awards implemented these principles.

Even at the peak of the wartime labor development (prior to the severe setbacks in steel and other manufacturing industries as well as the reaction to the Boston police strike), the social security and labor standards laws of the New Deal would have represented an achievement of historic proportions.

From a 1973 perspective on the New Deal, the social security–labor standards programs continue to loom as major achievements in American economic and social history. In the third of a century since their passage, these New Deal programs have been expanded and supplemented, but the basic elements remain intact. Congress has periodically extended coverage (e.g., to retail establishments, domestic service, and farms) and raised benefits without altering any significant principles.

Recent innovations, however, underline the fact that the New Deal represented a start rather than a conclusion. For example, the policy of nondiscrimination in employment because of race, sex, national origin, or religious belief, as expressed in title VII of the Civil Rights Act of 1964, was largely ignored in the 1930s. Similar gaps are indicated by the Equal Pay for Women Act of 1963 (a long-discussed but largely neglected issue in practice) and by the adoption of Medicare and Medicaid for the aged in the middle sixties, although even in 1973 national compulsory health insurance remains an elusive goal.

The Occupational Safety and Health Act of 1970, which may prove to be one of the landmarks of labor legislation, covers still another major area in which the New Deal program made relatively little progress. Public interest in occupational safety and health goes back to the pre–Civil War period, but responsibility for factory and business inspection and rule-making was left largely with the states. The result was a wide variation in the quality of rules and the effectiveness of enforcement. The U.S. Department of Labor's Division of Labor Standards attempted to raise standards and promote uniformity, but it had limited success. The growing need for a federal program, indicated in worsening factory accident statistics, led to the 1970 legislation.

EMPLOYMENT AND UNEMPLOYMENT

If the laws on collective bargaining, social security, and labor standards were among the crowning achievements of the New Deal, the inability to cope with the problem of unemployment was clearly one of its greatest failures. The statistics shown in table 1 require little commentary.[13] When one considers that in the depth of the short post–World War I depression the unemployment rate had been 11.7 percent and that in no other year since the 1893–96 depression had the rate reached 9 percent, the tragic dimensions of the Great Depression become fully evident.

TABLE 1

RATE OF UNEMPLOYMENT

Year	Total (thousands)	Percentage of Civilian Labor Force
1929	1,550	3.2
1931	8,020	16.3
1933	12,830	25.2
1935	10,610	20.3
1937	7,700	14.3
1939	9,480	17.2
1941	5,560	9.9
1943	1,070	4.7

The New Deal administration proved incapable of developing a national economic program to overcome the depression. Only World War II enabled that goal to be achieved. Nevertheless, several significant innovative steps were taken in the areas of work relief: public works, youth corps, and public employment exchanges or offices. Mass starvation was avoided through elaborate welfare and work projects, and public inclinations to rebel at the system of private capitalism that had broken down so badly were held to surprisingly small levels. Despite the fact that radical movements attracted many more adherents than in the past, Roosevelt's charismatic leadership and his willingness to introduce new ameliorative programs effectively undermined all of the challenges from the political left as well as the right. He conveyed a spirit of hope and confidence to the mass of Americans not shared by many of the intellectuals and upper-income stratum.

The New Deal attack on the relief problem started in 1933 with the Federal Emergency Relief Administration (FERA), experimented for a winter with the Civil Works Administration (CWA), and then in 1935 adopted the unprecedentedly massive Emergency Relief Appropriation Act (designed to provide 3.5 million jobs to people on relief) out of which emerged the Works Progress Administration (WPA). For men between 18 and 25, the Civilian Conservation Corps (CCC) also provided a substantial number of useful relief jobs. The National Youth Administration (NYA) provided financial assistance through part-time jobs to college students. A more conventional public works program (PWA), paying union prevailing wages rather than the much lower relief payments of the WPA and the CCC, moved slowly and on too small a scale to contribute significantly until the later years of the decade.

These efforts to remove people from the "dole" and to provide work that was useful and psychologically rebuilding created conflicts across the whole political spectrum. No American government had ever spent so much money on relief or on public works before, and there was a fear among the middle- and upper-income classes of national bankruptcy. AFL trade unionists (particularly in the building trades) saw the low wages of relief workers as a source of unfair competition, undercutting their job opportunities and job standards. Liberals and radicals, in contrast, contended that the bare subsistence payments were too low to sustain the workers and their families and that the program was far too limited to put the country on the road to recovery.

The solution to the unemployment problem, of course, was not to be found in relief measures. Even the ERA legislation, providing billions, could have merely a temporary stimulating effect. Moreover, it was not only too small but too short-lived to promote general prosperity. In 1937, fearing that costs were getting out of hand, the president ordered sharp cutbacks in relief and PWA programs; the taxes of the new Social Security system had a further deflationary effect; and the result was a sharp recession in late 1937 and throughout 1938. The New Deal administration was torn between its budget-balancing (traditional) and pump-priming (Keynesian) factions and shifted policies in a state of confusion and indecision. Finally, the onset of the European war resolved the economic dilemma.

In addition to its relief projects, one of the first New Deal efforts to counter unemployment was the passage of an act (in June 1933) to establish the United States Employment Services (USES) with a network of local offices throughout the nation. The public employment office was not a new idea. A state system had been established in Ohio in 1890, and a Federal Employment Service had been set up in 1907, originally to place new immigrants on farms. During World War I, the federal service became a truly national system and played a significant, if not wholly efficient, role in meeting wartime needs. After the war, however, Congress refused to support the service on more than a minimal basis (the appropriation in 1920 was $200,000, compared with over $5,600,000 in 1919). The state employment systems also deteriorated in size and scope. Thus the USES, utilizing federal grants-in-aid and minimum national standards to induce the cooperation of the states, laid the basis for a meaningful system of public employment offices. Later, the system was integrated with the unemployment insurance provisions of the Social Security Act. The USES was an important achievement from a long-run view, but its contribution to the unemployment problem was necessarily limited—it could not create jobs.

From the perspective of 1919, the unemployment of the Great Depression would have appeared a regrettable but unavoidable consequence of the business cycle that had characterized American economic life since the 1830s. Defenders of free enterprise would have agreed with radical critics that occasional great depressions such as those of 1893–96 and 1873–79 and more numerous shorter ones were inherent in capitalism. The belief of the late 1920s that depressions were a thing of the past had not yet gained support among prominent economists and businessmen. Americans enjoyed the artificial prosperity of the World War I years but knew in their bones that it could not endure. Within a few years, indeed, they suffered through the short but deep depression of 1920–22.

To 1973 eyes, however, the unemployment of the 1930s looks incredible and intolerable. In the thirty-odd years since 1941, the unemployment rate has not exceeded 6.8 percent. At least five recessions have been identified during this period, but the concept of a self-adjusting "business cycle" has been abandoned. When in 1946 Congress passed the Employment Act, which declared that the federal government would do everything possible to promote maximum employment, production, and purchasing power, and which established the Council of Economic Advisors as the economic intelligence of the president, the nation in effect rejected mass unemployment as an acceptable economic alternative. Even during the Eisenhower presidency (1953–60), when more conservative economic policies were followed, the government engaged in a high degree of economic interventionism. Conservative politicians in 1973 no longer attach prime importance to the balanced budget, and talk instead in "new economics" terms of high-employment budgets, full-employment surpluses, fiscal drag, negative income taxes, and annual income guarantees.

Despite its failure to cope with the unemployment problem, the New Deal did convey several economic lessons to the future. One was the need for federal government leadership in attacking the problem—it could not be left to private enterprise or to state and local governments. A second was the value of unemployment insurance and work relief to help tide people over periods of unemployment. A third was the importance of employment offices to help match unemployed people with available job opportunities.

LABOR IN POLITICS

The labor movement has been involved in politics since its beginning. During the 1930s, it greatly expanded political action and substituted for the traditional Gompersian policy of "reward your friends and punish your enemies" a deep and lasting attachment to the New Deal Democrats. A number of AFL leaders, including John Lewis, were Republicans during the twenties, but the collapse of Republican policy and the prolabor programs of the New Deal drove all but a few (such as Hutcheson of the Carpenters Union) into the Roosevelt camp. The organizing slogan "President Roosevelt wants you to unionize" was symbolic. The intense opposition of the American Liberty League and other business-minded organizations to New Deal labor bills, the inept employer campaign against social security in the 1936 presidential contest, and the revelations by the La Follette subcommittee of employer use of spies, strikebreakers, and provocateurs were hardly calculated to win worker support for the Republican party.

During the 1936 presidential campaign, CIO leaders, with the cooperation of some AFL unionists, set up Labor's Non-Partisan League to help reelect Roosevelt. William Green and other AFL leaders were soon to become highly critical of the league, although many AFL national and state affiliates originally cooperated with it. The league contributed a substantial amount of money (an estimated three-quarters of a million dollars) to the Democratic campaign and brought out a sizable labor vote, although Roosevelt's personal popularity was so great that his reelection was inevitable. During the Little Steel strikes of 1937, when the president made his "a plague on both your houses" statement, John Lewis bitterly recalled the United Mine Workers' and CIO's contributions to the 1936 campaign. Lewis's breach with Roosevelt widened during the administration's fruitless efforts to reunite the AFL and CIO. In 1939, after an apparent Lewis proposal that he be nominated vice-president on the Democratic ticket was rejected out-of-hand, he appealed to his followers to repudiate the president and vowed to resign as CIO president if Roosevelt were relected to a third term. Lewis's political stance as well as some of his CIO policies were not shared by a number of prominent CIO leaders. It was Lewis, not Roosevelt, whom the miners and other workers repudiated in the political arena.

The split in the labor movement led inevitably to AFL political organization to counter the CIO, but Labor's League for Political Education was not set up until the 1948 election campaign, following passage of the Taft-Hartley Act by a Republican-dominated Congress. In the decade between 1938 and 1948, the AFL functioned along more traditional lines. Roosevelt was sensitive to its problems, particularly after his efforts to repair the split in labor were frustrated by Lewis. When, in 1937–39, the AFL became unhappy over the decisions of the National Labor Relations Board, he skillfully changed the board's composition. Just as Sidney Hillman was his key link on the CIO side, so Dan Tobin of the Teamsters served as a major line of communication to the AFL. Thus, Roosevelt had overwhelming labor support in his third (and later his fourth) campaigns as well as in his first two.

A new political force in the 1930s was the Communists. Throughout the twenties, the Communist party had been a largely negative factor on the labor scene, creating internecine warfare in the New York garment trades with their policy of boring from within and then finding (after 1928) that their new policy of dual unionism was an exercise in futility. The Great Depression gave them a golden opportunity to carry on organizational activities first among the unemployed (1930–32), then among relief workers (especially on CWA and WPA projects), and, most importantly, with the new CIO unions in mass production and other industries. Other radical groups—Socialists, Musteites, Trotskyites—also intensified their efforts in the labor movement, although less effectively. As Karsh and Garman concluded, "By the end of the New Deal period, left-wingers controlled a larger portion of the American labor movement than at any time since the formation of the American Federation of Labor in 1886."[14]

On the political front, the Communists also found it more profitable to work "from within" than to carry on independent political action. Using the slogan of the popular front, they worked from 1935 under the New Deal umbrella in both the Democratic party and the Washington bureaucracy. Although they retained the organizational identity and structure of the Communist party, their vote-getting ability was far less significant than the influence they achieved through propaganda, control of popular front organizations, and positions in government and unions. It was to be short-lived. The Nazi-Soviet pact of 1939 threw the party into confusion and disarray, and exposed many of their machinations. And though they regained their equilibrium after the Nazi invasion of Russia in 1941, they were doomed to virtual extinction in the cold war era after World War II.

Looking once more at the New Deal from a World War I perspective, we find a considerable parallelism between the AFL relation with the Wilsonian Democrats and the AFL-CIO alliance with Roosevelt's New Deal administration. The ties would have seemed natural and consistent with the AFL's traditional political policy, to support labor's friends. There was little doubt in the 1930s which of the two major parties supported and fostered labor's aims (notwithstanding the temporary AFL dissatisfaction with the NLRB) and which party opposed them. The formation of Labor's Non-Partisan League (marred as it was by the split in the labor movement) would have seemed logical and realistic to organized labor in 1919.

The role and status of the radicals were a different matter. The Socialist party was badly split over Wilson's war policies, and its antiwar majority severely attacked Gompers for his support of Wilson. The IWW, which was the "red menace" of its time, was crushed by the acts and acquiescence of the Wilson government—a very different treatment than that accorded the Communists in the thirties. But then the administration and the radicals agreed on the menace of Nazism, whereas they differed on involvement in World War I.

In 1973, we see the labor politics of the New Deal as the foundation-stone of the labor–Democratic party coalition that has functioned almost intact for three decades. The growth of the union movement in strength, wealth, and political sophistication has made organized labor an increasingly important ally of the Democrats. In theory, the AFL-CIO remains politically independent; in practice, it has been a major support of every presidential candidate of the Democratic party since Roosevelt, except for McGovern in 1972. Although there are signs that the coalition of urban union workers and ethnic minoritites that Roosevelt forged may be in the process of disintegration, the breakup of the New Deal's labor–Democratic party alliance has not yet occurred. The only major difference from the thirties is the elimination of the Communist party from any serious role in American political life as well as from the labor movement.

CONCLUDING ASSESSMENT

Whether one attempts to assess the New Deal's impact on labor from a contemporary point of view, from the perspective of a decade and a half earlier, or with today's hindsight three decades later, two central conclusions stand out. One is that the industrial relations system of the United States was profoundly changed—structurally, legally, ideologically, and in terms of power. The people of the thirties knew it; the sense of a historical turning point was reflected in their attitudes and behavior. Roosevelt, the Hyde Park aristocrat, was assailed with incredible bitterness and passion as a traitor to his class while he was revered and idolized by the masses of ordinary workers. The rise of industrial unionism and the resultant split in the labor movement, the constitutional struggle over the New Deal's legislative program and the shift in the position of the Supreme Court, the destruction of company unionism—these and other dramatic events evidence a fundamental restructuring of the industrial relations system.

Three laws were at the center of the new system: the National Labor Relations Act, the Social Security Act, and the Fair Labor Standards Act. Each act had clearly traceable historical roots. Each responded to a need that students and reformers had identified and, in varying degrees, pressed for since the turn of the century. The Social Security and Fair Labor

Standards acts for the most part simply brought the United States to a welfare stage long occupied by Germany, Britain, Australia, New Zealand, Sweden, and several other nations. The NLRA was more distinctive. It threw the weight of federal authority behind unionism and collective bargaining, thereby establishing a bilateral process of decision-making that the labor movement had not been able to achieve by itself in most branches of American industry. However, labor had to pay a price. Henceforth and in increasing measure, the federal government was to serve as a third party in industrial relations, placing its mark not only on the rules of the game but also on the structure and some of the substantive results of bargaining and on many features of the labor movement itself.

The New Deal's labor program was partly a product of the thought and pressures of the union movement, but for the most part it was the result of the initiatives of the New Dealers themselves—notably politicians like Senator Wagner and President Roosevelt, administrators like Secretary Perkins, and legal and economic advisers and staff like Donald R. Richberg, William M. Leiserson, and Edwin E. Witte. The AFL had begun to cast off its ideology of "voluntarism" by 1932, but many of its older leaders were not able to discard a generation of suspicion about the role of government. Throughout the thirties, they tended to introduce qualifications and conditions to New Deal proposals rather than to project new ideas. The CIO leaders were less hampered in this respect; however, their central preoccupation during the decade was the problem of organization. For the most part, they strongly supported New Deal bills, but were not their innovators.

The second major conclusion of this essay is that although the New Deal failed to solve the problem of mass unemployment because of the timidity, uncertainty, and contradictoriness of its economic policies, it did not forfeit labor's support thereby. That organized labor, and particularly its leaders, held firm to Roosevelt's coat-tails is not surprising in view of the record described earlier. But Roosevelt also retained the unremitting loyalty of the working class as a whole, organized or not, who were the chief victims of the Great Depression.

Three reasons may help explain this worker attachment to the New Deal. One is the charismatic appeal of Roosevelt and his political skills. He exuded "hope." He was constantly introducing new ideas and new programs. The seven years between the first hundred days and the outbreak of war in Europe were full of excitement and drama that kept up people's expectations. Moreover, he was extraordinarily adept, as a politician, in placing and keeping the blame for the Great Depression on Herbert Hoover and his administration. He was greatly aided in maintaining this charge by the negative posture of Republican spokesmen against virtually all of the New Deal's labor bills. A second factor in the workers' attachment to the New Deal was the relief program. Despite the continuing high level of unemployment, almost all distressed families got some form of government assistance. Young people who could not break into the labor market at all were aided by the Civilian Conservation Corps and the National Youth Administration. The pay on relief jobs was extremely low, but it prevented starvation and supported personal dignity. In industry, the sharing of work through shorter work days and three- or four-day work weeks had a similar effect. A third reason for the New Deal hold on labor is that the alternative political choices were of limited appeal. The negativism of the Republicans has been noted above. The radicals were fragmented in a dozen ways, and their more realistic proposals, like unemployment insurance and social security, were adopted by the New Deal, thus depriving them of key issues. Demagogic personalities like Huey Long and Father Coughlin had followings, but they were largely confined to geographic sections, a religious group, or some other limited category within the electorate.

The New Deal could not restore economic vitality to the nation. The gross national product did return to 1929 levels in 1937, but then it slumped badly in the 1937–38 recession. Economists began to talk about the society's stagnation or maturation instead of its continued growth. Nevertheless, one lesson was learned. The federal government could not stand aloof from the nation's economic problems and institutions. It had to intervene directly and on a large scale, with new laws and programs as well as with conventional fiscal and monetary tools. Herbert Hoover had recognized this fact on a limited scale near the end of his term. The New Deal made it a cardinal point. Because of it, organized labor forged an alliance with the Democratic party that has lasted to the present time.

I am indebted to my colleague W. H. McPherson for reviewing this essay and making a number of helpful comments.

1. *The Roosevelt I Knew* (New York, 1946), pp. 239, 301.

2. See, for examples, Irving Bernstein, *Turbulent Years: A History of the American Workers, 1933–1941* (Boston, 1970); Walter Galenson, *The CIO Challenge to the AFL: A History of the American Labor Movement, 1935–1941* (Cambridge, Mass., 1960); and Milton Derber and Edwin Young, eds., *Labor and the New Deal* (Madison, Wis., 1957).

3. Leo Troy, *Trade Union Membership, 1897–1962*, National Bureau of Economic Research, Occasional Paper 92 (New York, 1965), p. 8.

4. Quoted in William E. Leuchtenburg, *Franklin D. Roosevelt and the New Deal, 1932–1940* (Torchbook ed.; New York, 1963), p. 177.

5. These statistics are based on the surveys by Leo Wolman and Leo Troy for the National Bureau of Economic Research; see Troy, *Trade Union Membership*.

6. See, for example, Bernard Karsh and Phillips L. Garman, "The Impact of the Political Left," in Derber and Young, *Labor and the New Deal*, especially pp. 108–11.

7. For historical background, see John R. Commons and John B. Andrews, *Principles of Labor Legislation* (4th rev. ed.; New York, 1936), and Arthur J. Altmeyer, *The Formative Years of Social Security* (Madison, Wis., 1966).

8. Declared unconstitutional by the Supreme Court, it was replaced in 1935 by legislation similar to the Social Security Act.

9. See Michael E. Schiltz, *Public Attitudes toward Social Security, 1935–1965*, U.S. Department of Health, Education, and Welfare, Research Report No. 33 (Washington, 1970).

10. Derber and Young, *Labor and the New Deal*, p. 229.

11. Samuel I. Rosenman, ed., *The Public Papers and Addresses of Franklin D. Roosevelt*, 13 vols. (New York, 1938–50), 9:407.

12. Hammer *v.* Dagenhart, 247 U.S. 251.

13. Stanley Lebergott, *Manpower in Economic Growth* (New York, 1964), Appendix Table A3, p. 512.

14. Derber and Young, *Labor and the New Deal*, p. 111.

Jerold S. Auerbach

Lawyers and Social Change in the Depression Decade

DURING THE GREAT DEPRESSION DECADE, THE AMERICAN LEGAL profession, structurally and ideologically committed to stability, underwent wrenching change. Its texture was woven from various strands—some dating from the turn of the century, others quite new: the impact of corporate capitalism on professional values and structure; the emergence of university legal education as the primary channel of access to the professional elite; social stratification that produced blocked mobility and generational conflict; and the employment crisis created by the depression in conjunction with the opportunity structure established by the Roosevelt administration. Although lawyers are functionally committed to a process of social ordering designed to mitigate abrupt or unpredictable change, the nexus between law and public life requires their profession to serve as a sensitive barometer of social change. Amid the turbulence of the thirties, the legal profession, buffeted by external pressures and rent by internal conflict, uneasily confronted both its past and its future.

During dedicatory exercises at the Law Quadrangle of the University of Michigan in 1934, Justice Harlan F. Stone delivered an address decrying the diminished public influence of the bar. Stone, nearing the end of his first decade on the Supreme Court, could view his profession with uncommon perspective. His experiences with the prestigious Sullivan and Cromwell firm, as dean of Columbia Law School, and as attorney general in the Coolidge administration had exposed him to the major sources of professional opportunity: private practice, legal education, and public service. From these, however, Stone drew scant consolation. Even prior to World War I, he had begun to mourn "a deterioration of our bar both in its personnel, its corporate morale, and, consequently, in the public influence wielded by it." Professional leadership had passed into the hands of the business lawyer who, at his best, was a "skillful, resourceful solicitor," but at his worst was "the mere hired man of corporations." Postwar developments heightened Stone's unease. Soon after his appointment to the Supreme Court, he declined an invitation to contribute an article on the bar to *Harper's*, explaining that any "worth-while article" would include sharp criticism. After sketching the outlines of such an essay, Stone drew back, telling editor Frederick Lewis Allen that if the author "is influential, you are not likely to get very much of an article; if he is critical, he is not likely to be influential."[1]

By 1934, however, Stone no longer cared to contain himself. The subject of his address, he confessed, "had been festering in my insides long enough so I had to get it out." In a blistering attack, subsequently published in the *Harvard Law Review*, Stone deplored professional defects that were inhibiting the ability of the bar to resolve "the problems of a sorely stricken social order." In a stratified, specialized profession the lawyer no longer served as the "representative and interpreter of his community." Instead, with success measured by income, he managed "a new type of factory, whose legal product is increasing by the result of mass production methods." His primary allegiance went to business clients, not to the professional ideal of disinterested service that once had elevated lawyers to a position of public influence and leadership. Stone sadly concluded that these changes had transformed "the learned profession of an earlier day [into] the obsequious servant of business, and tainted it with the morals and manners of the market place in its most anti-social manifestations."[2]

Stone's nostalgic *cri de coeur* for the golden age of American lawyers, before the country swallowed the forbidden fruits of industrialization, urbanization, and commercialization, had a familiar ring. Ever since the turn of the century, lawyers wedded to nineteenth-century myths and memories had mourned their loss of independence in an urban industrial age. Neither Tocqueville's celebrated praise for their profession nor Lincoln's rough-hewn example provided sustenance in the twentieth century; indeed, they only aggravated the lawyers' sense of loss. Yet Stone's lament, however poignant and pointed, expressed merely the least that might have been said about professional troubles at a time of national crisis.

In structure, the practicing bar resembled a pyramid. Its apex was the privileged preserve of white Anglo-Saxon Protestant lawyers, trained in colleges and in university law schools, who, as partners in law firms, specialized in the lucrative practice of corporate law. Far below, at its base, a horde of solo practitioners from ethnic minority groups, whose formal education often was limited to high school and night law school, scrambled for clients in the nether realms of criminal and civil practice. Strong and mutually reinforcing barriers perpetuated stratification. Social origins (in conjunction with financial resources) often determined access to those colleges and law schools whose certification was a prerequisite for a position with prestigious firms. The discriminatory recruitment practices of law firms weeded out aspirants with "inferior" social origins who might surmount financial and educational hurdles. Professional associations, disproportionately representative of corporation lawyers and their social values, devised educational requirements, bar admissions standards, and ethical norms that either inhibited access to the bar by the socially and ethnically disadvantaged or, when that failed, placed the onus of unethical behavior upon them. Intraprofessional mobility was virtually impossible. Those assured by their social origins of access to Wall Street firms would never slip to the status of marginal solo practitioners; nor would the latter, regardless of merit, ever rise to the professional heights. Professional stratification, with Wall Street practice at one level and solo practice at another, correlated closely with the ethnic stratification separating Anglo-Saxon Protestant from Russian Jew and Catholic. The profession, as law professor Karl Llewellyn perceived it, was split into its "blue-stocking . . . respectable bar" and its "catch-as-catch can bar."[3]

The depression threatened to demolish the lower professional stratum. Young lawyers, urban solo lawyers, and lawyers from ethnic minority groups were especially vulnerable. In California, among lawyers admitted to the bar between 1929 and 1931, 51 percent did not earn enough during their first year in practice to support their families; 37 percent did not do so in their second year of practice; and 33 percent still did not in their third year. One new California lawyer in ten received no income at all from practice; three in ten earned less than half their income from law work. Across the country in New York, more than one-third of those with incomes below $2,000 were solo practitioners; only 17 percent of firm lawyers earned that little. Conversely, although 9 percent of solo lawyers earned more than $10,000, 35 percent of firm lawyers did so. Jewish lawyers in New York City (approximately one-half of the metropolitan bar) discovered that their practice had become "a dignified road to starvation." The conjunction of aspiration, social origin, and professional stratification made this group especially susceptible to the pinch of hard times. In contrast to non-Jewish practitioners, they were less likely to be college graduates, more likely to have received training in night law schools, more likely to practice alone, and more dependent upon income from another vocation. Regardless of the number of years spent in practice, their income was "strikingly less" than that of their non-Jewish colleagues. At every income level below $5,000, the proportion of Jewish lawyers exceeded the proprtion of lawyers generally; above that figure, at every level, the proportions were reversed. Although they fared poorly in comparison with their metropolitan colleagues, their low income paralleled that of the profession nationally. Nearly half of American lawyers, in the mid-thirties, earned less than $2,000 annually. Young lawyers, the American Bar Association concluded after a study of the economic condition of the bar, comprised "a severely handicapped group," and "the proportion of lawyers in large cities who earn so little as to constitute a serious professional problem is very great."[4]

At elite levels, partners flourished while aspirants languished. Some firms doubtlessly lost lucrative corporate retainers after 1929, but bankruptcies, receiverships, and corporate reorganizations took up the slack until New Deal regulatory legislation stimulated litigation. As the historian of the Cravath firm observed, "depression-induced bankruptcies and New Deal agencies engulfed business and created such demands on the profession that competent legal assistance was at a premium." A prominent Seattle corporation lawyer, who subsequently became president of the American Bar Association, recalled that his firm was "very little affected" by the depression; in fact, its business increased. And Harrison Tweed of Milbank, Tweed, in New York, concluded that law firms always earn more "when times are very bad or very good." Those lawyers most likely to be adversely affected by the depression were young men seeking access to corporate firms. The Cravath firm and Sullivan and Cromwell, to cite two examples, sharply curtailed recruitment between 1931 and 1933. Exceptional applicants, observed a partner in Sullivan and Cromwell, would encounter slight difficulty, "but some of the others may be up against it."[5]

From many angles of vision—Stone's, the solo practitioner's, or the aspiring partner's—the legal profession had betrayed its promises. Dreams of personal independence, public influence, or social mobility were cruelly mocked by depression realities. Frustration and disenchantment quickly bred criticism: in a climate of hostility toward "economic royalists," lawyers were vulnerable for their service to businessmen. Any reevaluation of the American business system was bound to lead to a parallel reconsideration of the role of the profession that served it so conspicuously. Throughout the thirties, lawyers were raked by criticism—and by searing self-criticism, which reached its apogee when Yale law professor Fred Rodell advocated the abolition of the legal profession by making it a crime to practice law for money. The most frequent complaint, especially from law teachers, was complicity with big business. Harvard law professor Calvert Magruder told Maryland lawyers that the profession "must cease to take its ethics, its economics, and its political ideals from the banker." Adolf A. Berle of Columbia, writing in the *Encyclopedia of the Social Sciences*, accused the profession of having become "virtually an intellectual jobber and contractor in business matters." Commercialization had "stripped it of any social functions it might have performed for individuals without wealth." Little wonder that New York attorney Arthur Ballantine nostalgically recalled his own law student days, when "legitimate money-making was not . . . thought of as a crime, and proper service to business was regarded as service to society."[6]

There were many critics, but few perceived the relation between corporate counseling (a negligible dimension of the problem) and certain basic structural and organizational features of the legal profession. Present in good times as in bad, these features exposed an alarming gap between the professional ideal and reality, between promise and performance. It was, in the first instance, difficult to speak accurately of an American "bar." Karl Llewellyn of Columbia, who was an acute observer of his professional culture, described it as "an almost meaningless conglomeration" containing thousands of lawyers "without unity of tradition, character, background, or objective." Professional differentiation was a product of legal specialization, reinforced by social and ethnic stratification. It encouraged the channeling of the best professional talent into corporate counseling. This meant, in Llewellyn's words, "that the fitting of law to new conditions has been concentrated on *only one phase* of new conditions: to wit, the furtherance of the business and financing side, *from the angle of the enterpriser and the financier*. It has been focused on organizing their control of others, and on blocking off control of them by others." Bar organization, for Llewellyn, was the critical issue. "Our bar is organized, theoretically, in terms of an Adam Smith economy: individual initiative, small enterprisers, individual skill, work, and reputation. Its ethics are so organized. Its theory is so organized." If nineteenth-century theory stressed individualism within the context of self-contained communities, twentieth-century reality required organization in sprawling, interdependent cities. Yet the large law firm, a creative response to this need, had transformed "bar-leaders and aspirants to leadership *ever more* into specialized adherents of the Haves."[7]

Llewellyn's indictment was echoed throughout the thirties, when the legal profession was an inviting target for its "surrender" to business and law "factories" were as vulnerable to rhetorical attack as their industrial counterparts. Sophisticated critics cultivated anthropological analogies to explain professional defects. Fred Rodell likened lawyers to medicine men and priests, "who blend technical competence with plain and fancy hocus/pocus to make themselves masters of their fellow men. Thurman Arnold, law teacher at Yale and a student of folklore and symbols, airily compared the activities of the American Bar Association with the "quaint customs" of primitive Philippine tribes. Journalist Ferdinand Lundberg described the American lawyer as a member of "a privileged priesthood" who interprets "tribal customs and superstitions of the dim past with sacerdotal solemnity." But Lundberg, like others, missed the point when he asserted that the legal profession was "independent of society," and "psychologically, at least, quite outside of the social system."[8] The legal profession all too accurately mirrored American society; it enjoyed anything but an independent existence. Every essential feature of professional organization and structure reflected prevailing national values: stratification along ethnic lines; recruitment patterns that rewarded corporate counseling with the highest income and status; availability of legal services according to income rather than need; and an individualism that was anachronistic in the twentieth century. The corporation lawyer, paradoxically, was caught in an excruciating whipsaw. The most contemporary of his practicing brethren, he had long since adapted his practice to modern urban business conditions. Yet by doing so, his conspicuous commitment to business values made him an alluring target once the underpinning of prosperity was removed. And his predominance in professional associations, a reward for his innovative success in practice, exposed his social and political conservatism.

Nowhere was this contradiction more apparent than in the American Bar Association. Once the sanctuary of southern gentlemen who welcomed the annual respite provided by summer meetings in the pleasant resort of

Saratoga Springs, it had become the organizational voice of the most successful urban corporation lawyers. Unrepresentative of the bar, it accurately reflected the views of successful practitioners whose elite status it rewarded with membership and leadership in the association. Capitalizing first upon the patriotic fever of the World War I years, and then upon the antiradicalism and xenophobia of the postwar Red Scare, it had so commingled unregulated corporate capitalism and patriotism as to virtually equate reform with revolution and to transform advocacy of economic regulation into an assault on the Constitution. At the beginning of the depression decade, the association's *Journal*, conceding "a certain amount of business depression," reminded lawyers of their responsibility "to keep public sentiment and feeling on an even keel. . . . As a member of a profession which has always played a patriotic part in public affairs, he will hardly be insensible to rash experiments with American ideals."[9]

In the ensuing years, one association leader after another echoed this theme. The typical speaker began with an admission that the profession confronted sharp critics—invariably misguided and politically motivated. He then reasserted the responsibility of lawyers to lead the nation. Leadership required defense of "the fundamentals of the law from assault from without and intriguing falsities from within." The inevitable peroration warned of "an adroit, systematic and sinister effort to discredit and destroy the influence and the leadership of the stabilizing forces and institutions of American life"—the bar being conspicuous among them. Stabilization required defense of business values. "Our prime function is to implement the existing order," declared a Chicago lawyer. "Its sudden destruction . . . implies our own." Businessmen, wrote a New York attorney, "are still the most substantial and the most influential members of each community." Therefore, "it is the rehabilitation of the managers of the economic system with which the lawyer is primarily charged."[10]

Occasionally professional spokesmen harkened back to an earlier tradition that antedated industrial and corporate capitalism. John W. Davis, who described himself as "an unreconstructed believer in the things of yesterday," sought to recapture an era when honor and integrity prevailed and when young men succeeded by virtue of their character, morality, and hard work. Davis defended the virtues of small-town practice long after he had repudiated them for the luster and lucre of a Wall Street firm. Insisting that the profession offered spiritual rather than material rewards, he enjoyed telling young men that "a lawyer works hard, lives well, and dies poor." Success was within anyone's grasp: "whether one succeeds or not depends largely on himself." Davis's rhetoric substituted the simple past of an age of individualism for the complex present of organized business life. Others shared his ambivalence about the modern world. The depression moved James Beck, another traditional individualist, to question the exigencies of modern law practice. Corporation law firms seemed to him to undermine moral responsibility; Beck yearned nostalgically for the golden age of individual practice.[11]

Whether materialistic or nostalgic, the conservatism of bar leaders made it difficult for them to cope with social change. Few of them, complained the senior partner in a Chicago firm, understood that "the old methods will not serve." Within professional circles, criticism of the American Bar Association was frequently expressed, occasionally from unexpected quarters. James Grafton Rogers, prominent in ABA councils and a chronicler of association presidents, confessed that he felt "like giving up and starting all over to make a national lawyers society." A Dallas attorney concluded sadly that no one "pay[s] much attention to what the American Bar Association does." Too many of its members, a St. Louis lawyer told Thurman Arnold, wanted only to "ingratiate themselves into the good graces of Big Money." To critics, the association seemed little more than a spokesman for business interests. Partisan in its advocacy under the guise of defending patriotic values, it chose politics over professionalism. Yet it remained the only national voice of the American legal profession.[12]

It would be difficult to exaggerate the sense of personal and professional dislocation that elite lawyers experienced with the accession of the Roosevelt administration. Warnings of imminent cataclysm punctuated bar association proceedings and the pronouncements of the National Lawyers' Committee of the American Liberty League, organized in 1934 to defend the Constitution against the New Deal. An older generation of corporation lawyers was conspicuous in these groups; the cutting edge of their verbal assault against the administration was professional displacement reinforced by political opposition. As William L. Ransom, ABA president during 1935–36, wrote: "The American lawyer has traditionally been the aid and servant of private enterprise. As government comes into the picture . . . there is less of a place for the independent lawyer." Liberty League lawyers were more explicit in their hostility to the New Deal; indeed, they reached the brink of unethical conduct when they declared the Wagner Act unconstitutional before the Supreme Court reviewed it and offered free legal assistance to potential litigants. Earl F. Reed, counsel for the Weirton Steel Company, asserted the novel claim that once a lawyer told a client that a law was unconstitutional, "it is then a nullity and he need no longer obey that law." Its legal presumptuousness aside, Reed's statement was a vigorous reassertion of the primacy of corporation lawyers at a time when their values were challenged, their clients were pilloried, their accustomed deference was withdrawn, and their self-assumed role as defenders of American institutions was mocked. New Deal laws posed a moral no less than a legal challenge. As George Wharton Pepper, the eminent Philadelphia lawyer, told the Supreme Court at the conclusion of his oral argument in the *Butler* case, testing the constitutionality of the Agricultural Adjustment Act: "I am standing here to plead the cause of the America I have loved; and I pray Almighty God that not in my time may the land of the regimented be accepted as a worthy substitute for the land of the free."[13] Pepper's plea expressed the lawyer's fear of displacement in a society badly shaken, first by the depression and then by an energetic reform administration.

Years before Franklin D. Roosevelt's inauguration, professional associations had expressed concern about the growing concentration of power in Washington. The sudden proliferation of New Deal laws and agencies exceeded the worst fears of traditionalist lawyers, who proclaimed their commitment to a tidy separation of judicial, legislative, and executive powers. They viewed with alarm the growth of administrative law, which not only destroyed their prized symmetry but symbolized the expansion of governmental regulatory power into areas of American life traditionally free of public control. A "flood of administrative legislation" after 4 March 1933 threatened to erode established boundaries between government branches. The adjudicatory functions of administrative agencies endangered the judiciary, which, according to an ABA committee, was "in danger of meeting a measure of the fate of the Merovingian kings." Worst of all, perhaps, the administrators, often young lawyers from backgrounds quite dissimilar from theirs, felt professionally comfortable inside the administrative process and waved the banner of legal realism from their New Deal redoubts. The swiftness of change was unsettling. In an emergency, declared one association leader, it was essential "to hold fast to fundamentals, keep the faith, cherish the basic institutions ordained by our laws, and resist all violent onslaught upon those institutions and those ideals." Instead, the New Deal repudiated tradition and principle and, it seemed to some, even liberty and law. A Los Angeles corporation lawyer spoke for many of his professional colleagues when he predicted to John W. Davis that a continuation of the New Deal "may well result in the overthrow and destruction of American institutions and ideals, and indeed our very system of government. . . . The peril is as great, if not greater, than any war could bring."[14]

The crash, Arthur Schlesinger, Jr., has written, produced "a profound shaking up of American society: it led to a general discrediting of the older ruling classes . . . and a sudden opening of opportunity for men and ethnic groups on the way up in the competition for position and power."[15] The experience of the legal profession during the New Deal decade offers a striking example. A pivotal institution in that process was the university law school. Early in the twentieth century, law teaching became as professionalized as law practice. The growth of American universities, the introduction of the case method at Harvard (reflecting Dean Langdell's conviction that law was a science to be rigorously studied) and its rapid spread to other law schools, and the complexities of business organization in an industrial society, all pointed toward formal legal education by full-time teachers. In 1870, 1,600 students attended 28 American law schools; by 1900, 13,000 law students studied in 100 schools. The birth of the Association of American Law Schools in the first year of the new century testified to the emergence of professional consciousness among law teachers who, during the progressive era, self-confidently proclaimed their growing power and influence. Once law schools began to serve as a training ground for public service, and once law teachers became, according to Richard Hofstadter, "the keepers of the professional conscience," the gulf between teacher and practitioner widened. The business-as-usual approach of the practitioners offended their academic brethren, whose distance from the marketplace shaped their perception of practitioners, especially corporation attorneys, as money-grubbers and lackeys of big business. Practitioners reciprocated with an image of law teachers as utopian dreamers committed to the subversive view of law as an instrument of social change. Discord and animosity accompanied their struggle for power within the legal profession.[16] The dominant business values of the 1920s, which practicing lawyers shared, followed by the ferment of legal realism, the heady brew of law professors, pushed these rivals far apart.

Teachers repeatedly complained that professional leadership was reserved for lawyers with restricted social vision. Harvard law professor Thomas Reed Powell, who heard one ABA president advise his students to go to church and join Rotary clubs, concluded that the association presidency was reserved for men of "no distinction." His colleague, Zechariah

Chafee, Jr., told the members of a local bar association that professional leaders devoted their attention to "matters just as appropriate to plumbers as to lawyers." Dean Charles E. Clark of Yale Law School, speaking to members of the American Bar Association, maintained that their organization was nothing but "a social gathering of the older and financially successful lawyers." Teachers, convinced that practitioners were encumbered by self-interest and social myopia, insisted that only they possessed the necessary critical detachment and enlightened awareness to cope with social ills.[17]

Although teachers trained eminently practical lawyers, and certified their best students for positions with Wall Street firms, elite practitioners expressed unease whenever the accelerating pace of social change quickened the reform impulses of law professors. With the Roosevelt administration turning eagerly to law faculties and to recent graduates, rather than to the practicing bar, established lawyers knew that their public influence was waning. Their knowledge accounted for the tone of irascibility that characterized so many of their observations about law teachers. John W. Davis put it bluntly when he referred to "wild men" at Yale and Harvard law schools "whose social, economic and legal principles I distrust." Publicly, lawyers were more discreet. James Beck, confessing high regard for law professors for their "philosophic detachment" and for their renunciation of high fees, found them prone to "visionary ideas" which "are not helpful in the development of sound public opinion." An ABA member, reporting extensive correspondence with practitioners regarding their evaluation of recent law-school graduates, described "a schism between the thought of the law schools and the thought of the Bar." The notions held by professors might be "scintillating in their brilliance and evince profound learning, but at the same time display an utter lack of touch with the realities of the law."[18] It was one thing to teach law as it was; it was quite another to teach law as it ought to be, and to train men who might become critics rather than defenders of the old order.

Practitioners distorted the subversive influence of teachers, but they accurately perceived that economic collapse had undercut those patterns of deference and emulation that had placed the corporation president and his attorney in the pantheon of postwar heroes. They also knew that scattered through the world of law teaching were legal realists who repudiated law as a "brooding omnipresence," stressed its use as a flexible instrument for the resolution of social problems, and sharply challenged the prevailing wisdom regarding the nature of the judicial process. At a time when practition-

ers viewed the courts and the Constitution as their bulwark against revolutionary change, legal realists, who rejected the mechanical notion that
judicial decision-making rested solely upon syllogistic reasoning from
rules and precedents, doubtlessly sounded like the bar's bolsheviks.

Simultaneously, demographic changes were undercutting the foundations of the older professional culture. Fledgling lawyers from ethnic
minority groups, who were graduating from law schools in unprecedented
numbers, confronted imposing obstacles. Disqualified by their social
origins in the best of times, they now entered a professional world in which
restricted law firms were cutting back on new recruits and opportunities to
earn a living wage in solo practice were sharply constricted. Aspiring
Jewish lawyers bore the brunt of professional prejudice. They were disproportionately concentrated both at the top of their law school classes and at
the bottom of the metropolitan bar. Their presence in such profusion
threatened to unsettle the apex and the base of the professional structure. In
this setting, the New Deal loomed as a source of salvation to them and as a
menace to the established bar. Its alphabet agencies exerted a magnetic pull
on professionals who, by tradition, had been drawn to public service, by
training had been prepared for it, and by circumstance found curtailed
opportunities in the private sector. The New Deal needed talent; lawyers
needed jobs, which the New Deal provided. It also provided a program that
infuriated defenders of unregulated corporate enterprise, who were predictably enraged to see young Jewish lawyers drafting and enforcing
regulatory statutes. Consequently, the Roosevelt administration posed
serious challenges to the dominant professional culture and to its values
and symbols. It enabled a new professional elite to ascend to power, an
elite drawn from different social and ethnic strata and encouraged by their
teachers to seek professional fulfillment in the public sector.

Felix Frankfurter stood at the intersection of many of these trends. Back
in 1911, he had rejected the "drab uniformity" of his Harvard Law School
classmates by spurning private practice for government service. Practice,
Frankfurter complained, meant "putting one's time to put money in other
people's pockets." After working in the United States Attorney's Office
and in the War Department, Frankfurter turned to law teaching as the
career par excellence for involvement in public life. Inspired by the
Wisconsin Idea, he carved out a role for law teachers and law schools as
participants "in a great state service." During the postwar years, he often
expressed his disappointment at the role models provided by bar leaders.
He waited in vain for lawyers to protest against the "enveloping commer-

cialism and general corrupting atmosphere" of the Dollar Decade. The 1924 presidential candidacy of corporation lawyer John W. Davis angered him. Dismissing Davis as "the employee of Big Business," he complained that "it is good neither for these lads that I see passing through this School from year to year, nor for this country . . . that we should reward with the Presidency one to whom big money was the big thing." Years later, it still pained him that "the attractions of New York"—meaning Wall Street practice—lured the best Harvard law students of that generation. Frankfurter himself was responsible for placing many of them. He virtually served as an employment broker for his old friend Emory Buckner, partner in the Root-Clark firm in New York, and he performed a similar service for the Cravath firm, for his former mentor Henry Stimson, and for others who came to rely upon his appraisal of legal talent.[19]

The conjunction of the depression, with its attendant dislocations in the private sector of the legal profession, and the Roosevelt administration, with its special dependence upon lawyer's skills, propelled Frankfurter close to center stage. The personal and political affinity between the professor and the president provided him with a unique opportunity to focus his energies and experience as social critic, as teacher, and as job broker. Most disturbing to him was the role of the legal professional in public affairs during the pre–New Deal years. "One would be a complacent optimist," he and Nathan Greene had written in their important study of the labor injunction, "who would take pride in the influence exerted by the Bar upon our public affairs in recent times." He often referred to the antediluvian attitudes of bar leaders—especially their hostility to the nomination of Louis D. Brandeis to the Supreme Court, their complicity in the postwar Red Scare, and their indifference to due process during the Sacco-Vanzetti case. In letters to Justice Stone, he cited the "obtuseness" of the bar and "the inaccessibility of its mind to the needs of a rather rapidly changing world." Disdainfully, he described bar leaders as "about the least educable portion of the community."[20]

One year before Roosevelt's inauguration, Frankfurter expressed his conviction that "never has there been greater need in this country for the quality and the talents that the best in the law can give to society." Yet, he conceded, "I am more and more compelled to the conclusion that I am spending my time the better to fashion minds whose chief concern is the making of money." His model of state service—inspired by the Wisconsin Idea, nurtured by his admiration for Louis Brandeis and Henry Stimson, strengthened by his conviction that law school graduates were especially competent to assume the responsibilities of governance, and reinforced by his envy of the respect accorded to British civil servants—seemed doomed to failure. Expertise, Frankfurter insisted, was indispensable to efficient government in a modern society. But, he had written midway in the Hoover administration, "the whole tide of opinion is against public administration as a career for talent." When one of his former students rejected a position with the Reconstruction Finance Corporation for private practice, Frankfurter chastized "those worldly wise men in New York" who advised young lawyers to spurn careers in teaching or government. When another student, who chose the favored path, reported about his work on utilities regulation in Wisconsin, Frankfurter took obvious delight in "what 'the Wisconsin idea' meant in Action—the continuous and systematic utilization of the best available intelligence on the complicated social problems of the day."[21] It was this opportunity and challenge that the New Deal provided.

As Frankfurter surveyed personnel during the early weeks of the Roosevelt administration, he expressed dismay at "the lack of capable, free men among lawyers of parts" between the ages of thirty and fifty. Freedom meant "the resiliency of mind and judgment . . . that is ready to take in new facts and new forces and to realize that new accommodations have to be made, though made in the organic unfolding of valid past traditions and techniques." Lawyers, Frankfurter believed, should be "experts in relevance"; yet all too often they were practitioners of obstructionism. The Securities Act of 1933, drafted by his protégés Tom Corcoran and Ben Cohen, and by his Harvard colleague James Landis, provided prompt confirmation for his disaffection. The law upset Wall Street financiers and their lawyers; their hostility, in turn, peeved Frankfurter. Writing from Oxford, where he was spending the academic year as visiting professor, he complained that leading lawyers were behaving toward the securities law as they had behaved toward all regulatory legislation since the Interstate Commerce Act. Rather than demonstrate "sympathetic compliance," once "they and their clients got out of the storm cellar of fear . . . [they] began a systematic campaign to undermine the essentials of the act." In an unusually sharp letter he reminded Henry Stimson that prominent law firms "were in some cases the architects and in others the agents of practices which you would be the very first to regard as indefensible and anti-social." Accusing them of efforts to "chloroform" the act, he concluded with a denunciation of "exploiting businessmen and their leading lawyers." Their activities continued to nettle Frankfurter.

When Landis, who served on the Federal Trade Commission and the Securities and Exchange Commission to enforce New Deal securities legislation, described "the genius of the New York bar for devious misconstruction," Frankfurter repeated his comment approvingly and referred to their belief that "they serve God when their client is Mammon." Inevitably, Frankfurter concluded, financial lawyers would retard or defeat New Deal legislation—"unless those lawyers are matched at their own game, in advance, by the use of lawyers equally astute in the public interest and as ready to devote their time to the public cause as are Wall Street attorneys to the cause of Wall Street interests."[22]

This was not an idle hope, as the superb draftsmanship of the securities legislation demonstrated. The decisive contribution from Cohen, Corcoran, and Landis represented in microcosm the ethnic and institutional forces that would shape the legal ambiance of the New Deal. Cohen, the Jew, brought rare professional skills and personal qualities to his task (to supplement his considerable knowledge of the stock market obtained from his successful trading prior to the crash when he was in Wall Street practice). Corcoran, the Irish Catholic, came to the New Deal by way of a Wall Street firm and the Reconstruction Finance Corporation. (Some years earlier Frankfurter had said of him: "He is struggling very hard with the burden of inferiority imposed on him because of his Irish Catholicism by his experience at Brown, in Providence and in Boston.") Landis, the Harvard law professor, discovered in New Deal service that "the administrative process is, in essence, our generation's answer to the inadequacy of the judicial and the legislative processes."[23] Notwithstanding their considerable abilities and achievements, each, in different ways, stood partially outside the dominant professional culture and its values: Cohen and Corcoran as members of ethnic minority groups; Landis as law teacher. Established and successful, but apart, they personified the institutional sources of New Deal talent and the particular generational appeal that the Roosevelt administration exerted.

The younger the lawyer, the more likely he was to be attracted to the New Deal. Frankfurter had often heard from "some of the ablest younger lawyers in the big New York offices" who derived little satisfaction from their work. "Literally by the score they are sick of it all," he told Walter Lippmann. "That's one of the heartening things about the times—that the Government can avail itself of an abler lot of younger lawyers for key junior positions than has been true at any time since I left the Law School." In addition, there was the annual crop of fresh recruits, drawn to Washington by the special attractions of the New Deal and by restricted opportunities in private practice. By 1935, Frankfurter saw "impressive evidence that the more recent generations of law school graduates care about the law as a great social process and as opportunities for having a share in the effort to solve some of the most complicated riddles of modern society." Few individuals deserved as much credit for this development as Frankfurter himself. To a generation of law students, wrote one among them, Frankfurter conveyed the conviction "that there was no more challenging and exciting business in the world than the responsible, craftsmanlike handling of the power of the state."[24]

Frankfurter derived immense pride from the migration of lawyers to Washington. He knew that the success of the adminstration, to which he was deeply committed, depended upon its ability to compete with private interests "for the command of brains." Its outstanding achievement, in Frankfurter's judgment, was the extent to which Roosevelt "stirred the imagination of younger people to the adventure of, and the durable satisfactions to be derived from, public service." Here was the fulfillment of Frankfurter's teaching career. As he told one young protégé whose presence in Washington delighted him: "You know very well that I regard the building up of the equivalent of the British Civil Service in our country as second in importance to nothing affecting the public life of our nation." Aboard the *Britannic*, sailing to England for his year at Oxford, he expressed his satisfaction "that there are more intelligent and more purposeful and more disinterested men in the service of the country than there has been for at least half a century."[25]

The precise nature of Frankfurter's role in the New Deal was difficult to calculate amid the political hyperbole of the 1930s. Roosevelt's opponents depicted Frankfurter as a sinister, diabolical schemer: "*the most influential single individual in the United States*," whose " 'boys' have been insinuated into obscure but key positions in every vital department—wardens of the marches, inconspicuous but powerful," Hugh Johnson thundered after he left the National Recovery Administration. According to journalist John Franklin Carter, Frankfurter dominated "the infant industry of legal liberalism," supplying lawyers who were "sufficiently ingenious to justify the New Deal to the Courts and sufficiently radical to sympathize heartily with its purposes." Critics on the left, seizing upon the continuity of Frankfurter's job brokerage function, bolstered their contention that New Dealers were providing mild medicine for economic and social ills that could be cured only by drastic surgery. Thus, Fred Rodell, the prickly law professor at Yale, drew attention in an article entitled "Felix Frankfurter, Conservative" to the number of Frankfurter protégés who had served the Harding, Coolidge, and Hoover administrations or profited from Wall Street practice. For Rodell, the difference was merely quantitative, not qualitative.[26]

Frankfurter's self-assessment varied according to circumstance and audience. He persistently claimed that he initiated no recommendations regarding personnel or policy "unless asked." When public exposés appeared, he backed away even further. In the wake of Hugh Johnson's denunciation of him as the Iago of the administration, Frankfurter observed that many more of his former students held positions in Wall Street firms than in New Deal agencies. After editor Raymond Moley published a critical evaluation of his role, Frankfurter took vigorous exception —prompting Moley to remind him that "whether or not you regard yourself as the leader of 'the boys,' they certainly regard themselves as your disciples." The presence of his "boys" in such profusion—Dean Acheson, Cohen, Corcoran, Paul Freund, Alger and Donald Hiss, Landis, David Lilienthal, Nathan Margold, and Charles E. Wyzanski, Jr.—enabled Frankfurter to play a role and to deny it too. Corcoran, who functioned as his favorite personal, and personnel, ambassador to New Deal administrators, acknowledged his mentor's role and cheerfully carried out Frankfurter's instructions. ("He is a shrewd fellow generally and knows a good deal about Washington ways," Frankfurter told Jerome Frank, whom he had recommended for *his* job). Others performed similar service at Frankfurter's instigation. He could thereby honor his "fixed rule . . . not to make any requests of any of the officials." But he relied upon Corcoran, Paul Freund, Wyzanski, and others to "insulate my intervention."[27] By intervening covertly through intermediaries, Frankfurter maintained both his private influence and his public distance.

Several considerations dictated the need for camouflage. Frankfurter anticipated a diminishing willingness for public service if "this silly, uncritical, wholesale gibing at the 'brain-trusters' " persisted. He often cited the respect and esteem directed toward British civil servants, in contrast to the carping criticism that characterized the Washington scene. "One of the worst of American traditions," Frankfurter complained, was "that anybody could do everything, and that the government is no place except for the drone and the politician." Hopeful that the British model was transferable to the United States, and anxious lest young lawyers be deflected from government service, Frankfurter sought to mitigate his own role to remove a potential irritant upon public opinion. He knew that he was a symbol of "the Jew, the 'red,' the 'alien.' " In his judgment, he could best serve the president and his own policy objectives by working through others.[28] Frankfurter's strategic location within the profession and his unique access to the administration provided him with a dual opportunity: to cultivate a counter-elite that would mitigate the influence of the dominant professional leadership that he despised; and to place its members upon an alternative mobility ladder to social position and public influence within an administration that he revered.

These achievements were made possible by demographic and social trends that originated beyond the profession and affected university law schools, the key institutions of professional access. Samuel Lubell has written about the voting patterns of the children of the thirteen million new immigrants of 1900–1914 who came of age after 1930; concentrated in cities, they became "the chief carriers of the Roosevelt Revolution." More than voting patterns were affected by population changes. Between 1919 and 1927, there was a sharp spurt, exceeding 80 percent, in law school enrollments. And from 1920 to 1930, in a few eastern cities with a heavy concentration of immigrants, there was a substantial proportional increase in the number of foreign-born lawyers. In New York, where the number of lawyers increased by 57 percent during that decade, the number of foreign-born lawyers increased by 76 percent. In Philadelphia, the bar grew by 21 percent while the number of foreign-born lawyers increased by 76 percent.[29] Expanding law school enrollments, and the changing ethnic structure of the bar, threatened the professional elite ensconced in law firms and dominant in professional associations. Although it could, and did, easily defend these redoubts against intruders, it could not protect what it did not control. New Deal agencies were enemy country. They attracted younger lawyers who came disproportionately from ethnic minority groups; lawyers with relatively weak commitments to private practice in corporate law firms; lawyers trained in administrative law, skilled in legislative draftsmanship, exposed to the stimulating currents of legal realism, and eager to apply their expertise; and lawyers who responded with alacrity to a call for public service once a liberal reform administration came to power.

The establishment of a New Deal counter-elite among lawyers had nothing of an underclass rebellion about it. Lawyers who occupied responsible positions within the administration possessed impeccable professional credentials and were committed to quite traditional professional and social goals: opportunity, success, money, and power. Many of them had successfully carved out niches in the private sector. Others, especially from depression years graduating classes, could not do so. Circumstance, rather than choice, may have deflected them from private firms. Excluded from Wall Street and welcomed in Washington, they fused personal ambition, social mobility, and liberal reform in government service. Few of them, however, became career lawyers for the government. In time, with the expertise provided by their service in New Deal agencies, many entered corporation law firms. Professional democratization, never an articulated goal, was indefinitely deferred. The New Deal offered new positions of power to ethnically, not professionally, disadvantaged lawyers. It restricted mobility opportunities to those already designated as the most talented graduates of the best schools. The remainder of the profession was left to fend for itself; marginal lawyers remained forgotten professional men, and marginal clients were still without the legal services that corporations, and now the federal government, could command.

For lawyers, the newness of the New Deal resided in the multiple possibilities it afforded for personal and professional opportunity. Like a freshly cut diamond, it displayed many facets and attracted a variegated band of admiring attorneys. It could simultaneously appeal to an independent country lawyer whose model was nineteenth-century practice (Robert H. Jackson); to a legal realist who made intellectual leaps beyond most of his twentieth-century counterparts (Jerome N. Frank); to a craftsman who saw nothing incongruous in voting for Hoover and then committing his energy to the Roosevelt administration (Charles E. Wyzanski, Jr.); and to young, upwardly mobile, minority group lawyers.[30] Notwithstanding the variety and the inevitable exceptions, a common thread wound through many of their careers. Lawyers who felt displaced, and those who sought a place, turned to the Roosevelt administration. A drop of nostalgia blended with a torrent of anticipation to produce the characteristic New Deal tang.

Robert H. Jackson was an unlikely New Deal lawyer. The prototypical New Dealer was an upwardly mobile urbanite, a second-generation member of an ethnic minority group with superior academic credentials and, perhaps, some Wall Street experience. Jackson was the obverse: an upstate Protestant New Yorker who never attended college, never graduated from Albany Law School, served an apprenticeship in a Jamestown law offfice, and incessantly preached the nineteenth-century virtues of the small-town practitioner: "hard work, long hours, and thrift." The son of a Pennsylvania farmer, he would aptly be described as a lawyer whose "bent was to plow old pastures in a new way, not to leap fences and attack virgin soil. . . . It was his job to defend, not to formulate, policies."[31] The consummate advocate, he defended the New Deal as special counsel for the Securities and Exchange Commission, as assistant attorney general in the Tax and Antitrust Divisions of the Justice Department, and as solicitor general and attorney general. Regardless of office, Jackson remained the nineteenth-century liberal in the twentieth century. His anachronistic liberalism was apparent, even conspicuous. Yet as a New Dealer Jackson seemed to march in step with the times. This was less paradoxical than it appeared. His critique of the legal profession, a recurring theme in his public addresses, focused on the corporation lawyer as the personification of wrongdoing. His was the animus of Main Street, displaced professionally by Wall Street. Jackson's New Deal colleagues, who voiced similar complaints, fired at the same target for different reasons. Theirs was the cry of contemporary experience; his was the voice of nostalgic betrayal.

The nobility of the legal profession, for Jackson, derived from the work of general practitioners, who were "not submerged in a specialty nor dominated by a single overshadowing interest, who become champions of any just cause." Such men found no place in metropolitan law firms, whose distinguishing products were "the wide clientele and the narrow lawyers." Once a leader, the lawyer had become a mouthpiece. "More than any other class," Jackson insisted, "our opinions, as well as our services and talents, are on the auction block." In professional associations, "we generally pyramid conservatism until at the top of the structures our bar association officers are as conservative as cemetery trustees." Speaking to law teachers in 1934, Jackson acknowledged the benchmarks of change, especially the concentration of legal business and talent in large metropolitan firms and the consequent malaise of the middle-class bar, once the backbone of the profession. But he refused to retreat to the storm cellar of the nineteenth century; rather, he sought to transplant its virtues to a different era. He spoke of the government's need for lawyers who possessed education and experience, but were devoid of "mental ossification." Legalism "has a place in shaping any new deal. Why should the bar so largely renounce its function of shaping it to oppose it?" At present, he concluded, the bar "is one of the most stubborn, reactionary and short-sighted groups in our national life." But, he added with revealing ambivalence, "I should be sadly disappointed if my son should fail to join it."[32] Jackson, like the country lawyers he constantly praised, viewed law more as a religion than as a means of remuneration. "He embodied a significant part of the American dream," one of his admirers has written—"the storybook American boy who by dint of brains and work and pluck drives himself from an unpromising start to a glorious finish." For this very reason, he was, in the words of a less-unabashed analyst, the "Everyman of the law."[33] He won the highest legal prizes the Roosevelt administration could bestow, yet he was an incongruous New Deal lawyer. Misplaced in time, he seemed most contemporary when he spoke for the bygone liberal professionalism of an earlier era.

If Jackson carefully tilled old soil, Jerome Frank preferred to leap fences. A precocious graduate of the University of Chicago at nineteen, he hoped to become a novelist, unwillingly became a lawyer at his father's insistence, and developed a lucrative corporate law practice, first in Chicago and then in New York, which he never enjoyed. After the crash, when the concerns of his clients preoccupied him, he became increasingly restless. From psychoanalysis, he learned that lawyers chose "childish thoughtways in meeting adult problems." He wrote *Law and the Modern Mind*, an exciting venture into the psychology of jurisprudence, out of the desire "to see and have others see and help me see more clearly just what we lawyers are doing daily." Why, he asked Roscoe Pound, was "absolutistic thinking so difficult to surmount in cerebration about law? Why is certainty-hunger peculiarly vigorous in lawyerdom? . . . How make [lawyers] eager to think pragmatically, to use concepts operationally, instrumentally?" Frank, who delighted in tilting against "illusions about legal certainty [that] get the lawyers in bad with the public," rebelled against what he perceived as legal authoritarianism. Most lawyers and judges, he wrote in his book, insisted upon the certainty of law when it was, in fact, "largely vague and variable." They did so because they had "not yet relinquished the childish need for an authoritative father and unconsciously have tried to find in the law a substitute for those attributes of firmness, sureness, certainty and infallibility ascribed in childhood to the father." Frank demanded (and perceived in his fellow realists) "a skepticism stimulated by a zeal to reform, in the interest of justice, some court-house ways." He tried, in the words of his close friend Thurman Arnold, "to free the law from its frustrating obsessions. His jurisprudence was the jurisprudence of therapy."[34]

The more clearly that Frank perceived his daily activities, the more frustrated he became. Although he managed to write his book, maintain a voluminous correspondence, and engage in a busy practice, he complained, "Its hell how practicing law interferes with decent intellection." Shortly before the 1932 election, he confessed to being "so fed up with the tawdry aspects of practice" that he would welcome an academic appointment. Roosevelt's victory opened tempting possibilities. He offered his services to Adolf Berle; he suggested to Thurman Arnold that Yale, where

Frank lectured, organize its own brain-trusters; and he accepted with alacrity an invitation, extended at Frankfurter's behest, to draft farm legislation and then to become general counsel of the Agricultural Adjustment Administration. "Financially, it is a somewhat risky adventure for me," he conceded, "but I couldn't resist the opportunity."[35]

Frank personified the affinity between legal realism and the New Deal. Realists, he declared in a thinly veiled autobiographical statement, could easily become New Dealers because they were "less Procrustean and more flexible in their techniques" and because they judged legal institutions by their human consequences rather than by their Platonic essences. As experimentalists, they were skeptical of their own notions but not paralyzed by inaction. The lawyer who believed in "undeviating fixed legal principles," Frank's "Mr. Absolute," would be repelled by the New Deal. His adversary, "Mr. Try-it," could run social experiments for sixteen hours each day without strain or fatigue.[36]

Yet those very social experiments, as Frank conceded, were designed merely to harness private financial gain to social welfare. This presumably rash, brash experimentalist, freed from authoritarian dogma, only wanted *"the profit system to be tried, for the first time, as a consciously directed means of promoting the general good."* Therein lay the outer limits of his experimentalism—a point never perceived by those who criticized him as the New Deal's Robespierre. Frank suffered from a reputation exceeded only by Frankfurter's as the radical lawyer-ogre of the administration. Once the Agricultural Adjustment Administration became the battleground for a clash between southern tenant farmers and their landlords, Frank and his group of talented, socially committed young associates, sympathetic to the plight of the sharecroppers and eager to secure their legal rights, were suspect, vulnerable, and finally expendable, But Frank, who wrestled self-consciously with the boundary between policy preferences and legal judgments, demonstrated considerably greater restraint than his public reputation suggested. Policy considerations must affect a lawyer's opinion, he wrote, but they "should not play at all a dominant role in a lawyer's thinking." Frank insisted that his own advocacy was usually directed toward inducing his colleagues "to narrow the issues so as to confine the argument as far as possible to controversy *on traditional lines."* As he told Frankfurter: "I do not believe in trying to vindicate abstract principles and . . . to me the important thing is to win *particular* cases." Frankfurter knew that Frank wanted to win cases; he also saw that Frank was "a damned romantic intellectual." Frank conceded, yet denigrated, the romance. He described his work as general counsel as "heartbreaking days and nights spent with almost reckless financial sacrifice in aid of public causes [I] deem desirable." Yet, he hastened to add, one of his major aims was "to have our job done with legal accuracy—so that it would stand up in court."[37]

Therein lay the tension that tormented Frank as long as he remained in Washington. His commitment to realism and to experimentalism impelled him toward policy-making; his lawyer's commitments to process and precedent restrained him. More venturesome than most of his colleagues, he suffered from the knowledge of his radical reputation. Critical of lawyers' absolutes, he nonetheless was inhibited by the restraints of professionalism. An experimentalist about means, he unquestioningly accepted ends. Standing at the cutting edge of legal thought and of the New Deal, he demonstrated their compatibility and the strength that each derived from the other. Liberated by both, he was nonetheless bound by his commitments to professionalism and to capitalism. By 1935, he felt "functionless." He sensed that his effectiveness in Washington was at an end; but he dreaded returning to private practice, and he anticipated a hostile reception should he attempt to do so. "I'm badly bewildered," he told Frankfurter, "—and not a little frightened."[38] Frank, like the administration he served with such passionate distinction, was simultaneously liberated by lawyers' skills and inhibited by lawyers' values.

If the New Deal appealed to nostalgic liberals and to bold realists, it also attracted able legal technicians who found matchless opportunities for honing their skills and practicing their craft. Charles E. Wyzanski, Jr., grandson of a successful immigrant peddler and a product of Exeter, Harvard College, and Harvard Law School, was one of these. Drawn to law study after reading Zechariah Chafee's *Freedom of Speech*, he was a law review editor, clerked for both Learned and Augustus Hand, and practiced for three years in Boston's prestigious Ropes, Gray firm. When the Roosevelt administration came to power, Wyzanski's career was still in its formative stages. New Deal opportunities set Wyzanski's course. As solicitor for the Labor Department, he nearly tripled his salary and enjoyed immeasurable freedom to exercise his lawyer's craft. Wyzanski, who had voted for Hoover in 1932, did not go to Washington as a crusading reformer. But he took pride in the fact that "we were a level of employees that Washington hadn't previously seen." And the considerable demands upon his skills were exhilarating. Given twenty-four hours to draft the public works title of the National Industrial Recovery bill, he compared the travail to "plunging into the furnace."[39]

Wyzanski's instinct for craftsmanship made him eager for "more law work, and less administration." By 1935, he concluded that the solicitorship offered "less play to legal than to political and administrative currents." Moving over to the Justice Department, he compared his earlier government work, which taught him "to analyze quickly, to assume responsibility and to act courageously," with the greater fulfillment provided by "the intellectual satisfaction which comes from a chance to turn problems around so that every angle is displayed." He subsequently referred to the *process* of drafting the Wagner Act brief as the consummate experience of his Washington service: "We would talk back and forth at each sentence. . . . We were just a crowd hard at work . . . doing our best to understand the kernel of the thought, and then reducing it to the narrowest possible statement." This was the distillation of his law school training under Reed Powell, who, Wyzanski recalled years later, could "make you think twenty times before you write that sentence quite that way."[40] Wyzanski knew, in addition, that he was participating in the lawyer's resumption of his role as social mediator, a role weakened by lawyers for corporations who were "too loyal to a *part* of a community to see the new problems in the light of the *whole* community." New Deal social legislation represented an attempt to restore the equilibrium between public and private right. Thus, Wyzanski could fulfill the lawyer's historic mission in the process of maximizing his professional satisfactions. He could also set a valued precedent, for he treasured nothing more about his Washington experience "than the feeling that I have been part of a practice (which I hope will become a tradition), under which young men give part of their early manhood to public service."[41]

Although scores of young lawyers, and a sprinkling of older ones, went to Washington during the thirties, it is impossible to know how many responded to "public service," or how many would have agreed with Wyzanski's definition of it. "Public service" had complex meanings to lawyers from various backgrounds who reached Washington at different stages of their careers. A special fillip of excitement aroused successful, established lawyers who were secure and prosperous in private practice. Francis Biddle renounced his family firm in Philadelphia for "the sense of freedom, the feeling of power, and the experience of the enlarging horizons of public work." Lloyd Landau, president of the *Harvard Law Review* during World War I and subsequently clerk to Justice Holmes, was prepared to abandon a substantial private practice with a large annual income for the opportunity to serve under Frankfurter if his old mentor became

Roosevelt's solicitor general. A New York attorney, who had served in Washington during the war, wanted to return because he sensed that a position with the New Deal "might be even more of a thrill." Established law teachers found special gratifications. James Landis, who temporarily vacated his Harvard professorship, quickly discovered that he could enjoy "a larger share in the handling of government than I ever had after years in the handling of the Harvard Law School." Landis had dreaded interviews with Dean Pound; he never enjoyed the privilege of an interview with President Lowell; but he anticipated conferences with Roosevelt "with pleasure, knowing that there will be an exchange of views. . . . It is things like this that make life fun."[42]

Young men who went to Washington were exhilarated, edified, and often exhausted by the demands upon them, especially in the newer agencies. Abe Fortas, who worked under Frank in the Agricultural Adjustment Administration, "could see the new world and feel it taking form under our hands." A young lawyer for the National Labor Relations Board described his experience as "helpful to me as a lawyer and as one who is trying to understand some of the social forces at work. . . . I think my concepts are more direct and real than they were." Another NLRB attorney recounted a year "crowded with action and providing many opportunities for intensive labor."[43] For these lawyers, the opportunity to function provided the paramount satisfaction.

Other attorneys found the New Deal ideologically compatible—or sufficiently flexible to permit them to implement their own political and social commitments. Nathan Witt, galvanized by the Sacco-Vanzetti case, drove a taxi for two years to earn enough money to afford Harvard Law School. His greatest ambition, he told Frankfurter, was to devote his energies to "the public service of the law." This meant to work for minority groups, who were "most likely to complain of the failure to be accorded even-handed justice." Witt battled for sharecroppers in the AAA and for workers as general counsel for the National Labor Relations Board. Lee Pressman, his classmate and friend, followed a parallel path. Pressman received his decisive intellectual push from a course on labor unionism at Cornell. Unable to find work in labor law, because no firms specialized in the field, he did corporate receivership and reorganization work with Frank, until he eagerly escaped the "yoke" of private practice after Frank went to Washington.[44] Pressman, like Witt, joined Frank in the AAA; like Witt, he moved over to the labor movement; like Witt, he flirted with the Communist party. These second-generation radical children of immigrant

parents found the New Deal congenial to the investment of their legal skills
and to the nourishment of their radical political convictions.

Unlike Witt and Pressman, Thomas Emerson came from a venerable
family whose forebears reached New England three hundred years before
the Roosevelt administration reached the Potomac. Emerson, first in his
class at Yale Law School and editor-in-chief of the *Law Journal*, had his
pick of elite offers from the Cravath firm, Sullivan and Cromwell, Root-
Clark, and Davis-Polk. Uneasy about their routinized absence of individual responsibility for young lawyers, he chose to work for Walter
Pollak, a talented civil liberties lawyer who had argued the *Gitlow* case
before the Supreme Court, often acted as counsel for the ACLU, committed his firm to matters of "social significance," and believed in "justice
through the legal process." Emerson was not disappointed; his first case
was the landmark appeal of the Scottsboro boys in *Powell* v. *Alabama*. But
by mid-1933, after two years with Pollak, Emerson responded to the
excitement in Washington. Moving along Frankfurter's underground railroad—from Corcoran to Wyzanski to Donald Richberg to Blackwell
Smith, Richberg's assistant—he reached the National Recovery Administration and journeyed from there to the National Labor Relations Board. In
both agencies, Emerson delighted in the immediate delegation of responsibility to young lawyers, the tumult and the challenge, and the opportunity
to implement his own belief in law as "an instrument by which social
change can be effectuated."[45]

For lawyers from ethnic and racial minority groups, a position with the
New Deal offered another illustration of the relationship between law and
social change. Professional discrimination and job retrenchment virtually
eliminated the prospects of Jewish, Catholic, and Negro lawyers for
remunerative employment in the more lucrative sectors of the profession—regardless of their qualifications. For Jews, perhaps the most professionally ambitious minority group, the problem was especially acute.
Catholics and Negroes attended ethnic law schools—Fordham,
Georgetown, Howard—and followed established but narrow channels into
state and municipal politics, lower-level federal government employment
(for example, in the Federal Bureau of Investigation), or solo practice.
Prospective Jewish lawyers, however, competed successfully with the
Protestant elite in the national law schools, only to discover that a law
review editorship might be a necessary credential, but it was insufficient
for elite certification. An earlier generation of German Jews—Brandeis,
Louis Marshall, Julian Mack, and Samuel Untermeyer—had securely

established themselves. Against high odds, predepression Jewish graduates—Wyzanski, Ben Cohen, Pressman—also managed to carve out successful private practices. But the depression generation of talented Jewish law students was saved from professional extinction, insofar as it was saved at all, only by the New Deal alphabet agencies.[46] For no group of second-generation Americans did the New Deal serve as a more efficacious vehicle for social and political power than for Jewish lawyers, who in many instances possessed every necessary credential for professional elite status but one: the requisite social origins. The social structure of the profession excluded them from established elite positions; the social policy of the New Deal drew them to Washington. There they could quickly climb the rungs of an alternate mobility ladder to reach newly created elite positions.

Rampant anti-Semitism had long infested the legal profession. Teachers and practitioners with experience in job placement received constant confirmation of the national dimensions of the problem. In Boston, Frankfurter concluded, "none of the so-called desirable firms . . . will take a Jew." In New York, Emory Buckner, a partner in the Root-Clark firm, cited "a somewhat restricted area for Jewish boys." Although Buckner referred to his own firm as a "notable exception," he verified the existence of the problem when he described a Jewish lawyer in his firm as "devoid of every known quality which we in New York mean when we call a man 'Jewy.' " When Jerome Frank received a list of Yale graduates, those who were Jewish, although highly recommended, were specially identified. In Chicago, Jewish law review graduates of Northwestern were turned away from elite firms. Thurman Arnold, enthusiastically recommending a *Yale Law Journal* editor, emphasized that his Jewishness was his only handicap and that he was devoid of "Jewish characteristics." The dean of the law school at the University of North Carolina wondered how fair it would be to hire a Jewish editor of the *Harvard Law Review* for his faculty, given the "provincialism" of his community. And James Landis, who recommended a Jewish graduate of Harvard for a position on the Illinois faculty, emphasized: "I do not regard him as forward or pushing, and I should have no hesitation in saying that such Jewish characteristics as he possesses are not a handicap." In the spring of 1936, eight *Harvard Law Review* editors still were not placed for the following year—all were Jewish. Understandably, Frankfurter complained bitterly: "I wonder whether this School shouldn't tell Jewish students that they go through . . . at their own risk of ever having opportunity of entering the best law offices."[47]

The Jewish lawyer from an immigrant family who managed to secure a New Deal position recognized his own coming of age as an American. Malcolm A. Hoffmann, a Harvard graduate, described himself at the outset of his government service with the NLRB as "a young neophyte at the bar, a member of a minority religious group, a boy who had never seen the inside of a political club nor had power nor status in our huge egalitarian society." Governmental employment provided just that sense of power and status. It legitimized the aspirations of minority-group members and assuaged the disappointment that they encountered in the private sector. Roosevelt, cognizant of the social implications of government service, tried to tap that supply. "Dig me up fifteen or twenty youthful Abraham Lincolns from Manhattan and the Bronx to choose from," he told Charles C. Burlingham. "They must be liberal from belief and not by lip service. They must have an inherent contempt both for the John W. Davises and the Max Steuers. They must know what life in a tenement means. They must have no social ambition."[48]

Except for the absence of social ambition, Roosevelt procured the type of lawyer he sought. Indeed, in Washington the problem was too many Jews, not too few. Nathan Margold, solicitor for the Interior Department, and Jerome Frank, in the AAA, had numerous legal jobs to fill; both, however, were troubled by the overabundance of qualified Jewish lawyers and by the political liabilities inherent in placing too many of them on their staffs. The poignancy of the problem was compounded by the flood of requests from young, highly qualified Jewish lawyers who pleaded, usually with Frankfurter, for New Deal employment. Other minority-group members were, if anything, at an even greater disadvantage. An Armenian-born female law review editor from Wisconsin Law School, suffering from the double professional handicap of social origins and sex, asked in vain for help. Black lawyers not only were barred from white firms; they also suffered discrimination at the administration's own hands. One black attorney, seeking an NRA position, was kept waiting for three hours while every white applicant was interviewed; finally he was told that the position was reserved for whites only. Angrily, he confronted his painful dilemma: "One is driven either to hate his color or his country."[49] The New Deal opened the door to professional mobility—especially for Jews and, to a lesser extent, for Irish Catholic lawyers like Corcoran, Frank Murphy, and Charles Fahy, and, on rare occasion, for a black lawyer like William Hastie. But the great wall of exclusion, made more imposing by depression conditions, still surrounded the legal profession.

Driven to desperation, young lawyers in private practice began to consider structural reforms in the profession that would alleviate their own plight by extending the provision of legal services to neglected constituencies. The major theoretical impulse to their effort was provided by Columbia professor Karl Llewellyn, who was dismayed by the individualism of the bar and the corporate orientation of its professional associations. Early in the life of the New Deal he suggested government action. Between legal aid, available only to the most impoverished, and specialized corporate counseling, reserved for the most privileged, a vast area existed for "legal hygiene" that would inform middle-class people of their legal needs and rights and provide the services required to alleviate or secure them. In an article published in *Law and Contemporary Problems* in 1938, Llewellyn indicted the bar for its anachronisms and deceptions. Complaints about overcrowding masked low professional incomes. Complaints about ambulance-chasing diverted attention from inadequate legal services. Complaints about unauthorized practice by title companies or banks emphasized the danger "to the Bar's needed service being rendered" by camouflaging the danger "to the Bar's needed living being earned." Ethical canons prohibiting solicitation, suited for small-town life, victimized urban dwellers and city lawyers. Two-thirds of the bar and 80 percent of the public, Llewellyn estimated, needed each other but lacked both the contact and the means of making contact. Llewellyn closed with a vigorous plea for the establishment of legal service bureaus that would serve these unmet needs.[50]

Young urban lawyers responded with alacrity to Llewellyn's call. Writing from Chicago, Atlanta, Denver, and Philadelphia, they expressed interest in establishing low-cost legal service bureaus in urban neighborhoods far from downtown clusters of exclusive law firms. These struggling attorneys, prepared to seek out clients with legal problems, knew that expanded legal services would simultaneously serve clients' interests while enlarging their own opportunities. In this way, professional reform and self-interest dovetailed. One law student told Llewellyn that law clinics would provide "a wonderful chance for both the young lawyer and also the people who can't afford to pay large legal fees." And a Chicago attorney, eager to serve needy clients, conceded that clinics would also be "an excellent training ground for the young lawyer as well as a basis for a fair income."[51]

These various streams—restricted professional opportunities, an obsolete bar structure, the precarious status of minority-group lawyers, generational turmoil, and reform agitation—converged in the National Lawyers Guild, the first professional association to challenge the hegemony of the American Bar Association. Its membership was drawn primarily from those groups—especially Jews, Catholics, and Negroes—who were disproportionately confined to the lower levels of professional life. But its leaders, from the same groups, were men from the most progressive professional circles who, attainments nothwithstanding, found the American Bar Association professionally and politically objectionable: labor lawyer Frank Walsh; civil liberties lawyer Morris Ernst; New Dealers Jerome Frank, Abe Fortas, and Thomas Emerson; and black civil rights lawyer Charles Houston. These men, together with other New Dealers and law teachers, exemplified the rising elite within the profession—an elite distinguished by its youth, ethnicity, and sensitivity to jurisprudential and doctrinal innovation. For too long, guild leaders proclaimed in their "Call to American Lawyers," the profession's concern for liberty had been secondary to its concern for property. The guild's constitutional preamble addressed itself to lawyers "who regard adjustments to new conditions as more important than the veneration of precedent, who recognize the importance of safeguarding and extending the rights of workers and farmers . . . , of maintaining our civil rights and liberties . . . , and who look upon the law as a living and flexible instrument which must be adapted to the needs of the people." Rank-and-file membership was drawn from those groups that scrambled for position during the depression years and identified their struggle with the cause of liberal reform. A 29-year-old Catholic lawyer of "good but humble birth" eagerly responded to the guild's appeal. So did Negro lawyers, especially once the guild banished color as an informal qualification for membership—in sharp contrast to the American Bar Association, which, in 1937, had only two Negro members. Jewish lawyers, especially from New York City, enthusiastically enrolled as guild members. Within five months, 2,600 lawyers had joined; an overwhelming majority came from the lower economic strata of the profession.[52]

In 1939, the Philadelphia chapter of the guild implemented a neighborhood law office plan to provide middle-income groups with competent legal assistance and preventive legal services. The thirteen-member executive committee of the Philadelphia guild chapter consisted, revealingly, of eight Jews, three Catholics, and one Negro.[53] Here was the operative reality of law and social change during the 1930s. An insurgent professional association confronted the ethnic and social structure of the professional elite with a reform proposal that challenged traditional assumptions regarding the provision and adequacy of legal services. With stark clarity the lines were drawn: between American Bar Association and National Lawyers Guild; between age and youth; between the established Protestant elite and the aspiring ethnic outsiders; between service to wealth and service to needy urban masses; and between professional values suitable to a bygone golden era and those required in a heterogeneous, urban, industrial society. A single neighborhood project hardly affected an entire profession—but it did indicate the direction from which the future winds of social change would blow. The guild, Thomas Emerson would claim in retrospect, "was born in revolt—a revolt that embraced the entire intellectual life of the times."[54]

In significant respects, the New Deal was a lawyer's deal. The virtues and vices of the legal approach to problem-solving were readily apparent. A commitment to flexibility, to instrumentalism, to skeptical realism, and to administrative discretion, applied by lawyers who were (in James Landis's words) "bred to the facts," freed the New Deal from the debilitating paralysis so characteristic of the Hoover years. Yet no result was permitted to assume such transcendent importance as to rule out compromise. The lawyer's obsession with process may liberate his skills, but it also dominates his values and inhibits his social goals. Lawyers guided New Deal solutions between the bargaining extremes but toward the existing balance of power between competing interest groups. This trait gave the New Deal its opportunistic, shallow side and made it all too willing to capitulate to its opponents. The prototypical New Dealer may well have been "a freewheeler and an activist" with considerable discretion and responsibility, who played a "pervasive role" in the policy-making process. Yet there were clear limits, and indeed narrow boundaries, to that process. At most, the lawyer controlled the *pace* of change, not its direction—for the lawyer's characteristic function, even during the turbulent New Deal years, has always been to mediate and adjust those social forces set in motion by others.[53]

New Deal lawyers did not make the world over; they were neither empowered nor inclined to do so. Their profession was, however, profoundly affected by patterns of social change that reached fruition during the New Deal years. As new areas of law emerged with new arenas in which to practice them, and as new careers opened, new groups of lawyers jostled for power and elite status. Although the strength of an elite usually is measured by its ability to set the terms of admission into its circle of influence, its survival may depend upon its ability to adjust to outside pressures and admit challengers.[54] During the 1930s, the traditional professional elite retained its privileged bastions in corporation law firms, in bar associations, and in pressure groups like the Liberty League's lawyers' committee. But it could not halt the growth of parallel professional institutions that trained and certified a newer elite drawn from different ethnic groups and social classes. These rival elites—one private, the other public—coexisted in uneasy equilibrium during the New Deal years. Just as many members of new immigrant groups "made it" in the business world by developing their own areas of marginal entrepreneurial activity—Hollywood, for example, and organized crime—so many minority group lawyers, excluded from Wall Street firms, served the administrative needs of the New Deal, practiced labor law, or litigated civil rights and civil liberties causes.[55] Not until after World War II, when corporate firms perceived the utility for their own practice of the expertise developed by lawyers in New Deal agencies, could minority group lawyers gain access to the Protestant professional establishment. The New Deal certified its own lawyers for their eventual careers on Wall Street or on law faculties.

The growth of a parallel elite, followed by its assimilation into the traditional structure, had dual significance. First, it made possible a necessary degree of social mobility within the legal profession; exclusionary patterns of access were weakened, although hardly destroyed. But the traditional professional structure, which defined elite positions as those in the service of business corporations, was retained. The New Deal created new elite positions, while leaving that structure, and the values that sustained it, relatively untouched. Elite circulation was achieved at the expense of professional democratization. At the base of the professional pyramid, nothing had changed. The battleground was reserved for the apex, where old and new elites clashed. When the dust kicked up by their professional rivalry had settled, the old structure—altered but not replaced—was greatly strengthened by its newest inhabitants, who were, by their presence, its newest defenders.

Recently, the New Deal has been criticized for representing "a transfer of power from the man in the street to the man from the *Harvard Law Review*," a process that accelerated the creation of "a hierarchical elitist society."[56] This is a half-truth, but a suggestive one nonetheless. Power hardly was held by the man in the street before 1933, unless the street was named Wall, rather than Main. It would be more accurate to say that the

New Deal reshuffled elites in a hierarchical society. Between 1933 and 1941, professional power in the public arena shifted from a corporate elite, served by Wall Street lawyers, to a legal elite, dominated by New Deal lawyers. From the perspective of 1941, the magnitude of this shift can hardly be exaggerated. From our perspective, with American society again in turmoil and its legal profession again in ferment and disrepute, the trade-off of social mobility for professional continuity may yield a less sanguine assessment of the interaction between lawyers and social change during the New Deal years.

I am grateful to the National Endowment for the Humanities for a grant that made possible much of the research on which this essay is based.

1. Harlan F. Stone, *Law and Its Administration* (New York, 1915), pp. 165–66, 197; Alpheus T. Mason, *Harlan F. Stone: Pillar of the Law* (New York, 1956), pp. 375, 376–77 n.

2. Mason, *Harlan F. Stone*, p. 382; Harlan F. Stone, "The Public Influence of the Bar,"*Harvard Law Review* 48 (1934): 2, 3, 6, 7.

3. Karl N. Llewellyn, book review, *Columbia Law Review* 31 (1931): 1218. The primary focus of this essay is on the professional apex, where the struggle between old and new elites was waged. My secondary concern is with the professional base, where the deleterious effects of stratification and the unsolved problems that accompanied urbanization and immigration were most apparent. I have ignored the large middle group of small-city, moderately successful practitioners, which was least involved in, and least affected by, professional decisions with public policy implications. For recent studies of these strata, see Irwin Smigel, *The Wall Street Lawyer* (Bloomington, Ind., 1969); Jerome E. Carlin, *Lawyers on Their Own* (New Brunswick, N.J., 1962); Joel F. Handler, *The Lawyer and His Community: The Practicing Bar in a Middle-Sized City* (Madison, Wis., 1967).

4. James E. Brenner, "A Survey of Employment Conditions among Young Attorneys in California," State Bar of California, *Proceedings* (1932), pp. 32–38; Isidor Lazarus, "The Economic Crisis in the Legal Profession," *National Lawyers Guild Quarterly*, December 1937, pp. 18–19; James P. Gifford, "Lawyers and the Depression," *Nation*, 30 August 1933, p. 236; Melvin M. Fagen, "The Status of Jewish Lawyers in New York City," *Jewish Social Studies* 1 (1939): 74, 79, 81, 86–87, 92, 95, 104; American Bar Association, *The Economics of the Legal Profession* (Chicago, 1938), p. 47.

5. Robert T. Swaine, *The Cravath Firm and Its Predecessors, 1819–1947*, 2 vols. (New York, 1946), 2:461; Frank E. Holman, *The Life and Career of a Western Lawyer, 1886–1961* (privately printed, 1963), p. 271; Harrison Tweed, Columbia Oral History Collection (hereafter cited as COHC) (Columbia University Library), p. 66; Swaine, *The Cravath Firm*, 2:xiii–xx; Arthur H. Dean, *William Nelson Cromwell, 1854–1948* (New York, 1957), pp. 172–81; S. Pearce Browning, Jr. to James M. Landis, 2 December 1932, Box 4, Landis Papers (Library of Congress).

6. Fred Rodell, *Woe unto You, Lawyers!* (New York, 1939), pp. 249, 272; Calvert Magruder, "What May Society Expect of Our Profession?", Maryland State Bar Association, *Reports* (1932), p. 102; Adolf A. Berle, "Modern Legal Profession," *Encyclopaedia of the Social Sciences* (New York, 1933), 9:340, 343–44; Arthur A. Ballantine, "The Lawyer's Outlook Today," *American Bar Association Journal* (hereafter cited as *ABAJ*) 24 (1938): 1022.

7. Karl N. Llewellyn, "The Bar Specializes—with What Results?", *Annals of the American Academy of Political and Social Science*, May 1933, pp. 178, 179; Llewellyn, review, *Columbia Law Review*, p. 1218.

8. Rodell, *Woe unto You, Lawyers!*, p. 3; Thurman Arnold to Roy M. Hardy, 17 May 1937, Thurman Arnold Papers (University of Wyoming Library); Ferdinand Lundberg, "The Legal Profession: A Social Phenomenon," *Harper's Magazine*, December 1938, pp. 3, 11.

9. "In Time of Stress," *ABAJ* 17 (1931): 666.

10. Guy H. Thompson, "Address," New Jersey State Bar Association, *Yearbook* (1932–33), pp. 117–28; Clarence E. Martin, "The Law in Retrospect and Prospect," *ABAJ* 19 (1933): 137–41; Newton D. Baker, "The Lawyer's Function in Modern Society," ibid. 19 (1933): 261–64; Earle W. Evans, "Responsibility and Leadership," ibid. 20 (1934): 589–93; William L. Ransom, "Government and Lawyers," Iowa State Bar Association, *Proceedings* (1936), p. 88; Adrian Raymond, "Revolutions and the Profession," *ABAJ* 18 (1932): 864; Jacob K. Javits, "The Lawyer's Place in the Coordination of Government and Business," *Commercial Law Journal*, March 1938, p. 71.

11. John W. Davis to Walter Lippmann, 25 June 1935; Davis to Charles McKie, 4 March 1937; Davis to Vance McLean, 9 January 1933; Davis to Max Schiffman, 29 March 1935; Davis to W. Matthews, 15 November 1935; Davis to LeRoy E. Kexel, 18 July 1934; Davis to Edyth M. Martin, 23 August 1938, John W. Davis Papers (Yale University Library); Morton Keller, *In Defense of Yesterday: James M. Beck and the Politics of Conservatism* (New York, 1958), p. 220.

12. Charles LeRoy Brown to Donald Richberg, 16 August 1933, Box 1, Donald Richberg Papers (Library of Congress); James G. Rogers to David A. Simmons, 8 February 1935, B 19/8; Harry P. Lawther to Simmons, 26 March 1935, B 19/21, Simmons Papers (Barker Texas History Center and Archives, University of Texas at Austin); Roy M. Hardy to Arnold, 12 May 1937, Arnold Papers; Donald G. Blaisdell, *Economic Power and Political Pressures*. TNEC Monograph No. 26, 76th Cong., 2d sess., 1941, pp. 2, 9, 37; Joel B. Grossman, *Lawyers and Judges: The ABA and the Politics of Judicial Selection* (New York, 1965), p. 58.

13. William L. Ransom, "The Profession of Law: Its Present and Future," in Addison Reppy, ed., *Law: A Century of Progress, 1835–1935*, 3 vols. (New York, 1937), 1:152; George Wolfskill, *The Revolt of the Conservatives: A History of the American Liberty League, 1934–1940* (Boston, 1962), p. 72; Francis Biddle, *A Casual Past* (New York, 1961), p. 358.

14. American Bar Association, *Reports* (1929), p. 302; ibid. (1934), pp. 549–53; William L. Ransom, "Public Opinion and the Bar," *Texas Law Review* 12 (1933): 61; Walter Tuller to Davis, 2 May 1935, Davis Papers.

15. Arthur Schlesinger, Jr., *The Politics of Upheaval* (Boston, 1960), p. 96.

16. For a full account, see Jerold S. Auerbach, "Enmity and Amity: Law Teachers and Practitioners, 1900–1922," in Donald Fleming and Bernard Bailyn, eds., *Law in American History* (Boston, 1972), pp. 551–601.

17. Thomas Reed Powell to Felix Frankfurter, 13 February 1934, A-6, Powell Papers (Harvard Law School), referring to Earle W. Evans, "Lawyers and Legal Events," *United States Law Review* 68 (1934): 107; Zechariah Chafee, Jr., "What's the Matter with the Law?", Address to Worcester Bar Association (1934), Chafee Papers (Harvard Law School); ABA, *Reports* (1935), p. 180; Albert J. Harno, "Social Planning and Perspective through Law," *ABAJ* 19 (1933): 201–6, 250; Arnold to Hardy, 17 May 1937, Arnold Papers; Stone to Frankfurter, 9 October 1934, quoted in Mason, *Harlan F. Stone*, p. 384; John Dickinson, "The Professor, The Practitioner, and the Constitution," *American Law School Review* (hereafter cited as *ALSR*) 8 (1936): 479–86.

18. Davis to Julian S. Gravely, 25 February 1935, Davis Papers; ABA, *Reports* (1935), pp. 156–57; Walter P. Armstrong, "A Practicing Lawyer Looks at Legal Education," *ALSR* 9 (1940): 776, 780; Joseph Auerbach, *The Bar of Other Days* (New York, 1940), p. 18.

19. Frankfurter to Philip L. Miller, 31 October 1911, Roll 14, Frankfurter Papers (Harvard Law School); Frankfurter to Miller, 11 March 1913, Frankfurter Papers (Library of Congress); Felix Frankfurter, "The Law and the Law Schools," *ABAJ* 1 (1915): 538–39; Frankfurter to Charles C. Burlingham, 14 February 1924, Frankfurter Papers (Library of Congress); Frankfurter, "John W. Davis," *New Republic*, 23 July 1924, pp. 225–26; Frankfurter to Learned Hand, 3 October 1924, Frankfurter Papers (Library of Congress); *Felix Frankfurther Reminisces*, Recorded in Talks with Dr. Harlan B. Phillips (New York, 1960), pp. 190, 248; Martin Mayer, *Emory Buckner*, (New York, 1968), p. 141; Joseph N. Welch to Frankfurter, 27 November 1925, Frankfurter Papers (Library of Congress).

20. Felix Frankfurter and Nathan Greene, *The Labor Injunction* (New York, 1930), p. 227; Frankfurter to Stone, 2, 4 April 1932, Frankfurter Papers (Library of Congress).

21. Frankfurter to Learned Hand, 18 March, 30 January 1932, 104–22, Hand Papers (Harvard Law School); Frankfurter, "Democracy and the Expert," *Atlantic Monthly*, November 1930, pp. 652, 660;

Frankfurter to Henry J. Friendly, 17 February 1932, Frankfurter Papers (Library of Congress); Frankfurter to David Lilienthal, 6 April 1931, Roll 8, Frankfurter Papers (Harvard Law School).

22. Frankfurter to Lippmann, 17 April 1933, Frankfurter Papers (Library of Congress); Frankfurter, "Dean James Barr Ames and the Harvard Law School," in Philip Kurland, ed., *Of Law and Life and Other Things That Matter: Papers and Addresses of Felix Frankfurter, 1956–1963* (Cambridge, Mass., 1965), p. 32; Frankfurter to William O. Douglas, 16 January 1934; Frankfurter to George A. Brownell, 12 January 1934, Frankfurter Papers (Library of Congress); Frankfurter to Henry L. Stimson, 19 December 1933, 20 February 1934, Roll 25, Frankfurter Papers (Harvard Law School); Frankfurter to Landis, 22 January 1935; Frankfurter to James Couzens, 7 December 1933, Frankfurter Papers (Library of Congress).

23. Frankfurter to Max Lowenthal, 23 January 1926, Frankfurter Papers (Library of Congress); James M. Landis, *The Administrative Process* (New Haven, Conn., 1938), p. 46.

24. Frankfurter to Lippmann, 17 April 1933; Frankfurter to Stone, 14 November 1935, Frankfurter Papers (Library of Congress); James Willard Hurst, "Themes in United States Legal History," in Wallace Mendelson, ed., *Felix Frankfurter: A Tribute* (New York, 1964), p. 200.

25. Frankfurter to Franklin D. Roosevelt, 9 January 1937, in Max Freedman, ed., *Roosevelt and Frankfurter: Their Correspondence, 1928–1945* (Boston, 1967), p. 374; Frankfurter to FDR, 18 January 1937, Roll 3, Frankfurter Papers (Harvard Law School); Frankfurter to Milton Katz, 25 May 1936, Frankfurter Papers (Library of Congress); Frankfurter to Jerome Frank, 29 September 1933, Frank Papers (Yale University Library).

26. Hugh Johnson, "Think Fast, Captain," *Saturday Evening Post*, 26 October 1935, p. 85; John Franklin Carter, *The New Dealers* (New York, 1934), p. 309; Fred Rodell, "Felix Frankfurter, Conservative," *Harper's Magazine*, October 1941, p. 453.

27. Frankfurter to Max Lerner, 17 March 1937, Lerner Papers (Yale University Library); Frankfurter to Nathan Margold, 29 November 1932, Volume 615, American Civil Liberties Union Papers (Brandeis University); Frankfurter to Charles Clark, 18 February 1934, Frankfurter Papers (Library of Congress); Frankfurter to Charles Robee, 10 January 1936, Roll 16; Frankfurter to Raymond Moley, Moley to Frankfurter, 31 October 1935, Roll 4, Frankfurter Papers (Harvard Law School); Frankfurter to Frank, 24 April 1933; Frank to Frankfurter, 18 April, 1933, Frank Papers; Thomas Corcoran to Frankfurter, 22 April 1933, Frankfurter Papers (Library of Congress); Frankfurter to Charles E. Wyzanski, Jr., 30 December 1938, 1–5, Wyzanski, Jr. Papers (Harvard Law School).

28. Frankfurter to Henry W. Bickle, 30 January 1936, Roll 14; Frankfurter to Eugene Meyer, 24 May, 1938, Roll 15, Frankfurter Papers (Harvard Law School); Frankfurter to Grenville Clark, 6 March 1937, Frankfurter Papers (Library of Congress). In the subsequent cold war climate, Frankfurter went to considerable lengths to repudiate both his role and its policy implications. See especially *Felix Frankfurter Reminisces*, pp. 248–50.

29. Samuel Lubell, *The Future of American Politics* (New York, 1965), pp. 43–44; American Bar Foundation, Research Memorandum Series, No. 15: *Compilation of Published Statistics on Law School Enrollments and Admission to the Bar, 1889–1957* (Chicago, 1958); U.S., Department of Commerce, Bureau of the Census, 14th Census, *Population, 1920 Occupations* (1923); U.S., Department of Commerce, Bureau of the Census, 15th Census, *Population* (1933).

30. In the careers of Thurman Arnold and William O. Douglas, the challenge of western insurgency to the eastern legal establishment is discernible. Douglas, especially, liked to describe himself as a country boy; after his accession to the Supreme Court, he insisted that all his law clerks come from the Northwest, where students had limited opportunities to achieve such positions. Douglas to Llewellyn, 17 May, 1934, 6 July 1939, R, IV, 5, Llewellyn Papers (University of Chicago Law School).

31. *In Memory of Robert Houghwout Jackson* (Washington, D.C., 1955), p. 25; Warner W. Gardner, "Robert H. Jackson, 1892–1954, Government Attorney," *Columbia Law Review* 55 (1955): 438.

32. Robert H. Jackson, "An Organized American Bar," *ABAJ* 18 (1932): 383; Eugene C. Gerhart, *America's Advocate: Robert H. Jackson* (Indianapolis, 1958), p. 49; Jackson, "The Lawyer: Leader or Mouthpiece?", *Journal of the American Judicature Society* 18 (1934): 72; Jackson, "The Bar and the New Deal," *ABAJ* 21 (1935): 93–96.

33. Charles S. Desmond, "The Role of the Country Lawyer in the Organized Bar and the Development of the Law," in Desmond et al., *Mr. Justice Jackson: Four Lectures in His Honor* (New York, 1969), p. 25; Glendon Schubert, *Dispassionate Justice: A Synthesis of the Judicial Opinions of Robert H. Jackson* (Indianapolis, 1969), pp. 5–6.

34. Jerome N. Frank, COHC, pp. 1–13; Frank to Powell, 20, 24 November 1930; Frank to Pound, 30 November, 2 December 1930, A–5, Powell Papers; Jerome Frank, *Law and the Modern Mind* (Anchor Books ed., New York, 1963), pp. x, 6, 22; Thurman Arnold, "Judge Jerome Frank," *University of Chicago Law Review* 24 (1957): 635.

35. Frank to Powell, 2 December 1930, A–5, Powell Papers; Frank to Arnold, 20 October 1932; Frank to Adolf A. Berle, 9 November 1932; Frank to Arnold, 29 December 1932; Frank to Julian W. Mack, 17 April 1933, Frank Papers.

36. Jerome Frank, "Realism in Jurisprudence," *ALSR* 7 (1934): 1066; Frank, "Experimental Jurisprudence and the New Deal," U.S. Congress, *Congressional Record*, 73d Cong., 2d sess., 1934, 78, pt. 11:12412–14.

37. Frank, "Realism in Jurisprudence," p. 1067; Frank to Chester Davis, 9 February 1934; Frank to Frankfurter, 29 November 1935; Frankfurter to Frank, 2 December 1935; Frank to Frankfurter, 21 January 1936, Frank Papers.

38. Frank to Frankfurter, June 1935, Frankfurter Papers (Library of Congress).

39. Charles E. Wyzanski, Jr., COHC, pp. 6, 44, 92–93, 101.

40. Wyzanski, COHC, pp. 108, 149, 154, 175, 194, 274.

41. Wyzanski to Frankfurter, 18 March 1935, 1 January 1936, Frankfurter Papers (Library of Congress); Wyzanski, "The Lawyer's Relation to Recent Social Legislation," Kentucky Bar Association, *Proceedings* (1937), p. 127; Wyzanski to Frankfurter, 16 June 1937, Frankfurter Papers (Library of Congress).

42. Biddle, *A Casual Past,* p. 366; Lloyd Landau to Frankfurter, 4 February 1933, Frankfurter Papers (Library of Congress); Leonard Davidow to Frank, 26 May 1933, Frank Papers; Landis to Frankfurter Papers (Library of Congress).

43. Abe Fortas to Richard Rovere, 25 October 1946, Group 31, R Roosevelt Papers (Franklin D. Roosevelt Library); David C. Shaw to Landis, 25 March 1937, Box 13, Landis Papers; Milton Handler to Frankfurter, 22 February 1934, Frankfurter Papers (Library of Congress).

44. Nathan Witt to Frankfurter, 7 December 1931, Frankfurter Papers (Library of Congress); Lee Pressman, COHC, pp. 5, 8; Pressman to Frank, 12 April 1933, Frank Papers.

45. Thomas I. Emerson, COHC, pp. 1, 172–74, 177–79, 181, 196, 221–27, 265–66, 1759.

46. I am grateful to Professor John Murrin for calling some of these points to my attention during his comments on my paper "The American Legal Profession: Social Structure and Conservatism," Conference on American Legal History, Harvard Law School (1971).

47. Frankfurter to Samuel Becker, 28 January 1937, Roll 14, Frankfurter Papers (Harvard Law School); Herbert B. Ehrmann to Frankfurter, 4 January 1932, Joseph N. Welch to Frankfurter, 30 December 1931, 1–5, Ehrmann Papers (Harvard Law School); Emory Buckner to Frankfurter, 27 February 1934, Buckner to Edmund Morgan, 31 January 1930, Frankfurter Papers (Library of Congress); Charles E. Clark to Frank, 26 March 1931, Frank Papers; interview with Raoul Berger (1971); Arnold to J. G. Driscoll, 12 June 1934, Arnold Papers; Edmund Morgan to Frankfurter, 1 June 1932, Frankfurter Papers (Library of Congress); M. T. Van Hecke to Landis, 2 December 1932, Box 8; Landis to Albert J. Harno, 9 February 1931, Box 6, Landis Papers; Mary [?] to Frankfurter [April 1936], Frankfurter Papers (Library of Congress); Frankfurter to La Rue Brown, 13 January 1937, Roll 14, Frankfurter Papers (Harvard Law School). See also Roscoe Pound to Julian Mack, 26 November 1935, Mack to Pound, 27 November 1935, 2–4, Roscoe Pound Papers (Harvard Law School); Smigel, *The Wall Street Lawyer,* pp. 173–75.

48. Malcolm A. Hoffmann, *Government Lawyer* (New York, 1956), p. 237. For a strikingly similar statement by a young Jewish economist, see Studs Terkel, *Hard Times: An Oral History of the Great Depression* (New York, 1970), p. 266; FDR to Burlingham, 6 February 1936, Roll 3, Frankfurter Papers (Harvard Law school).

49. Nathan Margold to Frankfurter, 27 March 1933, Roll 21, Frankfurter Papers (Harvard Law School); Frank to Mack, 17 April 1933, Frank to Frankfurter, 18 April 1933, Frank Papers; Harry Sagotsky to Frankfurter, 6 November 1935; Benjamin Pollack to Frankfurter, 24 September 1935; Asher W. Schwarz to Frankfurter, 16 October 1935; Benjamin J. Levin to Frankfurter, 29 January 1936; Allan Rosenberg to Frankfurter, 8 June 1936; Jerome R. Hellerstein to Frankfurter, 19 April 1933; Jacob Salzman to Frankfurter, 15 April 1936; Vartak Bulbankian to Frankfurter, 25 February 1936, Frankfurter Papers (Library of Congress); Charles W. Quick to Pound, 24 March 1939, 6–4, Pound Papers; Nelson H. Nichols, Jr., to Charles Houston, 24 February 1934, C–81, NAACP Papers (Library of Congress).

50. Llewellyn to Landis, 3 November 1933, A,II, 57, Llewellyn Papers; Llewellyn to Harrison Tweed, 25 November 1935, H,III,2, ibid.; Llewellyn, "The Bar's Troubles, and Poultices—And Cures?", *Law and Contemporary Problems* 5 (1938): 109–17, 124–26.

51. James O. McCulloch to Llewellyn, 1 July 1938; Sharl B. Bass to Llewellyn, 20 April 1937; Elliott Goldstein to Llewellyn, 16 February 1940; Arthur A. Brooks, Jr., to Llewellyn, 27 January 1940; Herman Steerman to Llewellyn, 20 August 1937; Llewellyn to Tweed, 25 November 1937, H,III,2, Llewellyn Papers.

52. "A Call to American Lawyers" (1936–37), Frank Walsh Papers (New York Public Library); *National Lawyers Guild Quarterly* 1 (December 1937): 1, Walsh to Harold E. Neibling, 19 December 1936; J. Francis Reilly to Walsh, 18 December 1936; Walsh to William G. Rice, Jr., 4 January 1937; Membership Report, 5/31/37; Minutes of Executive Board Meeting, 6/26/37, Walsh Papers.

53. Robert D. Abrahams, "The New Philadelphia Lawyer," *Atlantic Monthly*, April 1950, pp. 69–72; Letterhead, Philadelphia Lawyers Guild, February 1938, A,II,36, Llewellyn Papers.

54. Thomas I. Emerson, "The Role of the Guild in the Coming Year," *Lawyers Guild Review* 10 (Spring 1950): 1.

55. Landis, *The Administrative Process*, p. 155; Milton Katz, "James M. Landis," *Harvard Law Review* 78 (1964): 317–18; Schlesinger, *The Politics of Upheaval*, p. 229; *Report of President's Committee on Civil Service Improvement*, 77th Cong., 1st sess., House Doc. No. 118 (1941), p. 31; James Willard Hurst, *The Growth of American Law: The Law Makers* (Boston, 1950), p. 366. Even public service was described as a means for *restoring* the lawyer's prestive and traditional leadership role. See Albert J. Harno, *Letters to the Law Alumni of the University of Illinois, 1930–1957* (Chicago, 1958), p. 38; William O. Douglas, *Being an American* (New York, 1948), p. 54.

56. Geraint Perry, *Political Elites* (New York, 1969), pp. 32–33.

57. See Christopher Lasch, *The Agony of the American Left* (New York, 1969), p. 137.

58. Charles A. Reich, *The Greening of America* (New York, 1970), p. 51.

Raymond Wolters

The New Deal and the Negro

"The test of our progress is not whether we add more to
the abundance of those who have much; it is whether we
provide enough for those who have too little."—Franklin
D. Roosevelt

DURING THE GRAY YEARS OF THE GREAT DEPRESSION, AMERICA'S
twelve million Negroes were the most disadvantaged major group in
American society—"the first fired and the last hired." Government studies
indicating the "color or race" of families receiving relief reported that
blacks were "added to the relief rolls twice as frequently [in proportion to
their number in the total 1930 population] by loss of private employment as
whites, and are removed through finding places in private employment
only half as frequently."[1] Black people naturally hoped that the programs
of Franklin D. Roosevelt's New Deal would be constructed in such a way
as to assist their recovery. They were encouraged by the president's 1932
campaign promise that Negroes would be included "absolutely and impar-
tially" in his new deal for the forgotten man.[2]

President Roosevelt's program was so diverse and multifaceted that it is
difficult to generalize about its impact on Negroes. Some New Deal
programs were clearly advantageous, others less so, and some aggravated
the condition of black people. Yet on the whole, the New Deal was as
notable for its lost and rejected opportunities as for its actual achievements.
Its recovery program was limited and cautious, of more benefit to organized workers and to those who had fallen from relative affluence than to
those at the very bottom of society. Despite its deficiencies, however, the
New Deal offered Negroes more in material benefits and recognition than
had any administration since the era of Reconstruction. In gratitude for

these limited but real benefits, many Negroes in the 1930s began to vote for the Democratic party for the first time. This major realignment in black partisan identification—the breaking loose from traditional loyalty to the Republican party and the subsequent and tenacious loyalty to the urban Democratic coalition—was one of the most important developments in the political history of the decade, but it is not evidence that the Roosevelt administration fulfilled the promise of its egalitarian rhetoric. It is, rather, testimony to the fact that Negroes had come to expect little from governments in Washington or elsewhere and recognized that the New Deal, with all its shortcomings, was better for them than the existing Republican alternative.

More than half of the nation's Negro population lived in rural areas during the 1930s, but less than 20 percent of the black farmers owned the land they worked. Most were employed as tenants and wage hands with yearly incomes of less than $200, and any attempt to describe how Negroes were affected by the Roosevelt administration's agricultural policies must focus on the extent to which these impoverished, landless farmers shared the benefits of the various programs. The most important of these programs, that of the Agricultural Adjustment Administration (AAA), was essentially an attempt to increase farm purchasing power by sponsoring acreage and production control. It was thought that crop reduction would lead to higher farm prices, and thus the AAA was authorized to disburse government benefit payments to farmers who voluntarily promised to cultivate only a portion of their acreage. All farmers—owners, tenants, blacks, and whites—had suffered as a result of disastrously depreciated crop prices during the depression, and it was assumed that they all would profit from a general rehabilitation of the rural economy. The purpose of the AAA, then, was not to redistribute income within agriculture but to increase general farm prices and farm income through crop reduction.

The New Deal's agricultural administrators feared that given the system of caste and class relations in the cotton South, where the great majority of black farmers were employed, landowners would not support the government's crop reduction program unless they were assured that it posed no threat to the traditional dependence of tenants. Cully Cobb, the head of the AAA's cotton section, was a Tennessee farm boy who was educated at Mississippi A. and M. College, and his two assistants, E. A. Miller and W. B. Camp, were also recruited from southern agricultural colleges. They knew that many southern landlords would oppose any government program that gave tenants, especially black tenants, an independent source of income, and they saw to it that the AAA's cotton contracts were drafted in such a way as to take account of southern traditions. These contracts provided that landlords would receive four and one-half cents from the government for each pound of cotton not grown, of which the tenant's share was to be only one-half cent, a considerably smaller portion than the fifty-fifty division the AAA was distributing to tenants producing other crops and a ratio that suggests a great deal about the caste and class biases of those who controlled the AAA's cotton program. Cobb and his assistants also knew that many planters would object to direct payment of government money to tenants and thus all government money was distributed to landlords, who were instructed to act as trustees for their tenants' one-ninth share—a procedure that was contrary to the traditional method of handling government funds and one that offered virtually limitless opportunities for graft and deception.

The AAA delegated primary responsibility for the adjudication of any disputes that arose in the course of the reduction program to local authorities chosen in elections at the county and community levels. Negroes were allowed, even encouraged, to vote for members of these local committees; but they were not permitted to participate in the nomination of candidates, and throughout the South not a single black farmer served on a county committee. Eighty percent of the committeemen were white landowners, and most of the remainder were white cash renters. If a tenant believed his landlord had given him an unfair acreage allotment or had failed to distribute his share of the government money, he was required to present his case before the county committee. Since the committees were composed of the landlord's own friends and associates, such complaints were rarely decided in favor of the tenant and often resulted in further harassment for the complainant. Mordecai Ezekiel, an adviser in the office of Secretary of Agriculture Henry A. Wallace, correctly assessed the situation when he noted that "there can be no question that farm owners, constituting less than half of those engaged in agriculture, have been the dominant element in the preparation and administration of AAA programs. . . . In certain commodities, notably cotton, this has resulted in their receiving the lion's share of the benefits."[4]

To compound the difficulties of tenant farmers, the cotton section, fearful of even seeming to threaten the existing plantation system, never took effective steps to ensure that tenants would receive their allotted small share of the government benefit payments. Cully Cobb and his associates knew that in most cases the landlord did not forward the government money to the tenant but simply credited the money to the tenant's account at the company store. But they steadfastly rejected suggestions that landlords be required to fill out detailed forms specifying the price and quantity of goods they had advanced to tenants, arguing that such procedures would lead to a "colossal and expensive task" of administration and would provoke a "negative reaction" among planters.[5] The practice of distributing all money through the landlords naturally invited fraud, and one of the AAA's own studies acknowledged that "there have been a considerable number of cases in which tenant farmers have not received the full amount specified by the cotton contract . . . Whether the tenant received anything at all . . . depended upon the charitableness of the landlord."[6] Yet the prevailing view within the administration was that the cotton reduction programs had succeeded in raising the price of cotton from 6 cents a pound in 1932 to 12 cents in 1935, and, as Assistant Secretary of Agriculture Paul Appleby noted, "this doubling in value of the South's chief crop and that particular crop in which colored people are most interested . . . has had a far-reaching favorable effect."[7]

In addition to failing to protect the interests of tenants and sharecroppers, the AAA adopted policies that encouraged evictions. Put in the most simple terms, it was impossible to reduce cotton acreage by 40 percent without also reducing the need for labor in the cotton fields. The leaders of the AAA recognized that crop reduction might cause substantial unemployment among farm tenants; hence, special provisions were written into paragraph 7 of the 1934-35 cotton contracts requiring that landowners "maintain on this farm the normal number of tenants and other employees" and that all tenants be permitted "to continue in the occupancy of their houses on this farm, rent free." Yet Cully Cobb and his colleagues in the cotton section believed that these stringent requirements would antagonize many southern planters and jeopardize the chances for voluntary cooperation. Consequently, they proposed that the qualifying words *"insofar as possible"* be affixed to the requirement that landlords "maintain . . . the normal number of tenants." They also knew that it would be extremely difficult to force a landlord to keep an undesirable tenant, and therefore they proposed that tenants be permitted to "continue in the occupancy of their houses . . . *unless any such tenant shall so conduct himself as to become a nuisance or a menace to the welfare of the producer.*" The AAA's legal division objected to these proposed qualifications, pointing out that the additional phrases were vague, left the landlord with the prerogative of determining what was "possible" and who was a "nuisance," and made it impossible to go to court and force a recalcitrant landlord to honor the protective sanctions of paragraph 7.[8] Nevertheless, Secretary Wallace and AAA administrator Chester Davis supported the cotton section on this issue, and the cotton contracts, as finally drafted, expressed nothing but the AAA's hope that tenants would not be evicted.[9] The result was predictable. Beginning in 1934, observers throughout the South reported that many landlords were evicting tenants and thereby reducing their acreage in the easiest and most economical manner. The full extent of tenant displacement became clear when the 1940 census revealed that there were 192,000 fewer black and 150,000 fewer white tenants than there had been in 1930.[10]

Admittedly, the AAA cotton reduction program was not the only cause of tenant displacement during the 1930s. The availability of relief, the mechanization of agriculture, and the movement of population from city to countryside during the depression were other factors that also undermined the tenant's position. Moreover, it should be remembered that there was considerable displacement prior to 1933 when low cotton prices forced the curtailment of the labor force. Yet the AAA cotton reduction program must be charged with responsibility for a significant amount of displacement. As Gunnar Myrdal has written:

> Landlords have been made to reduce drastically the acreage for their main labor-requiring crops. They have been given a large part of the power over the local administration of this program. They have a strong economic incentive to reduce their tenant labor force, a large part of which consists of politically and legally impotent Negroes. Yet they have been asked not to make any reduction. It would certainly not be compatible with usual human behavior if this request generally had been fulfilled. Under the circumstances, there is no reason at all to be surprised about the wholesale decline in tenancy. Indeed, it would be surprising if it had not happened.[11]

When it became apparent that black tenant farmers were not receiving a fair share of the government benefit payments and that some previous difficulties had been aggravated by the AAA, the established Negro betterment organizations moved into action. The NAACP proposed that federal officials accept responsibility for distributing larger payments directly to tenant farmers and recommended the appointment of qualified Negroes to administrative posts in all phases of agricultural administration.[12] Most of the NAACP's suggestions were not adopted, however, and the association then turned to publicizing "the oppression suffered by the Negro—America's real 'forgotten man'—under the New Deal." It condemned the "shameless and unrebuked stealing of government checks made out to sharecroppers and tenant farmers," and chastised the federal government for "ignoring . . . complaints against maladministration, fraud and dishonesty."[13] Walter White, the secretary of the organization, protested strongly against the eviction of black sharecroppers and personally urged President Roosevelt "to instruct A A A to hold up all payments until [the] present situation is straightened out."[14] Benefit payments never were suspended, however, and attorney John P. Davis of the Washington-based Negro lobby, the Joint Committee on National Recovery, reflected a growing disenchantment with the Roosevelt administration when he complained that the government had "failed absolutely to protect the equities of the tenant . . . and made it an easy matter for the cotton producer to defraud and cheat his tenants. . . . Yet the administration in Washington—like Pontius Pilate—washes its hands of the whole matter and leaves it to the consciences of the white plantation owners of the South to see that justice is done."[15] The delegates to the NAACP's twenty-fifth annual conference in 1934 officially declared that the "nearly six million Negroes dependent upon agriculture have found no remedy for their intolerable condition in this [AAA] program."[16]

The response of the Roosevelt administration to the growing criticism of its cotton reduction program was essentially twofold. First, beginning in 1936 the cotton contracts were rewritten so that tenants would receive at least one-quarter of the benefit payment directly from the government, and this amount was raised to one-half in 1938. Yet increasing the tenant's share of the government money gave landlords a greater economic incentive for evicting tenants, a danger that was particularly great because the 1936-39 cotton contracts failed to improve the inadequate security provisions that had been written into paragraph 7 of the earlier contracts. Thus, it is not surprising that tenant displacement continued *at an accelerated rate* after 1935; the orders to increase the tenant's share of the benefit payment evidently prompted many landlords to resort to wholesale eviction.[17]

A second indication of the administration's growing concern for landless farmers occurred in 1937, when the president threw his support behind Senator John Bankhead's proposal to create a Farm Security Administration (FSA) that would provide very liberal tenant purchase loans (3 percent annual interest with a forty-year period for amortization) and additional funds for rural rehabilitation, relief, and resettlement. Despite the fact that the FSA's programs, like those of the AAA, were administered locally, about 23 percent of its benefits in the South were distributed among Negroes—a figure that corresponds closely with the black percentage of the southern rural population. Although one could argue, as Walter White and others did, that even this share was inadequate because the Negro's needs were so much greater and because Negroes made up 40 percent of the South's nonlandowning farmers, it is nevertheless a tribute to the fair-mindedness of the FSA's administrators that Negroes received as large a share of farm security benefits as they did.[18]

The agitation of groups such as the NAACP was partially responsible for the sensitivity of FSA's officials to the special problems of black tenants. Equally important was the fact that Will W. Alexander was chosen as the first administrator of the FSA. Unlike his counterparts in the AAA, Alexander had strong convictions concerning the need for interracial justice and cooperation. He had served as executive director of the Committee on Interracial Cooperation, as a trustee for five southern Negro colleges, as president of New Orleans's predominantly black Dillard University from 1931 to 1935, and as deputy administrator of the Resettlement Administration in 1936-37.[19] During his service with Resettlement, Alexander was constantly plagued by the special problems of black tenants; and to keep himself informed, he appointed a Negro farm specialist, Joseph H. B. Evans, to serve as his administrative assistant. (By way of contrast, Rexford Tugwell was "unable to see what advantage there could be to Negro farmers in the appointment of a special assistant" in the Department of Agriculture, and Henry Wallace claimed that such an appointment would be "patronizing" or even "discriminatory.")[20] Alexander took Evans with him when he moved from Resettlement to Farm Security, and during the next few years other advisers on Negro problems were added to the FSA's central office staff in Washington. Moreover, by 1941 each of the three southern regional directors had a black assistant to advise him concerning the special problems of black tenants. Negroes shared in the FSA benefits to the extent they did only because the Washington and regional offices exerted great pressure on local authorities to grant benefits to needy farmers regardless of race.

Of course, the FSA was not without its shortcomings, the most important being the economic limitations that sharply restricted the scope of its operations. While 192,000 black farm tenants were displaced during the 1930s, the egalitarian but financially starved FSA was able to provide tenant purchase and resettlement loans to only 3,400 Negroes. At this rate, it would have required several centuries to provide farms for all the needy tenants, and there was a grain of truth in the view expressed by Congressman William Lemke of North Dakota: "If ever a mountain labored to produce a mouse this bill is it. We have heard a lot of lip service that we are going to make farm tenants farm owners. In the light of that lip service this bill is a joke and a camouflage."[21] In addition, the FSA cautiously refused to challenge the southern caste system. The FSA countenanced segregation when it decided that applicants for rehabilitation communities would have to be selected "according to the sociological pattern of the community";[22] it bowed to white supremacy when it appointed only 72 Negroes to its staff of more than 7,000 southern farm and home supervisors;[23] and it generally worked with carefully selected tenants who were likely to make a good showing on loan collection records rather than with the most impoverished and needy.[24] Yet these compromises were just that, compromises undertaken to preserve the life of a small program which, however limited, distributed more than 20 percent of its benefits to black farmers. Unlike the leaders of the AAA, who assumed that there was no need for special attention to the problems of black farmers since prosperity was supposed to trickle down to the tenants after the plantation economy had been revived, the FSA made as many special efforts to ensure the distribution of benefits among Negroes as were consistent with institutional survival.

The AAA's dismal neglect of black tenants invites criticism, but has often been excused on the ground that political circumstances restricted the practical operations of the New Deal in the South. Bernard Sternsher, for example, has claimed that critics of the New Deal have not dealt adequately, "in some instances hardly at all, with the question of what the New Deal *could have been*. . . . To say that [Roosevelt] should have been something other than what he was is like saying that if Charlemagne had been more imaginative he would have discovered America in 792."[25] Among the forces constraining the administration, none was more important than southern domination of key congressional committees. Most of these southerners were willing to support the New Deal; they were loyal to the Democratic party, and their sectional economy was desperately in need of federal aid. But most of them also shared the conventional racial attitudes of their section, and President Roosevelt believed he would jeopardize the essential support of these southerners if his administration made any direct efforts to alter the dependent condition of black tenants. When Walter White complained, as he did on several occasions, that the president "did not go as far as he had the power to go," Roosevelt replied that he had "to get legislation for the entire country passed by Congress. If I antagonize the Southerners who dominate Congressional committees through seniority, I'd never be able to get bills passed."[26] Consequently, according to Frank Freidel, Roosevelt had "to modify or water down the New Deal in its practical operation in the South."[27]

Granting that political considerations required caution in race relations, FSA's success in dealing with black tenants suggests that the AAA could have done much more through bold administrative action. Perfunctory criticism doubtless would have emanated from the cotton South if the AAA had appointed qualified Negroes to advisory posts or had protected landless farmers by refusing to release payments to evicting landlords, but this desperately impoverished section simply could not have afforded to refuse cooperation with a program that brought so many benefits.[28] The men in the AAA believed that southern poverty could be alleviated without forcing a modification of either the tenancy system or white supremacy. Blacks, on the other hand, insisted that economic recovery could not be achieved in the South unless special programs were inaugurated to protect black tenants by substantially altering the equilibrium in the tenancy system. The New Dealers insisted that they were not responsible for tenancy, but they never came to grips with the thrust of the Negro argument: that the system of tenancy made black poverty inevitable and that the existence of widespread Negro poverty sooner or later would contradict and undermine white prosperity. Negro leaders believed that during the depression tenancy would have collapsed under the weight of its own inefficiency if the federal government had not rescued it with benefit payments. They insisted that, as NAACP Assistant Secretary Roy Wilkins put it, "now, while the Government is pouring millions of dollars into the South, is the time for it to insist upon the correction of some of the evils of the plantation system as a condition of government aid."[28] Unfortunately, this argument had little impact on the New Deal's most prominent agricultural officials, who consistently maintained that their goal was to revive the plantation system, not to reform landlord-tenant relations. Like some modern historians, New Dealers denied that farm tenancy and farm poverty were inextricably intertwined and insisted that there were legitimate reasons for refusing to make race relations a paramount issue.[29]

Although members of the Roosevelt administration generally agreed that the economy was badly imbalanced because mass purchasing power was insufficient to consume the products of the nation's factories and fields, they were of three minds (with many nuances) when it came to prescribing programs for industrial recovery.

One small group believed that the balance between production and consumption could best be restored by vigorous trust-busting that would destroy oligopolies and force lower prices. However, this antimonopoly approach had little impact on the black community. Although the administration's occasional forays in antitrust prosecution had some effect on the economy at large and on the general price level, there is no way to determine the extent to which Negroes as such were affected.[30]

A second group of New Dealers, with quite different assumptions, insisted that the depression was caused by excessive competition that destroyed reasonable profits, undermined business confidence, and reduced the rate of investment in job-creating enterprises. The solution, according to this view, lay in government-sponsored trade associations that would prohibit unfair competitive practices and establish fair minimum prices that would ensure profits and thus revive investment. These associationist advocates of "fair" competition had a beneficial effect on the black community in that they humanized the competitive struggle and encouraged the spread of labor standards that had existed previously only in the most advanced industrial states. In the past, "rugged individualism" had all too often led to "ragged individualism" for black workers; and in the long run, Negroes stood to benefit a great deal from the surrender of laissez faire and the stabilizing of industry on a basis of fair labor standards.

Unfortunately, many businessmen used cooperation as an excuse for raising prices more than was necessary to offset the cost of shorter hours and higher wages, and some took advantage of cooperation to make arrangements whereby short-run losses were minimized by restricting production. This combination of high prices and diminished production naturally subverted the plan for increasing purchasing power. High prices reduced everyone's purchasing power, and low production quotas led to work stoppage and unemployment. Although the New Dealers were aware of these dangers, they felt there was no alternative but to hope that businessmen would see that their own self-interest demanded that they agree to establish fair wages and hours without at the same time raising prices unduly or restricting production. Hugh Johnson, the administrator of the New Deal's industrial recovery program, appealed to businessmen to "keep prices down, for God's sake, keep prices down." He warned that if no control were placed "on undue price increases so that prices will not move up one bit faster than is justified by higher costs, the consuming public is going to suffer, the higher wages won't do any good, and the whole bright chance will just turn out to be a ghastly failure and another shattered hope."[31] Yet Johnson's plea was generally ignored, and by 1934 members of the Roosevelt administration were sadly acknowledging that "in case after case the price charged to the consumer has gone up . . . more than the increasing purchasing power paid out in production."[32] Insofar as New Deal-sponsored cooperation encouraged higher prices and restricted production, it was a burden for everyone —white and black.

A third group of reformers thought that purchasing power could be increased most effectively by prescribing higher minimum wages, encouraging the development of trade unions, financing employment on public works projects, and dispensing relief. These reformers joined with the cooperationists to produce a hybrid system of industrial cooperation under the supervision of the government's National Recovery Administration (NRA). Declaring that the economy would be invigorated by "increas[ing] the consumption of industrial and agricultural products by increasing purchasing power," the first title of the enabling legislation authorized the NRA to license businesses that were complying with nationally approved standards (minimum wages, maximum hours, recognition of the workers' right to collective bargaining, fair prices); and only those firms would be permitted to engage in interstate commerce or to display the NRA's symbol of compliance, the Blue Eagle. A second title provided for the establishment of a Public Works Administration (PWA) with an appropriation of $3.3 billion to finance construction of "a comprehensive program of public works."[33] Negroes naturally hoped that the new program would revive the economy, and initially most of them supported the NRA. *Opportunity*, the journal of the National Urban League, claimed that "a minimum wage . . . and maximum hours of work . . . will be of immeasurable benefit to the Negro worker who above all others has borne the cruel weight of prolonged unemployment and its resulting misery and want."[34] Yet even at the outset of the New Deal a few perceptive black critics recognized that though the new program might ameliorate the perilous condition of the general population, it would not necessarily improve the position of black workers, because Negroes were affected by the factor of race as well as that of economic condition. It was not long before many black spokesmen were criticizing discrimination in public works programs and claiming that higher minimum wages led to the displacement of black workers who had been employed only because their labor was cheaper.

The pressure of unemployed whites desperately searching for any sort of work naturally increased during the depression, and even before the NRA, white workers were being substituted in jobs customarily held by blacks. Nevertheless, most Negro spokesmen opposed proposals to establish a lower NRA wage scale for black workers. They knew that some blacks would lose their jobs if such a differential scale were not established, but they feared that any racial differential would become the entering wedge of a drive to classify Negroes as inferiors who deserved only substandard benefits. Some blacks also opposed differentials because they thought that workers could improve their position only if they submerged racial differences and joined together in biracial trade unions. Robert Weaver, soon to become a special assistant in the Department of the Interior, believed it would be better to keep the two races on a parity than to create so wide a difference in pay that antagonisms would be aroused; he objected to a racial differential primarily because "it would destroy any possibility of ever forming a strong and effective labor movement in the nation."[35] And Robert Russa Moton, the principal emeritus of Tuskegee Institute, maintained that it would be better for Negroes to lose their jobs than to be "put down by organized labor . . . as a group of strikebreakers and 'scabs.' "[36] Southern businessmen naturally saw things differently. Contending that black labor was less efficient than white, that it cost less to live in the South, and that the whole sociological condition of predominantly agricultural areas would be upset by paying high NRA wages to a few Negroes employed in industry, they appealed for lower minimum wages for the South, and particularly for southern Negroes. But in every case, the NRA rejected southern requests for racial differentials.[37]

While rejecting appeals for explicitly racial wage scales, the NRA permitted a complicated series of occupational and geographical classifications that enabled employers to pay white workers more than blacks.[38] Several NRA codes provided that minimum wage scales would cover only certain positions in the industry—positions generally held by whites. Thus, most of the thirteen thousand Negroes employed in cotton textile mills were classified as "cleaners" and "outside employees," categories specifically exluded from NRA coverage; in foundries there were two classifications of molders, with the black "molder's helper" receiving a lower wage than the white "molder"; and black workers in cotton oil mills were said to be processing farm products and were classified as agricultural laborers beyond the pale of the NRA, even though they were working in industrial factories with vast machinery. In addition, more than one hundred NRA codes established geographical classifications that permitted the payment of lower wages in the South than in other sections of the country. Negro leaders noted, however, that the NRA's geographical classifications were extremely inconsistent and concluded that "the one common denominator in all these variations is the presence or absence of Negro labor. Where most workers in a given territory are Negro, that section is called South and inflicted with low wage rates. Where Negroes are negligible, the procedure is reversed."[39]

Given the social and economic conditions prevailing in the South, the NRA's implicitly discriminatory classifications should not be censured. Black workers certainly would have suffered if the government had forced the payment of equal wages at a time when there was a tremendous surplus of unemployed white workers. The NRA faced an insoluble dilemma: on the one hand, it would be criticized for displacing Negroes if it pushed black wages too high; on the other, it was criticized for allowing any differentials at all. Perhaps its solution to the problem—permitting classifications that applied disproportionately to blacks but refusing to allow a specifically racial differential—was the best arrangement that could be made under the difficult circumstances.

The NRA's general emphasis on minimum wages was more blameworthy. In the South, most factory jobs were restricted to whites, but thousands of Negroes nevertheless were employed by small marginal enterprises that had little capital and obsolete machinery and could compete with more modernized concerns only because they paid less for their labor. Given their antiquated assembly lines, these marginal concerns were plagued by low productivity. By specifying minimum wages per man-hour rather than per unit of production, the NRA placed these inefficient firms at a severe competitive disadvantage. In effect, it forced small enterprises to choose between modernizing and going out of business. Most New Dealers agreed with President Roosevelt that "no business which depends for existence on paying less than living wages to workers has any right to continue in this country."[40] They knew that the NRA's minimum wage laws implied economic death for thousands of marginal enterprises, but they were convinced that "such economic surgery is necessary in a competitive economy in order to preserve the health of the larger body."[41] These sentiments were on a high moral plane, but this should not obscure the fact that either the bankruptcy or the modernization of marginal firms endangered a disproportionate number of Negro jobs.

In Greensboro, Georgia, for example, twenty Negroes were employed by a cotton textile mill. Before the NRA, the daily wage of workers at the mill was about 75 cents for a ten-hour day; afterward, wages ranged from $2 to $2.40 for an eight-hour day. The machinery in this mill was obsolete, and the firm had been able to compete with modernized mills only because its labor costs were so low. With the coming of the NRA, the mill had only two viable alternatives: to evade the NRA's stipulations by taking advantage of the classification system and other loopholes, or to install more productive machinery and pay code wages to fewer workers. Late in 1933, the mill made the second choice. After the new machines were installed, the management calculated that the mill could produce the same amount of goods with twenty fewer workers, and the Negroes were released. Economic factors had dictated the installation of improved machinery; racial attitudes dictated the displacement of Negro employees first.[42]

Similarly, in Virginia, North Carolina, and Kentucky tobacco manufacturing was a major endeavor that since colonial days had depended overwhelmingly on black labor. As a result of the NRA, the average work week in tobacco stemmeries declined from 55 hours to 40, while wages were rising from an average 19.4 cents per hour in 1933 to 32.5 cents in 1935 (a rate that would be doubled by 1940 in response to the subsequent Fair Labor Standards Act). Faced with rising wages, the tobacco companies installed stemming machines and commenced a mechanization program that halved black employment by 1940 while the number of white workmen was increased by more than 40 percent.[43] Thus, although it can be argued that in the long run black workers profited from the NRA-encouraged spread of better labor standards, the immediate impact of minimum wage legislation was harmful. Insofar as the new standards were enforced, efficient, modernized, lily-white firms were given a competitive advantage that enabled them to bankrupt the marginal concerns that employed most Negroes. Under the circumstances, Negroes were fortunate that the NRA was riddled with so many loopholes and classifications, and encumbered with such inadequate enforcement machinery, that most marginal businesses were beyond the effective reach of the Blue Eagle and continued to employ black workers at substandard rates.

In the United States of 1930, twenty-three of every two hundred persons gainfully employed were Negroes. Of these twenty-three, nine were engaged in some form of agricultural work, six were employed in industry, six earned their living as household employees, and the remaining two were engaged in trade, the professions, or public service. A consideration of the manner in which these workers were affected by the NRA must take account of the fact that there were no codes of fair competition, and consequently no government-sponsored increases in wages, for workers engaged in agriculture, domestic service, or the professions. Moreover, as just noted, black workers employed in jobs supposedly covered by the NRA often had to submit to a complicated system of classifications that, in total effect, resembled a racial differential, or run the risk of displacement by unemployed whites. For most black people, then, the NRA meant an increase in the cost of living without a corresponding increase in wages, and they must have sympathized with the *Norfolk Journal and Guide*'s contention that the NRA was defective because it did not reach down

to the large body of farm and mill laborers or domestic servants. . . . As commodity prices rise—as part of the NRA plan—these people will have to pay more for their bread and meat and clothes and rent. . . . With all costs of living going up the living standards of Negro wage earners will necessarily be forced down. . . . Recovery cannot be accomplished by bestowing all of the benefits of NRA upon white workers and crucifying Negro workers on an economic cross, merely because it has become customary . . . to take advantage.[44]

During the two years of the NRA's existence, Negroes repeatedly insisted that some of the racial problems of the industrial recovery program could be solved if the government would appoint qualified Negroes to key positions in the administration. Within the entire NRA bureaucracy, however, there was only one Negro professional worker, Miss Mabel Byrd, a graduate of the universities of Chicago and Oregon and a specialist in labor relations. Miss Byrd hoped to be sent to the South to study the problems of black labor under the NRA, but her research trip was canceled when high officials decided they would be "playing with fire to send a northern Negro to the South, and certainly one trained in Chicago."[45] Hugh Johnson believed that it would be simply "preposterous" to have a study of Negro labor made by a northern Negro, and Miss Byrd was effectively shut out of the NRA's decision-making process.[46] She was ignored as much as possible, excluded from staff meetings, and late in 1933 informed that there was no work for her and that she would be relieved of her duties. This dismissal left the NRA without anyone specifically concerned with Negro problems and emphasized the recovery administration's indifference to the plight of the black worker. Indeed, as the NRA began its second year of operations, there was not a single Negro employed with a rank equal to that of a clerk, and the Negro press suggested that the initials "NRA" in reality stood for "Negro Removal Act."[47]

The NAACP condemned the recovery administration for its refusal "to name qualified Negro experts to positions of authority" and concluded that "the result of this discrimination has been the impoverishment of hundreds of thousands of black workers and a complete failure in remedying the serious condition of unemployment among Negro workers."[48] Some Negroes, such as T. Arnold Hill, the industrial secretary of the Urban League, admitted that because black industrial workers had been abused for generations the NRA was not responsible for all the Negro's disadvantages. But this was "cold comfort to the hard pressed Negro worker who is looking around today for some means of relief from his present intolerable situation." According to Hill, "Whether [the Negro's] plight began three years ago or three centuries ago, the fact is that [he] remains the most forgotten man in a program planned to deal new cards to the millions of workers neglected and exploited in the shuffle between capital and labor." It was Hill's view that "a government which is honest in its claim of a New Deal, and which wishes to improve the lot of the forgotten man, should protect those who are least protected." But, he concluded, "this has not been done. On the contrary, the will of those who have kept Negroes in economic disfranchisement has been permitted to prevail, and the government has looked on in silence and at times with approval. Consequently, the Negro worker has good reason to feel that his government has betrayed him under the New Deal."[49]

Although the NRA's minimum wage codes were ineffective in terms of stimulating recovery from the depression and failed to have disastrous consequences for marginal black workers only because they were generally evaded, spending for public works offered the government the opportunity to pump purchasing power into the economy without jeopardizing any existing jobs. Yet definite measures were needed to ensure that black people would benefit from public works programs, and, because each New Deal administrative agency established its own procedure for handling Negro problems, much depended on the extent to which the dominant personalities in the Public Works Administration were sensitive to the special problems of Negroes. In this regard, Negroes clearly benefited from President Roosevelt's decision to appoint his secretary of the interior, Harold Ickes, to the post of public works administrator. Ickes was particularly concerned with race problems, and had served as the president of the Chicago branch of the NAACP. He promptly appointed Clark Foreman (white) and Robert Weaver (black) as special assistants to keep him informed on race matters, and local committees in charge of public works in particular areas were encouraged to have Negro members to keep them posted on any special problems that developed. Given this commitment to working with and for Negroes, the PWA provided tremendous benefits for black workers, who, with an unemployment rate more than double the national average, stood to benefit disproportionately from the creation of employment on nondiscriminatory public works projects.[50]

The PWA had a dual purpose: building useful projects and providing employment for those in need of it. With regard to the first of these, most of the work was for projects that would benefit the entire population—roads, dams, post offices, government buildings—and there is no way to determine how Negroes fared as a group. All that can be said, as Ickes observed, is that "they, like the rest of the American population, now have much better facilities in many lines than existed before." Ickes insisted, however, that the PWA did not discriminate "against any project submitted by or for the benefit of Negroes"; and insofar as the color of its beneficiaries can be determined, blacks fared well under the PWA.[51] During President Roosevelt's first administration, the PWA spent more than $13,000,000 for Negro schools and hospitals, a greater infusion of federal funds than had occurred in the seventy preceding years since Emancipation. By 1940, one-third of the 140,000 dwelling units constructed by the PWA and the United States Housing Authority, which succeeded the housing division of the PWA, were inhabited by Negroes. One hundred and thirty-three of the government's 367 housing projects were for the exclusive occupancy of Negroes, and 40 more were for the joint occupancy of blacks and whites. Although many Negroes had reservations about using government money to finance segregated facilities, most knew that it would be foolish to refuse such aid; and they gratefully accepted segregated projects as better than nothing at all. Negroes received 58.7 percent of the federally subsidized housing in the South, and this again suggests that determined federal administrators could overcome much despite the constraints of sectional race prejudice.[53]

The second of the PWA's major purposes—giving employment to the unemployed—presented greater problems for black workers. Due to the exclusion of Negroes from many trade unions and the widespread belief that whites should be given favorable consideration in the allocation of scarce jobs, there was blatant discrimination in many government construction programs. As the PWA began operations, for example, only 11 Negroes were included among the more than four thousand workers employed at the $166,000,000 project at Boulder Dam.[54] Administrator Ickes was determined to prevent discrimination, and to this end he officially ordered that there be "no discrimination exercised against any person because of color or religious affiliation."[55] Yet this ruling established no criteria for determining the existence of discrimination, and many contractors managed to comply by accepting token integration. Several Negroes complained that in their areas, as Roy Wilkins described the situation in New York, "we have discovered some surprising attitudes on the part of construction firms who have erected post offices, court houses, parcel post buildings, etc. To illustrate what they consider 'no discrimination' we found that out of 122 bricklayers on a parcel post building, one was a Negro. The firm handling this contract claims that it was not discriminating."[56] To prevent discrimination effectively it was necessary to find some criterion that could be used to indicate when discrimination existed. Late in 1933, the PWA's housing division decided to include a quota clause in its contracts requiring that skilled black workers receive a portion of the payroll corresponding to at least one-half their percentage in the local labor force. Where it was considered necessary, similar contractual provisions were included to protect unskilled black labor. The advantage of this procedure, according to Robert Weaver, was that it did "not correct an abuse after the project is completed—as is usually the case when Negroes' rights are being protected—but it set up a criterion which is *prima facie* evidence of discrimination. If the contractor does not live up to this requirement, it is accepted— until disproved—that he is discriminating against colored workers. Instead of Government's having to establish the existence of discrimination, it is the contractor's obligation to establish the absence of discrimination."[57]

By and large, this technique proved to be an effective solution to a difficult problem. It was later adopted by the successor to the PWA's housing division, the United States Housing Authority; and as of December 1940, $2,250,000, or 5.8 percent of the total payroll to skilled workers, had been paid to black workers. Weaver could proudly note that "this represented a portion of the total skilled payroll larger than the proportion of Negro artisans reported in the occupational census of 1930."

Of course, this method of defining and enforcing nondiscrimination did not solve the problem of Negro unemployment. The objective of the minimum percentage quotas was to retain past occupational advances for Negroes in the 1930s—a period when there was intense competition for every job and when the rate of black unemployment was more than twice as great as that for whites. The clauses, Weaver acknowledged, were "a device to regain lost ground; they were not designed to open new types of employment." Much remained to be done with regard to opening new jobs and upgrading Negro skills, but Weaver was convinced that "it would have been most unrealistic to have attempted to secure significant occupational gains for a minority group in a period when there was mass unemployment."[58]

Beginning in the spring of 1935, certain functions of the PWA, along with some responsibilities of the Federal Emergency Relief Administration (FERA), were taken over by the Works Progress Administration (WPA).[59] Fortunately for Negroes, Harry Hopkins, the director of the WPA, was sensitive to their special problems and appointed a Washington teacher, Alfred E. Smith, as an administrative assistant to coordinate the activities of a staff of Negro advisers: James Atkins, a professor of English from Tennessee A & I State College, served in the adult education division as a specialist in education among Negroes; literary critic Sterling Brown worked as an editor of Negro material in the Federal Writers Project; T. Arnold Hill of the Urban League served as a consultant on white-collar workers; social worker Forrester B. Washington operated as director of Negro work in the FERA; and John W. Whitten was appointed to the post of junior race relations officer. In addition, several of Hopkins's white assistants, led by Aubrey Williams, a top aide in the FERA, were also greatly concerned with the special difficulties of Negroes and did what they could to help resolve problems. The WPA's central administration repeatedly exerted pressure on local authorities to give jobs to needy workers regardless of race.[60]

Largely as a result of these determined efforts, the share of FERA and WPA benefits going to Negroes exceeded their proportion of the general population. The FERA's first relief census reported that more than two million Negroes were on relief in 1933, a percentage of the black population (17.8) that was nearly double the percentage of whites on relief (9.5).[61] By 1935, the number of Negroes on relief had risen to 3,500,000, almost 30 percent of the black population, and an additional 200,000 blacks were working on WPA projects.[62] Altogether, then, almost 40 percent of the nation's black people were either on relief or were receiving

support from the WPA. Of course, even this was an unsatisfactory measure of participation because Negro needs were so much greater. The
FERA and the WPA constructed hundreds of badly needed Negro schools
and recreation centers and provided hundreds of thousands of relief grants
and jobs for black workers; but when matched against the needs of the day,
all this amounted to little more than the initiation of a mild beginning. Yet it
was only because of the fair-mindedness of the central administrations in
Washington and their willingness to exert pressure on local authorities that
blacks received as large a share of the benefits as they did.

The over-all statistics should not obscure the fact that welfare and work
relief practices varied widely, with the Negro's chance for securing government assistance depending on geographical location and the personnel
in the local relief offices. Blacks generally were well represented in the
North and in the urban areas of the South, but found it difficult to receive
government assistance in the rural South, where many landlords insisted
that precautions be taken to ensure that relief would not compete with even
the most menial employment. Thus, the average monthly expense for
Negro relief in Georgia's rural Green County in 1934 was only $2.30, and
in Macon County only $1.19.[63] The evicted rural black was in the impos-
sible position of having to seek relief as the only means of staying alive,
and yet having his landlord demand that any assistance be kept to a
minimum lest relief spoil the tenant or wage hand, if and when regular farm
work again became available.

In line with this conviction that government welfare benefits should not
be so attractive as to "ruin" those on relief rolls for private employment,
most employers in all sections of the country, and especially in the South,
insisted that wages for work relief be kept below the prevailing rates in the
private labor market. As a result, the WPA was forced to abandon its
original thirty-cent-hourly minimum wage and instead established a scale
that in 1935 ranged from a low of $19 a month for 130 hours of unskilled
work in the rural South to $94 for skilled technical work in the urban North.
As in the case of the NRA's classifications, these occupational and
geographical categories affected a disproportionately large number of
black workers. John P. Davis noted that the $19 rate would cover "71.5
percent of the [southern] Negro working population but only 26 percent
of the white working population."[64] Walter White warned that race prejudice would cause black workers in the South to be "uniformly classed as
unskilled" and charged the administration with surrendering "to the demands of Governor Eugene Talmadge [of Georgia] and Southern

officials."[65] But federal authorities thought it would be foolish to alienate southern support by paying government relief workers more than their counterparts in private enterprise. Indeed, government officials were so concerned with placating local powers that they acquiesced in the release of black workers from federal jobs at harvest time, thus forcing them to take low-paying, seasonal jobs in the fields. Yet in fairness to the work relief program, it must be emphasized that though the WPA was willing to compromise with local forces, it never accepted the $2 and $3 weekly wages that prevailed in large areas of the South and often made life more tolerable for rural workers than it had ever been before.

Negroes also complained of many specific abuses in the relief and work relief programs—so many that it would require a volume to describe and categorize all the charges. The NAACP, for example, charged that black women on work relief in South Carolina were forced to do road work and that female construction workers in Jackson, Mississippi, were supervised by armed guards.[66] The *Chicago Defender* alleged that only three Negro workers were employed in the construction of WPA's black Wendell Phillips High School in Chicago,[67] and other Negro newspapers repeatedly printed similar allegations. The National Urban League charged that there was definite discrimination against Negro employees on the Triborough Bridge project in New York City, on the Inter-City Viaduct in Kansas City, and on all public works in St. Louis.[68] The files of the NAACP and the Urban League are replete with similar charges, and Mary White Ovington, the treasurer of the NAACP, summed up the feelings of most Negroes when she wrote that "as to the Washington work relief, . . . it varies according to the white people chosen to administer it, but always there is discrimination." Government officials such as Aubrey Williams were forced to acknowledge that "most of the contentions are true."[69]

Yet it must again be emphasized that, in spite of its local shortcomings, the FERA-WPA progam of relief and work relief was of enormous importance in helping Negroes survive the depression. Although federal control of relief has often been criticized, it is clear that blacks were served best by federal, as opposed to state or local, control; and many Negroes must have come to believe, with Professor Rayford Logan of Atlanta University, that the black man benefited from the New Deal "in just the proportion that the federal government exercises direct control over [its] many ramifications."[70] Indeed, while the locally controlled AAA cotton reduction program was shoring up the plantation system by displacing labor and subsidizing landowners, the New Deal's relief and work relief programs were providing an unprecedented number of jobs for Negroes, especially in urban areas. Thus, as Donald Hughes Grubbs noted recently, "both the 'push' and the 'pull' forces impelling black urbanization were intensified as an aim or byproduct of national policy."[71]

The Negro's encounter with the New Deal's twin programs for youth, the Civilian Conservation Corps (CCC) and the National Youth Administration (NYA), underscored two important lessons suggested by the experience with the more comprehensive relief programs: the distribution of significant benefits, in spite of inequity and discrimination, to black youths who were represented proportionately in terms of their percentage of the general population but underrepresented in terms of actual need; and the crucial influence, for good or ill, that officials in Washington could bring to bear on local authorities. The CCC was organized in 1933 to help relieve poverty and provide training for young men by employing them in conservation work under joint civilian and military supervision at salaries of about $25 a month. Unfortunately for Negroes, the civilian director of the corps, Robert Fechner, a white Tennessean and a prominent official in the racially exclusionist International Association of Machinists, had so absorbed southern mores that he was determined to prohibit racial mixing and was extremely reluctant to press for either the acceptance of Negroes or the appointment of blacks as supervisors in the segregated colored camps. As a result, the benefits of the CCC in the South were limited at the outset almost wholly to whites; less than 3 percent of the first 250,000 corpsmen were black. The state director of selection in Georgia, John de la Perriere, explained that "there are few negro families who . . . need an income as great as $25 a month in cash"; and, moreover, "at this time of the farming period in the state, it is vitally important that negroes remain in the counties for chopping cotton and for planting other produce."[72] After much pressure from the NAACP and officials in the Departments of Labor and Interior, southern Negroes gradually were admitted to the CCC, and the percentage of blacks increased each year until by 1936 the Negro enrollment had come up to the proportion of Negroes in the total youth population. Altogether, almost 200,000 of the 2,500,000 men who served in the corps during its nine-year life span were black.[73]

Given the customs of the era and the army's traditional Jim Crow organization, it was inevitable that the southern corpsmen would be segregated by race; but the CCC's central administration required segregation wherever there were enough blacks to form a colored company, even in states where companies originally had been integrated and where in at least one instance the governor, Philip LaFollette of Wisconsin, specifically requested that camps in his state be integrated.[74] Accepting the conventional southern view of race relations, director Fechner believed it would be dangerous to allow any but the right type of whites to exercise authority in Negro camps, and the CCC officially prohibited black officials in any position of authority other than that of educational adviser.[75] The education was kept to a minimum and slanted toward preparing blacks for menial jobs.

Thus, although blacks were belatedly and grudgingly permitted to join the CCC, they were segregated in units with limited opportunities for training and advancement and never received the measure of relief to which their economic privation entitled them. Yet despite the missed opportunities and compromised ideals, the CCC did provide relief for 200,000 black youths; and "in doing so it fed many of them better than ever before, provided them with living conditions far superior to their home environments, and gave them valuable academic and vocational training." Despite all the special problems, as one black corpsman noted, "as a job and as an experience, for a man who has no work, I can heartily recommend it."[76] "The failure of CCC," John Salmond has judiciously concluded, "was not so much one of performance as of potential. Much had been accomplished, but much more could conceivably have been done."[77]

Established in 1935, the National Youth Administration set up two programs that were of great assistance to young men and women: a Student Work Program that provided part-time work at a small stipend for youngsters who otherwise could not attend school, and an Out-of-School Work Program for unemployed youths between the ages of 18 and 24. Fortunately for Negroes, Aubrey Williams, the Alabama-born grandson of a planter who had freed a thousand slaves, was appointed as executive director of the NYA, and Williams was prepared to use his considerable skill and influence to help Negroes receive a fair share of the NYA's appropriations. With the support of President Roosevelt, who wanted to avoid a repetition of the CCC's discrimination, Williams named Mordecai W. Johnson, the president of Howard University, to a position on the NYA's advisory committee and, more importantly, appointed Mary McLeod Bethune, the founder of Bethune-Cookman College and president of the National Council of Negro Women, as head of a specially created Division of Negro Affairs. Mrs. Bethune and her black staff, in turn, persuaded most state directors to appoint additional blacks as administrative assistants and committeemen, and eventually more Negroes were employed in administrative positions in the NYA than in any other New Deal program. Although the actual NYA projects were sponsored by people from the local communities, a situation that often complicated the work of these black officials, Mrs. Bethune and her staff enjoyed considerable success in their efforts to ensure a fair deal for black youth. From the outset, Negroes received about 10 percent of NYA's appropriations, with their share increasing to almost 20 percent in the early 1940s as a growing number of whites found jobs in the reviving economy.[78]

At the same time, there were limits to what the NYA accomplished for blacks. Unwilling to jeopardize the existence of the agency's southern operations, Williams and Mrs. Bethune accepted segregated projects, though they never followed the CCC's example of forcing segregation on unwilling localities. In addition, knowing that many whites were thoroughly convinced that blacks should be trained only for "Negro jobs," the NYA accepted a disproportionate amount of servile work; and consequently, as Mrs. Bethune observed, many blacks concluded that "all they can get is cooking, sweeping, and agriculture."[79] Yet these jobs were better than nothing at all, and wherever the local authorities were willing to cooperate, the NYA sponsored projects that held out a larger promise. In Texas, for example, the state administration headed by Lyndon B. Johnson operated fifteen Freshman College Centers that offered special college prep courses each year to about four hundred black high school graduates who were planning to go on to college.[80] The most important weakness of the NYA was not racial discrimination or insensitivity but the very limited scope of its operations. Despite the disproportionately high rates of unemployment for the nation's youth, and particularly black youth, it was not until 1940 that as many as 300,000 young people were served by the Out-of-School Work Program, while the larger student program distributed checks to only a third of a million students each school month from 1935 to 1939, and half a million in 1940 and 1941.[81] Negroes received a fair share of these valuable benefits, but the National Youth Administration was able to help only a minority of those who needed its assistance.

Of all the New Deal's many programs, none had a greater effect on the nation than the social security program, inaugurated in the summer of 1935. This program marked a decisive turning point in American development, a rejection of the older exaltation of individual responsibility and self-help and an acceptance of the government's responsibility for providing social security for the aged, the unemployed, the infirm, and the dependent. Since black people were numbered disproportionately among the socially insecure, they eventually profited from all aspects of the government's social security program. Although blacks were assisted by the welfare provisions from the outset, however, the old-age and unemployment insurance provisions initially covered only 10 percent of the black work force; and thus, ironically, for a few years more blacks felt the impact of social insurance in the form of higher consumer prices (as employers passed on the cost of social insurance for whites) than benefited directly from old-age pension or unemployment checks.

Although they endorsed the principle of social insurance, most Negro leaders objected to three specific aspects in the Roosevelt administration's program. In the first place, they warned that the decision to give the states responsibility for administering the unemployment and welfare programs would lead inevitably to discrimination against southern blacks. George Edmund Haynes of the Race Relations Department of the Federal Council of Churches testified before committees in both the Senate and House of Representatives, reminding congressmen that several locally administered federal programs had been plagued by "repeated, widespread and continued discrimination on account of race or color" and appealing vainly "for a clause in this economic security bill against racial discrimination."[82]

Second, Negroes called attention to the fact that agricultural workers were explicitly excluded from coverage by the program, and most domestic servants were implicitly barred by provisions that extended coverage only to those who worked for employers with at least eight employees. Noting that 65 percent of the nation's black workers were classified in these two categories (and at least another 25 percent of the Negro population was unemployed and thus beyond the pale of social security), the NAACP's Charles H. Houston concluded that "from the Negro's point of view" the administration's Wagner-Lewis social insurance program "looks like a sieve with the holes just big enough for the majority of Negroes to fall through."[83] The association's journal, the Crisis, complained that "just as Mr. Roosevelt threw the Negro textile workers to the wolves in order to get the [NRA] Cotton Textile Code adopted in 1933, by exempting them from its provisions, so he and his advisers are preparing to dump overboard the majority of Negro workers in this security legislation program by exemption from pensions and job insurance all farmers, domestics, and casual labor."[84] The Norfolk Journal and Guide used the same analogy when it concluded that "like NRA, this new economic panacea seems to be intended to bring security to certain people, but not to all."[85]

Third, Negroes objected to the provision that employee contributions for old-age insurance would be supplemented by taxes on the employer's payroll, and unemployment compensation would be financed entirely by payroll taxes. Such taxes, Negroes contended, were essentially indirect sales taxes that employers would pass on to consumers in the form of higher prices, causing greatest discomfort among the low-waged domestics and agricultural wage hands who would be "doubly exploited" because they did not receive any benefits from the new program but still had to pay higher prices for the necessities of life. Writing in the *Crisis*, Abraham Epstein called for the program to be financed by the federal treasury and pointed out that the refusal to finance the program through progressive taxes had the effect of placing the entire cost of social security on the workers and their employers and exempted the well-to-do from responsibilities they had shared since the establishment of the Elizabethan poor-law system. "No other nation," Epstein insisted, "has ever put into operation an old age insurance plan without placing at least some of the burden on the government in order to make the higher income groups bear their accustomed share."[86]

For these reasons, among others, the administration's Wagner-Lewis social security bill was, as William Leuchtenburg has written, "in many respects . . . an astonishingly inept and conservative piece of legislation."[87] Not surprisingly, most black leaders opposed the administration's bill and supported Representative Ernest Lundeen's proposals to provide generous unemployment and old-age benefits for all workers, with federal subsidies financed by taxes levied on inheritances, gifts, and individual and corporate income in excess of $5,000 a year, and with a firm prohibition of discrimination and uniform minimum standards of administration to be enforced throughout the country.[88]

But though regressive financing, local administration, and the exclusion of black workers were real weaknesses in the social security program, it does not follow that Negroes would have benefited from a more careful and fair drafting of the legislation. Unfortunately, most black workers were trapped by a "Negro wage scale" that in all but a relatively few cases ranged from $100 to $500 a year. These wages were simply too small to permit the slow accumulation of reserves that is the essence of *insurance*. As Charles Houston pointed out, the average monthly pension for the 10 percent of the black population that would someday be eligible for old-age annuities would be only $4.50, or $54 a year.[89] What Negroes needed was not insurance but recognition by the state of its responsibility to cover the overhead social costs of capitalistic production. That is, poor people, black and white, were in no position to provide for their own security during the depression, but depended on their more prosperous fellow citizens to accept responsibility for financing security for those who were elderly, sick, or unemployed.[90] In a word, they needed *welfare*, which the Lundeen bill proposed in the guise of social *insurance*. Given the opposition of the administration, though, the Lundeen proposal had no chance of passage, and the Wagner-Lewis bill was enacted into law.

Despite frequent discrimination and limited funding, the welfare provisions of the Wagner-Lewis program provided immediate benefits for many indigent, infirm, and dependent Negroes; and, in the wake of agitation and negotiation with federal officials over the course of the next four decades, the provisions for unemployment and old-age insurance were modified so as to provide greater coverage for blacks. By emphasizing the need for social insurance, however, the Roosevelt administration misrepresented the needs of the nation's poorest citizens. Although the New Deal provided an unprecedented amount of welfare through FERA, WPA, and other agencies, its welfare programs were always considered temporary expedients to tide the unemployed over until recovery had been achieved. Social insurance, on the other hand, was a permanent program; but because it was insurance, it meant little to those at the bottom of the economic ladder. Some advocates of the Wagner-Lewis program frankly admitted that though social insurance would do little for the indigent and nothing for race relations, it was nevertheless a desirable step forward. But others justified the program with exaggerated claims that it would bring a New Deal to the forgotten man. In retrospect, it would seem that this rhetoric had the effect of deflating discontent by offering hope to the indigent while offering real benefits to the lower middle class, recently fallen from relative affluence and with frustrations and aspirations that threatened to become disruptive. Thus, the administration protected the essentials of the established system, but in so doing it fell well short of its egalitarian promises. Here, at least, in the words of Howard Zinn, "what the New Deal did was to refurbish middle-class America, which had taken a dizzying fall in the depression, . . . and to give just enough to the lowest classes . . . to create an aura of good will. . . . The New Dealers moved in an atmosphere thick with suggestions, but they accepted only enough of these to get the traditional social mechanism moving again, plus just enough more to give a taste of what a truly far-reaching reconstruction might be."[91]

The gulf between egalitarian rhetoric and discriminatory practice was particularly wide in the Tennessee Valley, where Congress, at the president's suggestion, created the Tennessee Valley Authority (TVA) to pioneer the development of regional multipurpose projects. The TVA was authorized to conduct a wide variety of operations: the construction of dams, the supervision of flood control and irrigation, the production of hydroelectric power and fertilizer. But the TVA was concerned with more than simply the production and sale of power and fertilizer. As Arthur E. Morgan, the chairman of the authority, explained, "TVA is not primarily a dam-building job, a fertilizer job or a power-transmission job. . . . We need something more than all these."[92] It was an experiment in comprehensive social planning. "The President," Morgan claimed, "sees the Valley Authority as a means for displacing haphazard, unplanned and unintegrated social and industrial development by introducing increasing elements of order, design and forethought."[93] Morgan's ambitious hopes for regional planning were only partially fulfilled, but historians nevertheless have generally concluded that the TVA was "an eloquent symbol of the time,"[94] "the most spectacularly successful of the New Deal agencies."[95]

Despite the TVA's general obeisance to planning and the need to improve social as well as physical conditions, it was clear to the 250,000 black residents of the valley that the TVA envisioned a lily-white reconstruction. To be sure, on paper the authority prohibited racial discrimination and promised blacks a proportionate share of jobs, but it practiced discrimination in housing, employment, and training. Because many TVA projects were in remote areas where housing was not available, it was necessary for the TVA to build dormitories and camps for the construction workers and villages for the permanent work force. Yet the work camps were segregated, with blacks given inferior accommodations, and Negroes were barred altogether from the "model village" at Norris that TVA spokesmen proudly heralded as an ideal American community that would serve as a "yardstick" for other villages and point the way to new residential possibilities throughout the valley. Black spokesmen naturally were indignant, and Walter White pointed out that "in using Federal funds to establish 'lily-white' communities," the TVA went beyond segregation to exclusion.[96] But John Neely, Jr., the secretary of the authority's board of directors, candidly explained to John P. Davis, "You can raise all the 'rumpus' you like. We just aren't going to mix Negroes and white folks together in any village in TVA."[97]

As for jobs, the TVA claimed that Negroes constituted about 10 percent of the work force—a figure roughly equivalent to their proportion of the total population of the valley—but it admitted that the Negro percentage of the payroll was lower because blacks were concentrated in unskilled construction work. As a matter of fact, the TVA seemed incapable of thinking of blacks in any capacity except that of unskilled and semiskilled laborers. After making a firsthand investigation in 1938, Thurgood Marshall of the NAACP reported that "not a single Negro has a white collar job in the entire TVA set up except for about five Negroes in the training division," and "absolutely no Negro is included in the apprenticeship program"; he concluded that TVA's policy was to "freeze Negro workers into unskilled categories forever."[98] Similarly noting the practically complete exclusion of blacks except as laborers, Charles Houston reported, "There is not even a Negro messenger, a Negro file clerk in the entire TVA organization";[99] and Robert Weaver charged that TVA had "a jim-crow labor policy, and none of the benefits of separation."[100] TVA Personnel Director Gordon R. Clapp claimed that the authority was simply "showing reasonable regard and respect for [the] traditional and reasonable approach of a particular locality," and especially for the views of labor unions that objected to the training and employment of skilled Negroes even in the construction of Jim Crow dormitories and villages.[101] Spokesmen for the NAACP, however, insisted "that TVA is a Federal agency and that TVA jobs are Federal jobs, and as such do not belong exclusively to any one element of citizens regardless whether organized or unorganized."[102]

Claiming that the TVA was "a symbol of the failure of the government to hire Negroes in any capacity except unskilled and semiskilled"[103] and knowing that the valley was one of the few places in the South where protest might be effective, the NAACP made the Tennessee Valley Authority the focal point of a public campaign for more jobs for Negroes. Beginning in 1934, John P. Davis, Charles H. Houston, and Thurgood Marshall were sent to the valley to conduct investigations for the NAACP, and Robert Weaver made a similar probe for the Department of the Interior; and in 1938, Congress established a Joint Investigation Committee under the chairmanship of Senator Victor A. Donahey of Ohio.[104] These inspections confirmed reports about discrimination in housing, employment, and training and pointed additionally to such unfortunate practices as excluding blacks from the recreational areas developed by the TVA and the National Park Service near Norris Dam, employing Negroes in skilled work without comparable pay, and refusing to discipline foremen who harassed and abused black workers. To correct these conditions, Robert Weaver urged the TVA to appoint a director of Negro work and black administrative assistants with responsibility for training and employing skilled black workers and foremen, emphasized the need to make white personnel and staff members recognize that the authority's proclamations against discrimination were going to be enforced, and suggested that the TVA would do well to follow the example of the PWA's housing division and establish objective quotas to determine the existence of discrimination against skilled black workers. Chairman Morgan and the TVA refused to adopt any of these suggestions, however, and by 1938, most Negroes believed that discrimination was a firmly established policy. The majority report of the Joint Congressional Investigating Committee concluded, "On paper the Authority policy toward Negroes is one of no discrimination and a proportionate share of jobs. In practice the Authority has not felt able to enforce this policy as fully as could be desired. . . . The Authority cannot solve the race problem in a year or in ten years, but it can and should do more for Negroes than it is doing."[105]

TVA officials initially claimed that their discriminatory policies were the result of oversight, but that explanation hardly sufficed after the NAACP and other organizations repeatedly brought attention to the authority's unfair race policies. Then, beginning in 1934, the TVA claimed that it could not risk jeopardizing the existence of its entire program by violating the traditional customs of the South. Chairman Morgan, beset by fervent criticism from rugged individualists and staunch defenders of the property rights of competing private enterprises, would do nothing for Negroes that might further antagonize the public and endanger the TVA's daring experiment in regional planning. Instead, he attempted to justify the TVA's neglect of blacks, claiming that they would not be happy in integrated communities, that they would be served best by a cautious policy of "inching along" without arousing racist suspicions that the TVA was violating Tennessee's segregation statutes. He warned that the TVA's black critics were only "provoking . . . anti-Negro sentiment to a more determined attack."[106]

Blacks insisted, however, that local statutes did not apply to federal territory, and that the TVA was a federal agency and as such differed from private employers and was required to conform to national policy and the egalitarian clauses of the Constitution. Moreover, Charles Houston discovered evidence indicating that, far from following local customs, the TVA was injecting a policy of discrimination unknown in the area. Mixed crews and black foremen were frequently employed by nonunion enterprises in the valley, but the TVA's decision to employ union labor while avoiding any semblance of a pro-Negro position had the effect of increasing segregation and black servility "beyond the usual sectional pattern."[107] Similarly, Walter White pointed out that Norris was the only community of its size in the entire valley that completely excluded Negroes, and he condemned "the timidity of those entrusted with the responsibility of directing the policies of TVA."[108]

Beyond timidity, the authority, like many other New Deal agencies, was guilty of indifference and, paradoxically, insufficient planning. The TVA never developed a program for Negro participation because it considered the status of blacks as a matter of only marginal importance. The authority was concerned essentially with promoting the economic recovery of the Valley, and its officials openly claimed that they had "[no] special responsibility to attempt to revise or reconstruct the attitude of this area toward the race question."[109] Consequently the TVA never developed a comprehensive plan to include Negroes, but instead dealt with each race problem as a special case. Negro interests were sacrificed whenever they conflicted with the claims of better-organized and more powerful white groups.

The fear that any challenge to white racism would alienate the South and thus endanger the administration's entire program for economic recovery also dissuaded President Roosevelt from endorsing the major civil rights proposal of his time, the NAACP-sponsored anti-lynching bill. The president was no doubt appalled by the more than one hundred lynchings that occurred during the first five years of the depression, but he refused to create problems for himself by challenging white supremacy and patiently postponed a firm public condemnation of lynching until after two white men were victimized in San Jose, California. Moreover, he never put the anti-lynching bill on his list of "must" legislation and was not willing to speak out against the filibusters and threats of filibusters that prevented the proposal from coming to a vote in the Senate. The president wanted the support of northern blacks, but he did not want to anger the southern congressional delegations, which, despite some misgivings, always remained an important element in the New Deal coalition, voting for its domestic bills and, as the threat of war approached, for the president's foreign policy and defense program.[110] Roosevelt did not oppose those who were working for Negro rights, and on one occasion he told Walter White to "go ahead; you do everything you can do. Whatever you can get done is okay with me, but I just can't do it."[111] He even authorized his wife to "say anything you want [in favor of the anti-lynching bill]. I can always say, 'Well, that is my wife; I can't do anything about her.' "[112] But the president himself would do nothing, explaining, "If I come out for the anti-lynching bill now, [the southerners] will block every bill I ask Congress to pass to keep America from collapsing. I just can't take that risk."[113]

Negroes complained about the silence of "the Sphinx" in the White House, claiming that "the utterly shameless filibuster could not have withstood the pressure of public opinion had [the president] spoken out against it."[114] Yet this criticism missed the mark. Regardless of what the president had done, there was no real chance of cloture being voted and the anti-lynching bill passed. Indeed, there is considerable evidence suggesting that the leaders of the NAACP themselves recognized there was no realistic possibility of securing the legislation; they launched the anti-lynching campaign to keep the name of their organization before the public, to raise funds, and, most importantly, to outmaneuver militant black critics who were demanding that the association deemphasize agitation, courtroom activities, and congressional lobbying and devote more of its attention to the economic problems that plagued the masses of Negroes.[115]

Although the success of Will Alexander's FSA, Harold Ickes's PWA, and Aubrey Williams's NYA demonstrates that bold administrative action could moderate the restrictions of race prejudice and suggests that other New Dealers were using the threat of alienating racists to excuse their own lack of interest in altering prevailing forms of segregation and discrimination, it does not follow that President Roosevelt exaggerated the problems that would have ensued if he had thrown the influence of his office behind a bill considered anathema by the great majority of southern politicians. The fact is that presidents, working in the full glare of publicity and symbolically representing "all the people," do not enjoy as much latitude as administrators who work in relative obscurity and of necessity must specify the multiplicity of conditions under which government funds will be disbursed or curtailed. If President Roosevelt's record in race matters is to be faulted, it is not for failing to endorse a historically premature civil rights bill but for refusing to consider enlightened and fair racial attitudes an important prerequisite for all his administrative officers. The president failed to recognize that the special problems of black farmers and work-ingmen demanded special attention from sensitive administrators, and evidently accepted the facile belief that Negroes would benefit automatic-ally from the New Deal—not because they were singled out for special consideration but because they preeminently belonged to the under-privileged class that the government's recovery programs were designed to assist. Refusing to consider race a matter of vital importance, the president acquiesced in the Negro policies of his various administrators—malign neglect in all too many cases. Many blacks certainly must have wondered if the president, in his inner heart, really was interested in challenging white supremacy, and must have concluded with Roy Wilkins that "it will be found in the record of Franklin Roosevelt that he was no special friend of the Negro."[116]

Beyond this lay the more fundamental and basic deficiencies of "broker leadership." The New Deal was essentially an attempt to solve the nation's economic problems democratically, but such a "democratic" system usu-ally gives the greatest benefits to those who are well organized and politically influential. Since blacks were neither, they inevitably gained little. There were some administrators who were aware of the special problems of Negroes, and they were able to do something for blacks; but other officials were not particularly sensitive, and some were hostile. Essentially, the history of "The New Deal and the Negro" is a chronicle of the manner in which the concern or indifference of individual adminis-trators modified or reinforced an underlying disregard for those without power.

Despite the New Deal's checkered record—an amalgam of concern and assistance, on the one hand, with indifference and neglect, on the other —black voters during the depression abandoned their traditional allegiance to the party of Lincoln. By the end of the 1930s, Negroes were the most favorably disposed of all major social groups toward Franklin D. Roosevelt and the New Deal.[117] There can be no doubt that the benefits accruing as a result of the Roosevelt administration's relief and work relief programs were largely responsible for a major shift in black voting pat-terns. Many Negroes would not have survived the depression without relief, and the distress of the entire black community was alleviated by the administration's programs. Indeed, the impact of relief was so great that contemporary critics of the right and more recent historians of the left have concluded that Negroes were "politically purchased by relief."[118] But though considerations of immediate self-interest were undoubtedly influential with impoverished blacks (as they are with the great majority of all people), it is an extreme oversimplification to suggest, as Dorothy Thompson once did, that "the Negro vote which has traditionally been Republican, partly because of memories of the Civil War, but also because the Republicans paid more for it, has gone largely Democratic because the Democrats are able for the first time to compete—not with cash at the polls but with relief and WPA jobs."[119] Relief was one important factor, but only one, in a complex equation of components that produced the important transformation in black partisan identification.

One of the additional factors that influenced Negro voting behavior was a growing dissatisfaction with the Republican party. During the 1920s, many officials in this party of Emancipation had come to assume that Negro devotion was unalterable and could be renewed simply by reminding blacks of the oppression suffered by Negroes in the Democratic South and by occasional egalitarian speeches and the distribution of patronage to black politicians. Even these meager benefits were curtailed after the GOP's unprecedented southern success in 1928, when Herbert Hoover carried five states that had formerly belonged to the Confederacy, and Republican strategists evidently concluded that the party could permanently attract a large number of southern whites if it dissociated itself from the cause of Negro rights. Thus, President Hoover proceeded in such a manner as to earn Walter White's condemnation as "the man in the lily-White House."[120] Though fifty-seven Negroes were lynched during Hoover's presidency, the chief executive resolutely refused to condemn this form of mob violence.[121] Instead, he insisted on nominating for the Supreme Court a southern judge who had publicly called for the disfranchisement of Negroes;[122] he acquiesced in the segregation of "Gold Star" mothers sent to Europre at government expense to visit the graves of sons killed in World War I;[123] he kept political contacts with blacks to a minimum and refused to be photographed with Negroes until the last month of his second campaign for the presidency;[124] he threw his influence behind the lily-white Republican organizations in the South by consenting to the punishment of dishonest black politicians and allowing dishonest whites to flourish;[125] he sharply reduced the number of first-class appointments for Negroes;[126] and, finally, since blacks were in such desperate economic straits, President Hoover's resistance to federal relief hurt them more than any other group. This record naturally disheartened Negroes, and, except in a few cities where local Republican machines remained solicitous to please blacks, most Negro leaders concluded that the race had allowed the GOP to monopolize its vote for too long and that in the future Negroes should become more independent politically and should support the party that would best serve their immediate interests. The Republican *Chicago Defender* editorialized, "It is now apparent that we have had our political eggs in one basket too long. It is true that tradition has inclined the average Colored voter toward the Republican party, but changing conditions are forcing the thoughtful Colored man and woman to seek protection within the ranks of all parties. . . . The managers of the Democratic party now have an unparalleled opportunity—if they will grasp it. It is their privilege to profit by the blunders of the Republicans."[127]

One Democrat who was eager to take advantage of the opportunity was Joseph Guffey of Pennsylvania. In 1932, upon hearing Robert L. Vann, the Negro editor of the *Pittsburgh Courier*, condemn Republican neglect and indifference and urge blacks to "go home and turn Lincoln's picture to the wall," Guffey envisioned millions of Negroes voting the Democratic ticket and persuaded the reluctant James A. Farley and Louis McHenry Howe to establish the first really effective Negro division of the Democratic campaign committee. Vann was then brought to New York as the division's manager-in-chief, and after the campaign Guffey persuaded President Roosevelt to appoint Vann as assistant to the attorney general, a position once held by a black football star from Harvard and one that Guffey calculated as the best Washington job ever given to a Negro by the Republicans. At the same time, Guffey introduced a special agreement in Pennsylvania whereby Negroes were entitled to 10 percent of the Democratic patronage, "no more and no less." Guffey also insisted that public relief be distributed equitably and threw his support behind a civil rights bill making it a criminal offense for a Pennsylvania hotel, restaurant, or theater to refuse accommodations to Negroes.[128] Guffey was using patronage, public money, and civil rights legislation to court the Negro vote; and in the process, he was making Pennsylvania something of a test case of a strategy designed to lure Negroes into the Democratic coalition. Black voters, concentrated in overwhelmingly Republican Pittsburgh and Philadelphia, cast more of their ballots for Roosevelt in 1932 than for any previous Democratic candidate for the presidency; but the Negro trend toward the Democrats was less pronounced than that of the whites, and Hoover managed to carry every black ward in Philadelphia and one of the two Negro wards in Pittsburgh. Yet as Guffey continued to court black voters, the Democratic trend emerged more clearly; and Negroes contributed significantly to the upsets that sent Guffey to the United States

Senate and his running mate, George H. Earle, to the governorship. Throughout the remainder of the decade, President Roosevelt and his supporters made their best Pennsylvania showings in the black wards of Pittsburgh and Philadelphia, where they generally received about 80 percent of the vote.[129] Thus, Guffey's vision became a shining reality, and Guffey himself became one of the first of the new style of political bosses—liberal in rhetoric and policy and, unlike his conservative predecessors who served big business and raised slush funds in the offices of large corporations, dependent on grants from the federal treasury to support his multitude of clients.

Guffey's experience suggests the crucial importance of local political machines in facilitating or retarding the transformation of Negro partisan identification. Like other citizens, Negroes wanted the recognition and patronage that accompany political victory, and the Negro underworld depended on the sufferance and protection of the ruling machines. (With individual numbers syndicates employing as many as 1,500 policy writers in Chicago and New York, this consideration was of no small importance.) Thus, the transfer of Negro political allegiance to the Democrats was effected most conspicuously in northern cities where the Democrats gained power and where there was a minimum of discrimination in the practical operation of New Deal programs. This was true not only of Guffey's Pennsylvania but also of "Boss" Tom Pendergast's Kansas City and the New York of Jimmie Walker, where Tammany Hall cultivated blacks throughout the 1920s and where many Negroes voted the Democratic ticket in municipal and state elections long before the advent of the New Deal.[130] Conversely, in Chicago, where the local Democrats had traditionally been hostile to the aspirations of blacks and where the Republican machine headed by William Hale "Big Bill" Thompson was extremely eager to please black voters, Negroes lagged well behind whites in shifting to the Democratic party; it was not until 1940 (after a newly ascendant local Democratic machine headed by Mayor Edward J. Kelly had demonstrated its willingness to deal fairly with blacks) that FDR captured a majority of Chicago's Negro vote.[131] But whatever the local variations, the basic trend was consistent: despite tremendous economic deprivation and widespread disillusionment with the Republican party, blacks initially lagged behind whites in shifting to the Democratic party; but in 1936 and thereafter, Negroes became increasingly Democratic while whites were beginning to return to the GOP. The trend in national elections was unmistakably Democratic, even in Des Moines, where Negroes voted overwhelmingly

Republican in "off" or non-presidential years,[132] and in St. Louis, where blacks voted first against the Republicans and then against the Democrats in local elections.[133] Local factors could not stay the basic swing of the political pendulum, though they could influence the width of the arcs.[134]

There is some question, however, as to whether the Democrats were mobilizing the support of blacks who had formerly been Republicans or were organizing those who had not previously participated in the political process. There are, it is true, occasional critical elections in which a considerable number of voters break decisively with their past partisan identifications and form new and durable electoral groupings.[135] The depression witnessed the emergence of new political coalitions, and mobile Negroes fleeing the rural South and then encountering the contrast between the neglect of some Republicans and the concern of many northern Democrats were more likely than other groups to alter their traditional political allegiance.[136] Nevertheless, a growing body of political analysis suggests that most voters enter the electorate with a marked preference for one or the other of the major parties, and this partisan identification increases as the voters grow older.[137] Thus, it is interesting to note that John A. Morsell, a student of black voting behavior in New York during the depression, has concluded that "most of the Negro votes which went Democratic in the thirties had not been Republican before; they had not been in existence before." During the 1920s, many Harlem Negroes expressed their political dissatisfaction by staying away from the polls. With the depression and the New Deal, however, there was a politicization of the masses, a surging participation in politics on the part of young people in the process of establishing their partisan identification and among previously apathetic citizens. The number of votes cast in Harlem increased by 50 percent during the depression, while the total population increased by only 1 percent, and these new voters were overwhelmingly Democratic. By 1936, when Franklin D. Roosevelt's *plurality* in black Harlem exceeded the largest Republican *totals* of the 1920s, Negroes were securely ensconced in the New Deal coalition. But it seems likely that most of these black Democrats were not erstwhile Republicans who had turned Lincoln's picture to the wall but younger people and other new voters in the process of forming their political allegiance.[138] (That these new Democrats would adhere ever more tenaciously to their party as they grew older should occasion no surprise. The elaborate data collected by the Survey Research Center at the University of Michigan have demonstrated that once voters establish a prevailing disposition, they are only marginally affected by the immediate issues and candidates in an election.)

Granting the significance of Negro disillusionment with the GOP, the emergence of egalitarian Democratic machines, and the opportunity created by the migration- and depression-induced surge of new voters to the polls, there was still an area of discretion within which the personality and policies of President Roosevelt could exercise great influence. Roosevelt possessed, as Leslie Fishel has noted, a "consummate ability to personalize his understanding of human exploitation and underprivilege." His voice "exuded warmth and a personal inflection which brought him close to his listeners. His own physical affliction and the way he bore it earned him deserved admiration and gave encouragement to those who had afflictions of their own."[139] Yet FDR's personal charm had a negligible impact on the black community during the election campaign of 1932. Negroes recalled that Roosevelt had served as assistant secretary of the navy in the segregationist Wilson administration and had uncomplainingly signed and forwarded orders Jim Crowing the rest rooms in the buildings of the navy department.[140] As a candidate for the vice-presidency in 1920, he had boasted of having written a constitution for Haiti ("and if I do say it, I think it is a pretty good constitution") that placed this black Caribbean republic under the control of American financial interests and the United States Marines.[141] Negroes were far from reassured by FDR's periodic vacations at his "second home," a "segregated mud hole" at Warm Springs, Georgia, and they looked askance at his delight in "listening to the singing of Negro musicians dressed like old-time plantation hands."[142] They positively feared that, if anything should happen to Roosevelt, his running mate, John Nance Garner of Uvalde, Texas, would preside over a resurgence of Jim Crow discrimination in the nation's capital.[143] Although a majority of black leaders endorsed Roosevelt in 1932 on the ground that "a vote for Roosevelt means merely a protest against Hoover,"[144] about three-fifths of the black electorate remained loyal to the Republican party.[145]

In 1936, however, the Democrats captured about 75 percent of the Negro vote, ballots that were cast almost entirely in cities where there was relatively little discrimination and where the benefits of the New Deal were most apparent. By this date, moreover, many blacks had begun to react positively to Franklin D. Roosevelt as a human being. Despite discrimination in the implementation of New Deal programs and the administration's cautious fear of alienating the white South, the president did speak out forcefully against the crime of lynching,[146] even while he refused to use his influence in an effort to break the southern filibuster that prevented a vote on anti-lynching legislation. In notable contrast with President Hoover, Roosevelt frequently conferred with black leaders and graciously received Stenio Vincent, the black president of Haiti.[147] He had, moreover, appointed some Negroes to advisory positions in the New Deal, not just politicians brought in as patronage appointees but professional men employed for the express purpose of securing relief from flagrant discrimination and integrating Negroes into the administration's recovery program.[148]

Equally important, in terms of the blacks' increasingly favorable impression of the president, were the activities of the first lady, Eleanor Roosevelt. At the very outset of the New Deal, Mrs. Roosevelt arranged a special conference with black leaders to discuss the integration of Negroes into the New Deal's subsistence homestead program,[149] and thereafter she repeatedly manifested her concern for the special problems of blacks. She acted as an intermediary between Walter White and the president during negotiations over anti-lynching legislation and clearly indicated that her sympathies were with the NAACP.[150] While attending the Southern Conference on Human Welfare in Birmingham, Alabama, she conspicuously took a seat on the "Colored" side of the segregated auditorium and refused to move to the "White" side. When police threatened to cancel the meeting, she reluctantly moved her chair to the middle of the aisle separating the two sections and refused to move again.[151] When the Daughters of the American Revolution refused to permit the gifted black contralto, Marian Anderson, to give a concert in Constitution Hall, Mrs. Roosevelt publicly resigned her membership in the DAR and immediately set about making arrangements to hold the concert at the Lincoln Memorial.[152] Throughout her years in the White House, she broke with previous tradition by holding receptions for black leaders and student groups.

The impact of Mrs. Roosevelt's personal conduct and example is difficult to determine, but impressionistic evidence indicates that it was considerable. Roy Wilkins claimed that Franklin Roosevelt was a friend of the Negro "only insofar as he refused to exclude the Negro from his general policies that applied to the whole country," but Mrs. Roosevelt was a true champion of the race. "The personal touches and the personal fight against discrimination were Mrs. Roosevelt's. That attached to Roosevelt also—he couldn't hardly get away from it—and he reaped the political benefit from it."[153] The *Pittsburgh Courier* later recalled that "though her husband as President was given credit for sympathizing with the plight and aspirations of Negroes, it has since become apparent that it was she who made him conscious of the social injustices existing in the country."[154]

While New Deal benefits trickled down to the black community and while President and Mrs. Roosevelt assumed an increasingly egalitarian posture, the Democrats of 1936 organized an ambitious campaign for the Negro vote. Openly acknowledging that blacks held the "balance of power" in Pennsylvania, Ohio, Indiana, Michigan, and Illinois, campaign manager James A. Farley established two amply staffed Colored Democratic Divisions—under the general supervision of Robert L. Vann, with the Negro attorney Julian Rainey in charge of eastern operations and the first Negro Democratic congressman, Arthur W. Mitchell of Chicago, at the helm in the West.[155] These organizations waged an extremely effective campaign: they publicized the New Deal's benefits; secured an official endorsement from the Bishops' Council of the African Methodist Episcopal Church and testimonials from blacks as diverse as heavyweight boxing champion Joe Louis and Tuskegee Principal Frederick Douglass Patterson;[156] held dances, such as one at Philadelphia's Convention Hall that was free of charge to those who stopped by Democratic headquarters to pick up their tickets, and monster rallies, such as one gathering of 20,000 blacks at New York's Madison Square Garden where the Colored Committee ceremoniously unveiled a colossal painting of FDR standing to a height of twenty feet, his hands outstretched in benediction over a kneeling group of Negroes with the spirit of Abraham Lincoln hovering in the background.[157] Catching the spirit of the campaign, President Roosevelt himself addressed the assembled black students and faculty of Howard University and proclaimed that "among American citizens there should be no forgotten men and no forgotten races."[158]

Yet it would be a mistake to conclude that black voters were simply seduced by Democratic rhetoric.[159] They could not fail to observe widespread discrimination and had firsthand knowledge of the limited nature of the Roosevelt administration's recovery program. To reinforce this awareness, the Colored Divisions of the Republican party spent twice as much as their Democratic counterparts pointing out the deficiencies of the New Deal and enlisting the support of such celebrities as Mamie Smith and the Beale Street Boys, J. Finley Wilson of the Negro Elks, and Olympic sprint champion Jesse Owens.[160] Francis E. Rivers, a black graduate of Yale and the director of colored Republican operations in the East, sounded the keynote of the 1936 campaign when he declared that dependence on relief would inevitably lead to "political and economic serfdom." There could be no lasting solution to the Negro's economic problems, Rivers insisted, until black people were reemployed and integrated into the productive life of the nation, and he complained that the New Deal's AAA and NRA programs had actually reinforced the trend toward Negro displacement.[161] Continuing with this theme, Governor Alfred M. Landon of Kansas, the Republican nominee for the presidency, charged that the New Deal was using "relief rolls as modern reservations on which the great colored race is to be confined forever as a ward of the Federal Government, . . . excluded from the productive life of the country." Landon predicted that this policy would prove to be "not only disastrous to a great people, but of alarming consequence to our entire economic and social life."[162] Other black Republicans presciently warned that continued dependence on government largesse might destroy self-respect and independence and paralyze the will to work. In 1935, for example, Professor Newell D. Eason of Shaw University predicted that relief would pauperize the race by inculcating a certain contempt for work and a willingness "to cling to the minimum existence which seems to be guaranteed by the relief agency." Noting that relief grants often approximated the meager wages for which blacks had labored so industriously in the past, Eason thought it was understandable that "normal attitudes toward work are not being preserved," but he warned that in the long run black people would suffer most from any erosion of the traditional work ethic.[163]

In retrospect we can see that there was some merit to the Republican critique of the New Deal, but most Negroes of the depression decade could not afford the luxury of considering the long-range ramifications of the dole. They were in desperate and immediate need of welfare and government employment, and for most, as Lillian P. Davis noted, this relief was not just "a pittance to drag them through . . . but a godsend of plenty such as in all their lives for generations back they have never known before."[164] The *Baltimore Afro-American* spoke for most Negroes when it claimed that though "relief and WPA are not ideal, they are better than the Hoover bread lines and they'll have to do until the real thing comes along."[165] The *Pittsburgh Courier* reflected the prevailing Negro mood when it editorialized that as a result of the New Deal

armies of unemployed Negro workers have been kept from the near-starvation level on which they lived under President Hoover. . . . Armies of unemployed Negro workers have found work on the various PWA, CWA, WPA,

CCC, FERA, and other projects. . . . Critics will point to discrimination against colored sharecroppers, against Negro skilled and unskilled labor. . . . This is all true. It would be useless to deny it even if there were any inclination to do so, which there is not. . . . But what administration within the memory of man has done a better job in that direction considering the very imperfect human material with which it had to work? The answer, of course, is none.[166]

1. Federal Emergency Relief Administration, *Unemployment Relief Census* (Washington, 1933), report 2, p. 26.

2. *Baltimore Afro-American*, 24 Sept. 1932.

3. For a detailed and extensively documented discussion of the impact of the New Deal's agricultural recovery program on black farmers, see Raymond Wolters, *Negroes and the Great Depression: The Problem of Economic Recovery* (Westport, Conn., 1970), pp.3–79.

4. Mordecai Ezekiel to Henry Wallace, Memorandum, 5 Feb. 1936, Records of the Department of Agriculture, R.G. 16 (National Archives).

5. Jerome Frank to D. P. Trent, Memorandum, 5 Nov. 1934; Cully Cobb to Chester Davis, Memorandum, 26 Oct. 1934, Records of the Agricultural Adjustment Administration, R.G. 145 (National Archives).

6. Calvin B. Hoover, "Human Problems in Acreage Reduction in the South," 1935 typescript in AAA Records.

7. Paul Appleby to Walter White, 6 Mar. 1935, AAA Records.

8. Oscar Johnston to Chester Davis, Memorandum, 26 Jan. 1935; Alger Hiss to Jerome Frank, Memorandum, 26 Jan. 1935, AAA Records (italics added).

9. David Eugene Conrad, *The Forgotten Farmers: The Story of Sharecroppers in the New Deal* (Urbana, Ill., 1965), pp. 57–59.

10. The census data on this point have been conveniently summarized by Gunnar Myrdal, *An American Dilemma* (New York, 1944), p. 253.

11. Ibid., p. 258.

12. John P. Davis to Henry Wallace, 23 Apr. 1934; White to Wallace, 21 Feb. 1935, Agriculture Department Records.

13. NAACP Press Release, 1 July 1934; Resolutions of the 25th (1934), 26th (1935), and 27th (1936) Annual Conferences of the NAACP, NAACP Files (Library of Congress).

14. White to Franklin D. Roosevelt, Telegram, 18 Feb. 1935, OF 2538, Roosevelt Papers (Franklin D. Roosevelt Library).

15. John P. Davis, Speech to the 25th (1934) Annual Conference of the NAACP, NAACP Files.

16. Resolutions of the 25th (1934) Annual Conference of the NAACP, NAACP Files.

17. Wolters, *Negroes and the Great Depression*, pp. 58–60; Myrdal, *American Dilemma*, pp. 253, 257; Louis Cantor, *A Prologue to the Protest Movement: The Missouri Sharecropper Roadside Demonstration of 1939* (Durham, N.C., 1969), pp. 42–43.

18. Richard Sterner, *The Negro's Share* (New York, 1943), pp. 295–309.

19. For Alexander's career, see Wilma Dykeman and James Stokeley, *Seeds of Southern Change: The Life of Will Alexander* (Chicago, 1962). For a full discussion of "The Negro in the New Deal Resettlement Program," see Donald Holley's article in *Agricultural History* 45 (1971): 179–93.

20. Rexford G. Tugwell to Fred Hildrebrandt, 4 Aug. 1933; Tugwell to W. F. Reden, 7 July 1933; Wallace to Hildrebrandt, 28 Aug. 1933, Agriculture Department Records.

21. U.S. Cong., House, *Congressional Record*, 75th Cong., 1st sess., 1937, 81, pt. 6:6438.

22. Paul K. Conkin, *Tomorrow a New World: The New Deal Community Program* (Ithaca, N.Y., 1959), p. 200.

23. Wolters, *Negroes and the Great Depression*, p. 77n.

24. Sidney Baldwin, *Poverty and Politics: The Rise and Decline of the Farm Security Administration* (Chapel Hill, N.C., 1968), pp. 193–294, and especially pp. 217 and 255.

25. Bernard Sternsher, ed., *The Negro in Depression and War: Prelude to Revolution, 1930–1945* (Chicago, 1969), pp. 46–47.

26. Allan Morrison, "The Secret Papers of FDR," *Negro Digest* 9 (1951): 9; Walter White, "Roosevelt and the Negro," typescript, no date, NAACP Files.

27. Frank Freidel, *F. D. R. and the South* (Baton Rouge, La., 1965) p. 36.

28. Roy Wilkins to Oscar Chapman, 21 May 1934, NAACP Files.

29. Jerold Auerbach, "New Deal, Old Deal, or Raw Deal: Some Thoughts on New Left Historiography," *Journal of Southern History* 35 (1969): 21–22. A few New Deal officials could not accept these priorities, but they were either isolated or, as in the famous purge of 1935, forced to resign from the agricultural administrations.

30. For an extended analysis of the rationale behind the New Deal's industrial recovery program, see Ellis W. Hawley, *The New Deal and the Problem of Monopoly* (Princeton, N.J., 1966), pp. 3–146.

31. Arthur M. Schlesinger, Jr., *The Coming of the New Deal* (Boston, 1959), p. 131; Charles L. Dearing and Associates, *The ABC of the NRA* (Washington, 1934), p. 32n.

32. Gardiner Means, "The Consumer and the New Deal," *Annals of the American Academy of Political and Social Science* 173 (1934): 11.

33. U.S., *Statutes at Large*, 48, pt. 1: 195.

34. *Opportunity* 11 (1933): 199.

35. Robert C. Weaver, "A Wage Differential Based on Race," *Crisis* 41 (1934): 238.

36. *Pittsburgh Courier*, 30 Sept. 1933.

37. Wolters, *Negroes and the Great Depression*, pp. 98–113.

38. Ibid., pp. 124–35.

39. John P. Davis, Speech to the 25th (1934) Annual Conference of the NAACP, NAACP Files; Allan A. Banks, Jr., "Wage Differentials and the Negro Under the NRA," (M.A. thesis, Howard University, 1938). For example, in the fertilizer industry, where 90 percent of the workers were black, seventeen states were classified as southern and given wage rates 40 percent below those elsewhere in the country; yet in cotton textiles, where very few Negroes were covered by the codes, only eleven states were classified as southern and the wage rate was only 8 percent below that paid outside of the South. Evidence such as this convinced Roy Wilkins that the differentials, "while not labeled on the basis of color, have nevertheless operated almost exclusively on that basis." Roy Wilkins to Oscar Chapman, 21 May 1934, NAACP Files.

40. Samuel I. Rosenman, ed., *The Public Papers and Addresses of Franklin D. Roosevelt,* 13 vols. (New York, 1938–50), 2:251.

41. Joel Berrall to R. L. Houston, Memorandum, 10 Sept. 1934, Records of the National Recovery Administration, R.G. 9 (National Archives).

42. Arthur F. Raper, *Preface to Peasantry* (Chapel Hill, N.C., 1934), p. 241.

43. Herbert Northrup, *The Negro in the Tobacco Industry* (Philadelphia, 1970), pp. 26–29.

44. *Norfolk Journal and Guide*, 12 Aug. 1933.

45. Minutes of the 18 Sept. 1933 meeting of the Special Industrial Recovery Board, as published in the *Chicago Defender*, 23 Dec. 1933.

46. Horace R. Cayton and George S. Mitchell, *Black Workers and the New Unions* (Chapel Hill, N.C., 1939), p. 102n.

47. Wolters, *Negroes and the Great Depression*, pp. 135–48; William Pickens, "NRA—'Negro Removal Act'?", *World Tomorrow* 16 (1933): 539–40.

48. Resolutions of the 25th (1934) Annual Conference of the NAACP, NAACP Files.

49. T. Arnold Hill, "The Plight of the Negro Industrial Worker," *Journal of Negro Education* 5 (1936): 40.

50. Wolters, *Negroes and Great Depression*, pp. 193–203.

51. Ickes, Message to the 26th (1935) Annual Conference of the NAACP, NAACP Files.

52. Harold Ickes to George McGill, 13 Nov. 1934, Records of the Department of Interior, R.G.48 (National Archives): Sterner, *The Negro's Share*, p. 319.

53. Sterner, *The Negro's Share*, p. 319. Unfortunately, two other New Deal housing agencies—the Home Owners' Loan Corporation and the Federal Housing Administration—encouraged segregation. Organized on the basis of ordinary business principles and consequently concerned with protecting real estate values, the HOLC and the FHA prohibited all influences that were thought to endanger property values. Although the FHA *Manual* was careful not to refer to Negroes as an adverse influence, the discussion of natural physical protection contained the statement that "protection from adverse influences . . . includes prevention of the infiltration of business and industrial uses, lower class occupancy, and inharmonious racial groups." It recommended a number of deed restrictions, including "g. Prohibition of the occupancy of properties except by the race for which they are intended." FHA, *Underwriting Manual* (Washington, 1938), pp. 932, 935, 980.

54. William Pickens to White, Memorandum, 21 Sept. 1936; Wilkins to Charles West, 18 May 1936; Wilkins to Chapman, 21 May 1934, NAACP Files.

55. Ickes, Message to the 26th (1935) Annual Conference of the NAACP, NAACP Files.

56. Wilkins to Harry Hopkins, 30 Nov. 1934, Records of the Works Progress Administration, R.G. 69 (National Archives).

57. Robert C. Weaver, "An Experiment in Negro Labor," *Opportunity* 14 (1936): 298.

58. Robert C. Weaver, *Negro Labor: A National Problem* (New York, 1946), pp. 12–13.

59. For a discussion of the Negro policies of the FERA, see Sterner, *The Negro's Share*, pp. 218–38.

60. Alfred E. Smith, "New Deal Gives Negro Square Deal," in *WPA and the Negro*, 1937 pamphlet, Department of the Interior Records; Ralph J. Bunche, "The Political Status of the Negro," typescript, Carnegie-Myrdal Manuscripts (135th Street Branch, New York Public Library), pp. 1393–98.

61. Federal Emergency Relief Administration, *Unemployment Relief Census*, 1933, report 2.

62. Sterner, *The Negro's Share*, pp. 239–53.

63. Raper, *Preface to Peasantry*, p. 260.

64. John P. Davis, "Report of the Executive Secretary," 1 June 1935, typescript, Records of the Department of Labor, R.G. 183 (National Archives).

65. White to Roosevelt, Telegram, 21 May 1935, NAACP Files; "U.S. Adopts the Georgia Plan," *Crisis* 42 (1935): 17.

66. *Norfolk Journal and Guide*, 6 May 1933.

67. *Chicago Defender*, 16 Feb. 1935.

68. National Urban League, "The Negro Working People and National Recovery," typescript, 4 Jan. 1937; St. Louis Branch of the Urban League, "Report on Local Labor Conditions, 1934," typescript, NAACP Files; *Opportunity* 14 (1936): 316.

69. Mary White Ovington to Wilkins, 6 Mar. 1934, NAACP Files; Aubrey Williams to Hopkins, 30 Nov. 1934, WPA Records.

70. Rayford W. Logan, "The Negro and the National Recovery Program," *Sphinx*, March 1934, p. 10.

71. Donald Hughes Grubbs, "Tenant Farmers and the Second Reconstruction," paper presented to the Southern Historical Association, November 1971, pp. 9–10.

72. W. Frank Persons to John de la Perriere, Memorandum of Telephone Conversation, 19 May 1933; Persons to Frances Perkins, 1 June 1933, Records of the Civilian Conservation Corps, R.G. 35 (National Archives).

73. John A. Salmond, "The Civilian Conservation Corps and the Negro," *Journal of American History* 42 (1965): 75–88.

74. Philip La Follette to Robert Fechner, 19 Dec. 1938, CCC Records.

75. President Roosevelt was undoubtedly embarrassed by this racist refusal to appoint Negroes to administrative positions in the CCC, and he issued an executive order revoking Fechner's ban. Yet a de facto prohibition remained in effect, and the president evidently decided it would not be politically expedient to make a major issue of this point.

76. Luther C. Wandall, "A Negro in the CCC," *Crisis* 42 (1935): 254.

77. Salmond, "The Civilian Conservation Corps and the Negro," p. 88.

78. Allen F. Kifer, "The Negro Under the New Deal" (Ph.D. diss., University of Wisconsin, 1961), pp. 261–69.

79. Mrs. Bethune, as quoted by Kifer, "The Negro Under the New Deal," p. 133.

80. Kifer, "The Negro Under the New Deal," pp. 127–28.

81. Ibid., pp. 82–83.

82. George Edmund Haynes, "Lily-White Social Security," *Crisis* 42 (1935): 85–86.

83. "Statement of Charles H. Houston," prepared for Hearing of the Senate Finance Committee, 74th Cong., 1st sess., typescript, 9 Feb. 1935, NAACP Files.

84. "Social Security—for White Folks," *Crisis* 42 (1935): 80.

85. *Norfolk Journal and Guide*, 9 Feb. 1935.

86. Abraham Epstein, "The Social Security Act," *Crisis* 42 (1935): 333–34, 338, 347.

87. William E. Leuchtenburg, *Franklin D. Roosevelt and the New Deal, 1932–1940* (New York, 1963), p. 132.

88. Wilkins to White, Memorandum, 2 Feb. 1935, NAACP Files; T. Arnold Hill, "A Statement of Opinion on H.R. 2827 (Lundeen Bill)," 1935 typescript in Urban League Files (Library of Congress).

89. "Statement of Charles H. Houston."

90. Frank G. Davis, "The Effects of the Social Security Act upon the Status of the Negro" (Ph.D. diss., State University of Iowa, 1938), passim.

91. Howard Zinn, ed., *New Deal Thought* (Indianapolis, 1966), pp. xvi-xvii.

92. Schlesinger, *Coming of the New Deal*, p. 327.

93. John P. Davis and Charles H. Houston, "TVA: Lily-White Reconstruction," *Crisis* 41 (1934): 290.

94. Schlesinger, *Coming of the New Deal*, p. 334.

95. Leuchtenburg, *Franklin D. Roosevelt and the New Deal*, p. 165.

96. Walter White, Foreword to John P. Davis, "The Negro and TVA," typescript, 1935, NAACP Files.

97. Davis, "The Negro and TVA," p. 16.

98. Thurgood Marshall, Memorandum for Press Release, 11 Aug. 1938, NAACP Files.

99. Charles H. Houston, "Abstract of Proposed Testimony before Joint Congressional Investigating Committee," typescript, August 1938, p. 5, NAACP Files; Testimony of Charles H. Houston, U.S. Cong., Joint Committee of the Investigation of the Tennessee Valley Authority, Hearings pursuant to Public Resolution No. 83, 75th Cong., 3d sess., 1935, pt. 6, pp. 2347–90.

100. Robert C. Weaver to Arthur E. Morgan, 12 Feb. 1935, NAACP Files.

101. *Knoxville News-Sentinel*, 31 Aug. 1938.

102. Houston, "Abstract of Proposed Testimony," p. 7.

103. Charles H. Houston, Memorandum for the Files, 25 Aug. 1938, NAACP Files.

104. Davis and Houston, "TVA: Lily-White Reconstruction," pp. 290–91; 311; Davis, "The Negro and TVA," passim; Thurgood Marshall to Sylvia R. Frank, 10 Oct. 1938; Weaver to Morgan, 12 Nov. 1935, NAACP Files.

105. U.S. Cong., Joint Committee on the Investigation of the Tennessee Valley Authority, *Report pursuant to Public Resolution No. 83*, 76th Cong., 1st sess., Sen. Doc. 56, pt. 1, pp. 56–58.

106. John P. Davis, "The Plight of the Negro in the Tennessee Valley," *Crisis* 42 (1935): 315.

107. Houston, "Abstract of Proposed Testimony," p. 6.

108. White, Forword to Davis, "The Negro and TVA."

109. *Knoxville News-Sentinel*, 31 Aug. 1938.

110. Freidel, *F. D. R. and the South*, pp. 71–102.

111. Walter White, "Roosevelt and the Negro," typescript, n.d., NAACP Files.

112. Tamara Hareven, *Eleanor Roosevelt: An American Conscience* (Chicago, 1968), p. 123.

113. Walter White, *A Man Called White: The Autobiography of Walter White* (New York, 1948), p. 169–70.

114. White to Roosevelt, 6 May 1935, OF6-Q, Roosevelt Papers; *Norfolk Journal and Guide*, 2 Mar. 1935.

115. Wolters, *Negroes and the Great Depression*, pp. 302–52, 365–66.

116. Roy Wilkins, interview in the Columbia University Oral History Project, pp. 98–99.

117. On this point, see the public opinion survey in *Fortune* 18 (July 1938): 37.

118. Paul K. Conkin, *The New Deal* (New York, 1967), p. 75.

119. Dorothy Thompson, column, *New York Herald Tribune*, 11 Aug. 1936. The relation between the Roosevelt vote and the percentage of Negroes on relief was positive but not close. In Chicago, for example, about 60 percent of the black population was on relief, but Roosevelt's share of the vote was 24 percent in 1932, 49 percent in 1936, and 53 percent in 1940. Obviously, then, at least 10 percent of the Negroes on relief were voting Republican; and Harold F. Gosnell of the University of Chicago, perhaps the most eminent black political scientist of the 1930s, was "inclined to the view that a much larger proportion of the Negroes on relief actually voted Republican." One of Gosnell's able graduate students, Elmer Henderson, calculated that "about 16 percent of the variation in the Negro vote as between census tracts could be explained by variations in the ratios of those on relief." See Gosnell, "The Negro Vote in Northern Cities," *National Municipal Review* 30 (1941): 264–67, 278; and Henderson, "A Study of the Basic Factors Involved in the Change in the Party Alignment of Negroes in Chicago, 1932–1938" (M.A. thesis, University of Chicago, 1939).

120. White, *A Man Called White*, pp. 102–19. Richard B. Sherman has written a thorough account of black voters and the Republican party: *The Republican Party and Black America from McKinley to Hoover* (Charlottesville, Va., 1973).

121. *Chicago Defender*, 9 Dec. 1933.

122. Richard L. Watson, Jr., "The Defeat of Judge Parker: A Study in Pressure Groups and Politics," *Mississippi Valley Historical Review* 50 (1963): 213–34.

123. White to W. J. Rice, 29 Sept. 1932, NAACP Files.

124. *Norfolk Journal and Guide*, 22 Oct. 1932.

125. W. E. B. Du Bois, "Mr. Hoover and the South," *Crisis* 36 (1929): 131–32; Du Bois, "Mr. Hoover and the Negro," *Crisis* 38 (1931): 207–8.

126. Du Bois, "Mr. Hoover and the Negro," pp. 207–8; *New York Times*, 23 May 1932.

127. *Chicago Defender*, 11, 25 June 1932.

128. On Guffey, see Joseph Alsop and Robert Kintner, "The Guffey: Biography of a Boss, New Style," *Saturday Evening Post*, 26 Mar. 1938, pp. 5–7, 98–102. On Vann, see James H. Brewer, "Robert Lee Vann, Democrat or Republican: An Advocate of Loose Leaf Politics," *Negro History Bulletin* 21 (1958): 100–103.

129. On Negro voting in Philadelphia and Pittsburgh, see James Erroll Miller, "The Negro in Pennsylvania Politics with Special Reference to Philadelphia since 1932" (Ph.D. diss., University of Pennsylvania, 1945); Ruth Louise Simmons, "The Negro in Recent Pittsburgh Politics" (M.A. thesis, University of Pittsburgh, 1945); and James E. Allen, "The Negro and the 1940 Presidential Election" (M.A. thesis, Howard University, 1943), appendices 7 and 8.

130. For New York, see Earl Brown, "The Negro Vote," *Opportunity* 6 (1936): 302–4; and John Albert Morsell, "The Political Behavior of Negroes in New York City" (Ph.D. diss., Columbia University, 1951).

131. Among the many good studies of Negro politics in Chicago, see especially the works of Harold F. Gosnell and Elmer Henderson cited in note 119 above, as well as Gosnell, *Negro Politicians: The Rise of Negro Politics in Chicago* (Chicago, 1935); St. Clair Drake and Horace R. Cayton, *Black Metropolis* (New York, 1945), chap. 13; and Rita Werner Gordon, "The Change in the Political Alignment of Chicago's Negroes during the New Deal," *Journal of American History* 56 (1969): 584–603.

132. For the situation in Des Moines, see James Braddie Morris, Jr., "Voting Behavior in Four Negro Precincts in Iowa since 1924" (M.A. thesis, State University of Iowa, 1946).

133. For St. Louis, see Howard Fisher, "The Negro in St. Louis Politics, 1932–1940" (M.A. thesis, St. Louis University, 1951).

134. Samuel Lubell has written a brief but perceptive general account of the impact of the "Roosevelt revolution" on black voters, *White and Black: Test of a Nation* (New York, 1964), chap. 4.

135. On this point, see V.O. Key's seminal article, "A Theory of Critical Elections," *Journal of Politics* 17 (1955): 3–18.

136. The migration of Negroes from the rural South to the urban North also led to an erosion of parental control and family stability. This increasing family disorganization was reflected, as is well known, in higher rates of desertion, divorce, illegitimacy, and juvenile delinquency, and also in a growing political independence as young blacks were socialized outside the old (Republican) family traditions. On this point, see E. Franklin Frazier, *The Negro Family in the United States* (Chicago, 1939); and Henderson, "A Study of the Basic Factors," p. 47.

137. See, for example, Angus Campbell, Philip E. Converse, Warren E. Miller, and Donald E. Stokes, *The American Voter* (New York, 1960), especially pp. 120–67.

138. Morsell, "The Political Behavior of Negroes in New York City," pp. 53–61, 74.

139. Leslie H. Fishel, Jr., "The Negro in the New Deal Era," *Wisconsin Magazine of History* 48 (1964–65): 111.

140. *Chicago Defender*, 15 Oct. 1932.

141. White to Roosevelt, 28 Sept. 1932, PPF 1336, Roosevelt Papers; White, letter to editor, *New York Times*, 23 May 1932; *Chicago Defender*, 10 Sept. 1933.

142. White to Eleanor Roosevelt, 20 Oct. 1936, PPF 96, Roosevelt Papers; Freidel, *F. D. R. and the South*, p. 64.

143. *Chicago Defender*, 3 Sept., 5 Nov. 1932; *Norfolk Journal and Guide*, 5 Nov. 1932.

144. *Baltimore Afro-American*, 22 Oct. 1932.

145. Charles H. Martin, "Negro Leaders, the Republican Party, and the Election of 1932," *Phylon* 32 (1971): 85–93.

146. W. E. B. Du Bois, "Roosevelt," *Crisis* 41 (1934): 20.

147. *Norfolk Journal and Guide*, 28 Apr. 1934.

148. There are two good master's theses that tell the story of the New Deal's Negro advisers: William J. Davis, "The Role of the Adviser on Negro Affairs and the Racial Specialists in National Administration" (M.A. thesis, Howard University, 1940), and Jane Motz, "The Black Cabinet: Negroes in the Administration of Franklin D. Roosevelt" (M.A. thesis, University of Delaware, 1964).

149. Conkin, *Tomorrow a New World*, p. 200.

150. White, *A Man Called White*, pp. 166–70.

151. Hareven, *Eleanor Roosevelt*, p. 118.

152. Hareven, *Eleanor Roosevelt*, p. 119; Harold L. Ickes, *The Secret Diary of Harold L. Ickes: The Inside Struggle* (New York, 1954), pp. 612–15.

153. Roy Wilkins, interview in the Columbia University Oral History Project, pp. 51–52.

154. *Pittsburgh Courier*, 17 Nov. 1962. Joseph P. Lash has written a detailed account of Eleanor Roosevelt's relations with Negroes, *Eleanor and Franklin* (New York, 1971), pp. 512–35.

155. *New York Times,* 1 Aug. 1936; "Campaigning for the Negro Vote," *Newsweek,* 12 Sept. 1936, 18–19.

156. *New York Times*, 22 June 1936.

157. Miller, "The Negro in Pennsylvania Politics," pp. 243–44, 201; Allen, "The Negro and the 1940 Presidential Election," pp. 67, 70–72.

158. Rosenman, ed., *The Public Papers and Addresses of Franklin D. Roosevelt*, 5:537–39.

159. It seems to me that Barton Bernstein has made this error in his generally scintillating essay, "The New Deal: The Conservative Achievements of Liberal Reform," in Bernstein, ed., *Towards a New Past: Dissenting Essays in American History* (New York, 1968), p. 281.

160. *Baltimore Afro-American*, 7 Nov. 1936; Ralph D. Casey, "Republican Propaganda in the 1936 Campaign," *Public Opinion Quarterly* 1 (April 1937): 27–44.

161. *New York Times*, 7 Aug. 1936; William N. Jones, "Day by Day," *Baltimore Afro-American*, 24 Oct. 1936.

162. *New York Times*, 6 Oct. 1936; *Baltimore Afro-American*, 10 Oct. 1936.

163. Newell D. Eason, "Attitudes of Negro Families on Relief," *Opportunity* 13 (1935): 367–69, 379.

164. Lillian P. Davis, "Relief and the Sharecropper," *Survey Graphic* 25 (Jan. 1936): 22.

165. *Baltimore Afro-American*, 24 Oct. 1936.

166. *Pittsburgh Courier*, 11 Jan. 1936.

John A. Salmond

Aubrey Williams: Atypical New Dealer?

ONCE, WHILE ON A TOUR OF SOUTHERN STATES, AUBREY WILLIS Williams, then executive director of the National Youth Administration, stopped in Birmingham, Alabama, to talk to NYA project workers at a luncheon arranged in his honor. During the morning, he found that only white enrollees had been invited. He immediately told the Alabama state director, John Bryan, that unless Negroes were allowed to participate as well, he would simply refuse to appear. Bryan agreed, with obvious reluctance, to this demand.

But there was more to come. When Williams entered the hall where the luncheon was to be served,

> I saw Negroes standing at the sides and at the rear of the room. I looked to see if any were seated, but none were, and so I said to John, "John, God Damn it, you are determined to mistreat these Negro Youth. Well, you won't do it while I am here. You have tables brought in here and chairs for these Negroes to sit down and eat." Flushed and sweating, poor, big, six foot six and handsome John said, "They have already eaten." I said, "O! they have already eaten, nevertheless you have tables and chairs put in here for them and serve them, just as though they had not eaten and don't serve anybody until they are seated."

Tables duly arrived, the blacks were seated, and Williams gave his address.[1]

This incident reveals something of the impulsive, forceful, and uncompromising style of Aubrey Willis Williams. It is also a statement of his social concerns. Williams was a radical, he wanted a just and decent America, and he wanted it quickly. Yet he was not, as were so many of those whose ideas he shared, a critic of the Roosevelt administration. Instead, he remained within it because of his particular perception of its purposes. He believed in the social direction of the New Deal, and he believed in the social vision of President Franklin D. Roosevelt. His public life, therefore, provides yet another window through which this complex, multifaceted movement can be viewed.

Aubrey Williams's Washington career almost exactly spanned the New Deal era. He came to the capital only a few weeks after Roosevelt's first inaugural, and he left public office permanently in 1945, just days before the president's death. Never one of the president's "inner circle," this lean, rough-hewn, passionate southern social democrat, was nonetheless a public figure of considerable importance. Primarily this was because of the successive offices he held, but also because his close friendship with Mrs. Roosevelt gave him a pipeline to the White House that, at certain times, enabled him to wield an influence larger than his official position would suggest. Moreover, his bluntness, his outspoken identification with the poor, the weak, and the dispossessed, his unconcealed contempt for those who would equivocate in the face of human suffering, his impatience with "politics" and its practitioners made him always a center of controversy.

Few New Dealers caused conservatives more sustained anguish. To the reactionary Republican, Hamilton Fish, who represented the president's home district of Dutchess County, New York, Williams was "one of the most radical men in the country . . . one of the pinkest of this pink New Deal administration." The aging, irascible Democratic Senator Kenneth D. McKellar of Tennessee, by the 1940s one of the Senate's most influential members, claimed privately that this "wilful, suave, easy, generous oily" man "not only disbelieves in the divinity of Christ, but he disbelieves in the American form of government," and publicly that he had turned agencies under his control over to Communist fronts.[2] Representative Eugene Cox, a Georgia Democrat, was once so offended by something Williams said that he attempted to have his salary stopped by legislative action. Only a hastily arranged personal appearance before the Democratic House Caucus Committee put things right.[3] Indeed, few New Deal officials suffered so consistently as did Williams from right-wing snipers.

Yet, for every virulent detractor, there was an equally passionate defender. Harry Hopkins called him in 1939 "a very great man"; Eleanor Roosevelt said in 1945 that he was "above all . . . a citizen of democracy"; a friend, the liberal publisher Louis Weiss, referred to him as "a symbol of decency, a symbol of democracy."[4] Henry Wallace, somewhat obscurely, once stated publicly that William "understands the very heart of the Christian message as very few people in the United States understand that message . . . pushing for that ultimate balance that centers around the concept of the Fatherhood of God and the brotherhood of man."[5] With less emphasis on the infinite, Senate Majority Leader Alban Barkley of Kentucky, on the same occasion, declared that Williams personified "the finest efforts of human society to achieve equality of opportunity for all men at a time when concentration of power in the hands of the few has caused the most destructive war in history."[6] Democratic Senator Scott Lucas of Illinois, by no means a committed liberal, once told a hostile Senate committee, "If you could convict this man of anything, it would be that he is a humanitarian."[7] Williams, clearly, was not the sort of person people were neutral about.

Aubrey Williams was born, as he put it, "sometime between darkness and daylight," on 23 August 1890, in Springville, northern Alabama, the third in a family of seven. His father had been ruined economically and broken in spirit by the Civil War. Born to relative luxury on a plantation that was lost in the conflict, he "never got over the feeling of having the roots cut from under him and being adrift in the world," drank heavily, and wandered. Much later, Williams remembered his childhood "as one of living in many places and many houses, moving around, looking for a cheaper place to live."[8]

The family moved to Birmingham when Aubrey was five years old, and shortly thereafter he began to work full time, first in a laundry, then in a department store. Indeed, the amount of formal schooling he had until he was 21 was minimal—eighteen months, he later calculated—but family and friends kept the desire to learn alive. In 1911, he was able to enroll in a Tennessee mountain school, Maryville College, with vague thoughts of the Presbyterian ministry in his head, financing his education through loans and a succession of jobs from sign-painting to managing a summer Chautauqua. In 1916, he transferred to the University of Cincinnati, but remained only a few months before going abroad with the YMCA to work in the European battlefields. There he found he could not stay out of what he believed was a climactic struggle between good and evil. In 1917, therefore, he joined the French Foreign Legion, and in 1918, transferred to the American First Division, where he soon gained a commission.

After the war, taking advantage of a French government offer, Williams remained in Europe to study. He enrolled at the Sorbonne, then took a degree from the University of Bordeaux, before returning to Cincinnati to compete the requirements for a degree in social work. He married, moved to Madison, Wisconsin, in 1922, as executive director of the Wisconsin Conference of Social Work, and remained there for ten years, teaching part time at the University of Wisconsin as well. In 1932, at the height of the depression, he went to Chicago to work for the American Public Welfare Association. His first task was to organize the distribution of Reconstruction Finance Corporation–loaned relief money in the state of Mississippi. Working virtually on his own, he set up a statewide organization there; and later in that year, with the help of Colonel Lawrence Westbrook, a former Texas congressman and an expert in rural rehabilitation, he repeated the operation in Texas. On both occasions, his aid had been specifically requested by the governors; and on both occasions, he insisted that work relief would be the method of operation.[9] It was this activity that brought Williams to Harry Hopkins's notice. In fact, so impressed was the newly appointed FERA director, that he brought Williams into the organization in its first hectic days of May 1933. The New Deal phase of Williams's life had begun.

Williams's original task within the FERA organization was southwestern field representative, directing operations in Oklahoma, Texas, Arkansas, Louisiana, Mississippi, and Alabama.[10] But he was to remain there only a few months before Hopkins, as he (Williams) put it, told him to "get someone else to take over those states of yours, and stay here in Washington." He came reluctantly, intending to remain for a few months only. Instead, he stayed till 1943.[11]

Williams brought with him to Washington a conviction developed during his years in Wisconsin, and sharpened in Mississippi and Texas, that unemployment relief should involve work, not what he was later to describe as "the penny-pinching, pantry-searching system of direct relief payments"—the demoralizing, dehumanizing dole.[12] Placed in charge of the Division of Relations with the States, he immediately became the FERA's most outspoken advocate of a completely federally financed and administered work program, as opposed to the current policy of working through state organizations, providing them with matching or direct grants but permitting them wide latitude in deciding how funds should be distributed. The times were propitious. Hopkins himself was thinking along similar lines. Moreover, it was clear by late 1933 that something had to be done in a hurry to get the unemployed through the winter, and that existing programs were not up to the task. In October, therefore, Hopkins placed before the president a proposal to create immediately a massive, federally administered works program, lasting at least until the spring of 1934. It was accepted, and Williams was selected to organize and administer what was to become known as the Civil Works Administration.

The task was a daunting one. Millions of people had to be put to work in the shortest possible time. Administrators were needed, thousands of projects had to be developed, a whole line organization had to be created. Yet it worked. By the time it was terminated in 1934, this makeshift program, thrown together in a few frenetic days, had employed more than four million people. Not all the tasks they did were useful, there was inefficiency, there was "boondoggling"; yet, given the circumstances of its creation, it is its accomplishments, not its failures, that are the more impressive.[13] Moreover, the CWA did give some indication of what might be accomplished through a properly planned, federally administered work relief scheme. For Williams, it simply reinforced his conviction that it was in this direction that the federal government ought to move.

By early 1934, the mutual respect between Williams and Hopkins had ripened into a firm and lasting friendship. In January, Williams became deputy administrator of the FERA. He was also placed directly in charge of a program that had considerable future implications, FERA's college work scheme. Late in 1933, largely as a result of entreaties from a number of college presidents who had journeyed to Washington bearing alarming figures about dwindling enrollments, reduced alumni giving, financial privations, and student despair, a pilot program was set up at the University of Minnesota. Students who could prove need were given FERA grants in return for work. The program became national early in 1934, and more than 10,000 students were eventually aided in this way.[14] Williams, whose own formal education had been somewhat limited because of lack of funds, was enormously sympathetic to the scheme, though dissatisified with the narrowness of its scope. Yet it can properly be regarded as a prologue to the National Youth Administration.

It was during these early months that Williams first met Mrs. Roosevelt, who was eventually to be at various times his White House lobbyist, his publicist, his champion, and always his friend. His first experience of her was at a meeting she had called to discuss the problems of transients; there he was completely taken with her firmness and dignity, particularly the way she handled an intemperate personal attack by the redoubtable Cissy Patterson, the publisher of the *Washington Herald*. He told her so, and soon after was invited to dinner. Before long, he was receiving notes from her, usually requesting him to look into various relief-related problems, often involving blacks or young people. By late 1934, she was calling him by his first name, and their informal partnership was well established.[15]

The example of the CWA was not allowed to fade. Pressure for a fully federally financed and controlled work program built up steadily during 1934. Hopkins talked several times to FDR about it, and an FERA task force, including Williams and Corrington Gill, another Hopkins deputy, drew up various blueprints. The sweeping New Deal victory in 1934 clinched the decision. The Thanksgiving Day newspapers broke the story. The FERA was to be wound up and replaced by a new federally controlled work relief program. The cost was to be nine billion dollars.[16] The figures were not correct, though the intent had been accurately perceived. Roosevelt, in January 1935, asked Congress for the massive sum of $4.8 billion dollars for relief, the bulk of which was to be spent putting people to work. The long Senate debate, then the feud between Harold Ickes and Hopkins over dispostion of the money, held things up for a while, but Hopkins eventually emerged victorious, head of the Works Progress Administration, and with the bulk of the billions to spend on work relief.

Given Williams's commitment to a federal work relief scheme, his position within FERA, and his friendship with Hopkins, it is scarcely surprising that he was offered the position of deputy WPA administrator. What is surprising, however, is that he nearly did not accept it. As early as his Wisconsin days, he had shown genuine concern with a specific aspect of the economic situation, the particular plight of unemployed young people. His directorship of FERA's college work program had simply served to exacerbate this anxiety. He saw no reason that only those at universities and colleges should receive government aid, nor did he consider the CCC, already one of the most popular New Deal agencies, an adequate answer to the problem. From mid-1934, increasingly, he thought about, held conferences on, drew up plans for, a much more thorough-going, civilian-directed youth agency. He was not alone in his concern. John Lang of the American Student Federation, Katherine Lenroot of the Labor Department's Children's Bureau, and John Studebaker, commissioner of education all produced and made public in late 1934 or early 1935 proposals for a youth agency.[17] But it was Williams's idea that Hopkins liked, and it was Williams's blueprint that Mrs. Roosevelt, at Hopkins's request, took to the president. Finally, it was Williams's document on which the National Youth Administration, with its continuation of student aid, but its far wider aim of providing work experience for out-of-school youth as well, was based. The NYA was created on 26 June 1935 by executive order. It was to be virtually autonomous division of the WPA, and Williams was named its executive director in addition to his WPA post. But it was not envisaged that he could hold both jobs for long, and when Hopkins asked him which one he wanted, he chose the NYA. A date was set for him to wind up his WPA affairs, but at the last minute, Hopkins had second thoughts. In a cab on the way to the Chicago railway station he spoke his mind.

> "We don't have much time to talk," Williams recalled him as saying, "but I want you to come back as Deputy Administrator, you can keep the N.Y.A., but get an assistant to handle the details—I'm going back to Washington today. I'd like you to come back tonight if you can."[18]

And this was the way it worked out. Until he left the WPA for good in late 1938, Williams had comparatively little time to spend on NYA affairs; in effect, a succession of deputy directors ran the agency. The bulk of his energy went to the WPA, and there is nothing to suggest that he was unhappy with this arrangement.

Williams's function within the WPA organization was to superintend its day-to-day operations, leaving Hopkins free to concentrate on larger policy matters. It was he who made most of the public announcements, he who dealt with patronage and with congressional protests, he who had to mollify the various delegations of the unemployed. Moreover, from late 1936 on, Hopkins was increasingly away from his desk, as first his wife's, then his own, health deteriorated. After his successful operation and lengthy recuperation, the WPA administrator seemed to tire of his agency. In 1938, with his mind possibly on a presidential bid, heavily involved in the mid-term election campaign, and more and more adopting the role of general White House adviser, he was disinclined to bother too much about the program.[19] For this reason, Williams had far more independence and importance than his position would normally have allowed him. From mid-1937, he ran the WPA for his chief.

He became a public figure, giving speeches, holding news conferences, making statements, being quoted. Soon he had acquired an unenviable reputation as a man who spoke from the hip, so much so that *Time*, admittedly no New Deal mouthpiece, which in 1935 had described him as "a tall, gentle, tweedy, eminently useful citizen," by 1939 was referring to him as "foot-in-mouth Aubrey."[20] Williams never learned to curb his tongue. He sounded off. He attacked Congress and congressmen, he proselytized, he propagandized. Virtually incapable of making a set speech, he preferred thinking aloud, whether his audience were NYA state directors, WPA administrators, Negro educators—or a congressional delegation.

Two such statements of belief, in fact, cost him his position at the WPA. Late in June 1938, he was visited by a delegation from the Workers Alliance seeking an increase in WPA wage rates. This was a CIO-affiliated union of WPA workers, which was eventually to become totally controlled by the Communists. At this time, however, non-Communist elements in the leadership, particularly the president, ex-Socialist David Lasser, were grimly hanging on. Williams, who knew this, and who greatly admired Lasser, wanted desperately to give him some crumb of hope on the wage rate issue. Suggesting that the best approach was to elect a Congress in November sympathetic to the unemployed, he declared,

> We've got to stick together. We've got to keep our friends in power. . . . I don't need to tell you. You know your friends very well. Just judge the folk who come and ask for your support by the crowd they run with.[21]

He could hardly have chosen a more inappropriate time, or body, to deliver himself of this homiletic. Politics in the WPA was a very big issue indeed, mainly because of a series of newspaper articles alleging serious malfeasance and vote-buying in the Kentucky Democratic primary. In fact a committee chaired by Senator Morris Sheppard of Texas had just been constituted to investigate these and other charges against the WPA. This committee termed Williams's action "unfortunate," but declined to recommend further action against him. The press and public were not so tolerant. Indeed, Williams later conceded that he had been more criticized for that speech than for anything else he had ever said.[22]

Conservatives, of course, had a field day. For them, the speech confirmed what they had been saying all along, that the WPA was nothing more than a gigantic slush fund, with no more noble a purpose than to rally to the aid of New Deal radicals at the polls. The use of federal funds for partisan purposes was "shocking to the public conscience," spluttered the *Chicago Tribune*, declaring that Williams was "acting in an un-Christian and un-American manner."[23] One of the hundreds of individuals who wrote attacking him for the speech asserted,

> Your astounding speech yesterday leaves no conclusion in the mind of the writer but that this present New Deal administration is composed of the most unscrupulous crooks ever gathered under one banner.[24]

Liberals, on the other hand were dismayed, not so much by the sentiments expressed as by their timing. The New Dealish *St. Louis Post-Dispatch* considered it a bad tactical blunder, and private correspondents expressed similar sentiments.[25] Though the White House said nothing about these remarks—after all, the president was saying much the same thing as he went about his "purge" of 1938—it cost Williams dearly on Capitol Hill, where he was already out of favor because of his uncompromising opposition to political interference with his agencies. Indeed, the speech was still being raised against him seven years later.[26]

Hardly had the dust raised by this incident settled than Williams was in the news again. In November 1938, with Mrs. Roosevelt, he attended the inaugural meeting in Birmingham, Alabama, of the Southern Conference for Human Welfare. There they caused much consternation among the local police by sitting in the Negro half of the auditorium, and there Williams was reported as having told the assembled gathering that he believed "class warfare does a lot of good." Both Mrs. Roosevelt and he claimed later that he had been seriously misreported, but the damage had been done. The House Committee on Un-American Activities was just beginning its investigations, and its chairman, Texas Democratic Martin Dies, never one to miss an opportunity, declared publicly that the remark was simply added evidence that Red subversion had penetrated into the highest of public places. Again, the conservative press excoriated him, Hopkins criticized him bitterly in private, and the hapless Williams prepared to resign. The president would have none of it, however, and sent him off to Florida instead to investigate a charge against the state WPA of malfeasance by a number of its officials.[27]

Nevertheless, the speeches and the attendant publicity hurt him badly. When it was rumored that Hopkins was to be moved to the Commerce Department, Williams frankly presumed that he would be chosen to lead the WPA. But this did not happen. As Williams recalled it, "The President told me in simple honest words. 'I can't appoint you to succeed Harry, the situation on the Hill is such that I can't do it.' " Rather, he was to become head of an expanded and independent NYA. The publicity he had received in 1938, at a time when the WPA was under serious attack from the right, made it imperative that he be removed. Instead of the volatile, committed Williams, the safe, moderate Army engineer, Colonel F. C. Harrington, became the new relief boss.

Williams was bitterly disappointed, but philosophical about it. He recognized that the president had had no choice but to dump him. To a friend who wrote in commiseration, he replied that though "the associations I had formed and the opportunity to do things for great masses of people has been broken up and lost and probably will never return, I only have one regret and that is that I didn't handle this thing so that I wasn't unhorsed." Besides, "the President is still here, Mrs. Roosevelt is still here . . . and fundamentally, Hopkins is still here because his influence will still dominate the whole program . . . of that I am more and more sure."[29] Moreover, there was still the NYA, in a real sense his brainchild, but one he had little time to involve himself with in recent years. Now he would have the opportunity to make up for his neglect.

After a rather confused, slow beginning, due at least in part to Williams's inability to concentrate fully on the tasks of organization because of his WPA duties, the NYA had by 1939 established a solid, if little publicized, record.[30] Its college and high school aid programs virtually ran themselves. In return for a set amount of work per week, students were to receive sufficient money to bridge the gap between their own resources and their expenses. The program for out-of-school youth was harder to get off the ground. It began as little more than a junior CWA; the youths were placed on jobs with a high labor, low capital outlay content, constructing recreation areas, developing parks, and so on, with little element of training involved.

This approach, however, was never particularly popular with the agency. By late 1936, it was being discarded, replaced by the idea that the NYA should train people as well as provide them with relief. Keeping costs down was important but not at the expense of rendering the work experience vocationally useless. NYA enrollees should learn while on the job—"learning by doing" became its slogan.[31]

Moreover, by 1937, those who ran the NYA had realized that not all the unemployed young people lived in cities, and that the type of group project viable in urban areas had to be modified to suit rural requirements. So they began to set up hundreds of resident centers, to which enrollees from the surrounding counties could come. At first, these were usually established on the campuses of agricultural colleges, the youths being instructed in farm methods or home economics while helping out with the college chores; but it was not long before a more eclectic approach was devised, with the training program being derived as much from the needs of the surrounding community as from the home farm. Thus, for example, the young men at the Conway, Arkansas, resident center were trained in cabinet-making, forestry, carpentry, soil erosion control, sheet metal work, and auto mechanics, as well as in practical farming. The girls received instruction in child care, stenography, and librarianship, and everyone attended specially devised English, mathematics, and citizenship classes. The result was a widening of horizons, a broadening of employment opportunities.[32]

This was the agency's stage of development when Williams moved into it full time. It was a going and growing concern, full of ideas, solidly democratic in organization, decentralized in operation. The NYA had never been a tightly controlled agency. Williams had always believed that it could succeed only if local project supervisors were given the widest possible latitude in developing community-oriented work schemes. The NYA national office should, he believed, do little more than set broad policy guidelines, leaving state and local officials to fill in the details. Furthermore, he was insistent that an advisory council of local citizens be set up in each area where there was an NYA project, to work with the local director. By doing this, he hoped, the NYA would not seem like just another federally run program, but would take on the lineaments of a cooperative endeavor.[33]

Williams had no wish to alter these administrative arrangements now that he was able to spend all his time on NYA affairs, but he did want to change the agency's focus slightly. As early as 1938, a series of conferences had been held to discuss the potential need for an increased supply of skilled industrial workers should defense production rise as a result of events in Europe and Asia. Williams, realizing that the hopelessly moribund apprentice system could meet only a small part of the need, saw a chance for the NYA to fill the gap. It could become, he thought, an apprenticeship substitute, training young people in the use of machines, familiarizing them with shop techniques, and then turning them over to individual plants for more specialized instruction.[34]

Overcoming objections within the agency to these ideas, and with the full cooperation of the president, the secretary of war, and others involved in national defense, Williams quietly began acquiring machinery —scouring army surplus stores, old industrial plants, even junk yards —anything that could be refurbished and used as a training tool was pressed into service.[35] By mid-1940, when a general defense program was announced, the conversion of the NYA to a defense-oriented agency was well under way. Throughout 1941, its nondefense functions were progressively shed, and by 1942 it was solely involved in the war effort, introducing young people to machines, giving them basic shop training, then pouring thousands of them weekly into the shipyards, the aircraft factories, and the industrial plants of the nation. The NYA took boys and girls from the New York streets, the Kentucky hills, the Mississippi riverlands, and trained them, fed them, looked after their health, transported them to areas of labor shortage, and acclimatized them, before letting them go. It showed no prejudice against black enrollees. Alone of all the defense agencies, it made a particular effort to comb rural areas. It pulled people from isolated pockets into the industrial mainstream who otherwise would never have gotten there. It became a crucial adjunct to the defense effort.

But the NYA had made many enemies along the way. Institutionalized education, epitomized by the National Education Association, fearful of federal intrusion into its domain, had been uneasy about NYA from the start. Yet, as long as its function was seen as mainly one of relief, coexistence was possible. Once the NYA moved into the industrial train-ing area, however, the atmosphere changed. From 1940 on, the NEA, with its executive secretary, Willard E. Givens, leading the assault, aided overtly by the American Vocational Association and tacitly by Commis-sioner of Education John W. Studebaker, a bitter foe of Williams, attacked the agency continuously, often scurrilously. They charged inefficiency and duplication of function. Most serious of all, they insisted that it was but the thin end of the dreaded wedge of a federally controlled system of education.[36]

These forces found useful allies in Congress, especially within the Joint Committee for the Reduction of Non-Essential Federal Expenditures, set up in late 1941 as a gesture to the powerful conservative coalition in Congress. The chairman of this committee was Senator Harry F. Byrd of Virginia, and Senator Kenneth D. McKellar was one of its most prominent members. Both of these senators, as well as being fiscal conservatives out of sympathy with much of the New Deal's achievements, were men whom Williams had offended deeply by resisting their many demands over WPA patronage matters. It was scarcely surprising, therefore, that in 1942 and 1943, the committee recommended the NYA's abolition.[37]

Williams fought back as strongly as he could, aided by the rank and file of educationalists, by such congressional stalwarts as Senator Harry S Truman of Missouri and Representative John W. McCormack of Mas-sachusetts, and by individuals who saw the NYA's contribution to the war effort as crucial. But, especially after the Republican gains in the 1942 congressional elections, the cry for economy was too strong to be resisted, and the NEA propaganda too effective to be overcome. The NYA was abolished in July 1943, and shortly after, for the first time since 1933, Williams found himself out of public life.[38]

President Roosevelt offered to find him another government job immediately, but Williams, disillusioned by the events of the past months, and feeling the need to speak his mind more freely on public issues, declined.[39] Instead, he became director of organization for the National Farmers' Union, in the South at least, a declining organization of small farmers that George Tindall has aptly described as "carrying the Populist spirit into the twentieth century." Its president, James Patton, a member of the NYA's Advisory Committee, was a close personal friend of Williams, and prevailed upon him not only to accept a job with the NFU but, in 1944, to tour the South, living with tenant farmers, sharecroppers, and the like, in an attempt to form a CIO-type union of the dispossessed, building up from the grass-roots.[40] Williams was later to describe this time with the NFU as a "dismal period," and his efforts at organization "futile"; and, indeed, the brightest spot for him in 1944 seemed to have been the election campaign, when he was able to link up his efforts with the CIO's Political Action Committee, working very hard for FDR among poor southern farmers.[41] This work forced him to concentrate again solely on the problems of his native region. He was bitter about the legacy of one-party rule and racist politics, but he believed he did discern signs of change, the stirrings of a more liberal spirit. In a series of articles in Farmers' Union papers and similar journals, he spelled out this intuition:

> There seems to be a bottom-deep awakening, a breaking up of the thick shell that has for decades covered the South; a stirring, or to use a good Southern term of 50 years ago, a refreshing. . . . An unmistakable assertion of decency, and a turning on people who live by exploiting hatred, religious bigotry, by trading in people's prejudices and fears, is happening in the South today more than anywhere else in the Nation.[42]

These were bold articles, angry articles, challenging articles, the sort he had been unable to write during his years in government. They earned him plaudits among those liberals who saw them, but they were bound to be used against him should he ever return to public life. The chance to do so came sooner than he could possibly have imagined. Harry Slattery, the combative head of the Rural Electrification Administration, was finally forced out of office toward the end of 1944; and the president, despite the strongest objections of his secretary of agriculture, Claude R. Wickard, decided that Williams was the man to take his place. "He knows the country," he wrote Wickard in justification, "far better than almost anybody else. But," he added, "I do not know if he could be confirmed by the Senate or not."[43] Still, he felt disposed to try. On 22 January 1945, FDR sent Williams's name in nomination to the Senate. The final phase of Williams's public career had begun.[44]

Actually, Williams's nomination was at first almost ignored, because at the same time as he sent it to the Senate, Roosevelt had also requested that it confirm former Vice-President Henry Wallace as secretary of commerce. This provoked a bitter, bruising fight, as ideologically divisive as any in the New Deal era. Many liberals saw in Wallace the best hope for a New Deal future. Conservatives on the other hand feared that his nomination was a stark symbol of Roosevelt's intention to hew to a pronouncedly leftward course once peace had been won, and they determined to prevent his confirmation. Not until the smoke of this particular battle had cleared away was the Williams nomination even looked at, and then commentators predicted a similar struggle.[45]

They were proved correct. The Senate Agricultural Committee voted against confirmation after subjecting Williams to a shamefully conducted hearing in which his old WPA speeches, especially "keep your friends in power," were raked up again, his supposedly leftist leanings flaunted, and even his religious beliefs called into question. His enemies had, indeed, grown more powerful. Senator McKellar outdid himself in loutish manners, execrable taste, and complete disregard of facts. He alleged that Williams was an atheist, a financial incompetent, and a member of the Communist party. But the most damaging charge against the nominee was that of being an integrationist, and the Farmers' Union articles provided all the necessary evidence. These cost him crucial southern support.[46] Indeed, Senator Lister Hill's opinion was that more than anything else his opinions on race cost him the position. Certainly, there was no more dramatic moment in the whole REA hearing than when Williams, quiet and dignified, faced down a baiting by the Senate's prime racist, Mississippi's spluttering Theodore Bilbo. There he defended his various actions in support of social and economic justice for black Americans, advocated the complete desegregation of all public facilities in the District of Columbia, refused to retract a word of his Farmers' Union articles, and conceded his commitment to

the principle of doing away with discrimination in getting a job, I do not believe a person should be denied employment because of a man's race, creed or color. I hold that the sole basis of giving or refusing employment should be whether a man is able to do the work which he is to be hired to do . . . if he is discriminated against because he happens to be a Negro, then I think the Federal Government has the responsibility of stopping that kind of treatment of a man just because of his color. I think if we have in the country what we call a democracy, then there should be no discrimination against people on the basis of their religion, or their color; that it should be a man's ability to perform a certain piece of work that should govern.[47]

This stand earned Williams many plaudits in the liberal press. T.R.B., in the *New Republic*, said he had "never looked finer" in his long and honorable career.[48] Without doubt, however, it cost him the key committee votes of Senator John Bankhead—"This is too much, Mr. Williams," he expostulated to him privately, "I am withdrawing my promise to support your appointment"—Senator Richard Russell, and probably Bilbo as well. Bilbo, who had supported Henry Wallace in the earlier fight, claimed, at least, that he had been for Williams until the race issue became so important. Moreover, the outcry from the South was such that other relatively liberal senators—Arkansas's young J. William Fulbright was one such—deemed it politic to renege on earlier promises of support before the appointment came to a vote on the Senate floor.[49] There were so many issues involved—anger over Wallace's nomination, a desire to hit back at the Political Action Committee with whom Williams had been connected in the recent campaign, dislike of Williams's economic philosophy—that it cannot be discerned with any certainty just how decisive the racial issue was. Yet, it is arguable that, at the least, Williams's refusal to compromise turned the fight from a neck-and-neck affair into one where the other side had all the advantages. Again, as with his dismissal from the WPA in 1938, his outspoken identification with the underdog had cost him his position.

Back to the National Farmers' Union he went, but not for long. Soon he was home in his native Alabama. Marshall Field, the liberal publisher of the *Chicago Daily News* and New York's *P.M.*, helped him to acquire the *Southern Farm and Home*. He turned this innocuous, moribund magazine into a genuinely liberal voice in the maelstrom of postwar southern change. Increasingly, his liberalism focussed primarily on the race issue. He supported the 1954 Supreme Court decision in *Southern Farm and Home*. He was closely involved in the organization of the Montgomery bus boycott, which made Martin Luther King a national figure; he formed and ran a company to build low-cost, decent housing for Montgomery's blacks; he became an expert in civil rights litigation.

Williams suffered for this commitment. *Southern Farm and Home* lost circulation, advertising, and capital. Senator James Eastland's Internal Security Committee harried him so irritatingly that he was eventually forced to call on his old friend and NYA colleague Senate Majority Leader Lyndon B. Johnson in order to have Eastland called off—a favor he detested asking. After the bus boycott, Williams was virtually forced out of white society in Montgomery. "We lived as pariahs, alone", he later wrote, "except for a few brave white souls and those few Negroes who accepted us as equals and made us part of their home life and their day to day living".[50]

Late in the decade, lonely and racked by cancer, he and his wife returned to live in Washington, where he died early in 1965. The career of the self-styled "Southern rebel" had run its course.[51]

This outline of Aubrey Williams's public life tells us something about the man himself. His concerns, his successes, his failures, his friends, his enemies, all give us some insight into the quality of his mind, some understanding of what he valued, some indication of the attitudes and beliefs he brought to public life. Far more valuable, though, are his own words. At the end of his life, knowing he was dying, and desperately feeling the desire "to put something down in writing," Williams tried to explain what it was that "made me tick," that fed his continuing passion "to make life better, more just, to help make people more considerate of people, kinder, and more regardful of others." He did not get very far with it. A few fragmentary pages of personal statement are all that remain, but they are sufficient to show that this gaunt, compassionate, decent man, far from deriving his political impulses from the Marxist doctrines he was so often accused of promulgating, developed them from fundamentally American sources, sources he shared for the most part with those who criticized him so severely.

In the first place, there was Jesus. Williams was no Christian in the institutional sense; he hated most churches, and he rejected many doctrinal tenets. "I was never able to swallow this immaculate conception doctrine," he once wrote.

I had a feeling Mary, this is sacrereligious [sic] I know might have strayed into the woods when Joseph was working, many good women have. I thought of Jesus as a good pure Man "that so loved the world," but this business being the son of God I had trouble with from the start.

Immortal or not, Jesus was always for Williams the shining example to follow, "the greatest moralist" there had ever been.

Following close behind, however, was Jefferson. Of all Americans, past or present, whose example was worth emulating, who laid down the clearest, "guidelines for doing the right thing, the just thing, the fair thing," Williams put Jefferson at the very top. Indeed, he scarcely saw the need to spell out in detail what he owed to Jefferson. As a southerner, a liberal, and a defender of the "common man," his debt was too obvious to require extended comment.

Perhaps less usual for a southerner was his intense feeling for Lincoln—"A deathless heritage to all who shall fight for freedom." Williams was often compared to Lincoln physically, something he considered to be vaguely irreverent, for Lincoln had been his "ideal since childhood." Once Jonathan Mitchell of the *New Republic* wrote an article on Williams in which Aubrey's compassionate concern for the underdog was explicitly compared to Lincoln's. Thanking him, Williams wrote:

> Curiously he [Lincoln] always represented the Presidency of the United States. I do not think I ever felt that anyone else really occupied the White House, and also somewhat curiously I always feel that no matter who is there, Lincoln is always there. Others seem to me to have departed, but he still remains.[52]

Williams believed that these three men made him what he was. Yet, of course, there were many other influences that shaped him and gave direction to his social attitudes. One, obviously, was his region, the South. He was in many ways a product of the southern populist–progressive tradition, and nowhere is this more closely demonstrated than in his economic thought. Williams kept with him forever the southern populist-*cum*-Wilsonian distrust of great wealth, especially corporate wealth. There are echoes of this strain in most of his writings, and in many of his speeches, much that is redolent of the New Freedom—and of William Jennings Bryan. "I believe in free enterprise," he wrote in 1945,

> but I really mean free enterprise. I do not mean monopolistic enterprise that goes under the name of free enterprise. I believe that cartels and monopolies unless they are controlled and are broken up will lead to one of two things. They will lead either to communism or to syndicatism [*sic*] and I believe they constitute the greatest threat to private enterprise that we have today.[53]

When he came to Washington, few things disturbed him more than that men like Jesse Jones—"just about as crooked as a snake" and "about as sympathetic to the aims and purposes of the New Deal as a dog is to a cat that has just given him a bloody eye"—men who symbolized the worst aspects of corporate America, could wield so much economic power. His conviction that FDR tolerated such men solely for political reasons only partially mollified him.[54]

Williams came to Washington, despite his period in Wisconsin, more familiar with rural America than with cities, still fairly southern in his political attitudes. Indeed, he wrote much later, it was not until the New Deal years that he even fully realized the enormity of his region's mal-treatment of black Americans.[55] Change came quickly. Exposure to the views of friends like Hopkins, John L. Lewis, Representative John McCormack, Senator Robert Wagner of New York, David Lasser, the nature of his tasks in the WPA and the NYA, the opportunity to work at the national level, together added new dimensions to his responses. Soon, "more New Deal than the President,"[56] he was talking on a whole new range of problems, from public housing to public health. He became particularly involved with the young CIO wing of the organized labor movement, convinced that big labor was a necessary counterweight in an industrial society to big business, and certain that unions would form a crucial component of any lasting liberal political coalition. He once told his NYA state directors that

> this is a great hour and the people that are on our side are the people that make up such things as the World Youth Congress, that make up the Workers Alliance, that make up the C.I.O., they are the people that are fighting our fight.[57]

Indeed, Williams continually sought ways of strengthening the links be-tween the NYA and the CIO. John L. Lewis was a valued friend; his parting of the ways with Roosevelt in 1940 was a particularly bitter blow to Aubrey. Williams was closely involved with the CIO's Political Action Committee in 1944, and evidence of industrial labor's feeling for him can be easily gauged from a survey of the hundreds of telegrams of support he received from CIO locals during the 1945 confirmation fight.[58] Always retaining his particular sympathy with, and understanding of, the problems of his region, and eventually returning to them full time, Williams nevertheless became during the New Deal years a figure whose concerns were genuinely national.

Though others undoubtedly helped him gain perspective in the complex-ities of national problems, no one did more to sustain his commitment to the New Deal than President and Mrs. Roosevelt. Williams had not voted for FDR in 1932, preferring Socialist Norman Thomas, but he soon developed for him both great affection and an awe verging on the religious.

"I really rather worship that man," he once wrote. "He was just about what I wished I was . . . what a truly great and good man he was."[59] The two men disagreed often on specifics; Williams found the president particularly insensitive on the race issue, for example, and was often astounded and appalled by some of FDR's more unusual suggestions for relief projects—cutting and stacking all the grass along railway lines and a proposal to set up a national scheme of field kitchens that would dispense a "wholesome stew" daily to all who needed it were two particularly bizarre examples. Moreover, in the last resort, Williams always admitted that his first loyalty was to the unemployed, rather than to his president.[60] Yet he never lost his faith in FDR; he never seems to have doubted for a minute that they shared the same social goals, had the same dream of what America could become. Even at the crisis periods of his own life, this faith never wavered. In the painful interview preceding Williams's departure from the WPA, he told Roosevelt that he understood why he was being passed over, apologized for his indiscretions, and pledged continued and total loyalty. He believed that the 1944 election campaign was the clarion call for a renewed and widened New Deal offensive, something his appointment as REA administrator seemed, to him, to confirm. FDR, he thought, forced to work with reactionary forces during the war, had decided to break free as peace approached. Williams had been given the job, he believed, because the president wanted someone who shared his convictions, someone who would not compromise one iota with reactionary southern political leaders.[61] For Williams, unlike some other New Deal liberals, Roosevelt never lost his charisma.

Williams had total devotion, too, for Mrs. Roosevelt. Years later, in describing his "great love for her," he confessed to once feeling intense anger on seeing Bernard Baruch kissing her in friendship, because he believed him to be "a scoundrel, and unworthy of her affection." It is difficult to exaggerate the importance of this relationship. From 1935 on, the two worked as a team, reinforcing each other's resolve, pursuing basically the same egalitarian goals, interested in the same areas of concern—neglect and injustice, blacks, young people, the unemployed generally. Mrs. Roosevelt's influence on the development of the NYA was profound. When money was hard to get, she became a ceaseless lobbyist in the White House. Indeed, the president often referred to the NYA as belonging to "the other side of the house," and confessed that sometimes he agreed to an increase in an appropriation, or a change in regulations, simply to prevent the needs of the NYA from dominating yet another dinner conversation.[62]

It was to Mrs. Roosevelt that Williams turned for advice before making a decision he later described as "the thing I am most ashamed of in my life." This was when in the last days of the NYA's existence he agreed to drop all Japanese-Americans from the agency's rolls, thus unilaterally abrogating an agreement he had made with the War Relocation Authority to train a specific number of these youths. Congressional pressure was very strong. The NYA was fighting for its life, and enough congressmen had told him that unless the Japanese-Americans were removed they would not lift a finger to help the agency. Aubrey realized that to refuse this request was to consent to the Youth Administration's death-warrant. Yet, it went against the grain so much to make the concession that it was not until Mrs. Roosevelt joined the ranks of those urging him to do the expedient thing for once in his life that he signed the "shameful" order.[63] At the dinner held in Williams's honor by the National Farmers' Union after his rejection by the Senate in 1945, it was she who was the principal speaker. There she reasserted her faith in democracy—and in Williams.[64] Williams, for his part, continued to admire her, and to be influenced by her, till the day she died. Indeed, he believed the fact that she continued as a beloved public figure even after FDR's death to be "some grounds for hope for a better world."[65]

The South, Jesus, Jefferson, Lincoln, the Roosevelts, these were what helped shape Williams. Southern poverty instilled in him a sense of need, and great public figures gave him a sense of higher possibilities. Together they formed his driving dream, a dream so startling to some Americans that they engineered his permanent departure from public life in 1945. Yet, when its outlines are examined, no radical doctrines emerge. Predictably, given such essentially American sources of inspiration, Aubrey Williams's dream was a variation on very familiar themes indeed. Perhaps he gave it clearest articulation in those tortured weeks following March 1945, when he lost first a job he had long hungered for and then his president. In a long, often moving document, written for his files, he tried to set down an explanation of, and a justification for, his political beliefs, because "these beliefs and attitudes have been the subjects of a debate in our highest legislative body." Williams's document revealed that he believed in free enterprise, but with equal opportunity for all—no monopolies or gigantic corporations. He believed in strong labor unions. He believed in public housing, public health, and free public education, because "there are certain things that the government can do better than private industry can do." He believed in the right of all Americans to earn their own living and the duty of the government to provide for those unable to do so. He believed that the New Deal had, basically, been traversing the correct paths, if not as fast or as far as was necessary. He also believed, however, that the momentum it had engendered could not be checked, that "a new day" was dawning, and the "wider distribution of opportunity" would be a fact of postwar American life. Williams was obviously a social democrat and, in the context of his times, a radical, yet his radicalism clearly took well-worn paths. He was very much in the reformist mainstream, simply wanting to push his country closer to what he thought was its wellspring. He believed implicitly in an "American Dream" and saw as its fulfillment not something derived from revolutionary ideology but "a more far-reaching and more fundamental New Deal." Williams, despite the powerful emotions he aroused, really went no further to the left than a fully developed, essentially American, welfare state.[66]

One further aspect of his public career needs to be considered, his special concern for, and involvement with, the aspirations of black Americans. No New Deal official became more closely associated than he with the accelerating struggle for Negro rights, something the NAACP certainly recognized when it threw all its resources behind the fight to have him confirmed in 1945.[67] His most conspicuous activity in the race relations area took place within the NYA's framework. Very soon after its creation, Williams assured a conference of Negro leaders that "there would be absolutely no discrimination" within the NYA and as far as was humanly possible he kept his word.[68] In fact, he used the NYA as a means of altering traditional racial relationships, risking its popularity with southern politicians in so doing. Black Americans were enrolled, as far as could be managed, according to need, not in proportion to their relationship to the total population, as was the case with the CCC. A fund was created specifically to aid Negro college students. In 1936, a special Negro Division was created within the national office and placed under the directorship of the redoubtable Mary McLeod Bethune, a prominent Negro educator and a personal friend of Mrs. Roosevelt's. Williams insisted that all state directors form similar divisions in their state offices, that they be staffed by blacks, and that they be housed in the same office blocks as the general NYA quarters. Similarly with the committees set up on national, state, and local levels to advise NYA officials—these, too, were to have black members.[69] Not all state directors were happy with this sort of pressure, but they complied. At every meeting with his state staffs, Williams demanded an accounting of activities among Negroes, and those who showed less than total enthusiasm for the drive for equal treatment usually found themselves publicly rebuked and possibly threatened with dismissal.[70] In 1938, while opening a Negro youth center in Birmingham, Alabama, he said,

> I made up my mind long ago to use my power to help those at the bottom of the social and economic ladder in America. I have and will continue to play that part. I don't care who knows it. I want it. . . . I want to say as a Southerner I covenant that the black man shall have his share in that better life.[71]

Aubrey Williams tried hard to keep that covenant. Of course, it was not easy to do so. In the South, kicking as he was against that region's most fiercely held traditions, prejudices, and hatreds, he often had to apply the most drastic pressure in order to make the point. There was, for example, the incident in Birmingham, described at the beginning of this paper. He was told privately that this action had cost him the governorship of Alabama, which may or may not have been true. In any case, it clearly was not the sort of gesture to endear him politically. After a similar occurrence in Oklahoma, when he insisted that a resident center be integrated immediately, NYA staffers tore pictures of him to pieces, and Senator Josh Lee called for his immediate dismissal.[72]

Undoubtedly, some NYA officials always discriminated against blacks despite all Williams's pressures; yet it is indisputable that, of all the New Deal agencies, it had the best record in the area of racial justice. Certainly black Americans thought so. As the *Chicago Sunday Bee* once said

> No Federal agencies have been fairer to colored Americans than the N.Y.A.; none as tolerant. It is the N.Y.A. that has distinguished itself by placing Negroes in policy-making positions. The ideas and thoughts of Negroes were sought and used in building the N.Y.A. program from the bottom up. . . . The N.Y.A. is ahead of all the Federal agencies in working toward the full integration of colored people in the defense program and in American democracy. . . . Aubrey Williams has been to N.Y.A. what the Prince of Denmark has been to Shakespeare's Hamlet—he gave it life, substance and direction.[73]

Williams's concern for fair treatment for Negroes had implications far outside the NYA, however. In 1937 and 1939, he used his agency to sponsor conferences attended by blacks from all over the country where all facets of the Negro situation were probed, the first such meetings on Negro affairs ever called under federal aegis.[74] His friendship with the NAACP's Walter H. White, A. Philip Randolph of the Brotherhood of Sleeping Car Porters, and other Negro leaders meant that he was often able to act as a trouble-shooter in situations involving blacks. In 1939, he was called in to help deal with the sharecroppers' roadside demonstrations in the Missouri boot-heel district, for example, and was the man FDR sent to talk Randolph and White out of their protest march on Washington in 1941 when blacks were being excluded from defense industry employment—action that prompted "Pa" Watson's often-related outburst, "Hell, Williams will join them."[75]

Indeed, the whole chain of circumstances leading to the creation of the Fair Employment Practices Commission in 1941 stemmed largely from Williams's inability to place NYA-trained blacks in defense industries. Mrs. Roosevelt shared his anger at this, and the two of them organized a conference to which all federal officials closely involved with the war production program were invited. From the discussion there, a consensus emerged that the only way to get members of minority groups hired in any substantial way was for the president to issue a strong executive order. Williams was closely involved in its drafting, and was in the room when it was signed. He regarded it, despite its very obvious weak spots, as an impressive step toward equality of economic opportunity, and as one of his greatest personal triumphs.[76]

Williams's passion for racial justice led him into charter membership in the Southern Conference for Human Welfare. This same passion helped shape his activities during his stint with the National Farmers' Union. As earlier noted, it probably prevented his confirmation as REA administrator in 1945, and gave direction to his life in Alabama thereafter. He wore few convictions lightly, none less so than this one.

When Aubrey Williams died, in March 1965, the *Washington Post*, eulogizing him, said that his "courage was wrapped in extraordinary gentleness. . . . In all that he did he was impelled by the same warm humanity and social concern. Of Aubrey Williams it could truly be said, above all else he loved his fellow man."[77]

This was probably as accurate an assessment of the meaning of this man's life as could be wished for. Williams *was* brave, he *was* gentle, he *was* possessed of enormous social concern. He hated poverty, injustice, and greed; he believed passionately in the possibilities of the American dream and strove mightily to narrow the gap between that dream and reality. He was a democrat, not a Marxist. Despite all the trials public life brought him, the disappointments and defeats, he never seemed to have lost his faith in "the people's will," with all the romantic notions that this implies, or seriously doubted that the system within which this will was expressed in the United States of America was redeemable. He was a social reformer, then, not a social revolutionary, despite all the allegations to the contrary.

Williams was not a first-rank New Deal figure. He was never an important presidential adviser like his friend Hopkins. His activities were confined fairly exclusively to the fields of welfare policy, youth matters, Negro affairs, and, eventually, preparedness. Yet his influence within these areas was without doubt far greater than has generally been allowed.

Moreover, in his public life, he represented a side of the New Deal that has been far too frequently ignored in recent discussions of the era. Much contemporary writing has concentrated on FDR's failures, on the New Deal's essential conservatism. New Left historians in particular tend to see the period more and more as some sort of gigantic capitalist plot, in which the energies of the federal government were used not to promote peaceful social change but to shore up decaying and outmoded institutions. Indeed, the domestic problems of the 1960s are seen as directly traceable to the failures of the 1930s. In this view, the lack of social vision, the eschewing of significant social reconstruction then, has made social revolution necessary now.[78]

Historians like Jerold Auerbach have rejected this interpretation on the grounds that it is both unhistorical and myopic—that it blames pre-1941 reformers for post-1941 policy failures, and looks at a part and calls it the whole.[79] The public life of a man like Aubrey Williams does reinforce this line of argument. Williams was a social reformer, and, in the context of the period, a fairly radical one. Yet he held important offices throughout the era. He was frustrated at times, true, yet never seemed to have felt permanent disillusionment; indeed, he was confident in 1945 that a revival and a widening of the New Deal was imminent. He retained that confidence till the end of his life. For him, the New Deal was not a liberal failure, the president never a brilliant improviser of shifting principles but a man with whom he shared a common social vision.

Perhaps he was wrong, permanently dazzled by the Roosevelt charm, one of Paul Conkin's "tragic figures," looking "back in nostalgia to what they had dreamed, and what they had all shared and what they had longed for," talking "of how Roosevelt had he lived, would at last have led them into the kingdom . . . they cried aloud for their old commander and for the old crusade."[80] Perhaps this faith was hopelessly misplaced, perhaps his sense of direction was awry. But perhaps not. There is far too much work yet to be done before Conkin's mordant judgment can safely be accepted. For Aubrey Williams was a distinctive New Deal type, and there were thousands like him, working in local NYA or Farm Security Administration offices, or on the the Federal Writers Project, or the WPA educational program, or in the REA or FHA, doing a host of disparate things, all thinking of themselves in some degree as being part of a sweeping social movement, people who saw themselves as the local agents of general social change and who believed implicitly in its value. People like the minor NYA official who once told Williams that "working for you and for the attainment and development of the ideals that you made a part of N.Y.A. has been the greatest experience of my life." Or like Charles Davis, manager of a North Carolina NYA project, whose weekly reports always included some reference to the great movement "of which we are all a part." Then there were the NYA employees who, in 1942, when funds were tight, used their own money to finance some agency activities, out of loyalty "to the [New Deal] program, to their jobs, and to this cause."[18]

We need to know more about these people and their influence before we can begin to judge the New Deal from anything like a panoramic vantage point. It is in this context that the public career of Aubrey Willis Williams takes on a general importance, both as a symbol of this strain, and as an indicator of new paths of inquiry.

1. Williams left two collections of papers, the Aubrey Williams Papers (henceforth cited as Williams Papers) in the Franklin D. Roosevelt Library, Hyde Park, New York, and an uncatalogued, discursive collection of reminiscences, jottings, and so on, presently held for Mrs. Williams by Professor Sheldon Hackney, of Princeton University. This second collection I have referred to throughout as Williams-Private Material, and this anecdote comes from a typescript dated 18 July 1963. I thank Mrs. Williams for granting me permission to use this second collection.

2. U.S. Congress, Senate, *Congressional Record*, 76th Cong., 3d sess., 1940, 87, pt. 3: 3445; Kenneth D. McKellar to Horace H. Hill, undated, Box 335, McKellar Papers (Memphis Public Library). See also *Nomination of Aubrey W. Williams. Hearings before the Committee of Agriculture and Forestry, United States Senate, 79th Cong., 1st sess. on the Nomination of Aubrey W. Williams to be Administrator, Rural Electrification Administration* (Washington, 1945), pp. 170–71 (henceforth cited as *Williams: Nomination Hearings*).

3. Typescript, "The Communist Front Label," Williams-Private Material.

4. *Time*, 23 Jan. 1939; transcript of a "Testimonial Dinner to Aubrey Williams," given by the National Farmers' Union, in Washington, on 28 Mar. 1945, p. 11, Box 335, McKellar Papers

(henceforth cited as "Testimonial Transcript"); Louis Weiss to Williams, 23 Feb. 1945, Box 27, Williams Papers.

5. "Testimonial Transcript," p.15.

6. Ibid., p. 2.

7. *Williams: Nomination Hearings*, p. 312.

8. Biographical Notes, Williams-Private Material. Factual biographical material on Williams's early life, unless indicated otherwise, is drawn from the following sources: Williams's own writings in the Williams Papers and the Williams-Private Material; material found in the Records of the National Youth Administration in the National Archives (henceforth cited as NYA Records); a long article by Ernest Lindley in the *Washington Post*, 26 Dec. 1938; and material found in the transcript of *Williams: Nomination Hearings*. Williams was married and had four sons.

9. Westbrook, an Army reserve officer, later became one of Hopkins's assistants in the FERA and the WPA, with special responsibility for rural rehabilitation work. Like his chief, he combined a taste for high living with a deep commitment to the unemployed. See Williams-Private Material; Searle F. Charles, *Minister of Relief: Harry Hopkins and the Depression* (Syracuse, 1963), p. 130; and Arthur M. Schlesinger, Jr., *The Coming of the New Deal* (Boston, 1959), p. 352.

10. He later wrote a highly entertaining account of his trials and tribulations in this period, particularly with Governor "Alfalfa" Bill Murray of Oklahoma. See "The New Deal—A Dead Battery," in "A Southern Rebel," Box 44, Williams Papers.

11. Numbered typescript, "Mrs. Roosevelt," p. 2, Williams-Private Material.

12. *New York Times*, 16 Feb. 1936.

13. There is no history of the CWA. A good outline can be found in Charles, *Minister of Relief*, pp. 44–66.

14. Ernest K. and Betty Lindley, *A New Deal for Youth: The Story of the National Youth Administration* (New York, 1938), pp. 11–12.

15. "Mrs. Roosevelt," pp. 1–3, Williams-Private Material. See also the correspondence between Mrs. Roosevelt and Williams in Box 4, Personal, Williams Papers.

16. Charles, *Minister of Relief*, pp. 94–103.

17. See the various draft proposals to be found in Box 13, Williams Papers. See also Franklin D. Roosevelt to Harry Hopkins, 28 May 1935, Box 13, Williams Papers; Williams to "Tulla," 7 May 1957, Box 32, Williams Papers; Eleanor Roosevelt, *This I Remember* (New York, 1949), pp. 162–63.

18. Unpaged, unheaded handwritten account of the creation of the NYA, Williams-Private Material.

19. Charles, *Minister of Relief*, p. 202.

20. *Time*, 8 July 1935, 30 Jan. 1939.

21. *St. Louis Post-Dispatch*, 27 June 1938; *Williams: Nomination Hearings*, pp. 46–57.

22. *Williams: Nomination Hearings*, pp. 46–47; *New York Times*, 3 July 1938.

23. *Chicago Tribune*, 1 July 1938.

24. C. S. Boothby to Williams, 28 June 1938, Box 3, Williams Papers.

25. *St. Louis Post-Dispatch*, 28 June 1938.

26. *Washington Post*, 26 Dec. 1938; *Williams: Nomination Hearings*, pp. 46–47; "The Communist Front Label," Williams-Private Material.

27. *Chicago Tribune*, 22, 24 Nov. 1938; "The Communist Front Label," Williams-Private Material; James R. Kearney, *Anna Eleanor Roosevelt, the Evolution of a Reformer* (Boston, 1968), p. 87.

28. "The Communist Front Label," Williams-Private Material.

29. Williams to Mrs. Edith Foster, 7 Jan. 1939, Box 13, Williams Papers.

30. Isaac Sutton to Charles W. Taussig, 31 Oct. 1935, Taussig Papers (Franklin D. Roosevelt Library). Taussig was chairman of the Advisory Council of the NYA, a body of prominent citizens created to help form the agency's policies.

38. *New York Times*, 3 July 1943; *Congressional Record* (Senate and House), 78th Cong., 1st sess., 1943, 89, pt. 5:5949–65, 6578–638, 6941–7085; Group 75, Box 12 (Letters from Industry), NYA Records.

39. Williams to John A. Lang, 1 Oct. 1943, Box 2, Williams Papers.

40. George B. Tindall, *The Emergence of the New South* (Baton Rouge, 1967), pp. 130–31, 428; Williams to James Patton, 5 July 1943, Box 3, Williams Papers.

41. See "The New Deal—A Dead Battery," p. 42; Williams to Franklin D. Roosevelt, 17 July 1944, PPF 8939; 6 Sept. 1944, OF 5394, Roosevelt Papers (Franklin D. Roosevelt Library).

42. *Williams: Nomination Hearings*, pp. 93–94.

43. Roosevelt to Claude R. Wickard, 28 Dec. 1944, OF 1570, Roosevelt Papers.

44. *Washington Post*, 23 Jan. 1945.

45. Ibid., 3 Feb. 1945.

46. *Williams: Nomination Hearings*, passim.

47. Ibid., pp. 317–19; transcript dated 7/15/63, Williams-Private Material.

48. Transcript dated 7/15/63, Williams-Private Material. See also *New Republic*, 5 Mar. 1945, p. 333.

49. *New Republic*, 2 Apr. 1945, p. 436; transcript dated 7/15/63, Williams-Private Material; Richard Russell to Williams, 21 Feb. 1945, Box 37, Williams Papers.

50. Tape 6, 7 July 1963, Williams-Private Material; *Time*, 21 Nov. 1949. See also "Southern Exposure" and "Bus Boycott" in "A Southern Rebel," Box 44, Williams Papers, and *Southern Conference Education Fund Inc. Hearings before the Sub-Committee to Investigate the Administration of the Internal Security Act and Other Internal Security Laws of the Committee on the Judiciary, United States Senate, 83rd Congress, Second Session, on Subversive Influences cn the Southern Conference Educational Fund Inc.*, 18, 19, 20 March 1954 (Washington, 1954).

51. *Washington Post*, 5 Mar. 1965.

52. Typescript, "At Present, 1963—," Williams-Private Material. See also the handwritten material on Mrs. Roosevelt, p. 73, and Williams to Jonathan Mitchell, 23 Jan. 1939, Box 2, Williams Papers.

53. Statement of personal belief, Box 37, Williams Papers.

54. "A Southern Rebel," p. 85.

55. Transcript dated 18 July, 1963, Williams-Private Material.

56. *Philadelphia Record*, 23 Dec. 1938.

57. Minutes of conference of state and regional directors of the NYA, 9–10 Sept. 1938, Group 38, NYA Records.

58. Williams to Elizabeth Wickenden, 12 Nov. 1940, Box 5, Williams Papers. For the messages of support from CIO locals, see Box 37, Williams Papers.

59. Unheaded manuscript, Williams-Private Material.

60. Undated, unheaded manuscript (probably written in 1963), ibid.

61. Transcript labeled tape 15, ibid.

62. Handwritten material on Mrs. Roosevelt, pp. 61–66, ibid. See also Williams to "Tulla."

63. Unpaged typescript, "Early Life," Williams-Private Material.

64. "Testimonial Transcript," pp. 6–11.

65. Handwritten material on Mrs. Roosevelt, p. 64, Williams-Private Material.

66. Typescripts of "Personal Statement" and "The South," Box 37, Williams Papers. See also "What is America," Box 42, ibid.

67. See Leslie Perry to Julian Steele, 2 Feb. 1945, Box 37, ibid.

68. Minutes of conference of Negro leaders, 8 Aug. 1935, Records of Office of Negro Affairs, Group 116 (File of Early "Inactive" Correspondence), NYA Records.

69. Final Report of the Division, 1943, passim, Records of Office of Negro Affairs, Group 118,

and Survey entitled "Comparative Employment of Races on N.Y.A.," Working and Data File, Box 9, Group 75, NYA Records.

70. Minutes of conference of state and regional directors, 9–10 Sept. 1938, pp. 1–9, Working and Data File, Box 8, Group 75, NYA Records.

71. Negro Division Newsletter, 1 Feb. 1938, Records of Office of Negro Affairs, Group 116 (File of Early "Inactive" Correspondence), NYA Records.

72. Typescript marked tape 6, Williams-Private Material.

73. *Chicago Sunday Bee*, 30 Nov. 1941.

74. Directors' File of Correspondence and Reports on Negro Conferences, 1935–41, Group 117, NYA Records.

75. Louis Cantor, *A Prologue to the Protest Movement: The Missouri Sharecropper Roadside Demonstration of 1939* (Durham, N.C., 1969), passim; long handwritten account, "Negro Affairs," Williams-Private Material. "Pa" Watson was F.D.R.'s personal aide.

76. "Negro Affairs," Williams-Private Material. See also Joseph P. Lash, *Eleanor Roosevelt: A Friend's Memoir*. (Garden City, 1964), pp. 214–19, and the file of letters and telegrams between Mrs. Roosevelt and Williams on the FEPC's creation in Williams Papers, Boxes 3 and 4.

77. *Washington Post*, 7 Mar. 1965.

78. See, for example, Barton J. Bernstein's article on the New Deal, "The New Deal: The Conservative Achievements of Liberal Reform," in Bernstein, ed., *Towards a New Past: Dissenting Essays in American History* (New York, 1968), and Paul K. Conkin's illuminating little book, *The New Deal* (New York, 1967). See also Staughton Lynd, "Again—Don't Tread on Me," *Newsweek*, 6 July 1970, pp. 30–32.

79. Jerold S. Auerbach, "New Deal, Old Deal, Raw Deal: Some Thoughts on New Left Historiography," *Journal of Southern History* 35 (February 1969).

80. Conkin, *The New Deal*, pp. 104–5.

81. Margaret Griffen to Williams, 6 July 1943, Box 12, Williams Papers; Project Managers Reports File, Box 1, Group 75; Robert S. Richey to Dillard B. Lasseter, 20 Aug. 1942, Deputy Administrator, N.Y.A.—Wartime Correspondence, Group 42, NYA Records.

Richard Polenberg

The Decline of the New Deal, 1937–1940

IN THE FALL OF 1938, LESS THAN TWO YEARS AFTER FRANKLIN Roosevelt's triumphant reelection, Walter Millis noted that the New Deal had "passed into a purely historical importance."[1] That Roosevelt's second term witnessed a sharp decline in New Deal fortunes is beyond dispute. What is less clear is the nature of that decline and the reasons it occurred. The waning of reform apparently involved three distinct but related phenomena: mounting hostility in Congress toward presidential proposals, as reflected in the defeat, watering-down, or repeal of key New Deal measures; declining public support, as measured by the success of conservative Democrats and Republicans in the 1938 elections; and a growing tendency of the president and members of his administration to devote more of their energies to national defense or foreign policy and less to social reform. If, as Millis believed, the New Deal was over, liberals may themselves have been partially responsible.

To say that Roosevelt faced a recalcitrant Congress in his second term is not to imply that he faced a tractable one in his first. Although Congress enacted a great many New Deal measures in 1935, it by no means followed meekly in the president's wake. In the case of the National Labor Relations Act, congressional pressure pushed Roosevelt further in the direction of supporting trade unions than he wished to go. More often Congress weakened New Deal proposals before adopting them. In June 1935, the House, with the backing of more than half of its Democratic members, refused to accept the important "death sentence" clause in the administration's Public Utilities Holding Company Act. The Senate Finance Committee substantially modified the undistributed profits tax in the Revenue Act of 1936. One official who had helped draft the measure considered the final bill "better than nothing, but not very much better."[2]

Yet these difficulties differed in kind and quality from those Roosevelt experienced after 1937. Where in 1935 congressmen had sometimes stood to Roosevelt's left, after 1937 they invariably stood to his right; and where once Congress had diluted New Deal measures, now it defeated them. This happened for many reasons. To some extent, congressional behavior reflected resentment at the steady enlargement of executive authority during the New Deal and a desire to reclaim legislative prerogatives. In part, the very size of the Democratic majorities—in 1937 the House contained 331 Democrats and 89 Republicans, the Senate 76 Democrats and 16 Republicans—encouraged factionalism and discord. Then, too, congressmen elected by large majorities tended to be less dependent upon party leaders, and less likely to follow them, than those chosen in close contests. In 1936, outside the South, 140 Democrats were elected from safe districts, compared with 110 in 1934; by contrast, only 77 Democrats came from marginal districts, compared with 95 two years before.[3]

Roosevelt's problems, however, stemmed not only from the composition of Congress, but also from what he was asking it to do. The president's plan to reform the Supreme Court and to reorganize the executive branch of government never enlisted the support of important interest groups, but instead divided the liberal coalition and exposed Roosevelt to the charge of seeking dictatorial power. Proposals to construct low-cost public housing and to regulate wages and hours appealed primarily to the northern, urban wing of the Democratic party. Southern and rural representatives, who balked at these measures, also fought savagely against civil rights legislation. Each of these measures fostered Democratic disunity.

Roosevelt unveiled his plan to "pack" the Supreme Court in February 1937. Asserting that the Court carried too heavy a burden of work, the president proposed to add an additional justice for each one who did not retire at age seventy. A maximum of six new positions could be created, and the Court would revert to a smaller size upon the death or retirement of an elderly justice. This proposal reflected Roosevelt's conviction that various members of the Court—particularly Willis Van Devanter, George Sutherland, James McReynolds, and Pierce Butler—were reading their own political prejudices into the Constitution and were thwarting the popular will under cloak of judicial impartiality. The president also considered the justices personally vindictive. In 1935, the Court had gone out of its way to chastise Roosevelt for dismissing William E. Humphrey, a reactionary member of the Federal Trade Commission, even though in so doing the president had followed an earlier Court ruling.[4] The Court had then gone on to wipe out crucial New Deal legislation and to adopt a perverse line of constitutional reasoning that jeopardized the Wagner Act and the Social Security Act, and made it doubtful that federal regulation of wages and hours, if approved by Congress, would be upheld.

Several justices appeared to be following William Howard Taft's admonition that "the only hope we have of keeping a consistent declaration of Constitutional law is for us to live as long as we can."[5] Willis Van Devanter, for example, who was born during the presidency of James Buchanan, had intended to retire from the Court after the election of 1932. But he considered Roosevelt "unfitted and unsafe for the Presidency" and remained on the bench in order "to sustain and to inspire others to hold fast to principles that safely guide." Van Devanter thought he knew how to cure the depression: "Do business along sane and safe lines. The situation cannot be remedied by legislative or governmental action." Harlan Fiske Stone later claimed that Van Devanter "conceived it his duty to declare unconstitutional any law which he particularly disliked." Van Devanter finally resigned in the midst of the Court controversy.[6] Franklin Roosevelt was the first president since James Monroe not to appoint a Supreme Court justice during his first term.

Opponents of the Court plan criticized the president for making an issue of the justices' ages when he really objected to their ideology, and in retrospect it appears that this tactic deeply offended liberals, including 80-year-old Justice Louis D. Brandeis. Yet if Roosevelt's emphasis was wrong, in seeking to enlarge the Court he chose one of the less radical courses available to him and the only one that seemed feasible. Many of his critics preferred constitutional amendments requiring a two-thirds vote of the Court in order to declare an act unconstitutional, permitting Congress to override Court decisions, or broadening the constitutional power to regulate the economy. These proposals, Roosevelt believed, suffered from a common fault: they could probably not be approved—and could certainly not be approved quickly enough—by three-fourths of the state legislatures, where intense pressure would be brought against them. In addition, each amendment might create more problems than it would solve: to demand a six-to-three vote by the Court would mean little because five members could persuade another to join them so as to protect the Court's prestige; to permit Congress to overturn rulings would politicalize the Court and bring judicial review to an end; to broaden constitutional powers would be useless if justices with an ice-age philosophy continued to interpret those powers. In Roosevelt's view, the Court, not the Constitution, needed changing.[7]

Although Roosevelt delayed presenting any plan until he believed that the Court had alienated large numbers of farmers, workers, and debtors, few people associated Court reform with any immediate, tangible benefit. Nor is it certain that they would have supported the plan even if they had, for court-packing seemed a devious attempt to tamper with a revered institution. In the spring of 1937, the plan lost whatever momentum it had when the Court—largely because Justice Owen Roberts switched to the liberal side—upheld a Washington minimum-wage law for women, the Social Security Act, and the Wagner Act. Then, in May, Justice Van Devanter's resignation gave Roosevelt his first Court appointment. Even so, the administration continued to push a compromise plan that would have permitted the appointment of one additional justice each year for every member who reached the age of seventy-five. This seemed likely to pass because most senators assumed that Roosevelt would nominate Majority Leader Joseph Robinson of Arkansas for a vacancy. For all their rhetoric about judicial independence, most senators would probably have enlarged the Court to do a favor for a colleague; for all his talk about judicial rejuvenation, the president would probably have appointed a 65-year-old southerner whom he believed "not sufficiently liberal" in order to avoid a humiliating defeat. The charade ended in July when Robinson died of a heart attack, and the Senate defeated the bill.[8]

The Court debacle injured Roosevelt's standing with Congress and the public, although it is difficult to measure the extent of the damage because many who would have broken with the president in any event merely used the episode as a convenient pretext for doing so. Nevertheless, the struggle over the Court divided the Democratic party, alienated a number of men who considered themselves reformers, aroused a general distrust of Roosevelt's leadership, antagonized progressive Republicans, and taught conservative Republicans that their best strategy was to maintain a discreet silence and permit Democrats to battle among themselves. The Court fight, one historian has concluded, "helped weld together a bipartisan coalition of anti–New Deal senators."[9] After 1937, of course, the Court ruled that the Constitution sanctioned New Deal economic regulation, and in this sense Roosevelt did not come away empty-handed. The president, who did not make an appointment to the Court in his first term, made five in his second. As Hugo Black, Stanley Reed, Felix Frankfurter, Frank Murphy, and William O. Douglas took their seats, judicial barriers to the welfare state collapsed.

In Roosevelt's view, administrative reform was hardly less important than judicial reform.[10] In 1936, he had therefore set up the President's Committee on Administrative Management, composed of Louis Brownlow, Charles E. Merriam, and Luther Gulick. The committee's report, issued in January 1937, sought to remove administrative obstacles to the implementation of the New Deal. The report asked Congress to furnish the president with six assistants, expand the merit system, improve fiscal management, and establish the National Resources Planning Board as a central planning agency to coordinate government programs. The committee also suggested creating two new cabinet positions—Welfare and Public Works—changing the name of the Department of the Interior to the Department of Conservation, and giving the president broad authority to transfer agencies, including certain functions of the independent regulatory commissions. In this fashion, Brownlow's group hoped to make a permanent home for New Deal agencies and to create an administrative apparatus for the welfare state.

But reorganization ran into rough sledding, in part because a large number of pressure groups found fault with some aspect of Roosevelt's plan. Veterans' organizations, for example, regarded it as an attack on veterans' preferential treatment in the civil service and feared that the Veterans' Administration would lose its independence (and they their influence over policy) if it were shifted to the proposed Department of Welfare. The medical profession objected to the probable transfer of the Public Health Service from the Treasury Department, where it enjoyed considerable autonomy, to the Department of Welfare. Organized labor, particularly the AFL and the railroad brotherhoods, fought against removing the Employment Service from the Department of Labor or altering the status of federal boards concerned with railroad rates and labor conditions. Conservationists, forestry groups, lumbermen, and grazing interests worked around the clock to prevent the transfer of the Forest Service from the Department of Agriculture to the proposed Department of Conservation. However much these groups may have sympathized with the broad aim of improved administration, they resisted change because they had established close relationships with the federal agencies servicing them and did not want to see those relationships disturbed.

Each successful reform associated with the New Deal had enjoyed the support of some social group or geographic region. Reorganization lacked any such constituency. The bill, after squeaking by the Senate in a diluted form, went down to defeat in the House in April 1938 when more than one hundred Democrats deserted the president. Many congressmen claimed that a vote against the measure would reaffirm legislative prerogatives and serve as a warning to cocky New Deal bureaucrats. Others responded to pressure from their constituents, and still others welcomed the chance to administer a drubbing to the president. Congress's lack of enthusiasm for large-scale bureau shuffling also reflected the local basis of its electoral support and the nature of its demands upon the administrative system. A congressman who wished to obtain favors for his constituents often found that his ability to do so depended upon his familiarity with administrative agencies and, sometimes, upon his personal relationship with particular officials. Reorganization threatened to sever the intricate web of personal association so vital to a successful legislative career.

The conflict over reorganization resembled that over court-packing in that both failed to gain support from sizable interest groups, both divided liberals, both opened Roosevelt to the charge of dictatorship, and both led to stunning presidential defeats. But just as Roosevelt had eventually succeeded in making the Supreme Court over in the image of the New Deal, so he managed to introduce important administrative reforms. In 1939, Congress passed a seemingly bland measure that allowed the president to suggest reorganization plans subject to a veto by a majority of both houses, and to appoint six administrative assistants. Denied his goal of creating permanent departments at the cabinet level to oversee new federal programs in the fields of welfare, public works, and conservation, Roosevelt nevertheless set up a Federal Security Agency, a Federal Works Agency, and a Federal Loan Agency, and placed related bureaus under them. By shifting agencies to departments in which they logically belonged, he somewhat rationalized the administrative system. Finally, he established the Executive Office of the President and brought the White House Office, the Bureau of the Budget, and the National Resources Planning Board into it. If by 1939 Roosevelt faced a divided Democratic party and a hostile Congress, he also found a Supreme Court ready to endorse the welfare state and a bureaucracy better equipped to adminster it.

Democratic opposition to court reform and reorganization had crossed sectional and, to a lesser extent, ideological lines. This was not true of three other measures that divided the party into rural and urban, northern and southern factions. Two of the measures—the Wagner Housing Act and the Fair Labor Standards Act—had strong backing from the administration. A third—the anti-lynching bill—won support from northern liberals but not from Roosevelt. Yet all three demonstrated that as the New Deal became more responsive to the claims of its northern, urban constituency, it sacrificed support from both rural and southern representatives. Indeed, southern Democrats now found themselves in an unaccustomed position. Although they continued to control a large number of committees, their relative strength in the Democratic party had declined as a result of the 1936 sweep. As the size of the Democratic delegation in Congress increased, the importance of southerners in that delegation decreased. The demand for housing, labor, and civil rights legislation heightened the discomfort of southerners.

Housing legislation, first introduced in 1935, remained rather far down on the New Deal agenda until 1937 when Roosevelt endorsed a bill sponsored by Senator Robert F. Wagner of New York. Even then, differences between Wagner and cabinet officials stalled the measure. One problem involved the means of financing public housing. The New York senator called for a $1 billion program, with the government floating a bond issue and agreeing to meet interest costs and other expenses amounting to $35 million a year over a sixty-year period. Secretary of the Treasury Henry Morgenthau, Jr., protested that such an arrangement would "just shoot the government credit to hell." He wanted to finance a more modest program through taxation and direct appropriations, and not commit the Treasury to expenditures far into the future.[11] Another difficulty concerned administration. Secretary of the Interior Harold Ickes sought control over the U.S. Housing Authority, and Wagner wanted it independent. (Ultimately Congress placed the agency under Ickes, but Roosevelt appointed Nathan Straus, a Wagner protégé, to head it.)

In the summer of 1937, public housing ran the gauntlet of southern opposition. Despite Wagner's assertion that "New York is not the only benefactor [sic] under this proposed program," southerners believed that the bill would aid cities, and primarily large cities in the North. To prevent this, the Senate added an amendment requiring that the Housing Authority not spend more than 10 percent of its funds in any one state. The Senate narrowly adopted a proposal offered by Senator Harry F. Byrd of Virginia that limited expenditures for each family unit to $4,000, a figure that did not (or perhaps in Byrd's mind, did) take account of high construction costs in large cities. The Senate then passed the measure by a vote of 64–16, with

Byrd and Carter Glass of Virginia, Josiah Bailey of North Carolina, James Byrnes of South Carolina, Tom Connally of Texas, Walter George of Georgia, and Millard Tydings of Maryland in the minority. In the House, the fate of public housing rested with Henry Steagall of Alabama, whose Committee on Banking and Currency controlled the bill. At Roosevelt's insistence, Steagall brought the measure to the floor, and the House passed it in one day. In final form, the Wagner Housing Act authorized expenditures of $500 million, allowed the Housing Authority to advance loans amounting to 90 percent of the projects' cost, and limited costs to a maximum of $5,000 per family unit.[12]

Southern Democrats opposed wages and hours legislation just as strenuously as they had public housing. They feared that the measure would, by raising wages in the South, destroy the region's competitive advantage as a cheap labor market. Many also perceived a threat to the southern racial hierarchy. As Martin Dies of Texas put it, "You cannot prescribe the same wages for the black man as for the white man."[13] In the spring of 1937, southern Democrats on the House Rules Committee joined with Republicans to prevent the measure from reaching the floor even though it had passed the Senate. Although a discharge petition in November 1937 pried the bill loose, the House voted to recommit by 216–198. Seventy-four percent of the opponents represented rural districts; southern Democrats voted to recommit by a margin of 74–17. In May 1938, after another discharge petition gained enough signatures, the House passed the Fair Labor Standards Act, but one tailored to southern specifications. The bill, which regulated child labor and provided for a forty-cents-an-hour minimum wage and a forty-hour work week, exempted domestic workers and farm laborers, allowed wages to achieve the minimum level only gradually, and permitted regional wage differentials.[14]

In the struggle over wages and hours, as in that over housing, Democrats divided along sectional lines. Moreover, each measure appealed to the northern, urban working class, but not to organized interest groups. Tenants had nothing like the formal bargaining power of businessmen, workers, farmers, or, for that matter, conservationists. Setting a minimum wage primarily helped unorganized workers rather than union members. For this reason and for others, the American Federation of Labor at first opposed the wages and hours bill; the Federation relented only when the bill's sponsors agreed to place its administration in the Labor Department (with which the AFL felt comfortable) rather than in an independent five-member board as originally contemplated. Just as housing reformers differed over whether the Housing Authority should be autonomous or within the Interior Department, so sharp disagreements occurred over implementing the Fair Labor Standards Act. Both controversies reflected an awareness that administrative location could have a decisive effect upon actual policy.

Perhaps nothing exposed sectional divisions within the Democratic party more clearly than the issue of civil rights. In April 1937, after a mob of whites in Mississippi had set two black men aflame with blow torches and then hanged them, the House took up an anti-lynching bill. The measure, which made lynching a federal crime and prescribed punishment for members of lynch mobs, passed by a vote of 277–120. Every southern Democrat with the exception of Maury Maverick and Wright Patman of Texas voted against it. Democrats from northern, urban areas, on the other hand, gave it overwhelming support. In the Senate, civil rights forces hoped to find a southern or border state Democrat to cosponsor the measure with Robert Wagner "for its effect in minimizing sectional issues," but none would cooperate. Instead, the threat of a southern filibuster stymied the bill during most of 1937. A six-week filibuster early in 1938 killed the measure when a cloture motion failed to receive a simple majority, much less the two-thirds vote it required. Every senator from the South voted against cloture. During the debate, Pat Harrison of Mississippi had inquired whether the South's "love for the Democratic party" was to be lost through northern insistence on civil rights. The question may have been rhetorical, but southerners had begun to ask it.[15]

The problems that the New Deal encountered after 1937 went beyond congressional reluctance to enact certain legislation. To a considerable extent, Congress accurately reflected the popular temperament. Every opinion poll in 1938 and 1939 indicated much the same thing: between two-thirds and three-fourths of the American people preferred that the Roosevelt administration follow a more conservative course. In March 1939, more than twice as many people wanted the administration to improve existing laws as wanted it to pass new ones. The polls revealed class and party differences: Democrats and poor people more often favored a broadening of the New Deal than did Republicans and wealthy people. Even so, a larger percentage of Democrats and the poor thought the administration should be more conservative than thought it should be more liberal. These surveys, taken in the early days of public opinion measurement, can be challenged on the basis of their sampling techniques and the way in which they phrased questions, but the over-all pattern they reveal cannot be discounted. The New Deal declined after 1937 because most Americans did not want to extend it much further.[16]

There are many reasons why this should have been so. In some respects, the New Deal was a victim of its own success, for with recovery came a lessening of the sense of crisis upon which Roosevelt had depended in his first term. As William E. Leuchtenburg has pointed out, "The more prosperous the country became, the more people returned to the only values they knew, those associated with an individualistic, success-oriented society."[17] Moreover, Roosevelt's proposals for judicial and administrative reform promised few tangible benefits but seemed rather to demonstrate a lust for personal power—and this at a time when the success of European dictators (particularly Hitler's annexation of Austria in March 1938) aroused a deep suspicion of executive authority in any form.

The administration's response to the recession of 1937–38 also led to rather widespread disenchantment with reform. In the fall of 1937, the economy suddenly went into a tailspin. The rate of decline over the next ten months was sharper even than in 1929: industrial production fell by 33 percent, industrial stock prices by 50 percent, and national income by 12 percent. Nearly four million people lost their jobs, boosting total unemployment to 11.5 million. The slump occurred largely because the administration, in attempting to balance the budget, had cut expenditures sharply. The government's contribution to consumer purchasing power dropped from $4.1 billion in 1936 to under $1 billion in 1937.[18] Not everyone recognized this at the time. Most businessmen attributed the downturn to a lack of confidence in the Roosevelt administration. To encourage investment or expansion, they held, the government should cut spending still further, repeal taxes that burdened business, and declare a moratorium on reform. "More government spending is not a feasible way out," said George L. Harrison of the New York Federal Reserve Board. "Business is now hesitant about making long term plans partly because it feels it does not know what the rules of the game are going to be."[19]

Roosevelt resented the attempt to bludgeon him into sacrificing social reform, and may have been angered by the realization that the health of the economy, and therefore the success of his administration, depended largely upon the behavior of businessmen who hated the New Deal. Yet he was nevertheless reluctant to undertake a new spending program. To do so would be to confess that his early policies had failed; and in any case, the president was too much of a traditionalist to accept the Keynesian formula of planned deficits in periods of slack. He believed that pump-priming had been appropriate in 1933 "when the water had receded to the bottom of the well," but doubted its worth in 1938 "with the water within twenty-five or thirty per cent of the top." Some cabinet officials, notably Secretary of the Treasury Morgenthau, bolstered Roosevelt's fiscal orthodoxy. For several months, the president let things slide. As conditions worsened, factories shut down, and the stock market tumbled. In February 1938, Harold Ickes termed Roosevelt's policy one of "watchful waiting"; a month later Morgenthau noted that Roosevelt was "just treading water . . . to wait to see what happens this spring." Not until April, when it appeared that economic conditions could ruin the Democrats in the fall elections, did the president listen to advisers who favored additional spending. He then asked Congress to authorize a $3.75 billion relief appropriation.[20]

But by then the damage had been done. Those who had lost their jobs, whose businesses had failed, or who again had to apply for relief now blamed the Democrats, not the Republicans. "Whether we like it or not," said one man, "we can't help its being called the 'Roosevelt depression,' because he has now been president for over five years." Roosevelt's behavior contrasted sharply with the impression of energy and purpose he had conveyed in 1933 and seemed to show that the New Deal, having exhausted its fund of ideas, had nowhere to turn. Then, too, people had accepted earlier New Deal measures because they seemed to improve conditions; the recession tended to discredit those measures. Some also argued that the administration should lower its sights, forget about broad-gauged reforms, and cultivate the good opinion of the business community. "Congress cannot afford to waste time on NEW DEAL schemes and plans to bring about Utopia, but must get down to brass tacks to do something constructive to save business and industry," wrote a resident of Minneapolis.[21] If after five years of innovation 1929 seemed to be happening all over again, perhaps the time for further innovation was past.

Just as the downturn damaged prospects for reform, so too did the appearance of a virulent strain of nativism. In the two years before the outbreak of World War II in September 1939, nativist sentiment appears to have increased sharply. This affected the New Deal because in the minds of some people the Roosevelt administration was playing into the hands of the very groups that seemed to pose the gravest danger—Communists, Jews, and labor agitators. Charges that the president had surrounded himself with alien advisers and had embraced an alien ideology were by no means new; what was new was the frequency with which they were voiced and the degree of public acceptance they received. Unlike Roosevelt's first term, when such assertions found a hearing mainly among the very rich, after 1937 they won a wide audience among the middle classes and among immigrants, particularly Irish-Catholics and Germans.

As in the past, nativist fears were associated with working-class militancy. In 1937, a rash of sit-down strikes broke out. No fewer than 477 such strikes, involving 400,000 workers, took place, the most notorious of which was the General Motors sit-down in Flint, Michigan. Although the workers' goals were traditional ones of union recognition and improved conditions, their tactics struck terror into the hearts of property-conscious people. Most Americans assumed correctly that occupying a factory and holding it hostage violated the law, but concluded erroneously that the automobile workers were inspired by revolutionary intent. Two out of every three people favored outlawing sit-down strikes and employing force against unions engaged in them. "Armed insurrection—defiance of law, order and duly elected authority is spreading like wildfire," protested one group of citizens. Editorial writers charged Governor Frank Murphy of Michigan, who had negotiated a settlement at General Motors, with tolerating "the reign of lawlessness." Similarly, because Roosevelt refused to call out federal troops to evict the strikers, he was accused of cringing before the forces of anarchy and encouraging disorder.[22]

Labor turmoil cost the administration support primarily from the middle classes, rural areas, and the South. Yet anticommunism could also be a potent force among the urban working classes. This was particularly true among those of Irish and German ancestry, who often linked Communists with Jews and imagined both exerting a sinister influence over the Roosevelt administration. In 1938, Father Charles E. Coughlin, the radio priest, helped set up the Christian Front to combat the "Red menace"; he also serialized the notorious anti-Semitic tract, the *Protocols of Zion*, in his magazine. Boycotts of Jewish merchants became commonplace in some cities. The president of the Flatbush Anti-Communist League in Brooklyn said, "The first thing I do when I walk into a store is to call for a Christian salesman."[23] The German-American Bund, founded in 1936 by Fritz Kuhn, saw conspiracies at every hand. "A bulwark must be erected against Marxist, Communist and Jewish arrogance," Kuhn asserted. One of his aides referred to the president as "Frank D. Rosenfeld." Strongest in the Yorkville section of New York City, the Bund by early 1939 could attract over 20,000 people to its rallies.[24] Of course, most German- and Irish-Americans did not belong to these organizations, and immigrant groups had no monopoly on anticommunism or anti-Semitism. Nevertheless, by the late 1930s nativist anxieties were influencing the reaction of many to the president and his program.

The public's response to the House committee investigating Un-American Activities illustrated the administration's vulnerability.[25] Created in the summer of 1938 and headed by Martin Dies of Texas, the committee lashed out at New Deal programs, agencies, and officials. Dies insisted that Francis Perkins, Harry Hopkins, and Harold Ickes gave comfort to subversives. He claimed that Federal Theatre Project productions "were nothing but straight Communist propaganda." During the 1938 campaign, he provided a forum for witnesses who attributed communist leanings to New Deal candidates in Michigan, Minnesota, and California. Roosevelt rebuked Dies on two occasions when the committee behaved in an especially offensive manner. But the president attempted to avoid a direct clash, in large part because he knew that the committee had wide public support. In December 1938, a Gallup poll showed that three out of four persons who knew of the committee approved of its work. The survey indicated that Dies enjoyed nearly as much support among lower- and middle-income groups as he did among upper-income groups. Also, more than two-thirds of the Democrats in the survey favored continuation of the committee. In 1939, Dies acted less flamboyantly and investigated fascist as well as left-wing organizations. But before long he was back to his old tricks. "The President must surely realize by this time," he said in 1940, "that his left-wing followers in the government are the fountainhead of subversive activities."[26]

The president, already under fire from so many sides, suffered yet another setback in attempting to oust anti–New Deal Democrats in the 1938 primaries. Proceeding with some caution, the administration made no effort to unseat such well-entrenched conservative senators as Augustine Lonergan of Connecticut, Alva Adams of Colorado, Bennett Champ Clark of Missouri, and Pat McCarran of Nevada. Events then confirmed James Farley's warning that there was "no use going into a thing when you are licked at the start."[27] Roosevelt failed dismally in his effort to eliminate Guy Gillette of Iowa (who, though he had opposed the Supreme Court bill, hardly qualified as an enemy of the New Deal), Walter George of Georgia, Millard Tydings of Maryland, and "Cotton Ed" Smith of South Carolina. Many southerners appeared to resent the president's intrusion into local elections (what Walter George termed the "second march through Georgia"), particularly when the administration backed candidates with undistinguished records. Besides, most incumbents, no matter what their voting records, put themselves forward as independent-minded New Dealers. Those who benefited most from New Deal relief programs and composed the only likely constituency for the purge—Negroes and poor whites— hardly participated at all in Democratic primaries. In fact, opinion polls indicated that only 35 percent of lower-class Democrats favored the purge, compared with 30 percent of upper-class Democrats. Even among the unemployed and those on relief, less than a majority supported the president.[28]

The purge claimed only one victim—John O'Connor of New York City, chairman of the House Rules Committee. O'Connor, who had regularly sided with Roosevelt during his first term, had desperately wanted to be elected majority leader as a "stepping stone" to the speakership. He attributed his defeat in January 1937 to Roosevelt's intervention on behalf of Sam Rayburn. After that, O'Connor broke with the president frequently. In April 1938, he blasted the executive reorganization bill and also criticized Roosevelt's call for additional spending to end the recession. The administration then persuaded James Fay, a popular local politician who had nearly defeated O'Connor in 1934, to make the race again. A well-drilled group of party workers managed Fay's campaign, and Roosevelt remained very much in the background. Fay's campaign, moreover, centered as much on personal issues as on national problems. His supporters contrasted Fay's heroic World War I record with O'Connor's failure to serve overseas, and they criticized O'Connor for living on Long Island, far from his tenement-house district. Fay narrowly won the primary, and again defeated O'Connor—who had gotten the Republican nomination—in November. The outcome represented less a vote of confidence in the New Deal than a victory for those who skillfully exploited local resentments and had the superior political machine.[29]

The distress resulting from the recession, and a shrewd manipulation of nativist fears combined to sap Democratic strength in the elections of 1938. Republicans won a smashing victory: they gained 81 seats in the House, 8 seats in the Senate, and 13 new governorships. The strategy of linking liberal Democrats with communism, the CIO, and labor turmoil paid high dividends. In Texas, Maury Maverick's opponent in the primary termed him a "friend and ally of Communism"; in Montana, Republicans described Jerry O'Connell as "a stooge for communism"; in Michigan, Frank Murphy was branded a "traitor" for failing to take a hard line with the sit-down strikers. All three were defeated.[30] But if the voters had repudiated social radicalism, they had by no means endorsed economic conservatism. Few Republicans advocated the dismantling of the New

Deal. Instead, many supported the Townsend old-age pension plan, which would have provided $200 a month to everyone over sixty who retired (at a time when monthly pension benefits averaged $19.21). In 1938, the Townsend movement endorsed 169 Republicans of whom 101 were elected, and 77 Democrats of whom 43 were elected. Republicans blandly promised to preserve the worthwhile features of the New Deal but to curb its excesses, to expand benefits but to reduce expenditures. As a defeated Democrat ruefully put it, "The WPA workers were all dissatisfied with their wages and openly declared for the Republican candidate, who promised Townsendism, more wages for the WPA, and at the same time more economy."[31]

The Congress that assembled in January 1939 was quite unlike any with which Roosevelt had to contend before. Since all Democratic losses took place in the North and the West, and particularly in states like Ohio and Pennsylvania, southerners held a much stronger position. The House contained 169 non-southern Democrats, 93 southern Democrats, 169 Republicans, and 4 third-party representatives. For the first time, Roosevelt could not form a majority without the help of some southerners or Republicans. In addition, the president had to contend with several senators who, having successfully resisted the purge, no longer owed him anything. Most observers agreed, therefore, that the president could at best hope to consolidate, but certainly not to extend, the New Deal. James Farley thought that Roosevelt's wisest course would be "to clean up odds and ends, tighten up and improve things [he] already has but not try [to] start anything new." In any event, Farley predicted that Congress would discard much of Roosevelt's program.[32]

Congress wasted little time in proving Farley right. It demonstrated its resentment at what it judged the attempted politicalization of relief by passing the Hatch Act. Designed "to prevent pernicious political activities," the measure prohibited all federal employees, except for high-ranking members of the executive branch, from engaging in political campaigns.[33] In addition, the House launched investigations of two controversial New Deal agencies, the Works Progress Administration and the National Labor Relations Board. The chairman of each committee was a Virginian hostile to existing relief and labor policies. The House abruptly cut off funds for the Federal Theatre Project, which, because much of its activity centered in a few large cities, was the most vulnerable of all WPA arts programs.[34] The tax on undistributed profits, perhaps the most important New Deal innovation in the tax structure and one bitterly resented by businessmen, was repealed outright.[35] Congress also killed a request to increase expenditures for public housing. Early in August, Roosevelt learned just how far the pendulum had swung. The administration had requested an appropriation of $3.86 billion (of which $840 million was to be spent in fiscal 1940) for self-liquidating public works projects. Although this "lend-spend" proposal was a good deal more modest than the pump-priming of 1938, the Senate trimmed the bill to $2.4 billion, and the House voted not to consider it at all.

Yet the picture of a reform-minded president thwarted by Congress at best tells only half the story. By 1939, the administration had itself begun to draw in its horns. "We have now passed the period of internal conflict in the launching of our program of social reform," Roosevelt noted in his annual message in January. "Our full energies may now be released to invigorate the processes of recovery in order to preserve our reforms."[36] The president torpedoed efforts by liberals to offset the imbalance in old age benefits between rich and poor states by expanding the federal contribution to social security. "Not one nickel more," he said. "Not one solitary nickel. Once you get off the 50-50 matching basis the sky's the limit, and before you know it, we'll be paying the whole bill."[37] Similarly, he withheld support from Robert Wagner's National Health Bill, which would have established a program of medical insurance and authorized federal aid for child and maternity care, public health services, and hospital construction. Roosevelt dodged a conflict with the American Medical Association by endorsing instead a proposal to construct fifty hospitals; a modified version passed the Senate in 1940 only to die in the House.[38] Finally, the president looked with disfavor on additional deficit spending for social purposes. As he told Henry Morgenthau, Jr., in July 1939, "I am sick and tired of having a lot of long-haired people around here who want a billion dollars for schools, a billion dollars for public health. . . . Just because a boy wants to go to college is no reason we should finance it."[39]

Roosevelt's behavior reflected not only his deeply ingrained fiscal conservatism and his assessment of the mood in Congress but also his unwillingness to fight for lost causes, particularly when more vital causes were not yet lost. During 1939, the president's attention turned increasingly to foreign policy and national defense. His chief legislative goal was to gain revision of the neutrality laws so as to permit the United States, in the event of war, to provide arms on a cash-and-carry basis to England and France. It is unlikely that Roosevelt consciously sacrificed domestic reform in order to mollify southerners whose help he needed for neutrality revision; most southerners would have supported his foreign policy in any case. What is more probable is that Roosevelt did not wish to expend his limited political capital on issues of relatively low priority. Even so, Congress proved uncooperative. On June 30, the House insisted on an embargo on arms and ammunition; and shortly thereafter, the Senate Foreign Relations Committee, by a vote of 12–11, decided to postpone neutrality revision. Not until after the invasion of Poland when Roosevelt convened a special session did Congress lift the arms embargo. By then the president was, in the words of one southern conservative, "cultivating us in a very nice way."[40]

If his concern with foreign policy caused Roosevelt to court southerners, his interest in national defense pointed toward a rapprochement with the business community. As early as November 1938, when the president wished to embark on an ambitious program of aircraft construction, he recognized the importance of business expertise. "At my suggestion," Henry Morgenthau, Jr., noted, "the President is going to invite three of the leading manufacturers in America who are not interested in airplane activities to come down at a dollar a year and later take full charge of production after the Army has turned over to them the blueprints of the models that they want." In August 1939, Roosevelt chose Edward Stettinius of United States Steel to head a newly created War Resources Board. Other members included Walter S. Gifford, president of American Telephone and Telegraph; John Pratt, a director of General Motors; and Robert E. Wood, chairman of Sears, Roebuck. Indeed, some liberals complained that "Wall Street bankers" dominated the board, that it was the nucleus of an "extra-legal autocracy which, in war, would destroy both American democracy and the social reforms of the New Deal." By the end of the summer, Roosevelt, fearing that the board's proposals might seriously dilute his own authority in wartime, disbanded it. The board filed a report in November 1939 that was not released for seven years.[41]

New Dealers who feared that permitting businessmen to formulate wartime economic policy would jeopardize social reform nevertheless wasted little time themselves in climbing aboard the national defense bandwagon. In 1938, officials in the Works Progress Administration became deeply involved in a planned expansion of aircraft construction, in part because Roosevelt mistakenly assumed that the government would have to build and operate a number of plants and would therefore be putting jobless men to work. An army officer muttered that "Hopkins and Aubrey Williams are running the defense show."[42] After 1939, New Deal bureaucrats commonly justified their programs on the grounds of their contribution to preparedness. The Tennessee Valley Authority noted that it was "developing the power necessary for the large-scale operation of war industries in this well-protected strategic area." The National Youth Administration stressed vocational training programs that contributed to national defense. The Civilian Conservation Corps ordered drills for enrollees, provided instruction in reading blueprints, and performed tasks for military reservations. The turn in this direction reflected not only a genuine belief that such projects would do the most good but a recognition that they were more likely to receive funding from a stingy Congress.[43]

Bureaucrats ordinarily wish to please those who control the purse strings, and the taking up of defense-related tasks was but one means of currying favor with Congress. Another was to administer programs in a way that would gain congressional approval even at the risk of distorting the program's purpose. As Sidney Baldwin has shown, officials in the Farm Security Administration, anxious to establish a good record for repayment of loans, selected clients who were most likely to meet their payments. Landless farmers with the most training, experience, managerial ability, and initiative therefore received a disproportionate share of FSA loans. By January 1940, the agency had to remind its field staff to "dig deep enough into the low economic levels to reach the people who need our help the most." Since its constituents—20 percent of whom were Negroes and all of whom were poor and unorganized—exerted little political influence, the FSA remained wholly at the mercy of Congress.[44]

Moreover, by the end of the 1930s some New Deal administrators had become so deeply committed to their own agencies that, like government officials before and since, they placed the welfare of a particular agency ahead of all else. Then reform became a casualty of a bureaucratic tug-of-war. National housing, wages and hours, executive reorganization, health insurance—all became tangled in conflicts over whose bureau would control which function. Often these disputes involved substantive questions of policy; at other times they involved power for its own sake. One of the most debilitating of all these rivalries was that between the Departments of Agriculture and Interior over control of the Forest Service, an agency that Harold Ickes desperately wanted to acquire. The controversy, which smoldered all through the decade, reached its height between 1937 and 1939. Both departments dissipated energies on intrigue and lobbying that could have found more constructive outlets.[45]

As a vital reform movement, the New Deal lasted only five years. Every major reform linked with the Roosevelt administration—social security, the TVA, the Wagner Act, wages and hours, public housing—was on the books by 1938. The New Deal declined in Roosevelt's second term, however, not only because Congress was reluctant to enact additional legislation, but because the president was reluctant to request such legislation; not only because the middle and upper classes thought reform had gone far enough, but because racial and ethnic tensions divided the New Deal's own working class constituency; not only because outside pressures overwhelmed government officials, but because many of those officials pursued policies dictated by considerations of bureaucratic expediency.

1. Walter Millis, "The President's Political Strategy," *Yale Review* 28 (1938): 1–18.

2. Marriner S. Eccles, *Beckoning Frontiers* (New York, 1950), p. 264.

3. Edward Hanlon, "Urban-Rural Cooperation and Conflict in the Congress: The Breakdown of the New Deal Coalition, 1933–1940" (Ph.D. diss., Georgetown University, 1967).

4. William E. Leuchtenburg, "The Case of the Contentious Commissioner: Humphey's Executor v. U.S.," in Harold M. Hyman and Leonard W. Levy, eds., *Freedom and Reform* (New York, 1967), pp. 276–312.

5. Henry F. Pringle, *The Life and Times of William Howard Taft*, 2 vols. (New York, 1939), 2: 967.

6. M. Paul Holsinger, "Mr. Justice Van Devanter and the New Deal: A Note," *Historian* 31 (1968–69): 57–63.

7. Benjamin Cohen to Louis D. Brandeis, 30 July 1937, Felix Frankfurter Papers (Library of Congress); Franklin Roosevelt to Felix Franfurter, 9 Feb. 1937, in Max Freedman, ed., *Roosevelt and Frankfurter* (Boston, 1967), pp. 381–82; William E. Leuchtenburg, "The Origins of Franklin D. Roosevelt's 'Court-Packing' Plan," in Philip B. Kurland, ed., *The Supreme Court Review* (Chicago, 1966), pp. 347–400.

8. John W. Chambers, "The Big Switch: Justice Roberts and the Minimum-Wage Cases," *Labor History* 10 (1969): 44–73; Leonard Baker, *Back to Back: The Duel Between FDR and the Supreme Court* (New York, 1967), p. 249.

9. William E. Leuchtenburg, "Franklin D. Roosevelt's Supreme Court 'Packing' Plan," in Harold M. Hollingsworth and William F. Holmes, eds., *Essays on the New Deal* (Austin, Tex., 1969), pp. 109–12; Karl A. Lamb, "The Opposition Party as Secret Agent: Republicans and the Court Fight, 1937," *Papers of the Michigan Academy of Science, Arts, and Letters* 46 (1961); George H. Mayer, "Alf M. Landon as Leader of the Republican Opposition, 1937–1940," *Kansas Historical Quarterly* 53 (1966): 325–34.

10. The following account is based on Richard Polenberg, *Reorganizing Roosevelt's Government, 1936–1939* (Cambridge, Mass., 1966).

11. John M. Blum, *From the Morgenthau Diaries: Years of Crisis* (Boston, 1957), p. 289.

12. J. Joseph Huthmacher, *Senator Robert F. Wagner and the Rise of Urban Liberalism* (New York, 1968), pp. 224–30; Timothy L. McConnell, *The Wagner Housing Act: A Case Study of the Legislative Process* (Chicago, 1957).

13. James Patterson, *Congressional Conservatism and the New Deal* (Lexington, Ky., 1967), p. 195.

14. Paul H. Douglas and Joseph Hackman, "The Fair Labor Standards Act of 1938:I," *Political Science Quarterly* 53 (1938): 491–515; James Burns, *Congress on Trial* (New York, 1949), pp. 68–82.

15. Robert L. Zangrando, "The NAACP and a Federal Antilynching Bill, 1934–1940," *Journal of Negro History* 50 (1965): 106–17; Robert W. Dubay, "Mississippi and the Proposed Federal Anti-Lynching Bills of 1937–1938," *Southern Quarterly* 7 (1968–69): 73–89; Minutes, Board of Directors, 8 Feb. 1937, National Association for the Advancement of Colored People Papers (Library of Congress).

16. Hadley Cantril, ed., *Public Opinion 1935–1946* (Princeton, N.J., 1951), pp. 978–79.

17. William E. Leuchtenburg, *Franklin D. Roosevelt and the New Deal, 1932–1940*, (New York, 1963), p. 273.

18. Douglas A. Hayes, "Business Confidence and Business Activity," *Michigan Business Studies* 10 (1951): 11–15; Kenneth D. Roose, *The Economics of Recession and Revival* (New Haven, Conn., 1954).

19. George L. Harrison to Marriner Eccles, 3 Nov. 1937, Harrison Papers (Columbia University Library).

20. Harold Ickes, *The Secret Diary of Harold Ickes*, 3 vols. (New York, 1953–54), 2:317; Blum, *Morgenthau Diaries*, p. 415.

21. C. W. Hellberg to Merlin Hull, 6 Apr. 1938, Hull Papers (State Historical Society of Wisconsin); H. L. Prestholdt to Henry G. Teigan, 2 Apr. 1938, Teigan Papers (Minnesota Historical Society).

22. Sidney Fine, *Sit-Down* (Ann Arbor, Mich., 1969), pp. 228–30, 330–35; Donald G. Sofchalk, "The Chicago Memorial Day Incident: An Episode of Mass Action," *Labor History* 6 (1965): 3–43.

23. Charles J. Tull, *Father Coughlin and the New Deal* (Syracuse, N.Y., 1965), pp. 193–99; David H. Bennett, *Demagogues in the Depression* (New Brunswick, N.J., 1969), pp. 278–82; George Britt, "Poison in the Melting Pot," *Nation*, 1 Apr. 1939, pp. 374–76; Ronald H. Bayor, "Ethnic Conflict in New York City, 1929–1941" (Ph.D. diss., University of Pennsylvania, 1970); Sheldon Marcus, *Fathern Coughlin: The Tumultuous Life of the Priest of the Little Flower* (Boston, 1973).

24. Alton Frye, *Nazi Germany and the American Hemisphere, 1933–1941* (New Haven, Conn., 1967), pp. 80–91; Fritz Kuhn, *Awake and Act: The Aims and Purposes of the German-American Bund* (New York, 1936); Sander A. Diamond, *The Nazi Movement in the United States, 1924–1941* (Ithaca, N.Y., 1974); Saul S. Friedman, *No Haven for the Oppressed: United States Policy toward Jewish Refugees* (Detroit, 1973).

25. The following account is based on Richard Polenberg, "Franklin Roosevelt and Civil Liberties: The Case of the Dies Committee," *Historian* 30 (1968–69): 165–78.

26. Martin Dies, *The Trojan Horse in America* (New York, 1940), pp. 285–303; August R. Ogden, *The Dies Committee* (Washington, 1945).

27. Raymond Clapper Diary, 14 Sept. 1938, Clapper Papers (Library of Congress).

28. Luther H. Ziegler, "Senator Walter George's 1938 Campaign," *Georgia Historical Quarterly* 43 (1959): 332–52; Patterson, *Congressional Conservatism*, pp. 269–87; Charles M. Price and Joseph Boskin, "The Roosevelt 'Purge': A Reappraisal," *Journal of Politics* 28 (1966): 660–70.

29. Richard Polenberg, "Franklin Roosevelt and the Purge of John O'Connor: The Impact of Urban Change on Political Parties," *New York History* 49 (1968): 306–26; Roosevelt to Marvin McIntyre, 4 Aug. 1938, PSF 53, Roosevelt Papers (Roosevelt Library); John O'Connor to Roosevelt, 22 Apr. 1938, O'Connor Papers (University of Indiana).

30. Stuart L. Weiss, "Maury Maverick and the Liberal Bloc," *Journal of American History* 57 (1970–71): 892–95; Richard T. Ruetten, "Showdown in Montana, 1938: Burton Wheeler's Role in the Defeat of Jerry O'Connell," *Pacific Northwest Quarterly* 54 (1963): 19–28; Samuel T. McSeveney, "The Michigan Gubernatorial Campaign of 1938," *Michigan History* 45 (1961): 97–127; Milton Plesur, "The Republican Congressional Comeback of 1938," *Review of Politics* 24 (1962): 525–62.

31. Jay Franklin, *1940* (New York, 1940), pp. 111–13; Abraham Holtzman, *The Townsend Movement* (New York, 1963), pp. 101–29; Paul R. Greever to O'Connor, 8 Dec. 1938, O'Connor Papers.

32. Hanlon, "Urban-Rural Cooperation and Conflict," pp. 381–85; Clapper Diary, 7 June 1938, Clapper Papers.

33. Dorothy Canfield Fowler, "Precursors of the Hatch Act," *Mississippi Valley Historical Review* 47 (1960): 247, 259–62.

34. Jane D. Mathews, *The Federal Theatre, 1935–1939* (Princeton, N.J., 1967), pp. 249–76; William F. McDonald, *Federal Relief Administration and the Arts* (Columbus, Ohio, 1969), pp. 203–6, 238–39, 306–12, 533.

35. Walter K. Lambert, "New Deal Revenue Acts: The Politics of Taxation" (Ph.D. diss., University of Texas, 1970), p. 498.

36. Samuel I. Rosenman, ed., *The Public Papers and Addresses of Franklin D. Roosevelt*, 13 vols. (New York, 1938–50), 8:7.

37. Arthur J. Altmeyer, *The Formative Years of Social Security* (Madison, Wis., 1966), p. 112.

38. Huthmacher, *Wagner*, pp. 263–67; Daniel S. Hirshfield, *The Lost Reform: The Campaign for Compulsory Health Insurance* (Cambridge, Mass., 1970).

39. John Morton Blum, *From the Morgenthau Diaries: Years of Urgency* (Boston, 1965), pp. 41–42.

40. James T. Patterson, "Eating Humble Pie: A Note on Roosevelt, Congress, and Neutrality Revision in 1939," *Historian* 31 (1969): 407–14; John Robert Moore, *Senator Josiah Willam Bailey of North Carolina* (Durham, N.C., 1968), pp. 174–82.

41. Blum, *Morgenthau Diaries: Years of Urgency*, pp. 46–47; Albert A. Blum, "Birth and Death of the M-Day Plan," in Harold Stein, ed., *American Civil-Military Decisions* (Birmingham, Ala., 1962), pp. 63–87; Louis Brownlow, *A Passion for Anonymity* (Chicago, 1958), p. 425; William A. Weinrick, "Business and Foreign Affairs: The Roosevelt Defense Program" (Ph.D. diss., University of Oklahoma, 1971).

42. Keith D. McFarland, "Secretary of War Harry H. Woodring and the Problems of Readiness, Rearmament, and Neutrality, 1936–1940" (Ph.D. diss., Ohio State University, 1969), p. 175. See also Frank J. Rader, "Harry L. Hopkins, the Works Progress Administration, and National Defense" (Ph.D. diss., University of Delaware, 1973).

43. William E. Leuchtenburg, "The New Deal and the Analogue of War," in John Braeman, Robert H. Bremner, and David Brody, eds., *Change and Continuity in Twentieth-Century America* (Columbus, Ohio, 1964), p. 138. John C. Salmond, *The Civilian Conservation Corps* (Durham, N.C., 1967), p. 187. See also Richard Polenberg, *War and Society: The United States, 1941–1945* (Philadelphia, 1972), chap. 3.

44. Sidney Baldwin, *Poverty and Politics: The Rise and Decline of The Farm Security Administration* (Chapel Hill, N.C., 1968), pp. 217–21.

45. Richard Polenberg, "The Great Conservation Contest," *Forest History* 10 (1966–67): 13–23.

David Brody

The New Deal and World War II

In 1948, Bruce Catton published an angry book about the American war effort. *The War Lords of Washington*, written with an insider's perspective by a newsman (and later famed Civil War historian) who had served as information chief for the War Production Board, took as its central theme the wasted opportunities of World War II. Not that Catton denied the magnitude of the military achievement. On the contrary: "In terms of sheer physical effort, America did the greatest job in the history of the human race."[1] War production multiplied four times in the first year of war, and outdistanced the combined output of America's enemies. At the peak in 1944, the country was producing for the military effort alone at a rate nearly as high as the gross national product in 1929. The economy turned out a total of 300,000 aircraft, 100,000 tanks, 70,000 landing craft, and the atomic bomb. The accomplishment was all the sweeter because it confounded the initial pessimism about the country's vitality. After the fall of France, from all sides, from Charles Lindbergh on the right to Dwight Macdonald on the left, came dire warnings that American capitalism could never hope to match the dread efficiency of the Nazi war machine.[2] In fact, the American war effort, though slow to start and hardly lacking in mistakes, far surpassed either Germany's or Japan's in the efficient use of national resources for making war.[3] All this Catton granted. But he had another standard for measuring the American performance:

> Do we try to pick up all of our peacetime affairs, after the war, exactly where we were before, in exactly the same old way, as if nothing at all had been changed?
> Or do we, on the contrary, accept both change and the need for change, and use this tremendous effort which the people have made in such a way that the

nation can adjust itself to the new world which is coming in out of the mist and the smoke?[4]

It was a fair question. For war possessed immense potential as an agent for social reform. The Civil War had led to the freeing of the slaves, had opened the way to the Fourteenth and Fifteenth amendments and Radical Reconstruction, and had, as David Montgomery has demonstrated, generated a potent labor reform movement. World War I—a more pertinent example, perhaps—had given rise to much talk of "industrial democracy" and "reconstruction"; and the domestic war programs had been seen, not merely as emergency measures, but as experiments containing the seeds of permanent change. True, these high expectations were swiftly punctured by the postwar reaction. But, as William Leuchtenburg and others have pointed out, the war experience was recalled and actively utilized during the Great Depression, both as a precedent for massive government action in a national emergency and as a guideline for New Deal programs in agriculture, labor, industrial recovery, and other fields.[5] For our purposes, however, the more important fact is that World War I did generate a reform impulse: in an explicit way, Americans perceived of the war crisis as an opportunity for building a better society.

In Great Britain during World War II, this connection resulted in a profound change in social policy. From Dunkirk onward, English war leaders began to plan for postwar reconstruction. The official British history of World War II draws this conclusion.

> There existed, so to speak, an implied contract between Government and people; the people refused none of the sacrifices that the Government demanded from them for the winning of the war; in return, they expected that the Government should show imagination and seriousness in preparing for the restoration and improvement of the nation's well-being when the war had been won. The plans for reconstruction were, therefore, a real part of the war effort.

Even before Labour's victory in 1945 and the consequent move toward socialism, a bipartisan commitment had been made for basic reforms in housing, education, health, and social insurance that added up to the welfare state. Reflecting on these events and turning to the evidence of earlier wars (Plutarch's account of the evacuation of Athens during the Persian invasion in 480 B.C. especially influenced him), the eminent historian of British social policy during World War II, Richard M. Titmuss, later arrived at this generalization: that the impact of war on social policy was substantially determined "by how far the co-operation of the masses is essential to the successful prosecution of war. If this co-operation is thought to be essential, then inequalities must be reduced and the pyramid of social stratification must be flattened."[6]

The American experience in World War II, unfortunately, does not fit Professor Titmuss's generalization. Nothing like the magnitude of British reform occurred in the United States then, nor even, indeed, of the kind of abortive movements that had excited both Britain and America during World War I. This is not to deny the powerful impact of the second war on American life. Race relations, internal migration, the status of women, family life—all underwent profound and permanent changes.[7] The character of government also was altered in important ways. The authority and administrative structure of the office of the presidency expanded tremendously, and the "military-industrial complex" took its modern shape. Nor did the war fail to bring about consequential, long-term changes in some areas of public policy, such as the federal financing of scientific research, in the modern tax structure, and in the G.I. Bill of Rights. But all of these had been conceived as war measures, not as vehicles for domestic reform, even where, as in the case of the G.I. Bill, profound social changes did result. In fact, efforts to link veterans' benefits to a broad program of social legislation had made no headway.[8]

What was absent was any momentum to turn the war crisis to reform purposes. On the contrary, the prevailing tendency was to draw a sharp line between the war emergency—and the progressive measures it engendered—and normal times. "Why are the good things a part of war; why can't we have them in peacetime as well?", Philip Murray asked angrily at the moment of victory in 1945.

> Are we concerned about the health and care of mothers and children only when the husband and father is being killed or mutilated? Are we willing to provide housing on the basis of people's needs for it only when soldiers in foxholes have no home or place to lay their head? Are we agreeable to feeding people more adequately when they are making or using the engines of destruction but care nothing about nourishment of the same people when war is done?

"Our citizens are not foolish persons: they will ask all these and a multitude of similar questions." It was the negative side of Murray's outburst that was significant. The beneficial programs of wartime—child care, maternity benefits for servicemen's wives, housing, and much else—had been strictly temporary responses to an emergency situation. And, in 1945, the

American people had not yet begun to demand "that the fruit of victory [be] something better than we have ever had before."[9] As for Bruce Catton, he answered his own question: "We never let ourselves build a war effort that would bring us into the peace with a dynamic, this-is-democracy-in-action program."[10]

The burden of this essay is to explore Catton's proposition. He was, in fact, drawing too bleak a conclusion. For the war did make a positive contribution to American reform as a consolidating force for the New Deal. But it did not generate a new thrust forward.[11] On this main score, Catton was indubitably correct. The reasons for that failure are, of course, exceedingly complex; but it is possible, for purposes of analysis, to map out the three operative factors: first, Roosevelt's wartime administration; second, the organized groups or coherent interests capable of using the war to promote reform. The third variable—the impact of war in America —can perhaps best be treated, not separately, but in interaction with the first two.

The Roosevelt administration chose early and probably almost by reflex: it drew a sharp line between the tasks of making war and its commitment to domestic reform. When President Roosevelt spoke jocularly of Dr. New Deal and Dr. Win-the-War at his press conference in December 1943, he was in fact acknowledging the key distinction governing his wartime domestic strategy. Dr. New Deal, who had treated the patient for a grave internal disorder since 1933, "didn't know nothing" about broken bones, and so turned the poor fellow, when he suffered a terrible accident on 7 December, 1941, over to the orthopedic surgeon Dr. Win-the-War. President Roosevelt had occasion to express this idea in soberer terms. Rejecting as "premature" a proposal in early 1942 for a commission to advise him on ways to improve race relations, Roosevelt responded that "we must start winning the war . . . before we do much general planning for the future." He intended to avoid projects that lead away from "the realities of war. I am not convinced that we can be realists about the war and planners for the future at this critical time."[12] Harry Hopkins, Eleanor Roosevelt, wrote, "put the running of the war ahead of everything else. As far as he was concerned, war needs were paramount. My husband felt similarly." Mrs. Roosevelt thought they were wrong. She "could not help feeling that it was the New Deal social objectives that had fostered the spirit that would make it possible for us to fight the war, and I believed it was vastly important to give the people the feeling that in fighting the war we were still really fighting for those same objectives. I felt it was essential both to the prosecution of the war and to the period after the war that the fight for the rights of minorities should continue. . . . I thought the groundwork should be laid for a wide health program after the war."[13]

Why did Roosevelt and Hopkins not share this perception of the connection between war and reform? The nature of the New Deal itself must serve as the starting point. Lacking a comprehensive blueprint for change, lacking even any clear vision of the new society, the New Deal was essentially *reactive* in character; the Great Depression had given it direction and momentum. The outbreak of war in Europe rapidly deprived the New Deal of the crucial stimulus for action. As unemployment shrank during 1940–41 and virtually disappeared by 1943, as farmer purchasing power zoomed by 1943 to almost double the level of 1939, as industrial production rose to record heights by 1943, the urgency vital to Roosevelt's brand of reformism departed. Indeed, the crisis mode of thinking that had shaped the New Deal now worked counter to reform; war posed the great emergency now, and Roosevelt, temperamentally inclined as he was to deal with the immediate and the concrete, would not turn his attention from the war effort.

Nor did he easily accept his wife's conviction that a reform appeal would advance the prosecution of the war. In part, this too was a matter of temperament. He was not inclined, as Woodrow Wilson had done during World War I, to elevate wartime emotions into a domestic crusade. Characteristically, when a strike during the summer of 1941 was forcing the government to take over a vital shipyard at Kearny, New Jersey, Roosevelt prompted the head of the National Defense Mediation Board to appeal (unofficially) to the selfish interests of both sides: saying to the company, that goverment compensation for seizure would be less than it anticipated; to the union, that the navy would give it an inferior contract.[14] This matter-of-fact approach, characteristic of Roosevelt's wartime leadership, hardly left room for the heady promises of "reconstruction" made by Wilson and the Committee on Public Information during World War I.

More than temperament was at work here. Accommodation was the essential mode of New Deal operation. Roosevelt always sought—with declining success in later years, to be sure—to win the approval and cooperation of the groups affected by his programs. This remained preeminently his method in meeting the military crisis. When the War Resources Board in 1939 put forward its Industrial Mobilization Plan concentrating extraordinary wartime powers in the hands of a military-industrial agency, labor, agriculture, and liberals generally raised furious objections. Roosevelt hastily dismissed the board and shelved the plan. Likewise, Roosevelt opposed punitive measures against labor when strikes seriously impeded the defense effort in 1941.[15] But the primary test of the accommodating strategy was posed by the peacetime opponents of the New Deal. Could Roosevelt secure the total support of American industry? This seemed absolutely crucial to the president, and from the first he worked assiduously to carry businessmen fully with him into war mobilization. On one point they were peculiarly sensitive: a *Fortune* survey in November 1941 revealed that three-quarters of American businessmen feared that Roosevelt would use the war crisis for reform purposes.[16] This suspicion, easily aroused and ever present, severely circumscribed Roosevelt's sense of what might be done during the war.

So did congressional politics. Roosevelt's troubles here antedated the war, of course. The presidential party (as James MacGregor Burns would put it) had begun to lose ground on Capitol Hill almost as soon as Roosevelt had won his great victory of 1936. Sharp Republican gains in 1938, plus the emergence of the southern Democratic–Republican coalition, solidified the conservative grip on Congress. Roosevelt's own successes in 1940 and 1944 did not translate into appreciably greater power in Congress. And New Dealers suffered heavy losses in the crucial mid-war congressional elections in November 1942. The Republicans captured forty-four additional seats in the House (thirteen short of a majority), nine in the Senate (nine short of a majority). Democratic losses in the North, moreover, increased the relative power of the southern Democrats, and their sense of independence was further enhanced by wartime prosperity in the South and by suspicion of the administration's intentions on race relations. The conservative coalition reached the apex of its effectiveness in 1943–44.[17]

The Seventy-eighth Congress was remarkable for its fierce hostility to the New Deal. Roosevelt himself came to regard it as a Republican Congress, as well he might in view of the succession of defeats he suffered on Capitol Hill. The conservative coalition emasculated the Farm Security Administration and ended the Works Progress Administration, the National Youth Administration, and the Civilian Conservation Corps. Such New Deal agencies, asserted Congressman John Taber, "should be dropped, not only for the duration of the war, but forever."[18] The Seventy-eighth Congress overrode a presidential veto of the 1944 tax bill that

Roosevelt decried for "providing relief not for the needy but for the greedy." This was the first major revenue bill in history to become law over a veto.[19] In 1944 the Senate rejected the Murray-Kilgore bill strengthening unemployment insurance coverage of war workers during reconversion and extending federal responsibility on employment matters; the more modest George bill on this subject went down to defeat in the House after passing the Senate.

In 1942, one Republican House leader vowed to "win the war from the New Deal." If conservatives could not manage that, they could at least be sure to prevent the war from advancing the New Deal. When the Department of Labor requested an appropriation to investigate absenteeism in war work, objections were raised that Frances Perkins seemed "more concerned about social gains than in winning the war."[20] This kind of mistrust actually went back to well before the Seventy-eighth Congress. In 1940, a Defense Housing Act was passed to meet critical housing shortages in defense plant areas. At House insistence, the measure prohibited any conversion of defense housing to public-housing use after the emergency without specific congressional authorization. "The New Dealers are determined to make the country over under the cover of war if they can," warned Senator Robert Taft in January 1942.[21]

Severe congressional opposition would, at any time, have blunted Roosevelt's reform impulse. The New Deal was intensely *political* in its orientation, depending always on a close calculation of congressional prospects. Roosevelt was never inclined to take up a legislative battle that could not be won (or at least pay dividends at the polls): hence the virtual abandonment of New Deal expansion after the legislative and election setbacks of 1937–38. The paralyzing effect of Roosevelt's political realism was compounded by another kind of realism arising from the war crisis. The essential support that he needed from Congress, Roosevelt felt, was for his military program and for his internationalist diplomacy. And he was entirely willing to accept a trade-off on domestic issues. This is, in fact, what transpired. Congressional relations with the White House developed a remarkable schizophrenia—partisan and negative on matters of domestic policy, bipartisan and supportive in carrying on the war and making the peace. The president seemed satisfied. He was, of course, saddened at the loss of so ancient an ally as George Norris, whose defeat summed up the conservative mood of the country in November 1942. But, on the whole, he viewed with evident equanimity the outcome of that election.[22] Only on a few rare occasions was he roused to make a fighting issue of congressional conservatism, for he was getting what he really deemed essential from Capitol Hill.

Nor was Roosevelt inclined even to follow the initiative of congressional liberals when they took up the battle in June 1943. The Wagner-Murray-Dingell bill, which drew among other sources from the recommendations of FDR's own planners, proposed a comprehensive revamping of the nation's social security system: nationalizing those parts under state control; improving the benefits and expanding the coverage of existing programs; adding compulsory health insurance; and providing benefits for veterans. Roosevelt saw the omnibus measure only after it was drafted. He wished Senator Wagner "good luck with it," but lent it little or no administration support, notwithstanding that, as Wagner's biographer notes, the bill "quickly became the focal point of New Dealers' hopes for the postwar future."[23] The president was careful, in fact, not to put a reform stamp on measures he did actively support. When Frances Perkins was preparing a speech for social security changes, he asked her to emphasize "that this is not, what some people call, a New Deal measure."[24] And he was willing to trade the scheduled increase in social security contributions for Senator Vandenberg's support in foreign policy.[25]

The natural bent of the Roosevelt administration to abandon reform during a war crisis was, finally, deeply exaggerated by the way war actually came to America. For more than two years after the German invasion of Poland, the United States stayed formally at peace. Roosevelt led a country still largely isolationist in sentiment and unwilling to go on a war footing. Always far ahead of the country on the need for American intervention, yet never daring to call the country to arms, Roosevelt had to follow a tortuous course that, as events permitted, involved the country by slow steps in the Allied cause and that brought about a sadly incomplete form of mobilization. The logic against reform operated with peculiar force during the defense period, when Roosevelt was bending every effort to carry his domestic opposition (as well as much of the New Deal support) with him in the deepening world crisis. The defense experience in turn helped shape an accommodating pattern that would apply throughout the war. Once Pearl Harbor plunged the nation into war, division was replaced by unity, irresolution by a national determination to go all out in the war effort. This dramatic reversal, ironically, also worked counter to war reform. After 7 December 1941, Roosevelt never had to worry about justifying American involvement in the war. He did not need to generate war enthusiasm by grand promises of "reconstruction," as Woodrow Wilson had felt compelled to do during World War I. (Confidence in national unity, in fact, goes a long way toward explaining why World War II did not generate the kind of evangelism—repressive as well as progressive—that marked World War I.)

On the other hand, the urgency of the war emergency tended to strengthen Roosevelt's inclination to concentrate on the immediate and the critical, and hence to divorce the war effort from matters of domestic policy.

So, if World War II was to bring reform the effort would have to come, not from Washington, but from the private sector. Black protest suggested the possibilities. Outraged at being shut out of the defense industries in 1940–41, Negroes began to demand effective government action against discriminatory hiring, as well as an end to segregation in the armed forces. The founder of the March on Wahington Movement, A. Philip Randolph, concluded from a meeting with Roosevelt that talk would not bring justice. He came away from the White House, a subordinate later recalled, "understanding that the government was not going to give you anything unless you made them. . . . The President . . . was not going to take the leadership . . . unless he had to." He seemed, in fact, to invite Randolph to put pressure on him.[26] So black leaders rejected Roosevelt's plea to call off the march on Washington. And then the president, responding characteristically to political realities, issued on 25 June 1941 the historic Executive Order 8802 that prohibited job discrimination in federal government and in defense industry, and set up the Fair Employment Practices Committee as the policing agency.

Countering pressures from the South and from industry and labor placed severe limits on the concrete achievements of the March on Washington Movement. Roosevelt actually conceded a good deal less than the MOWM had demanded.[27] And Executive Order 8802 was only weakly enforced, starved as FEPC was for funds by a hostile Congress and housed as it was in a war administration anxious to keep the lid on the race issue. The crucial weakness was the dependence on moral suasion; not once was a war contract withdrawn for failure to comply with an FEPC order. Obviously, in the final calculation production needs outweighed racial justice. Manpower shortages actually played the more important part in breaking down discrimination in employment and segregation in the military services.

Executive Order 8802 nevertheless marked a major advance, not only for the immediate accomplishments of the FEPC, but as the first step in making public policy an instrument against racial discrimination. Thus, during 1943 the War Labor Board prohibited wage differentials based on race, the U.S. Employment Service began to refuse to process requests that specified the race of applicants, and the National Labor Relations Board ruled that it would not certify unions that excluded minorities. (This went some way toward satisfying an original MOWM demand for a change in the Wagner Act to deny coverage to unions barring blacks from membership.) And the precedent had been established for more effective and far-reaching use of public policy against discrimination in the postwar period, first at the state level and then increasingly by the federal government.

For purposes of this discussion, in any case, the significance of FEPC is as a demonstration of the mechanics of wartime reform. The Roosevelt administration continued to rely on broker politics, shaping policy by a close calculation of the relative power of claimant groups. And the war emergency altered the prevailing balance; disadvantaged groups now were in a more strategic position to press their claims for reform. The March on Washington Movement could hardly have posed so potent a threat before 1941. But would the opportunity be seized? On this crucial point, black Americans were in fact quite exceptional. For them, war generated militancy, in part because of bitter memories of World War I, in part because of the discrepancy between war ideals and realities at home, and, probably most important, because of the frustration at seeing opportunities open up and be foreclosed to them because of discrimination (and, in fact, black protest did tend to subside as the bars to employment and military service fell later in the war). With its emphasis on economic issues, on exclusively black participation, and on mass action, the March on Washington Movement pioneered a new pattern of Negro protest. It was during World War II, as Richard Dalfiume has stressed, that the modern civil rights movement got its start.

But for other Americans the war led not toward militancy but toward conservatism. This result occurred in two discernible ways. Most important, of course, war brought good times. Unemployment dropped from roughly 9 million in July 1940 to an irreducible minimum of under 800,000 in September 1943. Tenant farmers and migratory laborers moved in large numbers to defense centers—the sad oddysey of John Steinbeck's Joad family doubtless ended on time-and-a-half in some aircraft plant in southern California. Weekly earnings in manufacturing industries went up by 80 percent between January 1941 and January 1945, partly due to an eight-hour increase in the work week, partly to the advance of hourly earnings by nearly 60 percent. Since consumer prices rose by only 30 percent during this period, industrial workers experienced a very substantial increase in real income. And for many families, this was augmented by the entry of five million women into the labor force, as well as of large numbers of teen-agers. The upward-leveling effect of the war was most dramatically expressed in the shrinkage of the share of national income from 23.7 to 16.8 percent going to the top five percent of Americans between 1939 and 1944.

The political consequences struck home in the congressional elections of 1942. The Republican gains came not so much from any notable shift of voters as from the failure of Democrats to turn out at the polls. Comparing the 1938 and 1942 congressional elections, the public-opinion expert John Harding concluded *"that the main source of the Republican gains was the almost total disappearance of the WPA."*[28] (The Democrats also disproportionately suffered from the loss of votes of young men in the Army and of workers on the move.) Insofar as economic hardship had rendered voters and interest groups reform-minded, that factor was essentially neutralized by the war boom.

There was a second reason why key interest groups who might have done so did not think of the war in terms of reform. The New Deal had done its work too well, for it had already created the basic mechanisms through which both agriculture and labor could advance their interests in wartime. Organized agriculture was entirely content to function within the system of price support written into the second Agricultural Adjustment Act of 1938. Although designed to deal with the problem of surplus, the parity system could also be put to profitable use in a time of war shortage. The key was to get the basic commodities pegged at a high parity level. Prodded by farm spokesmen, Congress set the minimum for commodity loan rates at 85 percent of parity in May 1941, then raised it to 110 percent in January 1942. Given greater shortages of some nonbasic crops, these levels created an abnormally high floor from which incentives would then have to be generated to encourage shifts in production from less critical basic crops such as short staple cotton. This was hardly the best system for bringing agricultural production in line with war needs, or for advancing Roosevelt's campaign for price stabilization.

The American Farm Bureau Federation won some of the ensuing battles with the administration and lost a few. The Economic Stabilization Act of

October 1942 forced the parity level down to 90 percent; but agriculture got important concessions in return: first, the inclusion of labor costs in the parity formula, and, second, the provision that the price supports would continue for two years after the war as insurance against the price collapse that had befallen American agriculture after World War I. The results were likewise mixed on the struggle over the use of subsidy methods. The Farm Bureau Federation and its allies preferred price increases (beyond parity levels, of course), and were able to defeat an administration move in 1943 to use incentive payments to help shift agricultural production to meet essential war needs. On the other hand, subsidies came into wide use—at the rate of $1.6 billion a year in 1945—as a means of holding the line on consumer food prices.

On the whole, American farmers fared very well during the war: net income per person in agriculture in 1945 was three times the 1935–39 level, whereas annual income for industrial workers only doubled during the period. But the crucial point, for purposes of this discussion, was the way farmers sought to rely on existing mechanisms to advance their interests. Far from opening up new possibilities, the war reinforced adherence to the system of farm price supports gained during the New Deal. "Farm groups, with the exception of the Farmers Union, have no positive program for additional basic legislation," remarked a Wisconsin farm expert in 1947.[29]

Organized labor went through a comparable experience. The National Labor Relations Act of 1935 had already granted what trade unionists deemed essential, namely, effective protection of the right to organize and engage in collective bargaining. Their impulse was to exploit the defense crisis, not to seek reform, but rather to make better use of the existing framework, particularly since they had discovered that depression conditions limited the benefits to be derived from the Wagner Act. John L. Lewis gave the most striking demonstration of labor's aims. In early 1940, Lewis began to press President Roosevelt to repay political debts to labor: the CIO president wanted defense contracts withheld from any firm that was not complying with the Wagner Act. (Roosevelt's refusal partly explained Lewis's break with FDR during the presidential campaign.)[30] Lewis's extremism was perhaps exceptional, but not his eagerness to use the war emergency to advance conventional trade-union interests. All through the defense period and the war itself, the union movement carried on assiduous organizing work, exploiting labor's strategic advantages and making full use of the mechanisms of the National Labor Relations Board.

The result was phenomenal growth: membership went up from nine to fifteen million between 1939 and 1945.

No less important than numbers was the union stability gained during the war. Here, too, John L. Lewis was the bellwether. The defense emergency gave him the opportunity to launch a campaign for the union shop in the captive mines during the fall of 1941. In the face of unyielding steel companies, a storm of popular disapproval, and an adverse decision from the National Defense Mediation Board, Lewis pressed his advantage —three times he called his miners out on brief strikes—and forced the deeply resentful Roosevelt to undercut the NDMB, create a special arbitration board to decide the issue, and, by this strategem, give to Lewis the union shop in the captive mines. On the whole, the rest of organized labor took a more moderate line (and disavowed, in fact, Lewis's strong-arm methods, especially after the war began), but it too strove for union security. The result was a quite favorable compromise—maintenance of membership, that is, the requirement that made membership compulsory during the life of a contract for those already in a union—which the National War Labor Board employed to resolve the thorny issue of union security. By the end of 1945, this formula covered 29 percent of all workers under union contracts, and, especially in the traditionally open-shop industries, played a crucial role in putting trade unionism on a stable basis.[31]

Labor's organizational gains during the war, though deriving at least as much from emergency conditions as from the role of the NLRB, nevertheless were an extension of the growth process started by the Wagner Act and, more important, held labor's mind very much within the frame of reference under which that law had been adopted. The war was no time to fool with new ideas.

A negative part of labor's war experience reinforced that conclusion. To a markedly greater degree than for agriculture, labor had to accept a departure from normal practice in its affairs. Free collective bargaining, which the Wagner Act had been designed to foster, could not in fact be permitted to prevail during wartime. Labor leaders gave a voluntary no-strike pledge immediately after Pearl Harbor. On 12 January 1942, President Roosevelt created the National War Labor Board with the authority to settle "labor disputes which might interrupt work which contributes to the effective prosecution of the war." By common consent and by the use of presidential war powers, therefore, the right to strike came to an end (although violations of the rule, both actual and threatened, kept the strike issue inflamed throughout the war). The need to control inflation soon eliminated what remained of normal collective bargaining, namely, the freedom to make contractual agreements that did not involve labor disputes. With the passage of the Economic Stabilization Act of October 1942, government control over voluntary wage increases began, using as a guideline the Little Steel Formula that pegged wage stabilization at the level of real wages as of 1 January 1941. The application of this rule became very stringent once the president issued his "hold the line" executive order of 8 April 1943.

Compulsion of this kind, even admitting its necessity, would have been hard for American labor to accept under the best of circumstances. And, as it happened, circumstances seemed far from best to union leaders. They unceasingly charged the administration with unfairness: government statistics underestimated price increases; actual economic needs of workers received too little consideration; and, worst of all, salaries, profits, and prices lacked the stringent controls placed on wages. Wage-earners were making "a disproportionate sacrifice relative to other groups."[32] At least, the unions had equal representation with management on the National War Labor Board. But, as the stabilization policy tightened, control over wage regulation shifted to James F. Byrnes's Office of Economic Stabilization, where labor had no effective voice and little influence.

Labor's wariness was fostered, finally, by the visible hardening of public opinion against the union movement during the war. President Roosevelt, for example, received in June 1943 a confidential survey that asked leading people to estimate opinion in their congressional districts: 81 percent believed the local feeling was that the administration had "bungled" on labor; asked to select the major local criticism of the administration from a list, 49 percent chose "Labor Policies too Soft. Should Stop Strikes." This hostile sentiment, brought to white heat by John L. Lewis and his miners' strikes, resulted in the passage of the punitive Smith-Connally War Labor Disputes Act, which gave to President Roosevelt more power over strikes than he wanted (the measure passed over his veto) and, additionally, restricted the use of union funds for political activity. No wonder, then, that organized labor thought no farther than of a return to the status quo after the war. Most unionists applauded the lifting of controls over wages and strikes, and ignored President Truman's request that they continue the no-strike pledge during the reconversion period.[33]

For both agriculture and labor, therefore, World War II provided an experience of a quite different order than had World War I. In 1917, neither had yet found ways to counterbalance its structural weaknesses in the economic order. World War I had produced answers: price supports for farmers, protection of organizing rights for workers. From these starting points, effective public mechanisms had been perfected during the New Deal. The second war experience acted wholly to reinforce the adherence of both agriculture and labor to the existing framework.

So the cause of reform lacked either of the kinds of champion capable of promoting significant change through the American political system. Neither from the public sector nor from the private sector did there arise a compelling initiative to seize on the war crisis for reform purposes. The blunting of that possibility can perhaps best be studied in the handling of industrial mobilization—first, because this offered the central opportunity, and, second, because it did evoke one genuine proposal for basic change.

Late in 1940, Walter Reuther, then a youthful vice-president of the United Automobile Workers of America in charge of the union's General Motors division, came forward with an imaginative plan for speeding up the lagging program for aircraft production. At the time, the official program called for the construction of new facilities specifically designed for the manufacture of war planes. The projected plants would not be fully operative until late in 1942. Meanwhile, Britain was battling for her life, and the United States was drawing ever closer to war. Why not make use of idle capacity in the automobile industry? Himself an old tool-and-die man, Reuther had been studying the problem for months. Having gathered data on available plant facilities and skilled labor, and having conferred at length with design engineers and skilled machinists, he concluded that automobile plants could be readily converted to aircraft manufacture. The second part of Reuther's plan involved the pooling of the industry's technical resources and idle production facilities for this massive project. Plants of the various companies would be assigned the manufacture of plane parts, and assembly would take place at a few central points. (Reuther had in mind the idle Hupmobile plant in Detroit as the central motor assembly plant.) "We propose to transform the entire unused capacity of the automotive industry into one huge plane production unit," asserted Reuther. His dramatic plan advanced a third idea: an aviation production board, drawn equally from government, management, and labor, and with "full authority to organize and supervise the mass production of airplanes in the automobile and automotive parts industry."[34]

The Reuther plan was actually the foremost expression of a broader CIO approach to defense. The Roosevelt administration was obviously groping toward centralized direction of industrial mobilization, first in a very halting way with the revival of National Defense Advisory Commission in May 1940 (based on statutory powers going back to World War I), then somewhat more vigorously in the formation of the Office of Production Management in January 1941. On 18 December 1940, Philip Murray urged President Roosevelt instead to turn the defense effort over to industrial councils (such as the proposed aviation production board). The CIO chief wanted control to be housed in each industry, not in a Washington agency whose efforts were clearly "unwieldy, inefficient and unfunctional." A national defense board would retain supervisory functions, but not direct administrative authority over industrial activity. The ineffectiveness of the Office of Production Management quickly gave point to Murray's argument on this score. Finally, full labor participation both on the national board and in the industrial councils capped the CIO scheme. To achieve industrial peace, and the fullest effort from American workers, Roosevelt would have to give labor "a voice in matters of [industrial] policy and administration."[35] In the following months, CIO unions developed specific plans for steel, aluminum, farm equipment, and nonferrous metals, but it was the Reuther scheme that evoked the greatest interest. At a time when the nation's most pressing need was for aircraft production, no rallying cry could have been more arresting than Reuther's call for 500 planes a day within six months.

The CIO proposals stressed immediate problems. "Emergency requires short-cut solutions," said Reuther. "This plan is labor's answer to a crisis."[36] But it also laid the basis for far-reaching reform of the economic order. The struggle to organize the mass-production industries had generated an authentic thrust that went beyond pure-and-simple unionism. From among old labor progressive types such as John Brophy and Powers Hapgood who had rallied to the industrial-union cause, from young leaders such as the Reuther brothers and James Carey who had sprung from the rank-and-file, came a keen sense that the CIO was destined for more than business unionism.[37] If the reform impulse proved short-lived, if John L. Lewis and Sidney Hillman too quickly became fallen idols, if factional battles with the Communists consumed too much of the initial idealism, if the day-to-day practice of collective bargaining swiftly diverted energies into the conventional trade-union mold, CIO progressivism was nevertheless briefly a genuine phenomenon, and one still much alive when war broke out in Europe. The industrial council notion sprang from these labor progressives who saw in labor's participation in the management of defense industry the prospect of permanent economic reform.

"The heart of the Murray plan is the proposal for Industrial Councils," John Brophy explained.

> This matter of production cannot be handled by issuing orders at Washington. It can only be handled by men who are intimately familiar with the peculiar production problems of their own industries. . . . The participation of labor is particularly important in order to guarantee that profits are not placed above the national interest in this emergency. It is essential likewise to the full protection of civil and industrial rights of the American people.

The council plan would serve "as a valuable method for the post-war world." Observers saw the implications as well. The Reuther proposal, remarked Walter Lippmann, was "of such historic importance" because it represented "the first great plan which organized labor had offered in its status not of a hired man but of the responsible partner." The radical journalist I. F. Stone perceived in the Murray plan "the beginnings of a kind of industrial democracy far better suited to the spirit of the American people than either control by a few men through monopoly or control by a few men through a Socialist bureaucracy. . . . If our businessmen, our workers, our engineers, learn to work in harness together in the job of defending America, they will learn how to reconstruct America . . . in the flexible framework of a co-operative industrial democracy."[38]

The history of the CIO plan reveals in a concrete way the interplay of forces that blunted the reform potential of World War II. The fate of Reuther's conversion scheme tells part of the story. Anxious to speed up aircraft production, President Roosevelt liked the conversion idea and issued orders that it be given full consideration. Others in his administration, both liberal advisers and defense officials, were enthusiastic. But the automobile companies objected. They denied the technical feasibility of conversion to aircraft production: plant floor space was too small, machine tools not easily altered and in any case not up to the low tolerance requirements for plane engines, and mass-production techniques not applicable to the complex problems of aircraft manufacture. Underlying this was a denial that national needs called for so drastic a departure from business-as-usual. The auto makers gladly undertook large contracts for building new aircraft facilities, but they wanted their business in the civilian car market left undisturbed. Ironically, the defense program boomed domestic demand: cars were rolling off the assembly lines at an annual rate of 5 million by the spring of 1941, and the year would ultimately prove to be the second largest in the industry's history. The Reuther proposal actually did not call for any cutbacks in civilian production (one of the practical motives behind the plan was to create jobs for idle auto workers); but it did contemplate such far-reaching departures from normal industry practice as postponement of new models, leveling production over the whole year, and pooling of equipment and technical data. Moreover, the way would have been opened for readily shifting from civilian production as defense needs required it. The administrative arrangements that Roosevelt had set up to run the defense program virtually foreclosed the possibility of overriding the industry's resistance to conversion. The Office of Production Management was manned by executives drawn from business; and, as it happened, the head was William Knudsen, formerly president of General Motors. Knudsen and his associates took the same negative view of conversion as did the industry, and thereby assured the rejection of the idea.[39]

As 1941 passed, pressure built up on the auto industry for conversion from a different direction. Shortages of strategic materials raised demands from within the War and Navy departments for the curtailment of civilian output. Moving haltingly, the OPM in mid-April announced a 20 percent cut in auto production effective 1 August 1941. It was, ironically, the agency charged with civilian problems, Leon Henderson's Office of Price Administration and Civilian Supply, that forced the issue by ordering a 50 percent reduction in car output on July 20. Prodded into action, Knudsen gave the auto industry a quota of 51.4 percent of 1941 production for the year beginning 1 August 1941. But the curtailment was to be gradual, rising from only a 6.5 percent cut in the first quarter to 62 percent in the last. Nor did the administration have any substantial success in its intensifying efforts to bring about conversion in the auto industry (which was one of the aims of curtailment). Knudsen held back, and Roosevelt, despite his increasing restiveness, was unwilling to take the auto makers on directly. Until Pearl Harbor, they had their way; auto production went on essentially unabated almost up to the outbreak of war. Nothing told more about Roosevelt's accommodating strategy during the defense period than his failure to extract a greater contribution from Detroit.[40]

Pearl Harbor at last brought decisive action. The government quickly ordered a complete halt to car production and announced that it was prepared to place 5 billion dollars worth of military contracts with the industry. Spurred by these moves and by the crisis itself, the car makers proceeded to convert their plants rapidly to war production—not, to be sure, to the manufacture of complete aircraft, as Reuther had proposed, but to aircraft parts, tanks, machine guns, and so on. By June 1942, the industry was using 66 percent of its machine tools on military goods. Late in the war, the president of Chrysler boasted that his company had converted 89 percent of its automotive capacity to war work.[41] This order of productive achievement, reproduced throughout American industry, signified the country's willingness and ability to take extreme measures in the war crisis. After Pearl Harbor, it was agreed on all sides that the situation demanded a radical departure from business-as-usual—the more so, ironically, because so much had been left undone in the defense period.

But the barriers to reform did not come down: radical measures there would have to be, but not such as would threaten the status quo. The other side of the Reuther plan—the industrial council idea—provides us with a starting point. Industry was, of course, unalterably opposed to any notion of labor participation in management. In fact, sensitivity on this score evidently had something to do with the refusal to give the technical aspects of the scheme a trial. "They wanted to come into the shop as a union committee and try to design fixtures for the present machinery," Knudsen remarked in March 1941. "We had to stall on that one and say that it couldn't be handled." When Reuther renewed his demand for labor participation in industrial direction after the United States entered the war, General Motors President Charles E. Wilson answered sharply that "to divide the responsibility of management would be to destroy the very foundations upon which America's unparalleled record of accomplishment is built." If Reuther wanted a place in management, General Motors would be glad to hire him. (Reuther declined.)[42]

Throughout the war, business displayed intense hostility to any intrusion on managerial prerogatives. Even the War Production Board's modest program for plant joint committees ran into rough going and required repeated assurances that the sole objective was more production. Hence, for example, this statement by four national labor and business leaders a year after the campaign had been launched in 1942:

> The labor-management committee program . . . , endorsed by us, is not designed to increase the power or position of any union. It does not interfere with any bargaining machinery or undertake its functions. It is not designed to conform to any scheme that contemplates a measure of control of management by labor or labor by management. . . . It is the War Production Drive Plan to

increase production by increasing efficiency through greater management and labor cooperation.

"This is probably the most completely negative bit of sales talk in the history of salesmanship," remarked Bruce Catton.[43] At the president's National Labor-Management Conferences in 1945, business placed managerial inviolability at the center of its program for postwar labor relations.[44] Given Roosevelt's accommodating strategy toward business, its objections would have doubtless constituted a veto of labor participation in any case.

But, as it happened, countering pressure from the labor movement, which might have made some difference, was largely absent. The AFL expressed indifference; it preferred adequate labor representation on government agencies. William Green himself was puzzled: Why should labor be interested in a managerial role? When war came, the federation called for a truce in which neither labor nor management would exploit wartime controls "to prosecute either's advantage at the expense of the other." Within the CIO, too, conventional union elements were cool to the idea, and the left was hotly opposed from start to finish. Before 22 June 1941, the Communists branded the Murray plan as a form of warmongering and a scheme for labor speed-up. Afterward, they regarded it as a vexatious impediment to fullest cooperation for maximum war production. When the United Electrical Workers (UE) urged its locals to set up joint plant committees, it stressed one point: "The authority to run the plant is in the hands of management." To reassure employers who feared a loss of authority, Julius Emspak explained, "We made it perfectly and unmistakably clear that we are not interested in 'taking over' a plant; we have but one interest, and that is increasing the plant's production."[45] The industrial-council idea, in fact, drew its support almost wholly from the liberal wing of the CIO, especially from those elements identified with the Association of Catholic Trade Unionists. Philip Murray, a devout Catholic, said that his plan "follow[ed] . . . almost completely" Pius XI's social encyclical of 1931. Nor did most of its advocates give the industrial council proposal more than ritual support after the American entry into the war. Although the CIO actively revived the idea in 1944 as "one of the surest methods" for solving the problems of reconversion, no real attempt was made to formulate the plan into a workable program, and in the postwar years it served primarily to establish the progressive credentials of the anti-Communist left within the CIO. Only Walter Reuther made a fight for labor's right to participate in management after the war: that was the point, for example, of his unsuccessful battle to force General Motors to open its books for inspection as a condition for raising prices to meet UAW wage demands.[46]

On 28 March 1945, both the AFL and CIO had signed with the U.S. Chamber of Commerce a New Charter for Labor and Management that, while proclaiming full employment, high wages, and labor's right to organize, also proclaimed a free-enterprise system with managerial prerogatives protected and a minimum of governmental interference.[47] Labor's treatment of the industrial council proposal reveals the larger point: that it was a "satisfied" movement, quite incapable during World War II of seeking in the war crisis an opportunity to bring about reform.

With industry rigidly opposed and labor at heart apathetic, the Roosevelt administration would hardly do otherwise than turn down the industrial council plan. It was left to labor's own man in the defense administration, Sidney Hillman, to administer the final blow when, in mid-December 1941, he concluded that the country "cannot delegate to any combination of private interests final decision on matters of basic policy."[48] How, then, would industrial mobilization take place? It was part of Roosevelt's genius as a war leader to devise an answer that resolved the dilemma: to take radical action but not to threaten the status quo.

There were three components to Roosevelt's answer. The primary one was an extraordinary centralization of control over the war effort. On 16 January 1942, the president created the War Production Board and lodged in it all his constitutional war powers (as supplemented by Congress) as these bore on industrial mobilization. Executive Order 9024 directed the WPB chairman to "exercise general direction over the war procurement and production program . . . including conversion, requisitioning, plant expansion, and the financing thereof . . . and his decisions shall be final." Nor was this immense power to be delegated out to industry committees, as the War Industries Board had done during World War I. All powers of decision would remain in the hands of WPB personnel. One of Chairman Donald Nelson's first actions was to appoint a WPB official to take charge of the conversion of the auto industry and to dissolve the meeting of management and labor representatives considering this problem. Labor and industry committees would be strictly limited to advisory roles, Nelson said at the first meeting of the War Production Board. Over-all direction of industrial conversion and production went to a Division of Industry Operations, with industry branches in charge of each manufacturing industry.[49]

But if this centralization of power was unprecedented in its completeness, it was also emphatically temporary and narrowly confined to the specific task of war-making. This was among the reasons, Robert Sherwood has suggested, that Roosevelt deliberately separated the war agencies from the regular federal bureaucracy.[50] The War Production Board, moreover, carefully limited its decisions to matters touching the war effort. The board, for example, ordered that production be concentrated in full-operation facilities in such industries as sugar refining that were functioning below capacity. Should the owners of the idled plants be compensated for their resulting losses, either by government subsidy or by pooling the industry's income? The WPB turned down the idea because, as its general counsel remarked, "compensation involves policy questions with respect to social planning which should be determined by higher authority."[51]

This strategy expressed itself, finally, in the refusal to set aside the antitrust laws. By the time the defense crisis began in 1938–39, New Freedom proponents such as Robert Jackson and Thurman Arnold had gained the upper hand within the Roosevelt administration; and, with the appointment of John Lord O'Brian as general counsel of the Office of Production Management (and then WPB), they succeeded in committing the administration to operating within the framework of existing antitrust legislation for the duration. This did not mean that the normal rules of competition would continue to apply, but rather that the anticipated departures would be at the direction of government agencies, not of private industry as during 1917–18. Industry committees could only be advisory, the members would be selected not by trade associations but by the government, and recommendations would require the approval of the Department of Justice before WPB industry branches could act on them. To regularize the procedure for authorizing the necessary violations of antitrust laws, the WPB chairman was empowered in June 1942 to grant Certificates of Immunity, after consultation with the attorney general, for firms so operating at WPB request.[52]

By centralizing economic control in the government and by drawing a sharp division between the war program and permanent public policy, the Roosevelt administration devised a radical form of industrial mobilization that contained no seeds of reform. Government control over industry hardly seemed a desired blueprint for peacetime. And any thinking in this direction would be cut short by the emphasis on the strictly temporary character of the war program. There was a third component to the administration's strategy. The war program had to be so implemented as to give no alarm to the nation's industrial interests.

The starting point was the selection of a chairman for the War Production Board. Secretary of War Henry Stimson admonished the president not to pick anyone with an antibusiness reputation. Roosevelt had initially preferred Supreme Court Justice William Douglas (against whom Stimson was especially warning him), but he finally chose Donald Nelson, whose credentials could hardly have been better for meeting the conflicting requirements for a production czar. A former Sears, Roebuck executive, he was identified neither with Wall Street nor big business; he was held in high regard in New Deal circles; and, as executive director of the Supplies Priorities and Allocations Board, he stood out as an energetic all-outer during the irresolute defense effort.[53] But Nelson was also a safe man from the standpoint of those who would be subject to his sweeping powers. He was, for one thing, not personally inclined to use those powers unreservedly. Conciliatory and patient by temperament, Nelson sought to get "action in the democratic way without dictatorial tactics." Deeply imbued with the virtues of the American productive system, moreover, Nelson did not believe it was up to him "to *tell* industry how to do its job; it was our function to *show* industry what had to be done, and then to do everything in our power to enable industry to do it, placing our chief reliance on the limitless energy and skill of American manufacturers. . . . What we did was to establish a set of rules under which the game could be played the way industry said it had to play it."[54]

Business was quickly reassured by Nelson's manner of administration. Not only was the WPB staffed by men drawn from business, but key posts—over 800 by 1943—were held by dollar-a-year men on loan from their companies. Nelson defended the latter policy from persistent criticism by the Truman committee on grounds of expediency; essential high-level people would not come on low government salaries. Nor was WPB policy against heading industry branches with men associated with those industries regularly followed. Aside from the branch chief, in any case, staff tended to be recruited from the same industries. So the control emanating from Washington was a good deal more comfortable in practice than it might have seemed in theory. And the industry advisory committees, specifically excluded as they were from making or carrying out policy, in fact collaborated very closely with the WPB branches and exerted substantial influence over the decisions affecting their industries.

Labor received, by contrast, a quite different welcome on the WPB. Largely indifferent to the Murray plan as it was, the labor movement from the first did press for a major part in governmental direction of industrial mobilization. In a formal way, trade unionism came closest to that goal during the defense period when Sidney Hillman served as associate director general of the Office of Production Management. As it happened, Hillman's participation hardly satisfied organized labor: the AFL considered him a CIO man; the CIO had not chosen him; and Hillman, in any event, soon demonstrated by his performance that he was Roosevelt's lieutenant, not labor's. After the drastic administrative reorganization in early 1942, Hillman was bypassed and edged out of power. When he resigned in April, no labor man replaced him on the War Production Board. Donald Nelson, who prided himself as a friend of trade unionism, did favor labor's participation on the WPB, but in a subordinate, advisory role except on specifically labor matters. The director of the WPB Labor Production Division was selected in consultation with the AFL and CIO, and the two associate directors came directly from the two labor federations. But, since manpower responsibilities had been carved out of the WPB in April 1942 and transferred to the War Manpower Commission, the Labor Production Division was little more than an advisory and liaison agency. No success met the efforts to increase its authority, especially by giving it charge of the War Production Drive that was fostering labor-management plant committees. The touchy issue had to be kept free of even a hint of partisanship, Nelson felt.[55] Finally, in June 1943, Nelson created two new offices—vice-chairman for manpower requirements and vice-chairman for labor production—and appointed to them CIO man Clinton Golden and AFL man Joseph Keenan (thus satisfying the rival labor federations, if not the administrative need for a single unified office). Nelson also advanced the policy of appointing labor assistants to the industry branches. Ever since mid–1941, too, labor advisory boards had served as counterparts to the industry advisory boards.

But these concessions in practice fell far short of labor's ambitions. For one thing, strong resistance developed within the WPB. The Tolan committee reported in October 1942 that recommendations from the Labor Production Division were "ignored or shelved for long periods," and its employees "treated as outsiders and their presence resented by industry branch representatives."[56] Unlike the active industry advisory boards, the labor advisory boards quickly atrophied. They were treated, one labor man complained, as "undigested lumps in the stomachs of the management people."[57] Nor were they permitted, under Nelson's policy, to meet jointly with the industry advisory committees. Only late in the war, as business suspicions moderated and firmer guidelines came down from the WPB, did the labor advisory committees revive and the labor assistants assume real responsibilities in the industry branches. Even then, however, labor participation remained narrowly confined: only on specifically labor matters did union representatives receive policy-making powers; otherwise, with some exceptions in industry branches, they were limited to advisory roles.[58] Never did labor participation threaten the safe administration of the immense powers guiding industrial mobilization.

A more inadvertent development worked also to hold production control in a safely conservative channel. The sweeping power granted to the WPB in January 1942 gave the chairman clear supremacy over all agencies of the executive branch "in respect to war procurement and production." But Nelson favored the broad delegation of authority, and he applied this principle freely to the armed services. They continued to do their own procurement, and the Army-Navy Munitions Board soon received extensive priority powers relating to contracts let by the military services. Nelson expected, of course, that all participants would view "the war supply organizations . . . as a single integrated system operating under the general direction of the Chairman of the War Production Board in a unified effort to win the war and not as a group of autonomous or semi-autonomous organizations acting in mere liaison with one another."[59] The military people, however, held quite other ideas. All their mobilization planning of the interwar years had rested on the notion of military control. When President Roosevelt rejected their M-Plan in 1939, the army and navy chose the next best alternative: to carve out the widest scope and greatest degree of independence that civilian control would permit. General Brehon Somervell proved to be singularly aggressive in his pursuit of that goal for his Army Services of Supply at the expense of WPB authority. And the Army-Navy Munitions Board managed to maneuver President Roosevelt in June 1942 into granting the ANMB an independent priority over military production, and even a concurrent voice on priorities for civilian production. "ANMB now lay beyond Nelson's grasp," remarked the official historians of World War II mobilization.[60]

But the military had overreached itself. As its faulty judgments about the complex industrial economy and its own requirements threatened to reduce the war effort to chaos, Nelson moved to regain civilian control.[61] Having allowed the military to penetrate so deeply into production concerns,

Nelson probably had no other means to curb the services than by incorporating their key people and functions into the WPB. This he did in September 1942 by bringing in Ferdinand Eberstadt, chairman of the Army-Navy Munitions Board, to head the new Requirements Committee that would allocate scarce materials. To handle production scheduling, Nelson appointed Charles E. Wilson of General Electric as chief of the new Production Executive Committee. Although it was composed of representatives of the armed services, Wilson was himself an outsider; and when he moved to take over scheduling functions hitherto in military hands, the War and Navy departments strenuously objected. In the struggle for internal control that followed this reorganization of the WPB, Eberstadt and his military backers almost won; but at the last moment in February 1943, Nelson moved decisively, dismissed Eberstadt, and installed Wilson as executive vice-chairman of the WPB. Even so, the military had established itself as a major presence within the civilian agency controlling industrial mobilization.

This development reinforced the safe conduct of war production. For one thing, important internal shifts accompanied the battle for control of the WPB: key New Dealers such as Leon Henderson departed; Nelson placed operational control in Charles Wilson's hands and so undermined his own authority; and the industry branches, renamed industry divisions, assumed much greater powers. More crucial was the conservative perspective of the military men who would henceforth play a central role within the WPB. Nothing would have been more alien to their way of thinking than to see industrial mobilization as an opportunity for postwar reform. They were, first of all, resolutely single-minded in their advocacy of specifically military needs (sometimes, indeed, to the detriment of the over-all war effort). And they tended, moreover, to share the social outlook of business. In fact, key civilian officials—such as James Forrestal and Ralph Bard of the Navy Department and Robert Patterson of the War Department—had been drawn from much the same financial and corporate circles as their strictly civilian counterparts on the WPB. Between the military and the industrial people (including Charles Wilson) there developed a durable community of interest.

The testing came over reconversion. By mid–1943, with WPB priority and scheduling procedures perfected and war production moving into high gear, planning for the return to a peacetime economy commenced. When and how should surplus capacity and material revert to the civilian economy *during* the war period? This was an interim matter, to be sure, but not one taken lightly. On 30 November 1943, Donald Nelson laid down guiding policy: as manpower, facilities, and material became available in any area, the WPB would authorize the production of additional civilian goods, "provided such production does not limit programs of higher urgency." Nelson had rejected an alternative proposal that called for full programming of reconversion. "It has been my objective from the very start to confine detailed economic planning to war-time production. . . . To start out with the policy of planning our peace-time economy in detail . . . would do irreparable injury to the free enterprise system."

With this philosophy, the business participants in the WPB were of course in hearty agreement, but not with its uncompromising application to the first phase of reconversion. The consequences seemed sure not to be random. Since the nation's major producers dominated war production—67.2 percent of the prime contracts by value up to September 1944 went to 100 companies—small business stood to benefit most from Nelson's laissez faire approach. To forestall "competition's getting a jump" (as Lemuel Boulware put it), the big-business interests that dominated both the industry advisory committees and the machinery of the WPB initially advocated a plan that would protect competitive patterns by assigning production quotas on a prewar basis and by precluding new competition. But Nelson opposed any such guarantees. Companies should be permitted to shift to civilian production "whenever it is possible to do so, even though the effects on competitive situations may be painful." As for prohibiting companies from moving into new fields, Nelson rejected the notion out of hand because "there would clearly be grave danger of shackling the country with a regimented economy."[62]

During the spring of 1944, the business elements on the WPB backed away from making any overt plan to protect the competitive status quo during reconversion. The same end might be attained in a quite different way. The military had at once objected to Nelson's approach: early reconversion would undermine morale on the battlefront and at home, divert manpower from essential areas, and eat up scarce material needed for war production. The military addressed itself wholly to the impact on the war effort, of course, but the economic effect happened to fall neatly in with big-business desires. The postponement of reconversion would permit all producers to shift to the civilian market at the same time. There is no way of assessing business motives here: to what extent was delayed reconversion favored because of the force of military arguments? and to what extent because of competitive consequences? What is certain is that unity on this issue swiftly developed between the military and the industrial groups. In December 1943, Charles Wilson and General Lucius Clay moved jointly to have reconversion placed in the hands of Wilson's Production Executive Committee, which was essentially beyond Nelson's control and which included none of the WPB vice-chairmen who favored early reconversion. Nelson rejected the scheme. But, yielding to opposition within the WPB and himself anticipating no imminent reduction in military needs, Nelson made no move to implement the general policy that he had set forth on 30 November 1943.

Events soon forced his hand. In May 1944, the navy suddenly cut back fighter plane production at the Brewster Corporation, without any provision for utilizing the idled facilities or the 9,000 angry workers. Seizing the opportunity, the Production Executive Committee circumvented Nelson and gained unqualified control over the cancellation of munitions contracts, obviously a key determinant of the pace of reconversion.[63] But Nelson took hold of the other side of the process. On 18 June 1944, he announced a four-point program, including "spot" authorization by regional WPB offices for civilian production wherever manpower, material and facilities were not needed for war production. A furious storm immediately blew up in Washington. The military led the attack. Nelson's reconversion orders "may necessitate [a] revision in strategic plans which could prolong the war," charged Admiral William Leahy of the Joint Chiefs of Staff.[64] Although the industrialists in the WPB remained discretely silent in the public debate, they too opposed early action on a reconversion plan.

The alignment of forces was thus heavily one-sided. Not only were the military and industrial elements within the WPB against Nelson, but so essentially was his own superior, James F. Byrnes, director of the Office of War Mobilization, which had been created in May as a super-agency coordinating the war effort. The only solid internal support for Nelson's reconversion program came from three of the lesser WPB vice-chairmen—the two labor representatives and the redoubtable Maury Maverick, head of the Smaller War Plants Corporation, who candidly favored early reconversion because it would benefit small business and hence counterbalance the favoritism he felt had been shown big business in the granting of war contracts. Maverick, in particular, proved to be quite formidable, not within the WPB, to be sure, but in his skill at airing the controversy and gaining support in Congress. Senator Truman charged that reconversion was being delayed by "some selfish business groups that want to see their competition kept idle . . . [and] by Army and Navy representatives who want to create a surplus of manpower."[65] This kind of publicity (with the threat of senatorial investigation behind it) certainly had an impact: it led, among other things, to the angry resignation of Charles E. Wilson just as he was about to replace Nelson. But liberal criticism was more than counterbalanced by the campaign of the armed services to discredit Nelson's reconversion plan not only by a skillful patriotic appeal but also by manufacturing a production crisis that did not exist.

Within the mobilization establishment, the military-industrial coalition worked persistently to postpone and emasculate the Nelson plan. Byrnes countermanded Nelson's directive to make the four orders effective on 1 July 1944, staggering them instead and placing spot authorization last. Before it could go into effect, Byrnes on 4 August removed spot authorization from the control of the WPB regional offices and required certifications from the hostile War Manpower Commission. Then President Roosevelt, anxious to end the noisy dissension within his war administration, eased Nelson out of office on 18 August and sent him off on a mission to China. His replacement, Julius Krug, proved to be a good deal more amenable to the military-industrial viewpoint within the WPB. Spot authorization went into effect, but was so hamstrung as to hold actual reconversion to a snail's pace. When optimistic predictions for an early end to the European war proved wrong, Byrnes suspended spot authorization in many areas, and then virtually eliminated it after the German counteroffensive began in late December 1944 in the Ardennes. Only with V-E Day almost upon the country did industrial reconversion resume in earnest, so late as to impose no handicaps on the big defense contractors in the scramble for civilian markets.

This tortuous battle over early reconversion was perhaps less important in itself—Maverick's high hopes for a resurgence of business competition hardly would have materialized even if he had won—than for its delineation of the locus of wartime control over the nation's industrial economy. With business interests strongly entrenched in the mobilization structure, and reinforced by their working alliance with the military, the immense economic powers concentrated in Washington held no terrors for American industry. The radical means demanded by the war crisis could hardly be diverted to reform ends.

The ultimate testimony to the success of Roosevelt's strategy came only after his death. As the war drew to an end, no other possibility existed tha..

the swift dismantling of industrial control. There was no counterpart in 1945 to the enthusiasm felt by many business leaders in 1918 for the experiment in industrial self-government during World War I, nor for the desire to carry wartime arrangements over into peacetime instead of returning to the antitrust laws.[66] The War Production Board led to a dead end for American business: its single-minded desire was to revert to the status quo after the war. In September 1944, Julius Krug laid down detailed guidelines for the removal of WPB controls after V-E Day. Among Krug's operating assumptions, the official historians of industrial mobilization noted the following:

> The free enterprise system would remain the basis of our economic activity; should Government intervene to maintain high levels of employment, it would do so mainly by means of fiscal policy; controls would not be used to restore prewar economic relationships or to accomplish social or economic reforms; and wartime controls would be abandoned as rapidly as possible.[67]

The last point gave rise to a dispute that revealed the deep commitment to the quick restoration of the free-market economy. Important interests —the very ones, ironically, who had sought to lift controls to speed reconversion—now wanted to utilize the WPB in the transition to a peacetime economy. Within the WPB, these included the labor vice-chairmen, who were concerned about employment, the vice-chairman in charge of civilian requirements, and Maury Maverick, who feared that small business would lose out in the scramble for scarce raw materials. They were joined by Chester Bowles of the Office of Price Administration, who considered controls over production and resources an essential adjunct to price control to stem inflation during the reconversion period. This New Deal–oriented group stood little chance of success. Krug answered that, after Japan was defeated, he intended to "get rid of regulations and production limits as soon as possible. They automatically put ceilings on initiative, imagination and resourcefulness—the very qualities the country will need most . . . [for a] resilient and rapidly expanding economy."[68] Within the WPB, the industry divisions and the business officialdom wholeheartedly approved Krug's position. So did American businessmen generally, even small manufacturers who stood to benefit from controlled allocation of raw materials. A government survey found little business concern about the problems of reconversion: "Answers to questions about transitions would often begin thoughtfully but suddenly break into a flood of words about American principles."[69] After wavering,

President Truman permitted Krug to have his way. After V-J Day, the War Production Board swiftly lifted its controls and, before the end of the year, passed out of existence. The remarkable wartime undertaking ended with hardly a trace on the nation's public policy.

And yet, if World War II did not generate new departures, it did consolidate older achievements. The reform wave of the 1930s stopped at the war's edge, but did not recede. The consolidating process had been going on all along, of course. It had been a part of the New Deal genius to draw conservative interests into its orbit. The New Deal had, in fact, gained strength from the ease with which interest groups had accepted and sometimes taken over its programs. Nor had the Republican party ever dared base its national politics on reversing the gears of New Deal reform. If Thomas E. Dewey seemed to echo Roosevelt in 1944, so had Landon and Willkie before him. Still, the New Deal had not fully secured itself at the outbreak of European war. It had not yet established the legitimacy of the underlying assumption of governmental responsibility for the nation's economic well-being. Nor had it overcome business hostility, which, indeed, had deepened and grown more embittered in the middle years of the New Deal era. Both of these intractable problems yielded to the pressures of wartime. The war experience helped make possible the Employment Act of 1946 that legitimized the shift of economic responsibility to Washington.[70] In yet more decisive ways, it reconciled American business to the changes wrought by the New Deal.

The test case was New Deal collective-bargaining policy. No reform had evoked greater opposition from industry, for no other had so clearly deprived management of power and curbed its prerogatives. Opposition continued even after the Supreme Court validated the Wagner Act in April 1937. The next year, the National Association of Manufacturers, the U.S. Chamber of Commerce, and other segments of organized business launched a major campaign for a sweeping revision of the law. In the spring of 1939, both houses of Congress held lengthy hearings on the NLRB and the Wagner Act. Some hard-core employers resisted the law outright, especially by exploiting its weak spot—the requirement to engage in bona fide collective bargaining. In all the mass-production industries, there were major firms still successfully fending off unionization at the end of 1939. The majority of open-shop employers, of course, had bowed before the law of the land after 1937, but they had done so reluctantly. They continued to deal grudgingly and conditionally with the new industrial unions. Hardly anywhere in formerly open-shop territory could collective bargaining be said to be on a solid footing when war started in Europe.

The defense period swiftly broke open this uneasy stalemate. As manpower needs grew and Washington exerted influence, Ford gave in unconditionally to the UAW, the steel independents moved toward union recognition, and everywhere collective bargaining resumed for the first time since weak original contracts had been negotiated before the recession of 1937–38. Wartime carried this accommodating process much farther along. Now the government could—and sometimes did—coerce recalcitrant companies into full acceptance of trade unionism. The National War Labor Board virtually wrote the contracts in such unyielding cases as that involving Wilson and Company. On the whole, however, the war influence was benign, as indeed it had to be to work a genuine change in managerial thinking about organized labor.

For one thing, the industrial unions grew strong and became internally stable. The early militancy faded, Julius Emspak remarked regretfully, as war conditions encouraged a "nice, cushy, administrative apparatus form of organization, and [unionists] got accustomed to bureaucracies and paperwork and looking for things through magic formulae."[71] The subsiding of the bitter rivalry between the AFL and CIO further answered the reservations of open-shop management. By 1945, no grounds remained to sustain hopes that unionization might be reversed, nor fears that responsible relations could not be established with the industrial unions. The war experience also worked directly to break down barriers to the full acceptance of trade unionism. Although by the fall of 1942 the National War Labor Board tightly circumscribed collective bargaining, it did not permit the function to atrophy. The NLRB would not consider a case until there had been a direct attempt at settlement; and its awards invariably left some issues open for further negotiation. In this wartime school in collective bargaining, both management and labor received training on limited problems and under controlled conditions, and precedents were set on fringe issues (which labor emphasized because of the wage freeze) that would serve as guidelines for postwar negotiation. In a broader way, too, ingrained animosities dissipated in the war setting. The union campaign for a major role in war administration may have fallen short, but it did have the effect of exposing business to men from the labor movement. Stereotypes could hardly survive the close contact in a common effort on government boards and agencies. The performance of union representatives, noted a government report in 1944, "would convince any sincere doubters that they had worked for the general welfare rather than any special labor interest."[72] Even on the War Production Board, the most sensitive place because it housed the control apparatus over industry, the efforts to circumvent labor participation gave way to substantial acceptance; late in the war labor had gained a measure of the effective role it had been fighting for on the WPB.

Nothing better signified the wartime change in labor relations than the abandonment of the principle of the open shop (i.e., the right to work without regard to union membership). Employers did not accept gladly the imposition of the maintenance-of-membership rule by the NWLB. They protested, as a spokesman from Swift and Company said, that unions have "not yet reached the permanency of organization to rightfully demand such security."[73] The converse was, of course, that the gradual acceptance of this modified form of union security meant recognition of unions as an established fact. The NWLB did its part here: responsible behavior was its test of whether to grant a union maintenance-of-membership. And, if the rule was imposed, it did nevertheless represent something of a consensus, for the employer members on the NWLB did accept the principle (although not its application in many cases).[74] By the war's end, the open shop had lost its force as a rallying cry against trade unionism, and that fact reflected a quite profound change of heart within American industry. The President's Labor-Management Conference of November 1945, although torn on many points, was not divided on the central issues: business signified its genuine acceptance of trade unionism and the basic national labor policy.

Progress on the labor front was part of a much broader accommodation by business to the New Deal during the war. In 1944, President Eric Johnston of the U.S. Chamber of Commerce published a thoughtful book, *America Unlimited*, that revealed new modes of thought among at least more progressive American businessmen. The book, first of all, exuded a prideful spirit. "Credit for the most astounding production job in all history must go primarily to American capitalism," boasted Johnston, to "the initiative, resourcefulness, and ability of private business." Its confidence thus restored by wartime achievement, business could appraise the New Deal free of the corroding defensiveness of the depression years. Nor could old hostilities well survive the wartime atmosphere of common effort, especially not when business played so major a role in that effort. "The war has proved to us a fact which has been true all along, but concealed from sight—that the areas of agreement transcend by far the areas of conflict . . . on which the most diverse groups in our national community can meet as friends in search of solutions and not as enemies in search of lethal weapons." Johnston's book also corroborated an acute prediction that Thurman Arnold had made in *The Folklore of Capitalism* (1937): that a war might serve to cut through the received truths that had constricted the business response to the New Deal. A war crisis would force men to act in fresh and pragmatic ways and reduce their faith in old rules. Considering the problems of demobilization, Eric Johnston warned against "doctrinaire free-enterprise theory." "In this, as in all things, we must guard against the dangers of absolutist thinking, of putting theory above fact." Finally, Johnston perceived now the immense prospects of positive, intelligent action in the common interest. War had dealt the old economic fatalism a hard blow. "What the American people have done under the impetus of a war challenge they can do again . . . for a more abundant existence for the whole nation," argued Johnston. "The upsurge of energy, inventiveness, productivity evoked by an external enemy can and must be maintained for war against internal enemies such as poverty." The time had come for American business to accept the New Deal, concluded the Chamber of Commerce president.[75]

National crisis generated the liberating forces, but the guides that led business toward reconciliation with the New Deal came from the latter's own champions. In choosing not to turn the war to reform purposes, they laid the basis for acceptance of what had already been accomplished. The chief architect was of course President Roosevelt himself. At once setting to rest industry's fears and satisfying its need for a dominant role in the war effort, Roosevelt shrewdly created the conditions by which former enemies might let go the past in the crisis of war. Nor was this FDR's only contribution to the consolidation of the New Deal. If he did not press it forward, neither did President Roosevelt ever abandon the banner of reform.

In his annual message to Congress in January 1941, Roosevelt called for a postwar world based on Four Freedoms. One of these—freedom from want—developed into the notion of an economic bill of rights. President Roosevelt gave the theme its fullest expression in his State of the Union Message of 11 January 1944.

> True individual freedom cannot exist without economic security and independence. "Necessitous men are not free men." People who are hungry —people who are out of a job—are the stuff of which dictatorships are made.

In our day these economic truths have become accepted as self-evident. We have accepted, so to speak, a second Bill of Rights under which a new basis of security and prosperity can be established for all—regardless of station or race or creed.

Among these are:

The right to a useful and remunerative job in the industries or shops or farms or mines of this Nation;

The right to earn enough to provide adequate food and clothing and recreation;

The right of farmers to raise and sell their products at a return which will give them and their family a decent living;

The right of every businessman, large and small, to trade in an atmosphere of freedom from unfair competition and domination from monopolies at home or abroad;

The right of every family to a decent home;

The right to adequate medical care and the opportunity to achieve and enjoy good health;

The right to adequate protection from the economic fears of old age and sickness and accident and unemployment;

And finally, the right to a good education.

All of these rights spell security. And after this war is won we must be prepared to move forward, in the implementation of these rights, to new goals of human happiness and well-being.

"The most radical speech of his life," Roosevelt's biographer James MacGregor Burns called it. "Never before had he stated so flatly and boldly the economic rights of all Americans. And never before had he so explicitly linked the old bill of political rights against government to the new bill of economic rights to be achieved *through* government."[76]

President Roosevelt carried this lofty pronouncement one step toward realization. From an early point, he recognized the need to plan for the postwar period. The country had suffered after World War I from the lack of planning for peacetime, Roosevelt felt. This time around, in any case, there was no confidence in an automatic return to "normalcy." On the contrary, it was widely believed, even among economists, that the depression would resume unless the government acted. By this time, too, fairly coherent thinking had emerged about the kind of government program needed to attain full employment. Keynesian ideas had begun to penetrate White House circles in the later 1930s. The new economics received solid confirmation from the recession that followed the sharp cutback in public spending in 1937 and in the boom that began with defense spending. To some extent also, the Beveridge Report and other British social planning had some influence in Washington. All of these elements—the memory of World War I, the expectation of postwar depression, some confidence about solutions—prompted Roosevelt to initiate planning for postwar America. This job he lodged in the National Resources Planning Board as early as November 1940. The NRPB would lay plans for public works, expanded social security, and development of national resources; more broadly, it would oversee the planning activities of all agencies of the executive branch. The NRPB defined itself "as a clearing house for the plans and proposals for the avoidance of a depression after the defense period, and to open the road for economic freedom expressed in the new Economic Bill of Rights."[77]

The ambitious enterprise soon foundered. The object of deep suspicion from the outset, the National Resources Planning Board came under sharp congressional attack in early 1943. Roosevelt chose this moment to send to Capitol Hill two NRPB reports on social security expansion and on postwar planning. The resulting furor led to congressional refusal to fund the NRPB. The agency ended in August 1943, and with it went the key to the coordinated direction of postwar planning. Staking out its own claim, Congress set up special postwar policy committees dominated by conservatives; Walter George of Georgia headed the Senate committee, William F. Colmer of Mississippi the House committee. Roosevelt himself, having tended to keep the NRPB at arm's length all along, now abandoned further thought of over-all planning within his administration. Much of the responsibility went to the Bureau of the Budget, whose Fiscal Division was staffed largely by Keynesian economists.[78] But the Office of War Mobilization also took over important planning functions, and when Congress reconstituted it as the Office of War Mobilization and Reconversion in October 1944 with greatly increased authority, it became the primary planner of reconversion. Confining its attention to contract termination, disposal of surplus property, and the relaxation of economic controls, the OWMR approach was more to the taste of conservatives and won their hearty approval on Capitol Hill.

Why did Roosevelt permit his design to come to this faltering end? In part, doubtless, for the reason that James MacGregor Burns has suggested: namely, FDR's genuine ambivalence and skepticism about grand planning.[79] But the failure also expressed the lack of specific purpose behind postwar planning. The aim was, of course, to implement the economic bill of rights, but Roosevelt had divorced this lofty statement of principle from any program of action. For reasons explored earlier in this essay, he had imposed a moratorium on reform legislation for the duration of the war. Not only did no initiatives emanate from the White House, but no help went to congressional progressives when they took up the battle. Nor did Roosevelt even attempt to give his economic bill of rights any functional relationship to the defense effort as a rallying cry that would justify wartime sacrifice. No more than the enunciation of hopeful intent, the economic bill of rights could not sustain even the first step of planning for its implementation. There was not a shadow of the kind of detailed preparation for swift action under way in England at this time.

It may be, as Margaret Hinchey has argued, that Roosevelt intended to shift gears late in 1944.[80] The election gave him a handsome personal victory, the crucial help of the CIO's Political Action Committee strengthened labor's influence on administration policy, and the European war seemed about to end in victory. If Roosevelt had meant to act on the economic bill of rights, he was swiftly deflected. The German counterattack in the Battle of the Bulge suddenly revived FDR's sense of military urgency. His presidential messages of the new year dutifully referred to postwar concerns, but, as he told the nation on 6 January 1945, "it is obviously impossible for us to do anything which might possibly hinder the production for war at this time."[81] Not the economic bill of rights, but a national service law received Roosevelt's urgent endorsement. (The "work or fight" bill never did get through; bitterly opposed by organized labor, it bogged down in Congress and died in April as manpower needs subsided.) Thus, to the last, Roosevelt adhered to his wartime strategy of compartmentalizing social reform, and of keeping the door locked so long as defense needs remained paramount. By the time the final German thrust had failed, Roosevelt was off to Yalta; the problems of peacemaking absorbed him until his death in April.

Even so, by steadily holding up the banner of an economic bill of rights during the war, Roosevelt had contributed mightily to the consolidation of the New Deal. He had served notice on old enemies that they had better discard any lingering illusions and come to terms with the New Deal. The concept of economic rights went a long distance toward securing the legitimacy of the New Deal; Roosevelt had paved the way for the Employment Act of 1946. To some degree, too, Roosevelt's wartime pronouncements did lead into the future, laying down guides to fresh areas for action (such as health, education, and housing) and committing himself to renew the battle for social reform. Harry Truman so understood the economic bill of rights, and he conceived his duty to be to fulfill the legacy that FDR had left him. That sense of historic responsibility may well have made Harry Truman a more pugnacious fighter for reform than Roosevelt would have been had he lived.

The limits on American reform were, ultimately, a function of the limits of the American war experience. In England, World War II came as a holocaust: German bombings killed roughly 60,000 civilians and injured 235,000; destroyed 222,000 houses and damaged 4,698,000 others; and sent upwards of 3.5 million women and children fleeing to evacuation areas outside the bombing zones. Civilian America never felt the war in this direct, calamitous way. Quite the contrary, on the home front Americans tended to associate the war with good times—with an end to depression, with plentiful jobs, overtime, new opportunities. The shortages of consumer goods, the rationing, and the wage and price controls hardly counterbalanced the real economic benefits flowing to most Americans from the war. Dislocation and stress occurred, of course, in many spheres: in housing shortages, in urban conditions, in labor mobility, in family life, and in education. But these home-front problems could either be ignored as matters of public policy or handled in relatively limited and conventional ways. Not so England's evacuations, casualties, and homelessness. These demanded an extraordinary expansion and rethinking of public welfare policy. In his detailed study of this development, Richard M. Titmuss describes the results:

> By the end of the Second World War the Government had . . . assumed and developed a measure of direct concern for the health and well-being of the population which, by contrast, with the role of the Government in the nineteen-thirties, was little short of remarkable. . . . It was increasingly regarded as a proper function or even obligation of Government to ward off distress and strain among not only the poor but almost all classes of society. And, because the area of responsibility had so perceptibly widened, it was no longer thought sufficent to provide . . . a standard of service hitherto considered appropriate for those in receipt of poor relief. . . . The assistance provided by the Government to counter the hazards of war carried little social discrimination, and was offered to all groups in the community. . . .
>
> The evacuation of mothers and children and the bombing of homes during 1939–40 stimulated inquiry and proposals for reform long before victory was thought possible. This was an important experience, for it meant that for five years of war the pressures for a higher standard of welfare and a deeper comprehension of social justice steadily gained strength. And during this

period, despite all the handicaps of limited resources in men and materials, a big expansion took place in the responsibilities accepted by the state for those in need.

The reality of military disaster and the threat of invasion in the summer of 1940 urged on these tendencies in social policy. The mood of the people changed and, in sympathetic response, values changed as well. If dangers were to be shared, then resources should also be shared. Dunkirk, and all that name evokes . . . summoned forth a note of self-criticism, of national introspection, and it set in motion ideas and talk of principles and plans . . . to be repeatedly affirmed with the bombing of London and Coventry and many other cities. The long, dispiriting years of hard work that followed these dramatic events on the home front served only to reinforce the war-warmed impulse of people for a more generous society.[82]

Great Britain emerged from the war with the welfare state. In the United States, World War II made a more modest contribution: it finished old business so that the country could turn unencumbered to the postwar world.

1. Bruce Catton, *The War Lords of Washington* (New York, 1948), p. 306.

2. Robert Sherwood, *Roosevelt and Hopkins: An Intimate History* (New York, 1948), pp. 152–53; Dwight Macdonald, "National Defense: The Case for Socialism," *Partisan Review* 7 (1940): 250–66.

3. U.S. Bureau of the Budget, *The United States at War* (Washington, 1946), chap. 16.

4. Catton, *War Lords*, p. 226.

5. David Montgomery, *Beyond Equality: Labor and the Radical Republicans, 1862–1872* (New York, 1967), chap. 3; William E. Leuchtenburg, "The New Deal and the Analogue of War," in John Braeman, Robert H. Bremner, and Everett Walters, eds., *Change and Continuity in Twentieth-Century America* (Columbus, Ohio, 1964), pp. 81–143; Gerald D. Nash, "Franklin D. Roosevelt and Labor: The World War I Origins of the Early New Deal Policy," *Labor History* 1 (1960): 39–52; Tom Gibson Hall, "Cheap Bread from Dear Wheat: Herbert Hoover, the Wilson Administration, and the Management of Wheat Prices, 1916–1920" (Ph.D. diss., University of California, Davis, 1970).

6. W. K. Hancock and M. M. Gowing, *The British War Economy* (History of the Second World War: United Kingdom Civil Series, W. K. Hancock, ed.) (London, 1949), p. 451; Richard M. Titmuss, "War and Social Policy," *Essays on "The Welfare State"* (London, 1958), p. 86. For a theoretical treatment of a hypothesis similar to Titmuss's, see the work in comparative sociology by Stanislaw Andrzejewski, *Military Organization and Society* (London, 1954). And for a critique based on the British experience in World War I, see Philip Abrams, "The Failure of Social Reform: 1918–1920," *Past and Present*, No. 24 (April 1963), pp. 43–64.

7. See, e.g., Francis E. Merrill, *Social Problems on the Home-Front* (New York, 1944); William F. Ogburn, *American Society in Wartime* (Chicago, 1943); Robert J. Havighurst, *The Social History of a War-Boom Community* (New York, 1951); I. L. Kandel, *The Impact of War upon American Education* (Chapel Hill, N.C., 1948); Marvin W. Schlegel, *Conscripted City* (Norfolk, Va., 1951); and, for a useful guide to the literature, Jim F. Heath, "Domestic America during World War II: Research Opportunities for Historians," *Journal of American History* 58 (1971–72): 384–414.

8. Richard Polenberg, *War and Society: The United States, 1941–1945* (Philadelphia, 1972), p. 97.

9. U. S. Senate, Subcommittee of the Committee on Banking and Currency, *Hearings on S. 380: A Bill to Establish a National Policy and Program for Assuring Continuing Full Employment in a Free Competitive Economy*, 79th Cong., 1st sess. (1945), pp. 223–35.

10. Catton, *War Lords*, p. 311.

11. We are speaking here of immediate consequences, not of later reforms that might be traced back to origins in World War II; and we are treating reform as it was expressed in public policy.

12. Quoted in Richard M. Dalfiume, "The 'Forgotten Years' of the Negro Revolution," *Journal of American History* 55 (1968–69): 105–6.

13. Eleanor Roosevelt, *This I Remember* (New York, 1949), pp. 238–39.

14. Roosevelt to W. H. Davis, 1 Sept. 1941, OF 407B, Roosevelt Papers (Franklin D. Roosevelt Library).

15. Paul A. C. Koistinen, "The Hammer and the Sword: Labor, the Military, and Industrial Mobilization, 1920–1945" (Ph.D. diss., University of California, Berkeley, 1964), pp. 61–71, 98 ff.

16. "Quarterly Management Poll," *Fortune*, November 1941, p. 200.

17. Dewey Grantham, *The Democratic South* (Athens, Ga., 1963), pp. 69–75; John R. Moore, "The Conservative Coalition in the United States Senate, 1942–1945," *Journal of Southern History* 33 (1967): 368–76; James T. Patterson, *Congressional Conservatism and the New Deal: The Growth of the Conservative Coalition in Congress, 1933–1939* (Lexington, Ky., 1967); Donald R. McCoy, "Republican Opposition during Wartime, 1941–1945," *Mid-America* 49 (1967): 174–89.

18. Polenberg, *War and Society*, p. 80.

19. James M. Burns, *Roosevelt, Soldier of Freedom* (New York, 1970), pp. 434, 436.

20. Roland Young, *Congressional Politics during World War II* (New York, 1956), pp. 23, 62.

21. Polenberg, *War and Society*, p. 185.

22. Burns, *Roosevelt, Soldier of Freedom*, pp. 277–81.

23. J. Joseph Huthmacher, *Senator Robert F. Wagner and the Rise of Urban Liberalism* (New York, 1968), pp. 292–93.

24. Polenberg, *War and Society*, p. 87.

25. Margaret Hinchey, "The Frustration of the New Deal Revival, 1944–46," (Ph.D. diss., University of Missouri, 1965), pp. 51–52.

26. Benjamin McLaurin Memoir (1960), pp. 64, 296, Oral History Collection (Columbia University Library).

27. Richard M. Dalfiume, *Desegregation of the U.S. Armed Forces: Fighting on Two Fronts, 1939–1953* (Columbia, Mo., 1969), pp. 116–22.

28. John Harding, "The 1942 Congressional Elections," *American Political Science Review* 38 (1944): 56.

29. Walter W. Wilcox, *The Farmer in the Second World War* (Ames, Iowa, 1947), p. 387; see also chaps. 9, 15.

30. Lauchlin Currie to Roosevelt, Memorandum, 6 Mar. 1940, Roosevelt to Currie, Memorandum, 1 Apr. 1940, OF 2546, Sidney Hillman to John L. Lewis, 30 July 1940, OF 522, Roosevelt Papers; Allen Haywood to August Scholle, 31 Oct. 1940, John Brophy Papers (Catholic University).

31. James M. Burns, "Maintenance of Membership: A Study in Administrative Statesmanship," *Journal of Politics* 101 (1948): 114–16.

32. Joel Seidman, *American Labor from Defense to Reconversion* (Chicago, 1953), p. 118, and passim, chap. 7; also, e.g., Philip Murray to Roosevelt, 18 July 1942, PPF 6988, William Green to Roosevelt, 18 Dec. 1943, PPF 3189, Roosevelt Papers.

33. Oscar Ewing to Roosevelt, Memorandum, 16 June 1943, PPF 471, Roosevelt Papers; Seidman *American Labor*, p. 217 ff. For the claim that some CIO leaders, including Philip Murray, would have preferred to have the wartime stabilization system carried over into the reconversion period, see Nelson Lichtenstein, "Industrial Unionism under the No-Strike Pledge" (Ph. D. diss., University of California, Berkeley, 1974), pp. 684–86.

34. *New York Times*, 23 Dec. 1940.

35. Murray to Roosevelt, 18 Dec. 1940, 11 Mar. 1941, OF 2546, Roosevelt Papers; Philip Murray, *The CIO Defense Plan*, CIO Publication No. 51 (1941); Philip Murray, *Planning for Democratic Defense*, CIO Publication No. 59 (1941).

36. Henry M. Christman, ed., *Walter Reuther: Selected Papers* (New York, 1961), p. 2.

37. E.g., the editor of the *CIO News*: "The CIO offered everything I had worked and hoped for—an ambitious, practical, crusading movement to organize American working people for the betterment of their immediate conditions without setting limits to the aspirations which a well-organized, militant, intelligently led working class should have for the eventual transformation of society." Len De Caux Memoir (1961), pp. 4–5, UAW Oral History Collection, Wayne State University; also Len De Caux, *Labor Radical* (Boston, 1970).

38. John Brophy to CIO Industrial Union Councils, 17 Feb. 1941, Jay Franklin, "We, the People," typescript, May 1941, Brophy Papers; I. F. Stone, *Business as Usual: The First Year of Defense* (New York, 1941), pp. 238, 264, 266; Morton W. Ertell, "The CIO Industry Council Plan—Its Background and Implications" (Ph.D. diss., University of Chicago, 1955), chaps. 1 and 2.

39. On the vicissitudes of Reuther's conversion idea in 1941, see George R. Clark, "The Strange Story of the Reuther Plan," *Harper's Magazine* 184 (1941–42): 643–54; Eliot Janeway, *The Struggle for Survival: A Chronicle of Economic Mobilization in World War II* (New Haven, Conn., 1951), pp. 220 ff., 253 ff.; Catton, *War Lords*, chaps. 8, 9.

40. Barton J. Bernstein, "The Automobile Industry and the Coming of the Second World War," *Southwestern Social Science Quarterly* 47 (1966–67): 22–23; Roosevelt to H. L. Stimson, 9 July 1941, in Elliott Roosevelt, ed., *F.D.R.: His Personal Letters, 1928–1945*, 2 vols. (New York, 1950), 2:1183.

41. Koistinen, "The Hammer and the Sword," p. 695; Colston E. Warner et al., eds., *Yearbook of American Labor* (New York, 1945), p. 476.

42. Clark, "Reuther Plan," pp. 650, 653; *Minutes of the War Production Board* (Washington, 1946), pp. 237–38, 290–91 (hereafter cited as *WPB Minutes*); Stone, *Business As Usual*, pp. 239–41.

43. Catton, *War Lords*, p. 149.

44. *President's National Labor-Management Conference. Official Conference Documents* (Washington, 1945), pp. 44, 47.

45. Seidman, *American Labor*, p. 78; Philip Taft, *The A.F. of L. from the Death of Gompers to the Merger* (New York, 1959), pp. 210–11; Julius Emspak, "Labor-Management War Production Councils," *Science and Society* 7 (1943): 91, 95; Joel Seidman, "Labor Policy of the Communist Party during World War II," *Industrial and Labor Relations Review* 4 (1950–51): 55–69; Irving Howe and Lewis Coser, *The American Communist Party: A Critical History* (Boston, 1957), pp. 409–12.

46. Ertell, "The CIO Industry Council Plan," chap. 1; CIO, *Proceedings* (1944), pp. 89, 261; ibid. (1951), p. 2.

47. Koistinen, "The Hammer and the Sword," p. 754; Irving Howe and B. J. Widick, *The UAW and Walter Reuther* (New York, 1949), pp. 107–8; Julie Meyer, "Trade Union Plans for Postwar Reconstruction in the United States," *Social Research* 11 (1944): 491–505.

48. Quoted in Koistinen, "The Hammer and the Sword," p. 613.

49. U.S. Civilian Production Administration, *Industrial Mobilization for War: History of the War Production Board. . . . Program and Administration* (Washington, 1947), p. 208; Donald M. Nelson, *Arsenal of Democracy: The Story of American War Production* (New York, 1946), pp. 195–96; *WPB Minutes*, p. 2; Koistinen, "The Hammer and the Sword," pp. 613–14.

50. Sherwood, *Roosevelt and Hopkins*, p. 158.

51. *WPB Minutes*, pp. 168–69.

52. Richard Polenberg has pointed out the lax enforcement of the antitrust laws during the war, and the administration's hamstringing of Thurman Arnold's efforts (Polenberg, *War and Society*, pp. 77–78). This was wholly in keeping with the third phase of FDR's strategy, described in the next paragraphs. The significant point here is the determination not to suspend the laws nor to set aside permanent policy during the crisis.

53. Koistinen, "The Hammer and the Sword," p. 631; Janeway, *Struggle for Survival*, pp. 285 ff.

54. CPA, *Industrial Mobilization*, p. 209; Nelson, *Arsenal of Democracy*, pp. 208–9.

55. CPA, *Industrial Mobilization*, p. 247.

56. Ibid., p. 265.

57. Koistinen, "The Hammer and the Sword," p. 676.

58. CPA, *Industrial Mobilization*, pp. 749–50; Bruno Stein, "Labor's Role in Government Agencies during World War II," *Journal of Economic History* 17 (1957): 389–408.

59. CPA, *Industrial Mobilization*, p. 213.

60. Ibid., p. 221.

61. The crystallizing event was the feasibility controversy, in which Nelson asserted his right to set maximum production limits and cut back projected military requirements for 1943 from 93 to 80 billion dollars.

62. Nelson, *Arsenal of Democracy*, pp. 392, 398–99; Koistinen, "The Hammer and the Sword," pp. 704–5; U.S. Smaller War Plants Corporation, *Economic Concentration and World War II* (Washington, 1946), pp. 30–31; Barton J. Bernstein, "The Debate on Industrial Reconversion: The Protection of Oligopoly and Military Control of the Economy," *American Journal of Economics and Sociology* 26 (1967): 164.

63. Koistinen, "The Hammer and the Sword," pp. 709–10.

64. Ibid., p. 714.

65. Quoted in Bernstein, "The Debate on Industrial Reconversion," p. 167.

66. Robert F. Himmelberg, "The War Industries Board and the Anti-Trust Question in November 1918," *Journal of American History 52* (1965): 59–74; Melvin I. Urofsky, *Big Steel and the Wilson Administration: A Study in Business-Government Relations* (Columbus, Ohio, 1969), chaps. 5, 6, 8.

67. CPA, *Industrial Mobilization*, p. 818.

68. Barton J. Bernstein, "The Removal of War Production Board Controls on Business, 1944–1946," *Business History Review* 39 (1965): 248.

69. Ibid., p. 249; CPA, *Industrial Mobilization*, pp. 814 ff.

70. For a helpful brief survey of assessments of the Employment Act, see Barton J. Bernstein, "Economic Policies," in Richard S. Kirkendall, ed., *The Truman Period as a Research Field* (Columbia, Mo., 1967), pp. 98–99.

71. Julius Emspak Memoir (1960), p. 319, Oral History Collection (Columbia University Library). For a detailed account of the imposition of discipline on rank–and–file militancy by the CIO leadership, aided by the War Labor Board, see Lichtenstein, "Industrial Unionism under the No–Strike Pledge."

72. Quoted in Koistinen, "The Hammer and the Sword," p. 675.

73. Quoted in David Brody, *The Butcher Workmen: A Study of Unionization* (Cambridge, Mass., 1964), p. 210, and passim, chap. 10.

74. Burns, "Maintenance of Membership"; Seidman, *American Labor*, chap. 6.

75. Eric Johnston, *America Unlimited* (New York, 1944), pp. 29, 107, 116, 138. It was not much of a jump from these ideas to acceptance of the Employment Act of 1946; and some progressive businessmen—those represented by the Committee on Economic Development, for instance—gave support to the original and more radical Full Employment bill of 1945. See, e.g., the testimony of Ralph Flanders, Subcommittee of the Committee on Banking and Currency, *Hearings on S. 380,* pp. 356–69.

76. Burns, *Roosevelt, Soldier of Freedom*, pp. 425–26.

77. Hinchey, "Frustration of the New Deal Revival," pp. 3, 4, and passim, chap. 1; W. S. Woytinsky, "What Was Wrong in Forecasts of Postwar Depression?", *Journal of Political Economy* 55 (1947): 142–51; Alonzo L. Hamby, "Sixty Million Jobs and the People's Revolution: The Liberals, the New Deal, and World War II," *Historian* 30 (1968–69): 585–87.

78. The division's White Paper on Full Employment provided the basis for F.D.R.'s major

campaign statement on domestic policy, the Chicago speech of 28 October 1944, that held out the goal of "close to 60 million jobs" (Hinchey, "Frustration of the New Deal Revival," pp. 13–18).

79. Burns, *Roosevelt, Soldier of Freedom*, p. 353.

80. Hinchey, "Frustration of the New Deal Revival," pp. 48–49.

81. Samuel I. Rosenman, ed., *The Public Papers and Addresses of Franklin D. Roosevelt*, 13 vols. (New York, 1938–50), 13:516.

82. Richard M. Titmuss, *Problems of Social Policy* (History of the Second World War: United Kingdom Civil Series, W. K. Hancock, ed.) (London, 1950), pp. 506–8.

Eric Solomon

Fiction and the New Deal

Half the people without jobs and half the factories
closed by strikes. Half the people on public dole
won't work and half that couldn't work even if they
would. Too much cotton and corn and hogs, and not
enough for people to eat and wear.—William Faulkner, "Delta Autumn"

He did not think in any abstractions, but in deals, in
sales, in transfers and in gifts. He thought in shares,
in bales, in thousands of bushels, in options, holding
companies, trusts, and subsidiary corporations.
—Ernest Hemingway, *To Have and Have Not*

Some people would consider themselves lucky to've
missed the last decade.—F. Scott Fitzgerand, "The
Lost Decade"

FOR AMERICAN NOVELISTS, THE NEW DEAL, AS SUCH, WAS IN-
tractable material. For journalists, and for novelists writing nonfiction
about what they really saw in their travels across the country, the New
Deal, its agencies and programs, and personalities and plans, could be
clearly and effectively documented in their prose. Only a few novelists
focused on positive aspects of the Roosevelt administration; most fiction
written throughout the 1930s reflected anger at depression conditions and
disinterest at the efforts of the federal government to discover remedies.

Some reasons for novelists' lack of interest in the achievements of the
New Deal come immediately to mind. Literature generally takes a stance
of opposition to authority, to institutions, usually to government, as Shel-
ley insisted when he stated that all true poets must be revolutionaries.

Novelists of the period were ready to condemn capitalism as both a cultural and an economic failure, but they were not prepared to analyze or to assess governmental action. Left-wing novelists envisioned the New Deal bureaucracy as sustaining capitalist conventions; neutral, apolitical writers ignored matters of government; a few conservative novelists, as we shall see, attacked the premises of, and participants in, the New Deal.

Subjects close to the hearts and concerns of New Dealers were explored by novelists who cast shrewd or lyrical assessments of Depression America into their nonfictional works. Louis Adamic in *My America* (1938) listened to the voices of those on relief; James Agee studied closely the lives of southern sharecroppers, and from poetic pages in *Let Us Now Praise Famous Men* (1936–41) came a genuine sense of what the Farm Security Administration should attend to. There were more: Benjamin Appel, a naturalistic novelist whose usual materials were the lives and deaths of urban criminals, heard the stubborn anger of workingmen toward business and industry leaders in *Let America Speak* (1937); as did his temperamental opposite, Sherwood Anderson, chronicler of the mid-western small towns, who caught the feeling of factory strife in times of layoffs in his *Puzzled America* (1935). Theodore Dreiser's *Tragic America* (1935), John Dos Passos's *Journey Between Wars* (1938)—which reflected the growing sense of totalitarian threat—even Leonard Q. Ross's *The Strangest Places* (1939), all showed novelists searching for the facts of life in the United States that were going into agency files or Senate hearings.

Two occasional novelists whose reputations are properly based on their nonfiction touched on the New Deal in their journalistic efforts: Ruth McKenney and Edmund Wilson. McKenney's *Industrial Valley* (1939), a detailed report of the Akron rubber strike, was far superior in accuracy and perspective to the mass of strike novels that came from Marxist and/or proletarian novelists. And Wilson, in his essays and reportage collected in *American Jitters* (1932) and *Travels in Two Democracies* (1936), wrote brilliantly on the interests of the New Deal—banking, welfare, labor relations, social security, agriculture, the courts, the end of isolationism, the proliferation of government agencies and controls. Wilson assessed the function of Rooseveltian policies such as rural electrification, CCC camps, flood control, and relief from a left-of-center angle of vision that slowly moved from pessimism to optimism, from delineation of confusion to acceptance of planning.

Even writers who continued the nonpolitical techniques of fiction that had served them successfully before 1929 wrote fragmentary accounts of what they actually perceived in the America of the thirties. For Scott Fitzgerald, writing in *Esquire*, the Roosevelt years meant grim realism, the end of the jazz age at the Ritz, the return of the expatriates, Princeton classmates leaping out of windows, and his own personal depression—his Crackup. For John Steinbeck, on the other hand, the 1930s meant research into the circumstances of migrant workers in the Salinas Valley, a spate of articles in the *Nation*, which would provide the impetus to *In Dubious Battle* (1935), his fine novelistic treatment of a fruit picker's strike, and to *The Grapes of Wrath* (1939), the *locus classicus* of depression fiction, which bewails the sad epic journey of the Okies to California's lost Eden. By implication, Steinbeck's novels could be understood as providing support for New Deal operations: in both novels, it is the absence of federal controls—either in the realm of fair labor practices or decent provision for migrants—that brings about the desperate cries for security. Ernest Hemingway, his latent political consciousness shocked to activity by the tragedy of the Spanish Civil War, turned out some excellent pieces of war correspondence for *Ken*, the left's short-lived answer to *Esquire*. Like Steinbeck, Hemingway discovered in Spain the material for his most socially acute novel, *For Whom the Bell Tolls* (1940). His implications about New Deal foreign policy, however, could be seen as an attack on the Roosevelt administration: no help came from the American government in the fight against fascism. Thomas Wolfe was also shaken out of his self-concentration by what he saw in Munich, and much of his writing in *The Story of a Novel* (1936) reflected his alarm and doubts, which would be turned into fiction in his final, posthumous novels. Of our major novelists, then, only William Faulkner left no nonfictional views of the United States in the 1930s; but this was characteristic, for his writing efforts in the decade all went either into his fiction or his Hollywood scripts.

Naturally, the decades after the thirties saw a multitude of autobiographical returns by lesser-known novelists to the New Deal era. Once again, however, the writing of novelists such as Alvah Bessie, Josephine Herbst, Langston Hughes, Albert Halper, Mary McCarthy, or Richard Wright, for example, concentrate on such subjects as the Spanish Civil War, the attraction of the idea of the Soviet Union, the confusions of left-wing journalism; their interests were human rather than political, and they tended to avoid the problems raised by the mass psychological crisis that gripped the United States. The basic political activities of the Roosevelt years play a minor part in the novelists' memoirs.

As for the novelists of social protest, whether following the kinds of Marxist formulas well described by Walter Rideout in *The Radical Novel in America* or caught by the ideological conflicts delineated in Daniel Aaron's *Writers on the Left*—here again, the world of the New Deal, its reforms and legislation, its centralization and power, was largely absent. To be sure, the subject matter that engaged the Roosevelt administration pervaded the social novels of the 1930s, which treated the unrelieved distress, the destruction of self-respect and natural resources, the need somehow to curb capitalism in order to sustain it. Still, most of these writers did not issue a clear call for governmental regulation.

The plight of the farmer was documented fully by emotionally involved novelists such as Steinbeck, Edwin Lanham, (*The Stricklands*, 1934), or Martha Gellhorn (*The Trouble I've Seen*, 1936). The drift into a life of crime brought about by depression poverty not only motivated detective story writers like Dashiell Hammett or James M. Cain but also provided themes for a range of novelists who treated urban slum life, writers like James T. Farrell (*Studs Lonigan*, 1932–35), Richard Wright (*Native Son*, 1940), Benjamin Appel (*Brain Guy*, 1934), Daniel Fuchs, (*Homage to Blenholt*, 1934), or Horace McCoy (*They Shoot Horses, Don't They?*, 1936).[1] Poverty itself, of course, was a subject traditionally handled by American novelists of social protest. As FDR's inauguration speech called attention to the pervasive quality of fear among the American people, many novelists attested to the terrors of an absolute lack of cash. There were various novels of men (and women) on the road, drifters, at the mercy of a society's indifference or cruelty. Most of these novelists found little hope in the idea of government aid. They wrote of the impossibility of love or family life; thus, there was no future. Nelson Algren (*Somebody in Boots*, 1935), or Tom Kromer (*Waiting for Nothing*, 1935) testified to the implausibility of hope; Edward Newhouse (*You Can't Sleep Here*, 1934) came close to making a virtue of urban rootlessness. A rather special perspective, from a quietly lyrical novelist, was that of Thomas Bell (*All Brides Are Beautiful*, 1936). His young couple manage to survive, just barely, through hard work and lowering of aims.

Most novels that treated politics directly took for their subject matter characters and situations beyond the purview of the New Deal. The examples of Albert Halper (*Union Square*, 1933) or Tess Schlesinger (*The Unpossessed*, 1934) were typical, concentrating on leftist intellectuals playing with abstract ideas of social revolution and on the familiar events of marches and rallies. Equally extraneous to serious New Deal concerns was Sinclair Lewis's emotional warning about the dangers of native facism (*It Can't Happen Here,* 1935), even though it raised the specter that would be fleshed out by such Roosevelt opponents as Huey Long and Father Coughlin.

The condition of labor, on the other hand, long a staple of American realistic fiction, did attract a great deal of novelistic attention. More radical novels, more general social protest novels, focused on strikes, early and late in the 1930s, than on any other major theme. Even in the most sensitive of these novels—in the work, for example, of Robert Cantwell (*The Land of Plenty,* 1934), Walter Havighurst (*Pier 17,* 1933), or Jack Conroy (*The Disinherited,* 1933)—the kinds of solutions to labor strife represented by the NRA or the NLRB were not on the horizon. Instead, Cantwell's furniture factory workers, Havighurst's longshoremen, Conroy's auto workers are defeated and can only look forward to more lonely struggles. A later novelist like Meyer Levin (*Citizens,* 1940) found the work of the LaFollette Committee and Labor Department investigators unrewarding; in his pages the tragedies of the Republic Steel strike are not mitigated by the New Deal, nor is there any implication that such intervention could be of value.

Finally, reports from the inside were few. Such works as a novel by Norman Macleod (*You Get What You Pay For,* 1939), which glanced at the petty politics within a WPA writers' project, were ephemeral. For an insight into fiction's response to the New Deal, we can either seek out novelists who reflected in passing on the mood, the aura, created by the Roosevelt administration, or we can focus on the one novel, by John Dos Passos, that most directly attempted to come to terms with the New Deal itself.

In his recent study of Nathaniel West, Jay Martin pinpoints certain aspects of the 1930s that changed the nature of the previous decade's fiction, which tended to concentrate on formal experimentation and on themes of personal liberation. As a result of the depression, politics, the public realm, became acceptable as subject matter. There loomed a sense of disaster—even hysteria—("a profound sense of uneasiness," was Rexford Tugwell's term). Whatever sense of hope remained during this time of bleakness and despair did seem to come directly from the New Deal, from the controlling idea that the Roosevelt years would provide ways out

—ways out of poverty, racial strife, exploitation, war. Although writers turned to the American past to try to regain some lost sense of confidence (if, as Kenneth Roberts indicated, the American people had won the Revolution, they would win the depression, too); and although the novelists looked to "the people," to the facts of American lives in the mass—still, the feeling of apocolypse, of a coming world conflagration, grew.[2] And despite the optimistic murals on the walls of post offices and, for some, the excitement of the possibilities of a new collectivism, the very titles of books written to assess the American landscape show a dark vision: *Puzzled America, Tragic America, The Years of the Locust, The Bitter Years*.

Nathaniel West's four short novels, all published during Roosevelt's first three terms, mirrored the attitudes the New Deal was trying to cope with. Particularly in *Miss Lonelyhearts* (1933), West caught the emotional poverty of urban life, the spiritual emptiness and inner panic that the New Deal sought to counter. For West, who moved steadily toward the left during his short life, Roosevelt and the reforms he was presenting during the decade could not cure the American malaise of which the economic depression was merely a symptom. Too radical for a belief in the New Deal, too experimental to be accepted by the grimly serious Marxists of the Mike Gold persuasion, West found few readers for his final novel *The Day of the Locust* (1939; the title was similar to Gilbert Seldes's 1933 book on the depths of the depression, *The Years of the Locust*). This novel predicted an end to the hope that Roosevelt was radiating. West saw America as Los Angeles, a city given over to false illusions and dreams —in architecture, in clothing, in sex, in life—symbolized by the movie industry. All the illusions are destroyed by the book's end, with an ultimate riot and the apocalyptic vision of the burning of Los Angeles.

Symbolically, F. Scott Fitzgerald, who was also becoming disenchanted with the New Deal promises as he watched the promise of his own brilliant career of the twenties dribbling out in the subsequent decade to alcoholism, mental illness, and artistic failure, chose Hollywood for his metaphor of disappointment.

His novel dealing with the motion picture industry, *The Last Tycoon*, was unfinished at Fitzgerald's death in 1940, but in it he took a stance toward labor and management in Hollywood that resembled President Roosevelt's "plague on both your houses" remark (unlike Budd Schulberg's more positive approach to the Screen Writers Guild in his 1941 *What Makes Sammy Run?*). Fitzgerald's creative hero, the producer tycoon who resembles Irving Thalberg, is doomed because of both the opposition of corrupt union bosses and because of the crass economic thinking of the bankers in control of the film industry. As he indicates by a sequence in the opening pages of the novel, where an independent producer commits suicide because he has been destroyed by corporate powers, Fitzgerald felt that bigness of any kind, in government or business, was dangerous. Symbolically, the suicide takes place at the Hermitage, representing that same loss of the earlier American ideal that John Dos Passos lamented in his writing at the time.

Although he did read Marx in the 1930s and commented approvingly in his letters, Fitzgerald, unlike Dreiser or his own friends Wilson and Dos Passos, remained aloof from Roosevelt and the New Deal. Instead, the novelist recorded his sense of loss, of despair for the American dream he could no longer cherish. While his last completed novel *Tender Is the Night* (1934) reflected in the decline and fall of its hero Fitzgerald's own doubts about a capitalist system that used money recklessly, he created in his final short stories a thirties protagonist who was an emblem of defeat. Pat Hobby, a cynical, worn-out Hollywood hack writer, marked, in Fitzgerald's view, the place where the writers of his generation had to come out. The New Deal's hope and plans could not penetrate Fitzgerald's personal depression—which, he insisted in "The Crackup," symbolized the American collapse. Fitzgerald, as did most American novelists, took a critical stance toward his society, which allowed him to lament the mood of the depression and at the same time to reject the pragmatism of the New Deal. He explained his sense of the American mood in an essay, "Between Three and Four":

> This happened nowadays, with everyone somewhat discouraged. A lot of less fortunate spirits cracked when money troubles came to be added to all the nervous troubles accumulated in the prosperity—neurosis being a privilege of people with a lot of extra money. And some cracked merely because it was in the air, or because they were used to the great, golden figure of plenty standing behind them . . . almost everyone cracked a little.

William Faulkner used Hollywood during the 1930s to sustain him financially, but he consistently escaped back to Oxford, Mississippi, where he worked out in his best fiction his obsessions with a southern past of guilt, sin, redemption, and endurance that had little connection to the decade in which he was writing, much less to the New Deal. Still, as a southerner, Faulkner responded to the rural depression he saw around him, even though it was not new. In *As I Lay Dying* (1930), he wrote for the first time about poor dirt farmers; in *Sanctuary* (1931), he created his depression antihero, Popeye—a cold, mechanical, impotent killer—the man for whom society could do nothing. Throughout his 1930s fiction, Faulkner dealt with the dark side of American life, and his contemporary studies were bleak. In *The Wild Palms* (1939), a doctor becomes an abortionist-killer; in the stories that made up *The Hamlet* (1940), Flem Snopes, representing sheer avarice, economic exploitation at its impersonal extreme, started his series of victories over weaker and more trusting farmers. In *Pylon* (1939), Faulkner probed a special kind of poverty, that of penniless carnival figures, in this case barnstorming airplane pilots. Throughout his writing about his own times in this decade, Faulkner displayed a consciousness of the bitter truths of rural economics that was just as acute as James Agee's or Erskine Caldwell's. In the final years treated in *Go Down, Moses* (stories collected and published in 1942), the sharecroppers were still in slavery, this time to the company store.

Unlike Agee, however, and like the conservative Southern Agrarians who called themselves the Fugitives, William Faulkner had no use for the New Deal. In the novels that concluded his Snopes trilogy, he took potshots at Washington corruption, in the persons of senators and FBI men. In *Go Down, Moses*, despite his nostalgia for the loss of the wilderness, Faulkner rejected federal interference such as TVA or Rural Electrification, since the Big Woods should not be changed. In *Pylon*, he had a minor character (admittedly an unpleasant one) comment on New Deal agencies:

> "You're a government agent. All right. We have had our crops regimented and our fisheries regimented and even our money in the bank regimented. All right. I still don't see how they did it but they did, and so we are used to that. If he was trying to make his living out of the ground and Washington came in and regimented him, all right. We might not understand it any more than he did, but we would say all right. And if he was trying to make his living out of the river and the government came in and regimented him, we would say all right too. But do you mean to tell me that Washington can come in and regiment a man that's trying to make his living out of the air? Is there a crop reduction in the air too?"

So much for the FAA.

Ultimately, of course, William Faulkner came closer, in the most crucial southern question, to the New Deal policies than has been generally granted. For Faulkner, as for Roosevelt (if not for Mrs. Roosevelt) and most of his advisers, the race problem was too tough to handle directly. Both felt and projected deep sympathy for, and understanding of, the condition of blacks; neither really moved to positive action. For a southern writer, this attitude was understandable.

Thomas Wolfe and Ernest Hemingway, dissimilar in most ways, shared an acceptance, ultimately, of the seriousness of the American predicament, at home and abroad. In his posthumously published novels, Wolfe movingly described America's loss of innocence, perceiving the awful plight of the poor in the Brooklyn streets at the same time that he observed the growing threat of fascism in the Munich beer halls. His fiction did not stress his personal belief in Roosevelt and the New Deal, the belief he wrote about in a letter to Jonathan Daniels of 23 October 1936. There he stressed the importance of the election, because Roosevelt's administration, "whatever its errors of commission or omission may have been, had made the only decisive movement . . . in the direction of social progress and social justice since the administration of Woodrow Wilson."[3] To Thomas Wolfe, the New Deal meant one quality: a ray of hope that might break through the prevailing clouds of depression. The government could cure the two diseases he most feared, European fascism and American urban poverty. Toward the close of his last novel, *You Can't Go Home Again* (published 1940), Wolfe enunciated his fears and hopes:

> Then came the cataclysm of 1929 and the terrible days that followed . . . and I saw as I had never seen before the true and terrifying visage of the disinherited of life. . . . For while I sat the night through in the darkened rooms of German friends, behind the bolted doors and shuttered windows—while their whispered voices spoke to me of the anguish in their hearts—while I heard and saw these things, my heart was torn asunder. . . . For then it was, most curiously, that all the grey weather of unrecorded days in Brooklyn, which had soaked through into my soul, came flooding back to me. Came back, too, the memory of my exploration of the jungle trails of night. I saw again the haggard faces of the homeless men, the wanderers, the disinherited of America, the aged workers who had worked and now could work no more, the callow boys who had never worked and now could find no work to do, and who, both together, had been cast loose by a society that had no need of them and left to shift in any way they could—to find their food in garbage cans. . . .

If the situation in both America and Europe was grim—"how sick America was, and . . . the ailment was akin to Germany's— a dread world-sickness of the soul"—it might be hopeless for Europe, but not for

Wolfe's romantically conceived homeland. "America was still resilient, still responsive to a cure if only—if only—men could somehow cease to be afraid of truth."

Ernest Hemingway, however, could not share Wolfe's belief in the New Deal. Like Wolfe, Hemingway perceived the dangers of European fascism; but unlike Wolfe, the more-committed Hemingway saw hope in the attempts of the Spanish Republic to oppose the Fascist thrust. The careful inability of the Roosevelt administration to support Ambassador Claude Bowers's position and to give aid to the republic angered Hemingway. When he showed his film *The Spanish Earth* at the White House, he was attracted to Mrs. Roosevelt and to Harry Hopkins, but disliked the president; this dislike turned to bitterness after he called on FDR, in the pages of *Ken,* to oppose Prime Minister Chamberlain's embargo on arms to the republic. In many ways, the argument of Hemingway's major novel of the Spanish civil war, *For Whom the Bell Tolls*, was a denial of American possibilities in the battle against fascism. Not only did the American hero, Robert Jordan, fight alongside the Spanish Partisans, thus repudiating even the mythic commitment to America shown by the Lincoln Brigade, but he also died alone, unsupported by the sense of group solidarity ("This is the beginning, from *I* to *we*," John Steinbeck had written).

Earlier, in *To Have and Have Not* (1937), Hemingway expressed his disillusionment with "the American dream turned nightmare." He showed the effects of the depression on poor and rich alike, the one driven to undertake suicidal smuggling missions, the other driven to empty alcoholic self-destruction. His protagonists rejected the idea close to the New Deal, which Hemingway denigrated by the term "charity,"

> "You always worked, didn't you? You never asked anybody for charity."
> "There ain't any work," I said. "There ain't any work at living wages anywhere."
> "Why?"
> "I don't know."

Trying to make it on his own, Harry Morgan died. Was the New Deal an alternative to lonely piracy? Hardly. It is no coincidence that federal agents were able to seize Harry's boat because it was spotted from a WPA tractor. Hemingway firmly believed that certain veterans, working for the CCC, had been shipped to the Florida Keys by Harry Hopkins (where some died in a hurricane) because they embarrassed Roosevelt's New Deal.[4] In the novel, a vet remarks, "Well, Mr. Hoover ran us out of Anticosti [sic] flats and Mr. Roosevelt has shipped us down here to get rid of us." The rich were in trouble with the administration, too. A wealthy yachtsman must commit suicide because he was being hounded by "investigators from the Internal Revenue Bureau."

Ernest Hemingway, like Scott Fitzgerald, Thomas Wolfe, and William Faulkner, was essentially uninterested in politics in the party sense. According to Rexford Tugwell, Hemingway "was fascinated by the New Deal but not willing to undertake an understanding of its issues"; thus, he would not write directly about New Deal politics, no matter how disappointed he felt about Roosevelt's domestic and foreign policies. His friend and fellow novelist John Dos Passos had no such compunction.

John Dos Passos's shift from the radical stance of his early novels —which culminated in his most famous, and best, work USA—to an increasingly conservative position is well known. The author often explained that his attraction to radical figures such as Randolph Bourne or Bill Haywood came not from any youthful belief in socialism but from an unchanging commitment to the principles of Jeffersonian democracy. Whatever the reasons might have been, whether personal shock over losing a friend in the Spanish civil war (possibly the victim of a Soviet-inspired murder) or a more general disillusionment with the course of radical politics, Dos Passos in the novels he published from 1939 to 1949 included few heroes and one major villain: Franklin Delano Roosevelt—and, by extension, his New Deal bureaucracy.

In *The Adventures of a Young Man* (1939), the first volume of what would become the trilogy *District of Columbia*, Dos Passos disposed of the Communist party. His hero is betrayed by the party, as are a group of idealistic coal miners, in a version of the Harlan County strike; he is tricked by Columbia University intellectuals (who will later become part of "the Boss's" Brain Trust);[5] finally he is murdered by members of the party apparatus while fighting in Spain with the International Brigade. In *Number One* (1943), the author demolished the idea of a populist political leader by drawing a totally unsympathetic portrait of a Huey Long archetype—with none of the sympathetic understanding of good and evil shown by Robert Penn Warren in *All the King's Men*. But it was in *The Grand Design* (1949) that Dos Passos directly took on the New Deal.

Although there are heroes in the Roosevelt administration as viewed by the novelist, they are doomed to frustration by red tape and, ultimately, to elimination when the third term draws near because of venal electoral ambition. Paul Graves, a dedicated agronomist, and Millard Carroll, an idealistic manufacturer, spend years in the AAA bureaucracy. Both sustain visions, Graves of providing technical support to the small farmer, Carroll of extending American democratic principles throughout the world. At the end of *The Grand Design*, both have quit the government, one to join the navy, the other to return to his midwestern roots.

Most of the negative characters in the novel are caricatures: the Communist party is riddled with avaricious, hypocritical homosexuals; newspaper columnists and radio broadcasters are sensual self-servers. President Roosevelt himself is only a voice, mysteriously manipulating people through phone calls or dinners at the White House, always substituting his sense of expediency for the underling's idealism. His alter ego is Judge Oppenheim (an amalgam, it would seem of Samuel Rosenman and David Niles), who cajoles and charms in order to keep the New Deal operating. The most devastating characterization is that of Walker Watson, the physically ill, politically ambitious, folksy, idealistic dreamer who is secretary of agriculture. In appearance Harry Hopkins, in emotion Henry Wallace, the figure of Walker Watson sums up for Dos Passos the contradictions inherent in the role of New Deal bureaucrat. Although Watson wants every child in the world to be able to drink milk, more than that he wants power. For Dos Passos, further, the New Deal could lead to socialism, which would lead to communism. Thus, he displays the New Deal at its worst, torn by cheap political deals, feuds, and power struggles. Benign gentlemen farmers can do more to preserve farmlands than can unbalanced agricultural theorists in government agencies. By implication, then, the entire New Deal betrays both the painful actualities of depression wants and the wonderful illusions of a reconstruction of the American dream.

Dos Passos's opening lyric gives the reality and the hope. The real—

> sheets that told
> of panic at the locked doors of banks
> of stalled factories
> and foreclosures and sheriff's sales
> and dispossess notices and outofwork gangs threatening state
> legislatures and bitter throngs round courthouses
> and wheat and corn burned in the stoves

—includes descriptions of a banker's suicide, a job-seeker's weary return to his home. The hope—

> the smooth broadshouldered figure confident and tall of the President newly elected who strode out on the arm of his son erect almost jaunty in his legbraces. . . . The voice resounded in our ears, the pervasive confident voice: " . . . social values more noble than mere monetary profit. . . ."

—includes an overtone of doubt at Roosevelt's insistence on broad powers.

It is the idea of power, centralized power, bureaucratic agency power, that measures for Dos Passos the inevitable corruption that must engulf the New Deal. Dos Passos seems to paraphrase Lord Acton's dictum: bureaucratic power corrupts, New Deal bureaucratic power tends to corrupt absolutely.

> They were packed into bureaus and offices, two at a desk, four and five at a table in conference rooms . . . checking programs, industrial pricelists, fair trade practices, standards of wages and working conditions, poring redeyed over dogeared acts of Congress in the dense tiny print of the Government Printing Office, scanning codes that covered abrasives, advertising, aeronotics . . . wine, women, and woolen goods. . . . Lobbies interlocked; petitions, appeals, telegrams criss-crossed; pressure groups hired halls; telephones tangled in straining contest. When the parallellogram of forces stalled
> somebody took it to the White House desk, where smiling the President leaned back in his chair, drew on the cigarette in its long holder, tossed his chin and decided
> to appoint a new administrator, arbitrator, coordinator, to improvise a commission, to implement an agency, to draft a directive
> or to request new powers from Congress. . . .

As this description of the New Deal's beginnings closes with a dying fall, so the entire novel, *The Grand Design*, indeed, charts the increase of power, the continuation of the status quo ante Roosevelt as far as genuine social change is concerned, and, finally, the triumph of political power seizures over idealistic economic reforms.

Early in the novel, Brain Trusters gather to voice their convictions that the only real question to be answered concerns who among the upper levels of power should make the inevitable plans for recovery: robber barons or government in the people's interest. As a farmer puts it, however, the New Deal principles are acceptable but, "What worries me is the way you idealists work it out in detail. . . . Half the time you get the opposite results." This is the best Dos Passos has to say for the New Deal. True, the author clearly turns down the left's own rejection of the Roosevelt administration; the early Communist party line is put in the mouth of a hypocritical proto-Communist labor faker: "Roosevelt's New Deal, priming the pump, relief, was only a social fascist whiting of the sepulchre of depression." Dos Passos, through his two administration heroes in the AAA, attacks the New Deal for its size, with the inevitable problems that sheer bigness involves—red tape, delays in preserving the subsistence (family) farm, the necessity to postpone genuine social experiment and to settle, during the first term, for future formulas, since the Boss will "underwrite only what he thinks is politically practical." Roosevelt's interpreter in *The Grand Design*, Judge Oppenheim, keeps reassuring the idealists who worry about the staying power of the secretary of agriculture with the bromide that doubt is self-indulgence.

Jobs, Dos Passos infers, are not enough. Early on he explains,

> there's a job for everybody
> (if you can't do anything else you
> can take the applications of the others)
> to make America over.

The author makes less of Hitler's threat than that of the ways the United States is being manipulated into a war situation—an attitude quite similar to that expressed by Sinclair Lewis during the late 1930s when he was attracted to the America First platform. Dos Passos is less impressed by the enhancement of trade union–organizing possibilities than he is frightened by the opportunities afforded to criminals and Communists to take over the unions from the working men. He is less impressed by the gains made for the farmer and the laborer than by the fact that "one third of the farm families of the nation were slum families then and after seven years of the New Deal they still are. . . . I don't say that we've found the cure or that surplus crop disposal or tenant loans or resettlement are anything but palliatives, but I do insist that instead of doing too much we aren't doing enough."

Paul Graves, Dos Passos's agricultural expert, comes to realize that the agency is not reversing the trend of farm abandonment (which Steinbeck had eloquently described) and, indeed, that the New Deal hadn't really changed southern life. As the novel builds its case against Roosevelt, more and more Dos Passos's argument pinpoints one essential flaw—the disparity between real life, in the fields and factories, and the bureaucratic view of that real life, as seen from Washington offices, committee rooms, and Georgetown dinner parties. Of course, the division between illusion and reality is a staple of fiction as an art form, and Dos Passos employs the concept to supply structure to his New Deal novel. Although such a gambit may be artistically viable, it raises serious problems for the literary historian. Dos Passos's freedom, as a novelist, to juxtapose events—such as the Nazi's use of power to kill Jews and the AAA's use of power to kill pigs—to indicate the play of historical forces can be as irresponsible as the freedom taken by Marxist novelists of the period to insist that all bosses are evil (and doomed) and all workers are noble (and ultimately triumphant).

Toward the end of *The Grand Design*, an ex–New Deal lawyer, probably modeled on Thomas Corcoran, bemoans the coming entry into war, which will entail a new list of accommodations and postponements. "The day may come when we can reform our ranks and give the country a new New Deal, a real one this time." But in the novel, Franklin D. Roosevelt triumphs, Walker Watson never gets to be president as term after term piles up for FDR, the bad bureaucrats become more entrenched, the good bureaucrats (those precious few) pull out of the government, and the very title of the novel, *The Grand Design*, is ambiguous. Perhaps it is an idealistic design that failed; perhaps it is a realistic design that may succeed—and destroy the true Jeffersonian democracy that Dos Passos cherished.

It is an irony of history that John Dos Passos, not the young Dos Passos but the aging critic of socialism, should have written what still stands as the major fictional study of the workings of the New Deal.

In summary, when American fiction treated the New Deal, the approach taken was usually oblique. The depression itself was an omnipresent subject; as Daniel Fuchs put it in his novel *Low Company*, speaking of the poor and confused, "It was not enough to call them low and pass on." Novelists for the most part seemed more interested in problems—which allowed full play to the creative urge for detailed description and deep sympathy—than in solutions—which would have demanded political and economic analysis. The intellectuals of the left, from the *New Masses* to the *Partisan Review*, were more involved with sectarian splinter factions than with the New Deal's attempt at a broad concensus, even during the Popular Front period. Symbolically, Leon Trotsky was a more important figure than Franklin Roosevelt to the kinds of leftist writers described in Lionel Trilling's *The Middle of the Journey*. Thus, the day-by-day achievements and aims of the Roosevelt administration found their fullest literary expression in the Federal Theater's Living Newspapers, such as "One-Third of a Nation" or "Triple A Plowed Under," or in WPA murals on the walls of federal buildings. The important fictional portrait of the New Deal remains to be written.

1. "Hammett brilliantly defined the troubled aspects of this period of open criminal warfare, poverty, and festering political corruption. He laid a hard-boiled veneer over the despair of citizens who were disinherited and disenchanted. Clam up, he told them. Stay tough. Don't back down to anybody. . . . Then maybe, just *maybe*, you can survive" (William F. Nolan, *Dashiell Hammett: A Casebook* [Santa Barbara, 1970], p. 7).

2. "Plans of all kinds were a major form of mental activity in the thirties, the most hurried and hasty decade of intellectual restlessness in our history" (Jay Martin, *Nathanael West: The Art of His Life* [New York, 1970], p. 232).

3. Quoted in Elizabeth Nowell, *Thomas Wolfe* (New York, 1969), p. 342.

4. Carlos Baker, *Ernest Hemingway* (New York, 1969), p. 270.

5. Both John P. Marquand and Mary McCarthy shot ironic glances toward New Deal bureaucrats, the one disliking their clannish chumminess with "the skipper," the other rejecting their tweedy self-importance.

Notes on the Editors and Contributors

Jerold S. Auerbach, who teaches history at Wellesley College, is the author of *Labor and Liberty: The La Follette Committee and the New Deal* and editor of *American Labor: The Twentieth Century*, and is currently engaged in a study of the American legal profession and social change in the twentieth century.

John Braeman, professor of history at the University of Nebraska—Lincoln, is the author of *Albert J. Beveridge: American Nationalist*.

Robert Bremner is professor of history at Ohio State University, author of *From the Depths: The Discovery of Poverty in the United States* and *American Philanthropy*, and editor of *Children and Youth in America: A Documentary History*.

David Brody teaches history at the University of California—Davis and is the author of *Steelworkers in America: The Nonunion Era, The Butcher Workmen*, and *Labor in Crisis: The Steel Strike of 1919.*

Milton Derber, who is professor of labor and industrial relations at the University of Illinois, is coeditor (with Edwin Young) of *Labor and the New Deal* and author of *The American Idea of Industrial Democracy, 1865–1965*.

Ellis W. Hawley, professor of history at the University of Iowa and author of *The New Deal and the Problem of Monopoly: A Study in Economic Ambivalence*, is currently at work on a study of Herbert Hoover and the vision of associational capitalism, 1917–33.

James Holt, who teaches history at the University of Auckland in New Zealand, has written *Congressional Insurgents and the Party System, 1909–1916* and has served as a Research Fellow at the Charles Warren Center for Studies in American History at Harvard University.

Richard S. Kirkendall, professor of history at the University of Missouri —Columbia when he prepared this essay, is now professor at Indiana University and executive secretary of the Organization of American Historians. He is the author of *Social Scientists and Farm Politics in the Age of Roosevelt* and *The Global Power: The United States Since 1941* and editor of *The Truman Period as a Research Field.*

Richard Polenberg, professor of history at Cornell University, is the author of *Reorganizing Roosevelt's Government, 1936–1939* and *War and Society: The United States 1941–1945.*

Albert U. Romasco, of the history department of New York University, has written *The Poverty of Abundance: Hoover, the Nation, the Depression.*

John A. Salmond is dean of the School of Humanities at La Trobe University in Australia, and is the author of *The Civilian Conservation Corps, 1933–1942: A New Deal Case Study.*

Eric Solomon teaches English at San Francisco State College and has written *Stephen Crane: From Parody to Realism* and *Stephen Crane in England.*

Raymond Wolters, a historian at the University of Delaware, is the author of *Negroes and the Great Depression: The Problem of Economic Recovery* and *The New Negro on Campus: Black College Rebellions of the 1920s.*

Index